Dress & Gender

Dress, Gender, Transgender, and Crossdressing

Vol. 1

Crossdressing in Context

G. G. Bolich, Ph.D.

Psyche's

Press

Psyche's Press

Raleigh, North Carolina

©2006 G. G. Bolich

ISBN 978-0-6151-6767-1

Detailed Table of Contents

The Questions

Volume 1: Dress & Gender

i

Dress & Gender

Crossdressing in Context, vol. 1.

Preface & Introduction
to the 5 Volume Set

Preface

Can we be honest?

What can you expect?

Let's be candid from the start. The subject matter of this book is controversial. Worse, it is the kind of controversy that often moves beyond mere intellectual disagreement to result in broken relationships and sometimes violence. In preparing this work one particular remark has stayed with me. In a report on violence experienced by transgendered people, the authors wrote, "What is common to most studies of transpeople is their staggering irrelevance to the community at issue."[1]

My intention has been to set forth information that is not irrelevant, either to the transgendered, or to those who find themselves related in some manner to them—which I think is all of us. As the title suggests, this work is about raising questions and offering answers. In the effort to do so, I have drawn both on academic material and on accounts set forth by transgendered people themselves. For example, one question asks how crossdressers describe themselves (Q. 26), while the next offers the results of various formal psychological tests to answer the same question (Q. 27). I have throughout tried to let others speak for themselves. You will find brief quotes from various sources to offer a bit of the flavor of how these other voices sound. In summarizing studies, theories, or personal accounts I have aimed at being concise but fair—and pointed you in directions to follow in order to learn more. Because of the ubiquity of the World Wide Web, whenever possible indication has been made in the endnotes as to where material can be accessed online. At the same time, I have not shied away from offering my own critique of what others have said or my own assessment of the matters about which they speak.

Despite the large number of questions raised, this work barely scratches the surface of transgender realities, including crossdressing. I often refer to 'transgender realities' and I do so quite consciously. I want us to remember that we are examining *realities*—lived experiences that range from very temporary occurrences of minor personal significance to profoundly meaningful matters of personal identity felt and expressed every day. I want us to consider how the *trans* in *trans*gender can mean different things to different people. Nor do I wish us to

1

ever lose sight of how *gender* is basic to trans*gender*. And, because the organizing framework is built around crossdressing, we must also know something about the role clothes play in our lives.

Obviously, I am very ambitious. I hope you are as well. Even something that superficially seems easy enough to describe, like crossdressing, which after all is simply the act of dressing in clothes typically associated with a gender other than the one assigned the wearer, is not really simple when once looked at closely. To understand crossdressing—to begin to truly see transgender realities—takes work. I want to do that work alongside you, serving as a partner in dialog while also offering my modest services as a guide to the vast literature on the subjects considered. Since I am functioning as a guide, you have every right to ask about my qualifications.

Who am I to talk?

One question you may have right away is what my 'position' or 'bias' is on the subject. For example, you might wish to know if I identify myself as a transgendered person. Unfortunately, in my experience, many people screen what they are willing to expose themselves to as they study a controversial topic by using this kind of query. Of course, I know *you* are more fair-minded than that, but the next reader might not be. So, whatever my stance—or identity—may be will have to become a matter of your own judgment (or speculation) as you read the work. I have conscientiously spoken of 'we' and 'us' throughout the book, both when speaking of crossdressers and when referring to noncrossdressers. I wish to convey my conviction that the fundamental humanity that unites us is greater than the differences that we too often let divide, separate, and isolate us. It is a small world we all have to share and a short life we all live.

What I am willing to tell you upfront about myself concerns my qualifications for tackling the subject. I caution you not to infer anything about my being 'for' or 'against' crossdressing from these qualifications.[2] As you know, qualifications do not guarantee people holding reasonable positions or even necessarily knowing what they are talking about! Still, I think you have a right to know relevant portions of my background because they may speak to my level of preparation for talking to you about these things. I don't expect you to take my word on anything from blind trust, but I do hope your confidence in the reliability of my remarks will be strengthened both by my background and by the actual material I set forth.

My background includes more than 30 years working professionally with people, primarily as an educator, but also as a counselor. I hold advanced degrees in the fields of religious studies and psychology, and my teaching and counseling have been in both areas. Because some people view crossdressing as a psychological disorder, my experience in psychology seems relevant. Because some people regard crossdressing as morally or religiously wrong, my experience in religious studies seems relevant, too. In fact, between these two areas, I find most of the questions and concerns about crossdressing that I have encountered from students, clients, and others.

In terms of religious studies, I am seminary trained, holding a M.A. in Theology, and the Master of Divinity—or M.Div.—the degree used to prepare people for professional ministry. My first Ph.D., in Educational Leadership, also focused on religious studies, culminating in a dissertation in the area of New Testament introduction. I am trained in biblical and classical languages (Hebrew, Greek, Latin), and in both traditional and modern methods of translating and interpreting sacred texts. Beginning in 1974, as an instructor at a Bible School, I have taught courses in religious studies at undergraduate and graduate levels in a wide variety of settings, including churches and synagogues, community college, public university, private college, and seminary extension program. These courses have covered matters of ethics, ancient and modern world religions, theology, history, sacred texts, and the relation of religion to psychology. My area of particular interest and specialization has been the religious writings of the period extending from about a century or so before Christ, to the end of the second century after Christ. In addition to scholarly work, I also have been involved in ecumenical work, notably between the Christian and Jewish communities. As a counselor, many people have identified my background in religious studies as an important reason why they chose to come see me.

My second doctorate is in psychology (Ph.D.). I started working with people as a counselor in 1973, while still a college student, on a crisis line. As time passed, my interests began to turn more and more to matters of human development and human sexuality. As a counselor I gradually developed a specialization in Trauma Resolution Therapy, principally working with adult survivors of sexual abuse. Today I teach graduate students in counseling about human sexuality. Both as a teacher and as a therapist I have continually encountered curiosity about crossdressing and transgender people. Because of my additional background in religious studies this curiosity by my students and clients has often extended to specific matters of faith and practice as well as the more specific psychological concerns about whether being a transgender person or engaging in crossdressing is deviant, sick, sinful, or harmful.

Accordingly, this work grows out of many years of interest and experience. I think my background contributes some layers of knowledge that may not be as easily accessible to other professionals whose experience is confined to only one or another of the areas relevant to a full consideration of crossdressing. To these credentials I will add my intention of being fair-minded and honest throughout this work. I intend this work to be educational in nature. At the same time, I am aware that when educating people on controversial subjects it may not be either feasible or even particularly desirable to attempt being completely above the fray and studiously neutral. In truth, I am not neutral on the subject—and I do not know anyone who is. Even scholarly works serve social and political ends, and every work—including mine—must be soberly appraised for fairness. I have every confidence that fair-minded readers who pursue the logic and evidence set down within this work will be able to accurately assess the value of this endeavor.

Introduction

What do you need to know to get started?

Why does any of this matter?

Chances are you aren't looking at this unless you already believe the subject matters. I agree. The fundamental assumption of this work is that transgender realities matter to all of us, whether we are transgendered ourselves or not. They matter because such realities by their very existence pose opportunities for us to explore and expand our sense of sex and gender. In a culture like our own, where sex and gender are so central to the way we define our identities and relationships, such an opportunity must not be missed.

We must also acknowledge from the very beginning that any discussion of these things will generate feeling, and quite often strong feeling. How can it not when the stakes—identities and relationships—are so high? Transgender realities in a culture where sex and gender are rigidly paired at two poles raise a challenge to our sense of what we think and know. But more critically than challenging the narrowness of our perceptions, they prompt questions about our own felt sense of sex and gender. In short, transgender realities matter because they disturb senses of identity and relationship founded and attached to a bipolar duality allowing us only to be masculine men or feminine women.

It seemed to me in framing this work that the most natural and appropriate choice was to mirror what happens in us when we encounter transgender realities like crossdressing. So herein everything is framed by questions. Though 100 questions are used to create what you may think of as 'chapters,' there are literally hundreds of questions raised and considered in this work.

Why this title?

The scope of this work, with all its queries, can be overwhelming—but then sex and gender are precisely that in our culture. You may already feel in over your head just holding this material in your hands. The subject of 'transgender' and 'crossdressing' is perhaps a lot larger than you initially thought—and then 'gender,' 'sex,' and 'dress' are thrown in for good measure! My choice of titles, then, requires a word of explanation.

Crossdressing in Context is meant both to be descriptive and to be implicitly critical of most other works on crossdressing. There are a number of important contexts in which crossdressing must be situated and the separate volume titles indicate these. First and most immediately there is *dress*, especially clothes, without which crossdressing is impossible and by which *gender* is experienced and expressed. Perhaps the greatest failing of studies of crossdressing is the general neglect of the role played by apparel. It is certainly appropriate to focus on gender, but such a focus needs to begin with gender-differentiated clothing. The first volume explores dress and gender, separately and together, in the context of a rich experience and expressive system.

The second volume examines another principal context: *today's transgender realities*, the actual lived experiences of human individuals. This material opens by introducing basic terminology and provides an overview of crossdressing behavior. The next set of questions considers a variety of possible causes of transgender behavior like crossdressing. The volume continues by examining contemporary transgender experience from a variety of perspectives, including how transgender people experience it, examined by a variety of psychological tests, understood legally, and regarded by other people.

The third volume sets crossdressing and transgender realities in *historical and geographical* contexts. The volume begins with a history of transgender realities, revolving around historical depictions of crossdressing, from ancient to modern times. This material also includes special attention to the history of theater, including modern movies and television. The volume then continues with a survey of transgender realities around the world. Collectively, these materials demonstrate that transgender realities like crossdressing have been persistent across times and cultures.

The fourth volume highlights the importance of *religion*. Not only is personal spirituality and religious observance as valued by transgender people as by anyone else, the long history of religions around the world show an involvement with transgender realities that make this area of critical value in properly understanding phenomena like crossdressing. Acknowledging the cultural context in which this work is produced, the first religious sphere considered belongs to Western religions. Thus a careful examination of what the Bible says about crossdressing is followed by how biblical material has been commented upon by Christian and Jewish scholars through the centuries. Following this material a survey is made of the principal religions of the world, both East and West. As in volume 2, the evidence documents an awareness and dialog with transgender realities throughout history and around the globe.

The final volume acknowledges the weight of modern *mental health* in discussions about crossdressing and other transgender realities. Since the medicalization of sex has firmly joined crossdressing behavior to sexuality, this volume begins by examining the theories and evidence allegedly connecting crossdressing and sexual behavior. This is followed by a broader examination of the question whether transgender people, especially those who crossdress, are mentally ill. First this matter is explored by providing a broad historical context—the medicalization of sex—and examining how transgender people often come to mental health professionals' attention. Special terminology like 'gender dysphoria' is explained. The possible connection of transgender behavior to various mental disorders is considered. Then follows a review of contributions on the subject by various scholars since the late 19th century. Given the dominant position the American Psychiatric Association's *Diagnostic and Statistical Manual of Mental Disorders* (popularly referred to as DSM) has attained, a careful look at how crossdressing and other transgender realities have been handled by this model throughout its history also is provided. This, in turn, leads to looking at a variety of treatment approaches that have been tried with transgender clients. The issues involved in such treatment lead to a careful consideration about the wisdom of retaining in the DSM model the categories concerning transgender. Finally, the volume—and the work at large—concludes with a last consideration of whether transgender people need to be changed.

Collectively the four volumes represent one sustained approach to placing crossdressing in context. Although this work broadly is about all transgender realities, the focal point has been the behavior most visibly associated with transgender: *crossdressing*. I treat the subject of crossdressing both as a topic of great interest in its own right and as an entrance into transgender realities. As large as the resulting work is, it could be much larger with a more sustained examination of other transgender realities.

What are the goals of this work?

The structure of this work is dialogical in nature. Questions—many, many questions—are raised and considered. The choice of these questions and the way in which they are answered reflects various goals. There are several principal, intentional goals sought by this work, all with the purpose of establishing an understanding in context:

1. to put dress back into crossdressing by situating crossdressing within an experiencing and expressing system built around clothes as the primary vehicle for communicating gender, which is central to our sense of self and relationships;

2. to highlight and explicate the role dress plays both in our affiliations, such as our membership in a gender group, and in our individuality;

3. to explore the basic distinctions between 'sex' and 'gender' in order to better see what transgender is about and how crossdressing is related to each;

4. to use crossdressing—a transgender reality—as entry into other transgender realities, and to see how these realities are similar and dissimilar;

5. to clarify the meaning of terms (e.g., 'transgender,' 'transvestite,' 'transsexual'), while questioning their usefulness;

6. to document transgender realities, especially crossdressing, throughout history and around the world, and to do so with enough depth and breadth to convince even the most skeptical reader of the pervasiveness and significance of these realities;

7. to broaden our understanding of crossdressing by exploring and illustrating the many various motivations behind it and thereby to simultaneously challenge such narrow and erroneous beliefs as that all crossdressing is done because of disturbed gender identity or sexual perversity;

8. to keep in view always that transgender realities are inevitably human experiences, lived by real people, who are worthy of respect and dignity;

9. to set out and place in context the work of others who have written about transgender realities, especially crossdressing, and in doing so engage in dialog with them;

10. to let transgendered people speak for themselves, especially in addressing matters such as what it is like to live as a transgendered person;

11. to examine basic issues of concern to people, such as the morality of crossdressing, the way in which religious traditions have related to transgender realities, the legal issues connected to transgender experience, the relational aspects of being with a transgendered person as a partner, family member, friend, or helper, and the role of sexuality in the life of the transgendered; and,

12. to address the critical matter of the involvement of mental health professionals, including looking closely at the history of study by professionals about transgender (especially crossdressing), detailing the discussion of transgender in today's dominant diagnostic classification system, reviewing the history of treating transgender conditions, considering whether changes need to be made, and examining new models of therapeutic support.

To meet these dozen goals requires some space; hence the size of this work.

Yet, for all this, there are some things underdeveloped.

For example, you should know right off that this book is *not* principally about homosexuality. Because that is the transgender reality that receives by far the most attention this work is organized around a different principle: crossdressing. Yes, some homosexuals (but not all) crossdress. And yes, some crossdressers (but not all) are homosexual. Thus, homosexuals are included within this work. But they are not the focus.

What are 'transgender realities'?

The focus, through the lens of crossdressing, is 'transgender realities.' In choosing the term 'transgender realities' I want to emphasize the multiplicity of expressions that do not fit at the gender poles of masculinity and femininity. A prominent transgender reality—a behavior shared among many transgender people—is crossdressing. I treat all crossdressing as a transgender reality even though not all people whom crossdress identify themselves as transgendered. In other words, just as a self-professed vegetarian may occasionally eat meat, so a non-transgendered person may occasionally enact a transgender reality like crossdressing. In this work I use the broad transgender reality of crossdressing as both entry into other transgender realities and to remind us how pervasive transgender expressions are. But to properly comprehend them they must be retained in their natural contexts.

How is the work structured?

A glance at the questions in the Table of Contents shows an almost bewildering breadth of matters. They are organized into 100 specific questions, each of which entails asking further questions. Yet these questions collectively still by no means exhaust the subject. Instead they aim to reflect a logical organization of reflection based on a variety of the more commonly asked questions related to our interests. Those questions cover all kinds of topics, everything from sex and gender to morals and religion. It takes time to cover so much ground and the length of this work reflects my commitment to taking that time and offering at least enough to cover the basics and point the way to more research. However, this structure allows you to enter wherever you like and get answers quickly.

In truth, this study could be shorter. Part of the length is attributable to the structure. By setting everything as answers to questions and encouraging you to dip in wherever you like, an element of repetition is needed to ensure every answer stays embedded in context with enough detail to make full sense to you. So, in reading through the work in a progressive fashion the effect of this repetition will be felt, though hopefully not in too tedious a fashion. I have tried to be varied in restating matters, but if nothing else the repetition serves pedagogically to reinforce basic concepts and themes.

A significant factor adding to the length is my insistence on fleshing out each context with reason and evidence. Too many people disregard arguments because they only see one or two illustrative cases and fail to recognize them as signifying a vast number of others. I wish to create the sense for you of a phenomenon so common and richly varied around the world and throughout history that it cannot be casually dismissed or superficially examined. Comprehension requires a sense of the complexity and fullness of transgender realities like crossdressing. If you are impatient to press on you can do so, but if you are looking for detail, you will find it here.

I recognize that your interest may not be in all forms of crossdressing, but only a particular kind. You may even only want information on a very specific matter related to that particular kind. As I mentioned above, that is why the organization of this material has been set out as answers to questions. I think this is an intuitive and practical approach that will prove useful to you now with the questions you presently have and later with questions still to come. Hopefully, the net effect will be to also prompt other questions and lead you into a larger, ongoing investigation.

While I like to think the optimal way to use this work is to read it completely from start to finish, it may not be the best way for you at this time. Instead, you might wish to browse it, looking for specific information. This can be done through the questions, a complete list of which is found in the Detailed Table of Contents. Once you locate an interesting question, you can explore it through three levels of interaction. The quickest and most superficial level is 'The Short Answer' provided at the beginning of each answer section. In a few lines you will get a summary answer. Next comes 'The Longer Answer.' This offers a detailed discussion to more fully answer the question. Finally, by using the endnotes for each answer you can find important sources and resources as well as pursue the discussion on some finer points. In sum, the work is organized in a user-friendly manner to meet your needs now and later.

On the use and misuse of this work: Who makes the rules?

A final matter about using this work is important to me. Scholarly work is often proof-texted. In other words, readers pick and choose what conveniently supports the position they want to hold. I don't imagine that any of us entirely escape selective recall or purposeful choosing of 'facts' for presentation, but I ask that you play fair with the material included in these pages. A dialog requires two parties, and fruitful dialog mandates both parties be allowed to speak with an effort to hear them. When once the whole matter is on the table, or as much of it as can be had, then is the time for making a respectful decision based on evidence and reason. I covet for us all making careful judgments and always treating others with respect and charity.

I know—and so do you—that the matters discussed in this work often engage strong feelings in people. None of my goals include telling you how to feel. However you feel about the matters we discuss I will hope you subject those feelings to scrutiny, evaluate the evidence honestly, and behave with respect toward all. This really matters to me—too many people continue to be harmed. Let's think about this matter a moment longer.

One of the curious things about freedom is that most of us demand it in very liberal portions for ourselves, but are less charitable toward others. We want to be left alone to do as we see fit, while often insisting that other folk conform to our personal standards as to what is 'right.' Naturally, we generally have at hand one or another rationale for our judgments. Frequently, our logic centers in an opposition to someone else's behavior on religious or moral grounds. After all, it is unseemly to prioritize the fact that the behavior we condemn makes us personally uncomfortable, so we set that truth in second place and justify it by reasoning that we feel uneasy *because* the behavior is inherently—and to us also *obviously*—wrong. Thus we enjoy the best of all solutions: moral and/or religious justification for our felt discomfort. If we can get a law passed against the behavior then the justification for our feeling is further strengthened—as may be the feeling itself.

We may even find ourselves justifying unkind remarks, avoidance, harassment, discrimination, or physical violence. Once we convince ourselves something is wrong, it is easy to think whatever is done in opposition must be right. But two wrongs never make a right. No matter how we excuse ourselves, violation of another person's human rights is evil.

Unfortunately, our real motivations often remain unconscious. We don't see that our reasoning is actually just rationalization—a way of thinking that has as its real aim making us less anxious rather than knowing the truth. All we know is that by thinking and judging in certain ways we shield ourselves from uncomfortable feelings. While this may seem useful, when it leads to disruption in our relationships with others and prompts us to words and deeds hurtful to others, then we have become the very makers of evil that we despise.

We are best served in the long run by opening our eyes and trying to see matters as clearly as we can. So let us agree to start in as neutral a position as possible. Instead of assuming that crossdressing is 'right' or 'wrong,' 'healthy' or 'mentally ill,' let us just let it be—and then examine it as best we can. If the subject elicits certain feelings, simply let them be as well. In the privacy of your own reading there is no need to let these feelings be more than they are—one source of information among others. Feelings do not have to motivate you to do anything right now. Simply accept them or set them aside and move on to a sober consideration of the topic.

You can do this—and you *must* if you are to be fair to yourself and to others. I know that it is very likely you are holding this book either because you crossdress or someone you care about does. Your feelings may be clear, or they may be mixed, but they are not facts that by themselves must determine what you think or do. In fact, by learning more your feelings may change. So be patient with yourself and with others.

Ready? Then let's start asking some questions.

Crossdressing in Context

Dress, Gender, Transgender, and Crossdressing.

Volume 1 of a 5 volume set.
The set titles:

1 *Dress & Gender*
2 *Today's Transgender Realities*
3 *Transgender History & Geography*
4 *Transgender & Religion*
5 *Transgender & Mental Health*

Volume 1:
Dress & Gender

The
Questions

Question Set 1

What is all the fuss about clothes and gender?

We have all heard it: appearance matters. "Clothes make the man," Mark Twain politely agreed, before adding, "Naked people have little or no influence in society."[1] And that's where most of us leave it—with a chuckling acknowledgment that dress is essential, but with little awareness of just how essential. Indeed, on first impression it seems rather silly how people become so emotionally worked up over what someone else is wearing. After all, we are talking about *clothes*, not threats to world peace! So what's going on? What's all the fuss over how people dress?

There is something clearly important about clothes, beyond their utility of protection from the elements. Scholar and filmmaker Peter Wollen points out, "the single trait which most significantly distinguishes garments from other useful things is, plainly enough, the intimate nature of the relationship between the garment and its wearer."[2] These *things* we put on become a part of us, both representing whom we experience ourselves to be and expressing how we want others to experience us. How we dress matters to us, and how others dress also interests us. If this were not true, crossdressing would be a completely unremarkable phenomenon.

But crossdressing, at least in some contexts, arrests our attention. This happens because in our Euro-American culture dress is a chief way of presenting—perhaps enacting—gender. Because gender is so rigidly paired with sex, and because both stand so central to our sense of self and relationships, clothing garners significant meaning. If crossdressing had nothing to do with matters of gender and sex it would occasion little comment or interest—and perhaps not exist at all.

This observation must completely register with us if we are to grasp fully why crossdressing matters. It matters because we have made sex and gender central to identity *and* used dress as the principal avenue to express that fact. Clearly, the most obvious fact about crossdressing is that it involves a particular use of clothing.[3] So it seems particularly peculiar how most of the discussion about crossdressing centers around gender, sex, and sexuality without saying

17

much at all about clothing. Dress has become almost invisible in the formal discussion of crossdressing even though it is the obvious spark to our attention. The most credible explanation for this occurrence is the ignorance of most scholars on crossdressing behavior concerning the central role played by dress in human psychosocial existence. Mental health professionals and social scientists mostly ignore dress itself because they are unaware of its importance or dismissive of its significance when it comes to gender or sexual behavior.

Therefore, the first task of a new major review and appraisal of the subject of crossdressing must begin by addressing the most obvious gap in the scholarly literature on the subject: the role of dress. The first question set, which constitutes the entirety of volume 1, does just that. Here we will discover to some extent the centrality of dress in the human experience and expression of gender. We will consider to what degree this also is important to human sexuality. In so doing, we will reorient the scholarly discussion of crossdressing back to its foundation, the first and most basic context in which crossdressing occurs, the context of dress.

Since crossdressing is first of all a phenomenon involving dress, we will do well to start with clothes, though dress, properly speaking, involves other elements of appearance, too, such as ornamentation. But it will be enough for our purposes to stay focused on clothing. We will begin with a broad approach to clothing and progressively work our way to more detailed applications to our primary subject. In so doing we will be led into questions not only about clothes in relation to gender, but also about gender in other respects, including its relationship to sex and sexuality, and a consideration of a host of realities embraced by the term *transgender*. In short, though this volume is about dress, it is about dress as a context. Thus what we have to say about dress inevitably must be accompanied by remarks on gender, sex, and sexuality, since all of these things in their interrelationships serve as a foundation for comprehending crossdressing.

In entering the subject where we begin will guide where we can go. A logical starting point for a social scientist in studying dress is first exploring why what anyone wears matters. The significance, or meaning, of dress is a proper entry point into the world of crossdressing.

Q. 1

Why do clothes matter?

The Short Answer: To answer why clothes matter, we might ask why they even exist. A number of plausible hypotheses suggest themselves. First, we may wear clothes to protect ourselves from environmental pressures, such as cold or dampness. But even where such need is minimal, people wear dress. Apparently, clothing and accessories serve social functions. Among these are signifying membership in various groups, and status within those groups. Sex and gender groups are served by clothes differentiated to mark not only membership, but to signal availability, enhance attractiveness, and make value statements (e.g., about one's modesty). These explanations for why we wear clothes contribute to the reasons clothes matter to us. Collectively, they suggest that clothes and the other elements that contribute to dress occupy a central position in a complex and subtle expressive and experiencing system. This system provides a context in which personal experience acquires dimensions impossible apart from wearing clothes. The system also constructs a social context in which experience can be translated into expressions aimed at others. We are able through clothes to express ourselves to ourselves and to others. In so doing we communicate values, feelings, personality characteristics, social affiliations, and other important information. Unfortunately, what we intend and what others perceive is not always the same. Crossdressing represents a special way for experiencing and expressing, one capable of offering diverse and significant ways for both. Because it involves gender, a central characteristic of identity and relationship in our culture, crossdressing is especially apt to engage value systems. Varying value systems produce different interpretations—and judgments. This reality makes crossdressing prone to misunderstanding, controversy, and conflict.

The Longer Answer: Clothes matter. Even though many of us pay little attention to why clothes matter, we have little difficulty agreeing that they do. Most of us exercise conscious care in what we select to wear, and show different motivations and choices according to varying situations. We dress to be comfortable—wearing different amounts, fabrics and styles to be warmer or cooler. We tend to dress differently when we are alone than when we anticipate being around others. When we are around others we tend to dress to fit social expectations about the occasion and relationships, whether it be a group meeting of an association we belong to (e.g., church, club, military unit), a holiday festival, a family outing, or a night on the town. But we don't just dress with others in mind even when sharing an occasion with them. We both dress to suit our mood, and to alter it. We dress to reflect values. We dress to make statements, to ourselves and to others. And when it comes to others, we are discomfited when what we intend to communicate in dress is misunderstood, disliked, or rejected.

In short, what we wear matters. It does so in a number of different ways, especially with regard to relationships and identity. Since both of those also revolve largely around gender, one of the most important meanings of dress involves its role in the experience and expression of gender—and incorporates the values we organize with respect to gender (see the answer to Q. 4). In Western culture, personal and social identities—our very 'Self'—are constructed from the foundation of gender. This is hardly a new contention. Janet Spence in the mid-1980s observed how "gender is one of the earliest and most central components of the self-concept and serves as an organizing principle through which many experiences and perceptions of self and other are filtered."[4] Since that time our culture's wrestling with things like 'gender identity' has only furthered the prominence of gender to our sense of who we and others are.

Because our culture ties gender to biological sex in firm and narrow fashion, clothing inevitably acquires a connection to sex as well. So transgender realities like crossdressing, which pair sex and gender in unaccustomed ways, especially arouse anxiety and questioning. In crossdressing the stakes always associated with clothes become visibly heightened as issues of gender and sex come roaring into our field of attention. But lest we get too far ahead of ourselves, let us return to a more basic question.

How has dress come to occupy such an important role? Feminist scholar Carole Turbin offers a useful starting point by recalling us to the obvious: clothing is part of daily life, tactile and visual, often emotionally charged. Rather than diminish its significance, the ubiquity of clothes underlines their importance while lulling us into taking them for granted. Turbin remarks that the cultural meanings attached to dress are complex and multilayered because "clothing and textiles almost uniquely combine production and consumption, and private, bodily, intimate sensation, sexuality, and fantasy with public self-presentation."[5] Nowhere do such disparate elements converge more potently than in the connection of dress with gender. In any society where personal identity and significant relationships are structured around sex and gender, dress will occupy a critical role, both providing avenues into gender and ways to display it.

As soon as human beings began to cover themselves they appear to have formed ways to use those coverings to differentiate genders. Although the sexual body provides a practical foundation for gendered differences in dress, it is neither a sufficient nor even necessary condition for gendered clothing distinctions. First, this is because Nature's physical reality simply does not provide enough difference between sexual bodies, nor make those differences reliable enough to keep us from mistaking a member of one sex for another if there aren't other clues, such as clothing, with accessories, and gender-typed behavior.

Look around. Little effort is needed to recognize that bodies, especially at any distance, are highly variable in shape. In an age where men and women can both sport long or short hair, wear jewelry or forego it, and dress in shirts and jeans, a casual glance at someone a little ways away may not immediately reveal whether the person has a male body or a female one. Many women, for example, have narrow waists and small breasts. Some men have noticeable breasts. Many clothes disguise obvious sexual anatomy. In sum, it often isn't easy to immediately tell if someone is biologically male or female. So clearly visible gendered distinctions in clothing become important aids to identification.

But gendered distinctions do more than help identify sexual bodies. Dress also provides a way to convey ideas about how different genders should act and be perceived. Colors, textures, fit, and style all have both practical and psychological ramifications for how a particular gender will be regarded, including inferences about psychological makeup, social roles, and what work is deemed appropriate. When, for example, women are strongly urged to wear long dresses of delicate fabric, a clear social message is being sent about the 'fragile' or 'weaker' sex. Such clothing also restricts the kind of movements—and hence work and leisure activities—the wearer can perform. Dress thus both sets and reinforces cultural ideals. But it also permits challenge and revolution. When women set aside skirts for pants they made statements about identity and capability that continue to reverberate. Both conformity and nonconformity to gendered distinctions in dress contribute to our cultural discussion about gender. As fashion styles across societies and times show, the importance of the sexual body itself waxes and wanes but gendered distinctions remain with us forever.

If we are to understand transgender realities, which do not conform to the sex and gender pairings regarded as normative in our culture, we must comprehend crossdressing. That effort in turn requires we delve into matters of psychology and sociology, look at human sexuality and gender, consider history and culture. But none of these things are enough. Investigations into crossdressing—perhaps the central behavior associated with transgender realities—inevitably fall short if they neglect consideration of clothing and dress behavior. In fact, for this reason alone most treatments of crossdressing (and thus of transgender and gender) fail to adequately comprehend their subject. There is only one proper place for an investigation of cross*dressing* to begin, and that is with conscientious effort to understand why clothes matter and what they have to do with gender, transgender, and crossdressing.

Why did we begin to wear clothes?

This question might not be the first one that comes to mind. Yet it is an entirely logical place to start. Why did we ever adopt clothing?[6] Would we have done so if it served no purpose related to our survival? That seems unlikely. So if related to our survival, how do clothes serve us?

Paleoanthropologist Ian Tattersall, curator for the division of anthropology at the American Museum of Natural History, argues that our use of clothing reflects a "fundamental human urge."[7] But an urge for what purpose? A variety of answers have been suggested over the course of time, but they converge in a common conviction that clothes came into existence because they had to. The 'urge' that impelled our ancestors was an invention born of necessity. Yet human beings have complex needs, both physical and psychological, ranging from the need to protect our delicate skin to finding ways to fully experience and express ourselves.

One intriguing proposal set forth by researchers at the Max Planck Institute for Evolutionary Anthropology dates the origin of clothing to some 72,000 years ago (+/-42,000), a date determined by genetic dating of body lice, which live in clothes.[8] This would make the appearance of clothing a relatively recent matter. By itself this research doesn't answer *why* clothing was adopted. The obvious explanation, and the one commonly put forward by anthropologists, is that as human migration extended from warmer climates to cooler ones, clothes became a survival matter. After all, we enter the world covered by skin rich in sensation but largely inadequate to protect us from environmental factors such as the heat of the sun or the cold of night. Some manner of *protection* for our skin was necessary if we were to enjoy much range of activity. Since this probably happened much longer ago than the lice theory suggests, clothing is generally thought to have appeared a million or so years ago.

However, there is no compelling reason to conclude that all clothing originated from this one survival function. In those climates where clothing is little needed, if at all, for protection from the elements, clothes are still common. In fact, clothing made from natural fibers like linen and hemp are not merely comfortable, but *healthy*. Our bodies feel—and function—differently in apparel made from natural materials as opposed to synthetic fibers.[9] Yet our range of clothing choices embraces all kinds of fabrics, fits, and styles. This complex reality suggests some other reasons have been at work in the adoption and development of dress.

Perhaps clothing was created to serve sexual differentiation. Two major theories about clothing take their cue from this fact. One suggests that morality inspired coverings. *Modesty*—the hiding from visibility of the parts of the body associated with sexuality—then provides another rationale for dress. Perhaps this need for modesty itself was born from a sense of shame associated with sexuality, as many read the biblical story of Adam and Eve (see the answer to Q. 4).

Another theory also highlights the role sexual differentiation plays but from a different perspective. At the beginning of the 20th century, renowned sociologist William Thomas observed that unlike many animals, humans are without "natural glitter, with no plumage, no spots or stripes . . . . But, thanks to his hands, he has the power of collecting brilliant objects and attaching them to his person, and thus becomes a rival in radiance of the animals and flowers." [10] With such words he placed himself in the midst of an ongoing debate that had emerged forcefully in the 19th century over the origin and purpose of clothes.[11] Rather than serving the moral desire for modesty, clothes can be viewed as providing *ornamentation.*

Clothing may have originated not from a desire to hide sexual anatomy because of modesty, but in order to enhance its attraction. Artful concealment increases curiosity to see what is hidden; the unobtainable becomes more desirable. As Thomas observed, clothes do provide ornamentation to human beings. Just as in the wild animals use natural ornamentation in their competition for sexual partners, so human beings may conceal and reveal body features associated with sexuality to facilitate successful mate attraction.

When once we begin to think along the lines of ornamentation or modesty we enter a wide realm of possibilities that all reflect *social* needs. Clearly sexual relations are one such need. They are hardly the only such one. From ornamentation's basic purpose may have evolved other functions, such as signifying social status—which evolutionary psychologists also associate with mate selection strategies. Clothes also prove readily able to signal social affiliations, demonstrating tribal membership or caste status, and so forth. The pliability of clothing to serve social needs stems from the manifold possibilities offered by color, texture, and style. Even the amount and placement of covering is significant. Indeed, although other animals (e.g., hermit crabs) may adopt coverings from materials found in their immediate environment, humans seem unique in the richness of their fashioning of materials to cover themselves, in whole or in part, from materials found near and far, natural and artificial alike.

There are other instrumental social possibilities that may explain the origin of clothing, at least partially. The idea that moral concerns prompted adoption of dress need not be limited to worries about sexuality. Morality typically is conjoined with religion. Perhaps clothing originated in response to some *religious* inclination; certainly numerous particular kinds of dress owe their origin to this motivation. Similarly, ancient *magic* may have prompted creating items of dress. Even today people around the world have various superstitions about particular kinds of fabric or ornamentation or arrangement of clothing. Dress, combining both the material world and the imaginative realm, is ideal for realizing magical principles.[12]

The social embraces the *personal.* Is it possible the first clothing came simply from a person's desire to be seen as an individual? Regardless of socially imposed standards in dress people appear always to have found ways to bend the standards to serve personal needs and desires. Ironically, fashion may derive its power from its ability to serve two fundamental purposes simultaneously: it lets people express individuality while staying in step with a desired cohort. Beyond that fact, a mountain of evidence from ancient sources and our contemporary reality strongly support the notion that people use dress to encounter and realize aspects of themselves, to alter personal moods and characteristics, and to display a sense of individuality.

So we have several plausible answers for the origin and continuing purposes of clothing. As seen above, the origin of clothing is typically viewed in connection with one or another function. Thus George Bush and Perry London, in musing on the theories of clothing's origin, conclude the theories fit one or another of three functions: protection, concealment/display of various regions of the body, or differentiation of individuals and/or groups.[13] Whatever the original purpose was (and it is doubtful we will ever know for sure), clearly our relationship with clothes is now very complex. As much as any one of us might glory in the nude body, few of us can imagine daily life without not merely coverings, but coverings of manifold types. Indeed, we have formed a reciprocal relationship with dress where our choices influence what is made and selected, while simultaneously influencing our perceptions of ourselves and of others.

The original act of covering ourselves became elaborated in Western culture into what we now term *fashion*. In this work, fashion relies on its intrinsic sense of 'making' or 'shaping'; with respect to clothes, fashion shapes styles, some of which for a period of time become a prevailing custom in dress by virtue of their popular esteem and, typically, widespread adoption (or at least desire to be adopted).[14] We also may regard clothes fashion as instrumental in shaping, as well as reflecting, social views of gender. This contention leads to another query.

Why do we need fashion?

If the original motivation for people creating clothing was simple—and it may or may not have been—its uses probably soon extended further. In the West, by the mid- to late 14th century, these uses, coupled with advances in tailoring, brought about what we know as 'fashion.'[15] Over the following centuries fashion and the processes attached to it (i.e., the production and consumption of clothing) have proved of enormous economic weight and social prominence. From the beginning fashion, in the words of fashion scholar Ann Priest, functioned "to create uniformity amongst equals whilst at the same time differentiating status and background, signposting preferences and commitments."[16] In this complex symbolizing of status and values fashion both reflects culture and shapes it. Put another way, fashion serves both as mirror and crystal ball, or as Joe Au summarizes the thinking of contemporary Italian fashion designers, "fashion is about current social attitudes and the future direction of the society."[17]

Joanne Finkelstein observes that fashion remains underestimated as a social force despite its apparent success engineering social practices even as it collects monetary rewards. Amazingly enough, a large part of fashion's appeal is its promise to enable each individual to stand out though, as Finkelstein notes, the central irony of fashion is that what it actually accomplishes better is social homogenization. Individualism exists in the context of a shared code about what is valued and how dress symbolically represents that.[18]

Of course, for those familiar with sociologist Georg Simmel's theory of fashion, the irony—or perhaps more accurately the *tension*—observed by Finkelstein makes sense. Simmel puts at the heart of the fashion process twin human desires: to be like others and to be unlike them; to imitate and to individuate. In his famous 1895 essay on fashion, Simmel formally expresses these as "the tendency towards social equalization" and "the desire for individual differentiation and change."[19] Accordingly, fashion can facilitate both individual expression and social affiliation—twin processes essential to this work's conception of the role of dress.

Clearly fashion invites us to focus on the symbolic power wielded by clothes.

Apparel is material, and it serves physical uses, but through color, design, and so forth it also readily lends itself to symbolism. Accordingly, as Patty Brown and Janett Rice remark, all clothing possesses both physical and behavioral dimensions. These combine to evoke sensory, emotional, and cognitive responses both in the wearer and in others.[20] Yet the way clothing does this is not uniform. As Finkelstein points out, "all fashions are ambivalent because the question of whether they are meant to be confrontational or affirmational is indeterminate."[21] Any fashion statement can be misconstrued no matter how carefully contrived.

Both the choice of what is worn and the elaboration of basic covering provide a means of signaling things to others. In fact, if you prefer to distinguish between mere covering and actual clothes, then perhaps the origin of clothing *per se* occurred when some group chose to use particular animal skins to set themselves apart.[22] At the same time, though, dress is a symbolic expression of an individual's relationship to his or her culture,[23] a way of belonging while standing in some independence. It is easy to see ideas of distinction, symbolic expression and self-identification expanding, with manners of dress conveying all of these and other aspects of culture. In fact, so potent is fashion that it has even been used successfully as a therapeutic tool.[24]

One fundamental emphasis in Western culture is the distinction between the sexes through the construction of separate gender identities and roles, with differing sets of expectations. In recent millennia this has seemed principally conducted through a hierarchical gender order. A vertical social order emphasizes the need for clear-cut distinctions in order to guard the privilege of those on top while keeping others in their place. Clothing provides an obvious tool in the construction of gender-based-on-sex distinctions. Dress offers a way to signal sex differences, build gender presentations, and then elaborate gradations in gender so that, for example, a gentleman of the upper class is a different sort of man than a ruffian of the lower class.

As best as we can tell, gendered differences in clothing have always been present. Apparently so, too, has been transgendered dress. Both seem omnipresent in cultures around the world and throughout history. Art historian Margaret Miller observes, "the sense that vestamental coding should clearly distinguish the sexes seems to be one of the rare universals of human culture, but almost equally universal is the periodic need to break the opposition embedded in the code by the introduction of a third element that is neither one sex nor the other but somehow mixes both." [25]

Later, we shall examine that phenomenon in multiple ways, through examining more closely how gender and dress are related, to studying instances of crossdressing throughout history and around the word. But we need first to catch a broader sense of the multiple roles and wide cast made by fashion. In addition to making gender distinctions, through clothing fashions human beings can make statements about other social affiliations and, ultimately, personal identity. In interactions with others clothing can signal all of the above, and more—a reality modern social psychologists are still exploring. [26]

What role does dress have in personal experience?

Clothes have become more than a means of expression. They also serve as conduits for experience tied to the clothing itself. Clothes contain and constrain the body, offering not only covering but limiting motion. [27] Clothes can both link and separate public and private, simultaneously preserving privacy and revealing the inner person. [28] They also function psychologically as a boundary, not only for the body, but for a sense of self, especially the public self. [29] With respect, for example, to sexuality, only a single cloth covering the genitals is needed to effect a boundary—often also a calculated barrier—that must be crossed or removed for intercourse to occur. [30] That boundary becomes a part of the experienced and expressed body.

On the one hand, this makes fetishism possible. The intimate proximity between material object and physical sex lends itself to the one becoming symbolically substituted for the other. The clothing next to the genitals becomes part of the sexual body, which is why lingerie attains an erotic quality. On the other hand, the use of clothing to connect with and explore the body self remains much broader than what fetishism entails. In fact, clothing is even broader for experiencing sexuality than the little aspect fetishism embraces. [31]

Each day, in some way or another, we encounter something in our dress. On one level we engage in delicious sensing of the look, smell, and feel of what we wear, because these things have become for a time a part of us. The color, texture, and fit of what we wear can excite or calm us. It can help us prepare for hard physical labor or facilitate relaxation. In some limited but important way we become the clothes we wear as much as they become a part of us. We conform to the expectations associated with the clothes we wear.

Our involvement with clothes is one way to experience the Self. How something feels on our skin, or how it changes our appearance, provides new self-realization that reinforce, expand, or alter our perception of ourselves. Through clothes we embrace (or at least encounter) our clothed self—physically and psychologically—as well as display matters about that self. In this respect, *experience* through clothing is more basic than the *expression* we discussed above. Through our manner of dress we can explore and engage a rich world of sensory experience while simultaneously exploring and engaging our sense of self and the social world around us.

The ways in which both experiencing and expressing have become anchored to clothing are diverse and complex. Influenced by culture—and influencing it—none of us are free from expectations about how we dress. At the same time, we manipulate via dress the process of personal exploration and self-actualizing. Likewise, we convey ourselves through both our conformity and rebellion to the rules about proper dress in our culture. If we are to understand crossdressing, we must see how personal experience can trump social expectations, generating a will and a way to resist and overcome social dress rules. Crossdressing entails involvement with clothes and uses of them to display who we are in ways that many among us find foreign—and perhaps upsetting. Yet, as we shall see, these experiences and expressions are widespread across cultures and range throughout history. They are an important aspect of our human story.

How does clothing affect our experience and how we express ourselves?

We care about what ourselves and others wear because of the importance of what can be realized and conveyed through clothing. Clothing purchases are hardly random—making it all the more surprising how little study has been conducted concerning the psychological factors at play when consumers make their choices.[32] Perhaps we are so accustomed to the role of dress in our lives both personally and socially that despite our care in selecting apparel we actually give little conscious thought to the myriad ways we find experience in and through clothes, or use clothing to express something. Much about the system with clothes at its center remains unconscious to us. When we do consider our clothes we may often do so naively and simplistically, making unwarranted assumptions about what others will perceive.

Likewise we are prone to errors when we infer what others intend to manifest through their manner of dress. We can benefit from better grasping how we interact with clothes, how they serve as conduits of exploring the self and relationships, and how we rely on dress to convey a multitude of basic and important matters. Understanding such things will put us in better touch with our own self and with other selves. Among other matters, clothes can communicate group affiliations, express personal identities, and suggest ways of relating. These factors all also apply to crossdressing.

How *does* clothing affect our experience and expression? An old saying runs, 'Clothes make the man' (or woman). Often called 'a second skin,' clothing shapes and alters appearance; this 'making' produces a presentation, perhaps more or less calculated, that others perceive and judge. What we wear commonly intends to make a personal statement directed to others—and others are often keenly interested in getting the message. Clothing, in this regard, is central to a sophisticated sending/receiving system of human expression.[33] Of course, as we noted earlier, we interact with clothing for more than expressive purposes. We also use dress as a conduit to important self-discoveries and enjoyable self-encounters. So this 'system' we will discuss is really both an experiencing and expressive one, with both aspects anchored in clothing.

The relationship between experience and expression is reciprocal. What we experience may unconsciously leak out in our expression or burst exuberantly and consciously forth. What we express generates and shapes internal experiences. In a very real sense every experience of dress is an expression and every expression an experience. So as we focus on the expressive side of the equation we remain attached to the experiencing aspects. This fundamental truth needs to be kept in mind as we proceed.

What are the elements of this experiencing and expressive system?

What we need is some rudimentary map to guide us. This requires a modicum of patience to ground ourselves in a bit of theory. While the purpose of this volume is not to elaborate a comprehensive theory of dress, we would be naïve to presume we don't all have at least some implicit theory of dress already. Far better we should spend a little time articulating the basics of a theory to guide us anew than to fall prey to our existing ideas, which may be largely unexamined or tested.

Let us start with the most basic term: *system*. As pointed out earlier, clothing does more than just protect us from the elements. It really doesn't have to do more—we might have settled for rather shapeless and colorless coverings that just kept us warm and/or hidden. But we did more than that. Characteristically, we imbued dress with meaning and incorporated clothing into the wide and complex symbol system we use to communicate with each other. In the process we also found ourselves experiencing the colors, textures, forms and fashions of dress itself. We also discovered that through these things we had new ways of experiencing self and relationships.

This occurred in various ways in different cultures. We could say with justice that this system is really many systems. But the underlying human process creates enough fundamental similarities to make it accurate to think of a universal system expressing itself in several cultural manifestations. This is why crossdressing in one form or another seems to crop up everywhere, irrespective of a particular culture's unique presentation of this universal system.[34]

We might also fairly say that the 'system' is an organic one, growing and developing through time. Clothing anchors this system as the concrete physical reality to which are attached all manner of symbolic meanings, social expectations, and utilitarian uses. As a system, this is a network of reciprocally interacting aspects fluidly related to one another. In other words, clothes, symbols, social rules and the practical uses for articles of clothing all influence each other. They do so dynamically, with changes occurring that reflect themselves through alterations of symbolic meanings, adjustments in social expectations, changes in how certain clothes are used, and in the manner and form of the clothes themselves. (Thus, with reference to crossdressing, important aspects of its identification and manifestation vary in different times and places.) Yet, despite the shifting, dynamic nature of these interrelationships, they persist and thus really are an identifiable 'system.' As such, in any specific time and place this system can be relatively marked out and delineated.

Obviously, navigating such a complex system is hazardous. Our brief investigation of it here will not solve that problem, though it may make movement within the system easier. In the world of lived experience, experiencing clothes and the expressiveness associated with what we wear never gets so easy we can afford complacency. The chief reason for this continuing difficulty lies in why the system is so complex: it is both *social* and *personal* with each dimension remaining largely *unconscious*.

A Largely Unconscious System

We will begin with this last aspect. This system commonly operates without our being very conscious of it. While that does not make our experience of what we wear any less real, it can and does complicate things. Unaware of all that is happening when we put on clothes, we may dismiss important aspects of the experiencing that takes place, truncate the experiencing possible to us, or misattribute to other things the effects experienced.[35] By raising unconscious matters to consciousness we increase our chance to exert a measure of control so that we are not blindsided by the frequently irrational character of these forces.

But that means probing to discover these unconscious contents. Susan Kaiser, a professor of textiles and clothing, as well as scholar of women and gender studies, explores the unconscious aspects involved in our interactions with clothes in a classic text. She notes the roles played by cultural ideas of sexuality and gender in shaping fashion, among other factors. [36] Though we may be mostly unaware of such influences they exert their force in shaping both our personal unconscious and what psychiatrist Carl Jung called the 'collective unconscious.'[37]

Jung also champions the notion that our individual psychological selves unconsciously seek balance, or equilibrium through the expression of 'inferior' (less developed) psychological functions. One aspect of our psychological selves is gender. Jung proposes that males need to experience and express the *anima*, or feminine aspects of self, to reach balance; females need to experience and express the *animus*, or masculine aspects of self.[38] There are undoubtedly many ways such a task can be accomplished and clothing provides one such conduit. Through dress—'*cross*dressing' if we wish—we can experience and express another gender than our assigned and expected one. Perhaps in some way, or to some degree, the unconscious force of Jungian archetypes (*anima, animus*) are at play within this system we are exploring, manifesting at times in crossdressing.[39]

On the other hand, our awareness of clothes can get us into trouble too. We may intentionally seek experiences through clothes that others won't share, or mean to express things that others don't (or won't) understand. Similarly, we may seriously misjudge the experience or expression of someone else related to how they dress. Finally, we don't want to exclude the possibility that sometimes what we, or someone else, wears doesn't intend anything, either consciously or unconsciously. Making absolute or universal judgments only makes for trouble!

Dual Dimensions: Social and Personal

Although partly unconscious, this system is also partly conscious. Nevertheless, in discussing the social and personal aspects of the system we would do well to remember that both possess conscious and unconscious dimensions. Social and personal duality may be simplistically portrayed like this:

❑ *Social* aspects of the system:
- *social experiencing*—the role of clothing as a conduit for shared experiences; and,
- *social expressiveness*—the role of clothing in displaying social aspects of the self, such as our group affiliations and identities.

❑ *Personal* aspects of the system:
- *personal experiencing*—the sensual experience of wearing various kinds of clothing and the experienced changes in self from so doing; and,
- *personal expressiveness*—the use of clothing to make personal statements regardless of conformity to social rules.

Social Aspects of the System

What beguiles us into thinking we understand the experience of clothes and what they express is the truth that the system formed around clothes is a social one and that we are conscious of this to some degree. That means shared rules and features that we can participate in and generalize. For instance, in various cultures specific colors have taken on symbolic meaning, and this meaning is conveyed to clothes, where it becomes another aspect of what the clothing means to the wearer and to others. To the extent we grasp such matters in a culture and embrace them, we can utilize them in our clothing choices both as a means of manipulating our experience (e.g., through choosing colors to boost our mood), or to express ourselves (e.g., through displaying a color to tell others how we feel).

Yet, as researchers Craig Thompson and Diana Haytko point out, the ways we talk about fashion—'fashion discourses'—afford so many different interpretive positions that an astounding range of juxtapositions are possible, including opposing values and beliefs. Somehow we need to honor both our individual experience and our obligations to society (largely met through our membership in various groups).[40] Accordingly, our notion that there is a shared set of meanings around dress may not be incorrect, but it will lead us astray if we suppose that such a set prevails for all people all the time. Rather, the social system of dress is best seen as an ongoing conversation in which the few general lines of discourse we discern are always set against a backdrop of babble.

That said, most of us remain interested in catching what basic threads of the discussion we can. With that in mind, let's consider findings in a foreign culture that may strike us as not so different from our own. In 2002, research involving 400 Korean women surveyed in a mall setting, MiKyeong Bae, Seong Sin Lee, and Sun Young Park found moderate to strong relationships between consumer purchases of a clothing item (jacket) and ten factors of clothing orientation. Their Factor 1, 'Clothing Involvement,' includes three items expressed as statements people may make:

❑ People form their opinions from me and my clothing.
❑ Clothing lets me express myself.
❑ You can tell a lot about a person by clothing.[41]

Consumers endorsed such views, but not as strongly as Factor 5, 'Benefit Sought 1,' which included such items as the following:

❑ Name brands represent social status.
❑ I wear clothes to attract the opposite sex.
❑ I wear clothes to look better.[42]

These 'benefits' reflect psychological perceptions in line with the beliefs espoused in the first factor.

While the Clothing Orientation Scale's ten factors include items related to enjoyment of shopping, perceived price, perceived value and so forth, what we are interested in is the apparent connection between beliefs about clothes and the benefits consumers believe they attain in a social context. The plausibility that our purchases of clothing are motivated in part by such social factors seems unassailable. We use dress as a means to enhance our standing in a social context, through identification with a desired social status, expression of our 'best' self, and so forth. We also use dress to advertise ourselves, including our sexual availability—another way of employing dress to create a shared experience.

Personal Aspects of the System

But some of the 'benefits' consumers seek are as directed at the self as at others; they are both social *and* personal. For example, also among the 'benefits' of Factor 5 are the following:

❑ Self-respect is raised by clothing.

❑ Wearing name brands raises self-esteem.[43]

Self-esteem and self-respect are important personal psychological characteristics.

Some might object that attaching any degree of self-respect and self-esteem to dress is shallow, the kind of superficial action we might associate with childhood or adolescence rather than maturity. Yet the research cited above included adults. Furthermore, other research indicates the same forces at work among older men and women. A study reported in 2000, involving 978 men and women over age 65, discovered that apparel significance was positively related to a number of factors, including self-esteem.[44] Most of us, children or adults, young or old, think our clothing matters and hence most of us find a connection between our dressed appearance and internal, psychological factors.

Another study, reported in the mid-1990s, found among young adults six 'social psychological' functions related to clothes as possessions—and three of these are explicitly personal:

❑ to express an individual sense of self-identity or unique personality;

❑ to provide a record of one's personal history and memories; and,

❑ to bolster mood and self-confidence.[45]

We need, then, to acknowledge the personal, highly individual aspect of this system alongside the social aspects. Each of us has an intimate and unique relationship to clothes. In that relationship we carry our own meanings, degree of importance, and felt sense of dress. We may use these together with our clothes to boost our self-esteem and self-respect. Though our relationship to clothes is shaped in part by cultural forces, it also is marked by idiosyncratic choices and preferences, personal experiences, and developmental factors. Our personality, upbringing, and actual life experiences all shape our relationship to clothes. We bring all of these things to this experiencing and expressive system.

Naturally that gets us into trouble. None of us does exceptionally well in figuring out where the boundary line between personal and social lies. Indeed, it shifts due to the relative influence each side exerts on us at any given time. Sometimes we are most guided by cultural expectations and rules; other times we defy those same forces in our effort to be who we are. In the middle of all this who can fault us for being confused? But if we have trouble always discerning what is going on with ourselves when we put on clothes, how much more should we be wary of assessing what is going on with others!

When we relate to others, clothing inevitably enters in. We experience others, in part, through their 'second skin.' We interact with them guided both by what we are wearing and what they are wearing; different dress styles strongly influence the course of an interaction. In fact, the subtle but potent impact of clothing on relationships can be glimpsed especially in a common relational gesture: the gift of clothes. Pulitzer prize winner Alison Lurie is surely correct in the observation that "such a gift is a mixed blessing, for to wear clothes chosen by someone else is to accept and project their donor's image of you; in a sense, to become a ventriloquist's doll." [46]

By the very nature of what we are covering in this book we shall devote most of our attention to the social side of this system, especially the expressive subsystem. The distinguishing feature of the personal side is just that—it's personal. As such it is highly individualistic and variable. While we should grant that any distinction between social and personal is bound to be somewhat arbitrary, since both merge in intrinsic and vital ways, the attempt to distinguish them is important because it keeps us honest: we simply aren't as good at managing this system as we might like to be (or think we are).

The Role of Fashion

On the social side of this system, human beings created fashion. However else that term is used, [47] one sense is this: fashion is the shaping of styles of dress to express customs and conventions among people. In so doing, fashion differentiates. It makes distinctions among social classes, age groups, and cultural groups. It also divides folk along gender lines—a particular concern for us since the term 'crossdressing' connotes a violation of these lines. In this sense, fashion is inseparable from crossdressing, at least anywhere that gender distinctions in clothing are socially dictated.

Of course, where we are today in our culture is just a point along the way. Fashion did not arrive full-blown on the scene. Today's fashions have continuities and discontinuities with past fashion that may prove important to understanding some things about crossdressing (cf. the answer to Q. 9). But wherever such investigation might lead us, we must first consider the most rudimentary elements of the social expressive subsystem built around clothing.

Elements of the Expressive Subsystem

Most simply, this social expressiveness as a subsystem has the following elements:

❑ *a point of origin*—this is the person and the clothing as a unity;
❑ *rules*—these are the conventions and customs of fashion;
❑ *points of reception*—these are the observers who witness an expression; and,
❑ *a context*—a specific situational matrix involving all the other elements.

While this expressive subsystem obviously is more complex than this rudimentary picture and merits more elaboration, for our purposes these few elements will suffice.

Many authors have referred to this system as a language. Lurie, for example, begins her book *The Language of Clothes* by referring to this use of dress as an "older and more universal tongue" than speech.[48] Lurie's interest lies in the vocabulary and grammar of this language, which is influenced by both the social and personal dimensions noted earlier so that this universal tongue is actually many languages. There is much to admire in such an approach. But it is hard to ignore Fred Davis' contention that if dress constitutes a language it is certainly an ambiguous one.[49] I prefer the term 'expression' to 'language,' or even 'communication,' because these other terms connote a consciousness and intention often lacking in our dress. While what we wear may be said to always communicate, it does not always do so in ways we are conscious of or intend. Since we generally use a term like 'language' to refer to intentional efforts to transmit information from one to another person, that term doesn't fit as well for what I mean as does 'expression.'

Expression involves representation and revelation. The 'communication' may be as natural as what a daisy in a field provides: an unself-conscious disclosure of its character. We witness the daisy and receive meaning from its disclosure even though it is not intentionally saying anything to us. This, I think, is what separates an expressive system from a language communication system. In a similar manner, clothing can reveal and represent us in an unself-conscious disclosure of our character and affiliations. The preeminence is not in the intention to send a message, nor is the emphasis on what a witness receives. Rather, the focus is on the point of origin.

In the expressive system envisioned above, the person and what is worn constitute a unity. This unity is inseparable from what is being expressed; we become what we wear. The 'second skin' of our clothing is *us*. The same power we use to transform ourselves through clothes may transform the way others see us. This is exactly why what we wear has the power to shock and upset others. We cannot easily or completely separate the wearer from what is worn. The denial of what someone wears is the denial of the person. Conversely, to accept what another wears is to offer at least implicit acceptance of that person's self. Although we may be largely unconscious to this dynamic, it lies centrally located in the dilemma we face in responding to a crossdresser.

So far our focus has been upon the point of origin, but already we have found that witnesses to the expression—our third element—cannot be ignored. Sometimes our clothing expressions are self-referential; we are our own witness, and the only one. [50] But frequently others see us in the garb we have chosen and, whether we mean any message or not by our choices, others may infer meaning. How they do that relies on the second and fourth components of our system.

34

Rules provide guidelines for interpreting clothing expressions. [51] These rules derive from multiple inputs. Culture is a primary source, both directly through fashion norms within a society and indirectly, through such things as gender expectations. Thus, as Alison Lurie observes, "Most men, however wet or cold they might be, would not put on a woman's dress, just as they would not use words such as 'simply marvelous,' which in this culture are considered specifically feminine." [52] Clothing rules set boundaries and establish conventions that direct our thinking. That makes them perfect for creative manipulation in the interest of highly personal statements.

We follow, bend, or break the rules of our groups whenever we dress. In any given moment our pursuit of self-expression can mean any of these alternatives—following, bending, or breaking the social conventions and customs of a group we are part of. For example, a crossdresser in the company of other crossdressers is following the conventions of dress for that group while simultaneously breaking the customs of fashion for a wider social group. Since the fashion conventions of the culture exert broad force, as individuals we may seek the support of smaller groups where we can together bend or break social customs we have not the will or strength to do by ourselves.

The example just given also illustrates the importance of context, our fourth element. Context includes both the specific situation and setting, plus the values and experiences that those involved bring to both. We look to situations and settings to provide contextual clues, [53] but what we select as relevant and how we manage that information is shaped by our own experience and values. At both the point of origin and all points of reception context is utilized to provide clues to decide which rules are most salient and how they should be applied. Because rules tend to be informal, they have a degree of flexibility that relies on context. Because there are enough rules to create a hierarchical structure, context also allows a reordering of rules so that—theoretically at least—various ones can take precedence in one situation but recede in another. [54]

What are two important things clothes express?

What we have been talking about has prepared us to be explicit about specific things this expressive subsystem is about. Remember, because fashion differentiates it is a wonderful vehicle for expressing ways in which groups differ from one another and, within groups, how individuals vary from one another. Thus, dress serves as an expressive system for both collective entities ranging from cliques to cultural groups, and for every one of us as individuals. Put another way, the following emerge as two fundamental reasons why dress matters:

❑ Clothes offer experiences that aid self-identity and personal expression.
❑ Clothes facilitate social affiliations and identify them.

In subsequent questions these reasons are explained further.

35

But before we turn to those reasons, we should also note that associated with affiliations and individuality are other important matters. Gender, for instance, is one affiliation, and in our culture is central to individuality as well as being an integral aspect of many (perhaps all) other affiliations. Obviously, in trying to understand crossdressing the relation of dress to gender will be a central concern for us (see, for example, the answers to Q. 67). Concerns about gender reflect in dress and raise questions of value, ethics and morality (see the answer to Q. 4). All these matters contribute to the context in which crossdressing occurs—and within which it must be interpreted.

Q. 2

How do we experience clothes?

The Short Answer: While the elements of dress are made to serve human purposes, they retain an independent reality that influences our selection and use of them. The varying properties of items of dress create different sensations (notably tactile, visual, and auditory), which elicit perceptions. These perceptions are guided by values and expectations that are both personal and social. When these elements are distilled in any given context they create dress experiences. At a fundamental level not merely the symbolic meanings we attach to dress, but the physiological experiences too, contribute to what we discover in wearing our clothes. We may be said both to dialog with clothes through our dress behavior, and to use them to dialog with our own selves and other selves. In fact, many of our dress experiences involve directly and potently our sense of self. Or perhaps we would do better to say 'senses' of self, for the diversity in clothing styles, garments, and colors available to us mirrors the incredible variety possible in our individual selves. To make only one distinction, we construct both personal and social selves—and dress facilitates exploring, realizing, and conveying each. Every encounter with apparel provides an experience, and every experience can contribute to self-perception, self-identity, and self-expression. Those who wish to do so can choose from the immense possibilities afforded by dress to display virtually any sense of self they desire to express. Clothing offers a robust system for self-expression and communicating the self to others. Although cultural pressures through fashion help steer us into the kind of selves we think society desires, we can choose individual paths that produce unique experiences and distinctive self-expressions. In this endeavor some utilize crossdressing.

The Longer Answer: Who will argue that apparel does not afford us ways to express our individual selves? Self-expression is one of the greatest benefits people report they gain from dress. Unfortunately, the idea is so commonplace it may actually mask an important corollary: through dress we *experience* the self. This experiencing is more than a substrate for expression; it is its foundation. Dress affords us daily occasions of important self-experience, which may be self-exploration as we try on new garments, self-reassurance in the comfort of

37

familiar clothes, or any number of other experiences that hinge on wearing something.

But already we have jumped ahead. Let's retreat to a sensible starting point: our embodied selves. Though the self is a construct, like all constructs it arises from an observable reality. The first thing we can say about the self is its most noticeably observable aspect—the human body. Each of us *is* a body; "the body constitutes the environment of the self," as sociologist Joanne Entwistle aptly puts it. Yet, as Entwistle immediately adds, "human bodies are *dressed* bodies."[55] Our physical selves interact with a material world, and the principal medium between the rest of that world and us is the clothing we select to wear.

Where otherwise bare flesh must receive the brunt of environmental input, clothes intervene, both shielding us from stimuli and creating stimuli of their own. Both a second skin and a separate skin, clothing is the most immediately relevant physical presence to the self each day. Whether we think that we should select clothes to fit us, or we choose to modify ourselves to fit clothes (sometimes with the help of other clothes[56]), we continually interact with the elements of dress.

While the physical properties of what we put on should not be ignored (though they commonly are by social scientists), the symbolic properties achieve preeminence in making dress a potentially rich field for self-experience. Social theorist Anthony Giddens points out that as a symbolic display, dress is "a way of giving external form to narratives of self-identity."[57] The stories we tell ourselves about our self become reflected in our apparel choices and then, however imperfectly, sent to any observers. Internal experience accompanies an external behavior, the wearing of clothes, which is a billboard medium to project the self publicly.[58] As Entwistle succinctly writes, "dress is both an intimate experience of the body and a public presentation of it."[59] And Giddens is right in his choice of terms: no matter how private we intend it, how alone we may be, dress is *display*. We may be our own intended audience, but we must at least imagine other observers.

Through dress we are offered first an opportunity to experience the self in some way dependent on the clothes we wear, and then further the chance to try to express this self we experience. In asking how we experience clothes we must address both personal and social dimensions, both our experience of the self through dress and our efforts to communicate the self to others through dress expression. Although self-expression is treated separately below, in reality it constitutes an important part of self-experience. But we shall begin by establishing how self-experience through dress is even possible.

How does clothing affect our physiology and psychology?

Clothes as a Self-boundary

Self-experiencing via dress is possible because clothes have an independent reality. The self is formed and develops by boundary constructions, which require the existence of other things and people to form. Everything we encounter contributes in some way to our construction, maintenance, or development of self-boundaries, and thus indirectly to the self-contents within those boundaries. But not everything does this with equal potency. Of the objects that populate our ordinary world, clothes prove the most significant in boundary formation. This conclusion is driven by the intimacy we have with apparel, which resides so close to us it constitutes a second skin. In putting on dress we construct a body boundary that is part of our self's boundary system.[60]

Within that system self-contents are shaped. Apparel does more than block or mediate sensory signals from the environment. They provide sensory stimulation. Thus clothes offer something tangible, with traits that embody symbolic meanings. In putting clothes on we create a boundary that extends our body boundary system and protects it, incorporates the sensations provided by the clothing, and simultaneously appropriates any symbolic meanings associated with the apparel for the self-contents within the boundaries of the self. Simply said, clothes become part of the self both by acting as a self-boundary and by lending their physical properties as well as their symbolic meanings.

Yet clothes themselves remain devoid of selfhood. We may attribute some degree of personality to them, but we remain aware they have no personhood. Despite the fact we encounter their sensory properties, borrow their meanings, and make use of them as a boundary, we remain in important ways separate from them. Put bluntly, we may make clothes temporarily part of who we are, but they no more become us than we become them. We *wear* clothes, perhaps in some moments even *embody* their symbols—an outcome allowing us with gendered dress to inhabit to some degree the gender attached to the clothes. But they are always a skin that can be shed. And when we shed that skin we set aside what the clothes afforded us. In every wardrobe change we possess the potential to construct a new self-presentation, albeit a transient one.

The Impact of Clothing on Physiology & Psychology

Interestingly, the 'skin' we put on with clothes interacts with our natural skin producing physiological and psychological effects that vary with the composition of the apparel. As in music, where it is not only the notes, but the spaces between them that matter, so in apparel it is both contact with skin and space away from the skin that matter. As noted by Elise Dee Co, "against the skin constantly throughout the course of a day, clothing provides perhaps the most persistent tactile stimulation." However, as Co reminds us, clothes can be shaped to create space as well as skin contact. The allowance of 'ease,' added space to facilitate movement, is as important to comfort as the sensation of cloth on the body.[61]

Much of the time our attention to such matters is limited just to our perceived comfort. This single dimension has been a special focus of both consumers and manufacturers for some two centuries at least. But even this narrow interest points us to a reality we can build upon: physiological factors such as pressure on the skin, the dryness or dampness of the material, its smoothness or roughness, the way it conducts or retards heat transfer, and so forth, all contribute to our assessment of comfort.[62] Additionally, activation of the senses of sight and hearing also elicit bodily responses. Physiological cues prompt psychological assessments—in this case of comfort, but of many other matters, too.

Given that we are investigating the contention that we experience the self in clothes, both physiology and psychology are important. They may converge in *interoception*, the entire body's sense of its physiological condition, which includes psychological motivation through feelings aroused by this sense.[63] Modern science provides tools allowing us some direct study of physiological changes produced by clothing and indirect, but evidentiary-based inferences about psychological changes. The result is powerful confirmation of what everyday experience teaches us: change clothes and change the self's experience; change gendered dress and change gendered self-experience. Such changes start with the skin.

The Impact of Clothing Fibers & Fabrics

The human skin is our largest sensory organ. Putting on clothes alters this organ as new sensory information is provided. Receptors in the skin transmit information to the brain about the stimuli provided by the clothes. Some of these nerve signals relay information to the brain's somatosensory cortex about the contact and pressure of the garments. Other signals travel to the insula (insular cortex), a part of the brain's limbic system. The insula processes information in order to provide for sensory experience an emotional context; it helps interpret the felt experience of the clothing. Mediated in the brain, the signals sent by apparel stimulate various body processes. These processes not only relate to matters such as the comfort felt in certain apparel, but also contribute to health.[64]

Polish researchers Malgorzata Zimniewska and Ryszard Kozlowski reported in 2004 a variety of studies conducted on physiological changes attributable to fibers used in clothing. In one study, volunteers slept in a laboratory where environmental controls were strictly monitored. The only condition varied was the fabric composition of the bedding: linen, cotton, or polyester. The experiments revealed that subjects using linen or cotton bedding slept deeper, with a lower body temperature and a higher immunoglobulin A (IgA) content, all indications of a more restful and healthier sleep. They compared these results with research done by others that found cotton pajamas, compared to polyester pajamas, significantly changed sebaceous gland activity in the skin. These changes were associated with less stressful sleep and, with enhanced sebaceous gland activity, better skin defense against bacteria and other environmental contaminants.[65]

In another study reported by Zimniewska and Kozlowski, male volunteers were tested to see what physiological differences occurred in various trials (resting, mild exercise, and post-exercise recovery), where the subjects wore either linen garments or ones made of polyester. The researchers were specifically interested in the effect of wearing these materials across situations on the body's total antioxidant status (TAS), which is part of our natural defense system. They found TAS lower for those who wore polyester across the trials compared to those wearing linen.[66]

Other studies found similar results favoring the health properties of linen over polyester. For example, muscle fatigue appears greater in individuals who wear polyester over several hours. Natural fibers like linen and hemp offer protection against ultraviolet rays of the sun. Such materials are, in fact, the best protection for the skin when outdoors.[67] In sum, natural fibers, by producing physiological changes conducive to health, prompt psychological changes such as feelings of being more rested, comfortable, vigorous, and so forth. These kinds of studies provide a physiological foundation that contributes to our better understanding the psychological effects of clothing. As researchers on clothing luxury aptly put it, "Physio- and psycho-pleasures are linked with each other through bodily wellbeing."[68]

Some research indicates that physical properties of fabric can be reliably correlated to touch sensations such that varying the fabric will predictably change the descriptors used by people handling it. In general, this research shows, people's expressed preference for fabrics increases as the perception of surface roughness decreases; we like smooth over rough fabrics.[69] In sum, then, the above evidence demonstrates how clothing interacts with our skin to produce sensations our brains interpret and fit in a psychological context of pleasure or displeasure, mood maintenance or changes, and so forth.

But touch is not the only sense enticed by clothing. Human beings tend to value sight most strongly of the senses and the visual appeal of garments is instrumental in their selection. Clearly the sensory input provided by the eyes matters as psychological judgments are being formed. Studies have demonstrated, for instance, that visual perception of the texture of the textiles used,[70] and sight-based associative aspects like colors (discussed below), which yield psychological import based on symbolic meanings,[71] are both important to us.

Likewise, the sound a garment makes elicits a psychological response. In a report issued in 2005, researchers evaluated the rustling sounds of polyester warp knitted fabrics using a psychophysiological technique. In the study, 14 women were exposed to the recorded sound of 3 different structural types of warp knitted fabrics (reverse locknit, double denbigh, and sharkskin), all made from the same fiber (75D polyester filament yarn). The women, while attached to physiological monitors, were asked to rate various sensations (softness, pleasantness, comfort, noisiness, annoyance, clearness, and highness) associated with each sound. The results support that such rustling sounds not only elicit physical sensations, but that these are variably differentiated as pleasant (e.g., the rustling sound of double denbigh) or unpleasant (e.g., sharkskin).[72]

All of these studies, and others, have this in common: they demonstrate how physiology influences psychology.

Fibers, Fabrics & Gender-differentiated Clothing

We should not find it hard to believe this process is incorporated in gender differentiating clothing. Anyone who has examined a range of masculine and feminine apparel readily recognizes the differences extend beyond style and color. Most noticeable may be things like the use of lace, a dependable gender marker of femininity these days. But we notice a difference too when we handle clothing. Devoid of visual cues, the feel of the fabric used, often remarkably different between masculine and feminine garb, can lead us to distinguish among items and make judgments as to their gender association.

People recognize this situation, of course. Many fibers and fabrics are accorded as belonging more to one gender than another. Some research has examined this phenomenon. For example, clothing scholar Mary Lou Rosencranz, in the early 1970s, reported studies on gender associations with fibers. On one end of the spectrum, wool was judged the least feminine; on the other end, lace and especially silk were judged the most feminine.[73] Given the properties of these fibers the symbolic connection is unsurprising. Softness, sensuous luster and luxuriousness—all qualities silk has in abundance—are associated with femininity.

The far greater range of clothing choices for women finds parallel in the wider use of alternative fibers and fabrics. Synthetic fibers are more likely to find their way into feminine apparel; in blended fabrics feminine clothing is likely to have a higher percentage of synthetic fibers. Individual items made entirely of synthetic fibers are also more likely to be gender-differentiated as feminine. Perhaps the synthetic material most likely to come to mind in this regard is nylon. Created in the 1930s, touted as a 'miracle fiber,' nylon stockings debuted at the San Francisco Exhibition of 1939. In the postwar period nylon established itself as a feminine essential and has remained perhaps the one fabric most readily associated with women by virtue of its use in hosiery. However, it also has been used in feminine lingerie, swimsuits, maternity wear, and sweaters.[74]

Consider, too, acetate yarns. Cellulose acetate is a manmade fiber of natural origin used in various fabrics. It provides a number of desirable characteristics including a silky feel, elegant drape, and comfort. In clothing it most often occurs in women's formal wear, nightgowns, blouses and sweaters. In sum, it serves feminine fashion much more than masculine.[75] The same might be said of a number of other fibers as well as weaves like satin.

The situation with synthetic fibers extends to natural ones. Although silk once was prized for upper class masculine fashion, and men today still can find silk shirts and underwear, in our modern Western culture it is more likely to be found in feminine apparel. In fact, silk remains esteemed as the ultimate luxury

42

fiber, suited for wedding clothes and the finest lingerie. The gendered reality is that the lustrous smoothness and softness of silk may feel pleasurable on any skin, but qualities like 'smooth' and 'soft' are in our culture associated with femininity.

Some natural fibers, like cotton, are widely used in both masculine and feminine apparel. That does not mean, however, that gender differences do not exist. For example, among children boy's clothing is far more likely to be 100% cotton than is girl's clothing. The greatest use of synthetic fibers is found in girls' apparel, particularly skirts.[76] By the time boys become young men (ages 25-34) it is little surprise to find they have the strongest preference for natural fibers.[77] Women and girls show a keener interest in the fiber composition of clothing, an interest fueled by many factors, but not least the greater range of choices open to them.

Because fabrics and the fibers they use have different properties, they produce different effects. The experienced sensations are incorporated into the store of associations we carry about gendered clothing. Though we ordinarily do not distinguish the feel of fabric from other properties such as color and style, when we pause to do so the differences between masculine and feminine clothing are apparent. Because the human skin is our largest sensory organ, and because physiological effects prompt psychological ones, it is reasonable to infer an effect from the feel of fibers contributes to a feeling of gender. To the extent that gender is constructed from body sensations, the feel of fabric is a relevant, if largely ignored, factor to consider.

Application to Crossdressing

The influence of the physiological changes elicited by clothing, prompting changes in psychological affect and cognition seem obviously pertinent to understanding crossdressing, yet there appears to have been no careful study of this. By now we should feel compelled to acknowledge this important fact: dress is gender-differentiated not merely by its look but also by its feel on the skin. More than merely an *expression* of beliefs about the genders, differences in the look and feel of clothing may be presumed to elicit varying physiological and psychological *experiences* in the wearer. Because different kinds of clothing are culturally associated with one or another gender, so also will be the effects produced experientially by wearing them. In other words, wearing dress associated with a different gender teaches the wearer to experience that gender.

Logically, if a boy—for whatever reason, constitutionally or environmentally—is exposed to feminine apparel and finds the resulting experience richly satisfying, because the feel and look of the clothes prompts changes physiological and psychological associated with pleasure, then the boy will seek to repeat such experience. The initial experience may be largely independent of either consciousness of gender differentiation in dress or concern about gender differentiation. In short, the initial experience may have little or nothing to do with

43

gender *per se*. The child may not be seeking to express anything; the experience is satisfying in and of itself because the clothes in their independent reality offer a venue for pleasurable sensation. This child's body interacts with the physicality of these clothes such as to produce a pleasing experience. The experience is not one of crossdressing so much as simply an experience of dressing. The pleasure in such clothing can persist into adulthood, but this pleasure becomes embedded in layers of meanings informed by the relation of dress to gender.

Though little explored, there is evidence for this contention that the sheer pleasure of the clothes themselves motivates crossdressing. For example, in a report published in 1996, based on data from more than 1,000 British men, medical writer Vernon Coleman found that of five possible reasons for crossdressing provided to respondents the one that was endorsed most frequently (by 77% of the men) was 'like the feeling of women's clothes.'[78] Many male crossdressers testify they find the variety and sensuousness of feminine clothing appealing. Unfortunately, virtually always others construe such declarations as meaning the crossdresser finds the apparel sexually stimulating. Certainly that occurs—just as it does for noncrossdressers—with some items, but there is much more to sensual satisfaction than sexual arousal.

However, because the clothing used by the crossdresser *is* gender-differentiated, gender sooner or later becomes more prominent and most crossdressers learn to identify gender expression as the motivation for their behavior. In part this may be a defense against a different construal by others—that the motivation has more to do with sexual deviance than variant gender. We would be wrong to deny that some crossdressing finds in the clothes a source of erotic pleasure. But we also would be wrong to assume that all pleasure in crossdressing is sexual in nature.

For some children the original sensual experience of apparel in its own right is translated into a pleasurable feeling associated with sexuality. There may be a variety of ways this comes to pass, and we shall consider the matter elsewhere (see the answers to Q. 21-22, 86-90). However it happens, over time the preoccupation with this particular form of sensuous satisfaction through dress may develop into what mental health professionals term 'transvestic fetishism' (see the answers to Q. 88, 96). But this is by no means the only possible path developmentally.

For other children whatever sexual component may emerge stays secondary to gender issues. Crossdressing cannot help but teach gender to some degree because we have made gender-differentiated clothes so intrinsic to gender. We learn early that putting on the gender clothes is putting on the gender. The assigned gender may prove taxing enough that the original pleasure experienced directly in the clothing, apart from gender meanings, becomes attached to those meanings. Thus the relief and generalized pleasure associated with temporary affiliation with another gender through periodic practice of crossdressing is a natural development from the former pleasure in the clothing in its own right.

44

Many identified as transvestites (see the answer to Q. 18) identify both cross-gender identification and stress relief as component features of their crossdressing.

For yet other children the experience is deeply tied to a developing sense of gender at variance with birth-assigned gender. The experience of gender-differentiated clothes resonates with a sense of gender identity to such an extent the body itself feels wrong and the child becomes someone identified as transsexual (see the answer to Q. 19). In these cases the original pleasure of certain apparel is conjoined to a deep, abiding sense of rightness about wearing such clothing as belonging to a fixed, intrinsic, and pervasive sense of the gendered self. It is functionally irrelevant whether the clothes experience or gender experience comes first because the two are so intertwined that the individual is unlikely to endorse the behavior as crossdressing. How can one crossdress when choosing to wear the apparel assigned to the gender being inhabited all the time?

The point is this: comprehending the influence of dress on physiology and psychology offers a plausible hypothesis for a common ground underlying the multiple developmental pathways of transgender connected to crossdressing. For at least some crossdressers, early experience of clothing associated with each gender may have produced significantly varying results. A preference for the experience accompanying dress assigned to the other gender presents then a psychological challenge to the individual. The different ways in which the individual solves this challenge leads to one or another transgender identification. For as long as dress remains gender-differentiated, any continuing experience of dress associated with a gender other than the one assigned at birth will necessitate some personal reckoning of gender that makes some transgender identity likely, if not inevitable.

The Impact of Color

While it is easy to comprehend the direction of physiological influence on psychology, it is equally important to recognize psychology influences physiology. The effects of experience and expectation, for example, may actually alter sensation; they certainly can alter perception. The most obvious case can be made for the effect of colors. Frank Menke nicely describes the reciprocal interaction: "The human reaction to a color, a color combination, and to the environment is always initially a psychological one, but it can also result in a physiological reaction. . . ." He points out that we can easily imagine a red tomato without the stimulus of an actual tomato nearby; the color is in our brain. The sensory impression of the external world is one thing; the feeling generated within the self, replete with associative memories and symbolic meanings, quite another. Though we may impute our own associations to colors, many of our psychological reactions seem to be inherited—the consequence of our species' evolutionary heritage.[79]

Because colors first derive from the natural world, and some aspects of Nature may serve as prototypes for color association, our inherited stock of symbolic meanings may rest within a range of stimuli largely accessible around the world. Red, for example, is seen in fire and blood—two potent realities fundamental to human life. Little effort is required to connect 'red—fire/blood—danger' in an associational chain. Similarly, blue abounds in sky and water, natural phenomena easily attached to words like 'cool' or 'clean.' So blue evokes vastly different associational chains from the color red. For blue, a chain might be 'blue—water—clean,' an association involved in purification rituals around the world.

Associational chains can be forged in many directions, including important social realities like gender. Long before we can easily differentiate male bodies from female ones, infants are conveniently color-coded to assign them gender and set them on a prescribed course of identity and role-playing. But it isn't merely babies we color code. To some degree we do so with adults as well. In general, darker colors and solid color patterns are more associated with masculinity while lighter colors and mixed color patterns are more associated with femininity.[80]

Our psychological sets toward certain colors prompts certain physiological changes. In a multitude of contexts the color red tells us to be wary, and we respond physiologically with increased arousal. When we say we 'see red' we mean we are angry—a pattern of physiological responses embedded in psychological ones. Yet dark red is likely to evoke different associations than bright red, and elicit different body responses. On the other hand, a color related to red, like soft shades of pink, may evoke an opposite response from agitated arousal by eliciting calm. While somewhat context-dependent (an attractive woman in a red dress, for example, prompts a different reaction than a red light, even if the shade of red is the same), color associations tend to be relatively fixed within a range of limited possibilities.

Social behaviors like color-coding babies contribute to our very early socialization into color associations. Some research indicates children by school age already have established strong color preferences and associations. In a study published in the mid-1990s, groups of children ages 5 and 6½ displayed some general agreement that brighter colors are more likely to produce positive feelings than darker colors, but also showed gender differences, with boys being more likely than girls to have positive responses to darker colors.[81] Another series of studies with children found that they use color to predict someone's sex and to form impressions about persons whose sex is known. In particular, these studies demonstrated the reliance of children on *clothing* color to assist themselves in sex determination and inferences about the characteristics of others. The use of stereotypes in this regard begins at least by preschool age.[82]

Adults perpetuate color associations. For instance, medical professionals strongly endorse white for uniforms because of the color's association with cleanliness and sterility.[83] Not unexpectedly, children and adult patients also endorse this color-to-uniform association. A study conducted in England reported in the mid-1990s that 70% of children and parents rated doctors' dress as 'important,' and even more children than adults regarded it as 'very important.' Further, the white coat was associated with competence and concern.[84] The way both professionals and patients respond to dress cues, including colors with strong symbolic associations, cannot help but influence psychologically-derived physiological changes.

Other Factors

Color is not the only pertinent example of psychology influencing physiology. British textile researchers Pat Dillon and Wendy Moody, with engineering colleagues, found that evaluations of fabrics with differing surface textures made by participants in a study were influenced by a number of factors besides the physical properties of the fabric. Among these were degree of experience handling fabrics and expectations arising from gender differences. Some of the difference between men and women may be explained by experience with fabrics (i.e., women typically have more), and some of it by physical differences (i.e., men's and women's hands differ in size); as a result, men found fabrics to be 'heavy, rough, and soft,' that women called 'light, smooth, and hard.' More than mere physiology is at work. "As well as gender issues," the authors remark, "social and cultural factors, past experiences, memories and experience with fabrics [all] have bearing on the responses" people make in evaluating fabrics.[85]

Research conducted in another culture helps reinforce these ideas. Nazlina Shaari and colleagues investigated women's responses to traditional clothing in Malay society from a *Kansei*[86] perspective. They were able to construct four classifications according to the responsible stimulus that collectively capture both conscious and unconscious responses to the clothing:

❑ *Somatic* (or *physiological*) stimulus: the tactile sensory impression left by the clothes on the skin;

❑ *Cognition* stimulus: psychological elements of expectation derived from emotional reactions acquired through personal knowledge and experience;

❑ *Pleasing* stimulus: the aesthetic sense or value conveyed by attributes of the clothes such as their material and shape; and,

❑ *Social* stimulus: the pleasure felt either from social interaction while wearing the garment or from the sense of social affiliation, identity, or status associated with the garment.[87]

These four typologies clearly show both physiological and psychological influences. In the team's view, they rest on a foundation of both haptic[88] (primarily physiological) and appearance (primarily psychological) values.

In our own society, consumers show distinct awareness of, and differing attitudes toward, fabrics. These attitudes tend to be persistent and consistent, reflect expectations about garment uses and comfort, and influence purchases.[89] While physical properties such as those described above are important, they are embedded in a dense cultural matrix. In turn that matrix centers in our notions about gender. We choose what we wear, and assess its comfort and appropriateness, not merely along conscious lines of perceived fit, use, and so forth, but also according to partly conscious, partly unconscious gender values and expectations. Our minds are active partners in dialog with body sensations.

Culture, Clothes, & Crossdressing

Once more we can imagine how this may work in crossdressing. Pleasurable, body-based sensations are translated into perceptions strongly informed by cultural notions of gender. Reciprocally, these cultural ideas influence perception. This can mean learned dislike, or at least disavowal, of the look and feel of clothing connected to another gender. A boy, for example, may learn to regard the feminine look and feel of girls' clothing as undesirable. The consequence may be a perception that something once worn with pleasure is now regarded with disgust; the actual sensation may be affected by the predisposing belief based on acculturated gender identification. In like manner, originally less pleasant clothing may become preferred because the gender status it confers is highly desired.

The Gestalt of Dress

Thus far we have concentrated on individual elements. Psychologically, separate properties such as color, fabric, fit, and style, together with their associated symbolic significance, create a *Gestalt*—a perceptual whole—which we experience directly through our senses and mediate meaningfully through our thoughts and feelings. The individual elements may emerge to the foreground of consciousness in any given situational moment, then recede into the background, but it is the *Gestalt* from moment to moment that constitutes the experiential skin of dress. Putting it on alters our experience of the self. Neither the physical properties of the apparel nor the meanings associated with them can be meaningfully separated; the *Gestalt* holistically integrates all. As a result, our experience is robust because any dress ensemble is replete with physical and psychological properties we are incorporating temporarily to our self.

One partial manifestation of this *Gestalt* is the silhouette (see the answer to Q. 6). The silhouette is like a shadow on a wall. It casts an illusion representative of more than the sum of its parts. Like a shadow, the silhouette suffers from too close inspection; it has its most power at a distance or by a casual glance. Also like a shadow, the silhouette can be manipulated, making it ideal for crossdressers and noncrossdressers alike to accomplish some semblance of the effect they seek in dress. The silhouette is a physical projection of an imagined self.

Any dress *Gestalt* relies on a generous portion of fantasy; we perceive what we want to perceive as much as we are able—and our skillful use of dress facilitates this process in imagining, experiencing, and expressing our ownselves. Thus, one way our experience of the self may be altered by what we wear is in what we imagine ourselves capable of when aided by dress. For example, a study published in 1994 examined 880 senior physical education students in Taiwan with reference to their relation to an item of sportswear—the T-shirts worn daily. Both physiological and psychological aspects were investigated. The students endorsed the connection between these two aspects by reporting their belief that functional and comfort attributes of sportswear contribute to better athletic performance. Actual physical properties of the clothing—such as how absorbent it was, its softness, and its air-permeability—all had a greater effect on psychological perception than such factors as price, brand, or overall look of the garment.[90] Whether or not the physical properties of the clothing in fact make performance better, they are believed to do so. Both physical and psychological elements contribute to a dress *Gestalt*.

How can dress alter our experience of gender?

Let us now attempt to relate what we have considered to the experience of gender. We enter the world and whether our genitalia clearly indicate our sex or not, we are designated either 'male' or 'female' and assigned a gender presumed to unfailingly coincide with that sex: 'masculine' for male, 'feminine' for female.[91] Once an assignment has been made, we are expected to develop a gender identity coinciding to it and to practice gender roles socially assigned to it. In sum, we are expected to be boys who grow into men, or girls who grow into women.

Dress is utilized by society with reference to gender in multiple ways, a few important ones including these:

❑ dress *differentiates* the genders;
❑ gender-differentiated dress *establishes* social beliefs and expectations;
❑ such dress *guards* and *maintains* those beliefs and expectations;
❑ such dress also *encourages* gender identity formation; and,
❑ such dress *facilitates* gender expression.

Gender differentiation through clothing is presumably based on the physical differences between males and females. For example, females typically have larger breasts and wider hips, which feminine fashion accommodates and often accents. However, actual gender differentiation in dress extends beyond physical differences to incorporate social beliefs. For instance, girls and women are expected to be more docile than boys and men so feminine clothing is more likely to restrict movement, either through physical constraints like corsets or modesty concerns like skirts. The wearing of gender-differentiated dress perpetuates social beliefs and expectations about gender, whether the wearer endorses all such beliefs or not. Social responses to such dress in particular guard cultural values associated with gender by rewarding dress conformity and punishing dress transgression. Early and persistent exposure to this process quickly educates most of us to what is permissible to wear, and what is forbidden, and our acquiescence encourages our affiliation with our assigned gender and thus, presumably, the healthy development of our gender identity. This identity we then proudly—or at least matter-of-factly—display in our dress. Thus dress becomes a daily and preeminent mechanism for gender expression.

The dependence on dress to aid gender has critical consequences. On one hand, it offers powerful, rich opportunities for gender self-experience and expression. On the other hand, it proves its vulnerability to manipulation for gender transgression as well. We can dress to conform to beliefs and expectations about gender and affirm them. Or we can dress to challenge those same beliefs and expectations. Such challenges may be mild, such as a girl or woman persistently selecting bifurcated garb like jeans to live an active life. Or it can be more serious, like men or women avoiding strongly gendered apparel and aiming instead for a more androgynous appearance. Or it can be blatantly transgressive, as when men dress in drag to critique the culture.

However, this exposition only highlights the role of gender-differentiated dress in self-expression. That remains only one facet of self-experience. Gender-differentiated dress offers entry into whatever gender the wearer desires to experience. As we have seen, clothes have their own properties, which influence our physiology and our psychology. Gender-differentiated clothes, by their distinction in various ways, physically thrust us into separate gender realms. For example, one among several ways that masculine dress is differentiated from feminine dress is in the side of the garment upon which buttons appear. Such a simple difference brings noticeable effects, especially to one not accustomed to the other gender style. Multiply this difference many times, through aspects like differences in color, weight of material, shape, fit, and drape of the clothing, and so forth. The result is that putting on clothes associated with another gender creates a *felt* difference; physiology and psychology alike are in play.

The notion that we use clothes to construct gender should not surprise us; it is inherently human to use tools to make things, including psychological things. Sociologist Diana Crane reminds us that while clothes are artifacts—produced by human agency—they are also creative agents capable of crafting behavior either by imposing social identities, or by empowering the assertion of latent social identities.[92] Earlier we saw that one way our experience of our self can be altered by what we wear occurs through what we imagine ourselves capable of when we put on certain clothes. Actors accomplish this regularly through costume. So do the rest of us when we choose, for instance, 'power clothing' for a business presentation or otherwise 'dress for success.' Cross-dressers are doing no differently, save that they are crossing gender lines imposed on them by others instead of staying inside them.

The physical properties of gendered clothing, added to the symbolic associations, afford strongly gendered elements of experience. A man may never know what a female body feels like, but he can know what feminine clothes feel like. Though the sensations may be somewhat different on his male body, the femininity of the clothes lends itself to his experience in some manner. In fact, it may do so in a felt way to such a degree that 'he' becomes 'she.' A male transvestite may only borrow the feminine gender for a time, and then only very partially. A transsexual male, whose inner sense of gendered self is feminine, experiences the kind of psychological right fit in feminine clothes that is complete and persistent, despite the inadequacy of the body sex.

All that we discussed above about the physiological influences on psychology and the reciprocal influence of psychology on physiology apply to transgender experience of clothes. That does not mean all such experiences are the same, either in intent or outcome. The transgendered person may seek the sensations, body alterations, and associative meanings in order to temporarily escape the confines and burdens of his or her own gender assignment—but not necessarily. The experience also may be sought to broaden, deepen, and enrich an appreciation for both the assigned gender and the one to which the clothes belong. It may happen because the individual desires to experience freedom from both masculinity and femininity by mismatching body sex and gendered dress. Or, of course, it may transpire as a way of enacting a desired or identified gender different from the one assigned at birth.

Given what we know about dress and how we can experience it, we should not be surprised that gender-differentiated dress can lead us into gender-differentiated experience. Indeed, we should be surprised at any contention that it cannot, that gender experience is inherently alienated from dress so that wearing clothes assigned to another gender cannot produce any sense of gender difference at all. Crossdressers regularly report—and we have no reason to disbelieve them—that they experience changes in body, mind, and feeling when they crossdress. Further, those changes are associated with the sense of other gender lent them by the experience of the dress they are in. No matter how we might wish to relegate this solely to the realm of personal imagination, too much evidence exists of real and perceivable changes associated with the crossdressed state.[93]

How do we dialog with dress?

In using dress to experience our individual selves we find an instrument that shapes us even as we attempt to make it our own.[94] At the same time, the act of dressing, even when private, is a public event. "As the self is dressed," writes social psychologist Gregory Stone, "it is simultaneously addressed, for, whenever we clothe ourselves, we dress 'toward' or address some audience whose validating responses are essential to the establishment of our self."[95] Because of the independent reality of clothes we are compelled to conduct a dialog with what we wear before we can express anything to others and complete important self-experience.

We want others to know us as we know ourselves and we use dress to facilitate that outcome. But this is not a straightforward process. "Clothes," declares culture scholar Katya Mandoki, "not only speak for themselves but they speak on our behalf, they describe us, commit and betray us. We try to monitor and control our clothes to have them say only what we intend them to say, but not always successfully."[96] We must on one side negotiate with our dress and on the other side negotiate with the perceptions of others.

As we experience ourselves through what we wear, we also express that understanding to ourselves. In other words, we talk to ourselves as we dress and then wear our clothes. Much of that self-conversation concerns our efforts to enhance ourselves before we extend ourselves out into the world. We dress to construct a particular self.

Mandoki explains this power of clothing as residing in 'social imaginaries'—a phrase originated by Henri Lefebvre—imaginative collective and personal constructions of a social nature. Social imaginaries modify the appearance of reality but not its makeup; they are knowingly fictional but provide hope they can be realized. Like alchemy, social imaginaries make clothes into amulets—the wearer is magically transformed. Clothes associated with particular qualities (e.g., youth or success) become, when donned, imaginative conveyors of those qualities to the wearer. We may know that the facts say otherwise, but the apparel blurs the boundary fixed between improbable and possible; social imaginaries "are like a game of 'as if' that ends losing the 'if.'"[97]

Yet the tactile reality of the garb itself keeps us grounded in a certain experience that isn't at all fictional. The clothes are what they are, and by fitting ourselves into them we enter a bounded world of color, shape, tactile sensation, and range of movement. This realm has its own rules and demands. We may bring imagination, but the clothes constrain and direct it. Thus, whatever we hope and intend to express, whatever we desire to experience, the real garments we put on still speak for themselves—and to us. Our dialog with what we wear not merely offers opportunities for experience and expression but necessitates both.

As we will see more in answering the next question, our conversation in and with dress may be about the groups we affiliate with, whether gender, professional, or otherwise. When we talk to ourselves about ourselves, and listen to what our clothes say, we cannot avoid some reflection about the self in relation to others. Though we use dress as self-talk, constructing experiences to explore or express our sense of self, that self is never entirely a private one. Quite naturally and inevitably we extend the conversation with and about our self to others. When we do so, we are using our dress not only to identify our affiliations but also to express our individuality.

Renowned British fashion designer Paul Smith, who in 2004 was European fashion's biggest success in Japan, speaks of a common perception in declaring, "Clothes are a part of self-expression, and they can show your personality or individuality."[98] Similarly, Joe Au's efforts to formulate a grounded design theory for how Italian fashion designers work identifies social attitude as the major construct guiding them; 'social attitude' means, "fashion is a tool of self-expression and is considered to be a means by which people's lifestyle and personality may be demonstrated."[99] More colloquially expressed, Susan Kaiser writes, "Clothing is a shortcut to perceiving an individual's personality." [100] Or, as Elizabeth Reitz Mullenix succinctly puts it, "Costumes, like actions, identify character."[101]

This notion presumes that we form over time reliably consistent patterns of disposition and behavior—'personality'—capable of reflection in dress. What we don't often pause to consider is that personality is textured from repeating experiences of the self. Thus, if dress can show our personality, it is revealing persistent self-experiences. Ironically, most of these are accompanied by dress (i.e., we were wearing clothes when we had such experiences), and many are actually associated with dress (i.e., the dress—whether in color, style, texture, or *Gestalt*—was an integral part of the experience). The latter situation makes possible forging a symbolic connection so strong that the dress can substitute for the experiences, which means standing in for an aspect of the personality. In this way we can literally dress to be shy or outgoing, sad or happy—we choose the clothes that engage those parts of our self-experiences that elicit the part of our personality we desire to experience in expression.

How do clothes express personality?

Probably most of us agree our dress shows our personality. Certainly we act as though we do. Not only do we assume we can show our personality in what we wear, we likewise commonly either infer, or impute, qualities of character or personality traits to others based on what they are wearing. As best we can tell, this is a universal tendency. That does not thereby make it a successful practice, but it does indicate it is an important one. How accurate are we in perceiving someone's personality from what they are wearing? Moreover, when we move from inference to imputation, how fair can we be?

Inferring Personality from Dress

First, how might we establish whether we can accurately infer personality characteristics from dress? There may be more than one way. We might administer personality tests and then correlate the results with actual clothing preferences. Or we might ask observers to interpret the dress they see and then gauge that against the dress wearer's self-perception. Fortunately, some efforts have been made along both lines.

Rosencranz in the mid-1960s reported on various empirical efforts to establish how dress correlates with personality features. For example, she points to the use of the California Psychological Inventory (CPI) to study personal preferences in dress color and design. In a study the CPI was administered to a group of young adult students. It was found that females with CPI scores for high sociability preferred deep shades and saturated colors; those with low sociability preferred tints. CPI scores for high conformity were associated with a preference for smaller, less bold designs than those who scored low conformity. Those with CPI scores for high femininity preferred more small designs.[102]

Rosencranz also reports research done using projective testing of personality to ascertain degree of clothing awareness and any possible association with other variables, such as status. A version of Henry Murray and Christiana Morgan's Thematic Apperception Test (TAT) was developed at Michigan State University and called the 'Clothing TAT.' It is comprised of 7 drawings on cards displaying incongruity between clothing and some other attribute such as age or sex, or incongruity in the dress between two people, or between the apparel and the background. Requiring 30-90 minutes to administer, in the study reported by Rosencranz it was given to 82 women in south-central Michigan selected by stratified random sampling. On average, about a quarter of the comments made concerned clothing. One card (VII) depicts a man in a skirt. It was remarked upon by 80% of the women. Results showed a correlation between women with high clothing awareness scores and upper social class status.[103] Such research certainly suggests that personality, dress, and social factors interact even at an unconscious level—an idea consistent with our recognition that the experiencing and expressive system built around dress is partly unconscious (see the answer to Q. 1).

In addition to studies using personality tests, there is some research conducted along the second line described above. It offers qualified support to the idea that we can be accurate in observation—at least to some degree. For example, a study reported in 1992 asked observers to evaluate the information presented by clothing selected by others as representative of their personalities. The observers were able to accurately decode the cues in the clothes and perceive a social identity significantly correlated with the wearers' own views about themselves. Unfortunately, such results have not been consistently found in experiments. The best we can affirm is that there does seem to be a relationship between personal identity and the clothes we choose, but this relationship is not easily deciphered. [104]

Technological Enhancements: The Emotional Wardrobe

New technological developments may ease this dilemma—or further complicate it. Early in the 21st century, a group comprised of experts in fashion and textile design alongside others expert in electrical and electronic engineering, allied to find ways to create what they term 'The Emotional Wardrobe.' Such clothing incorporates technological interfaces between the wearer and the apparel such that the apparel can visibly represent the wearer's emotional state. Moreover, the interface is also designed to stimulate the wearer's emotional response. Body sensors in the garment translate physiological data into patterns of color through light emitting diodes (LEDs) embedded behind contours in the dress.[105] The implicit conversation between wearer and worn is thus made more explicit, bringing it more fully into consciousness, and changing thereby its dynamics. Perhaps such clothing will facilitate more accurate communication between people using dress.

Imputing Gender Values to Dress

Certainly, as it is now, there is an oft hidden dark side to this matter. Not merely personality traits but moral character may be imputed to the wearer of certain clothes (see the answer to Q. 4). This possibility is inevitable when fashion styles are enforced upon a person, or group, as is the general case with highly differentiated gender garb. Cultural stereotypes about masculinity and femininity attach themselves to the clothing associated with each so that putting on the clothes means putting on the stereotypes, and the more so to the degree the clothing is viewed as especially masculine or feminine. Of course individuals can self-consciously select clothes to accept and appropriate this perception, but it still happens, whether willed or not.

Accordingly, cultural values that uphold a hierarchical gender order where masculinity carries power and privilege will lend their moral weight against expressions of masculinity by those assigned feminine gender. Thus women who appropriate masculine occupations, manners, or dress are subject not merely to resistance, but also to sanctions. Part of the punishment is the imputation of undesirable personality traits or moral flaws, as witnessed in expressions such as 'She's a pushy broad,' rather than 'She's assertive.' The message is clear: good girls dress femininely and grow up to be women who know and keep their place.

When Mullenix remarked, "Costumes, like actions, identify character," she had in mind a letter written by renowned activist Elizabeth Cady Stanton, who complained how contemporary women's dress mirrored her social condition: her clothes, Stanton wrote, "deprive her of freedom of breath and motion." Feminine dress put women into a position of dependency on men.[106] Their dependent character was written into their apparel—an imputation of a trait assigned and reinforced through dress.

Of course, the same holds true—and all the more so today—for men who select apparel seen as feminine. Crossdressing, whether done by the 19th century woman or the 21st century man, may be an act of individual expression, but it cannot escape some observers making unfavorable imputations about the wearer's character. Hence all crossdressing carries an embedded double semantic text, the desired self-expression and the social imputation, which in our society has been generally negative. No wonder crossdressers may struggle with identity issues—the very instrument they use to build and express a positive self-identity is constantly at risk of being appropriated by others to impute a very different and negative statement of identity.

Factors in Voluntary Self-expression Through Dress

However, let us return to the idea of dress willingly used for self-expression, no matter the risk of its reception. Comprehending the interplay between the elements of an expressive system is difficult, even if you keep it as simple as earlier outlined. In reality, many elements exercise influence. While observers often number many of the same factors, they typically highlight one or another matter as especially important. There may be as many hypotheses on the topic as there are observers. Still, a cursory review of a few writers on the subject can help orient us.

In their effort to set out a theoretical framework for grasping the connections between dress and identity, Mary Ellen Roach-Higgins and Joanne Eicher enumerate a list of factors associated with each. For instance, 'dress' includes how we modify our bodies and use supplements to clothing. These effects elicit sensory responses from others, and such become part of the interactions we have with one another. Knowing this, we dress with some sense that how we do so helps establish a certain identity for us. This other major part—'identity'—likewise involves a number of factors, such as positions we hold in various social structures (e.g., family), fashion standards and social mores, economic status, age, and so forth. [107]

The fashioning of social identity through dress is not a straightforward matter of choosing clothes we think will project who we really are—a commonplace idea about what personality is. The word 'personality' derives from 'persona' and refers to an actor's mask—an apt lineage when we consider how we use apparel. As Alison Guy and Maura Banim contend, women's relationships with their clothes may be organized around coexisting views of the self, of which 'the woman I am most of the time' is only one. Other self-views motivating dress behavior may be 'the woman I want to be' (recalling us to Mandoki's 'social imaginaries'), and 'the woman I fear I could be.'[108] Clothing provides a mask to project different personas, and helps craft them—an ongoing challenge fraught with peril, but also offering excitement and opportunities for growth.

Mandoki argues that ordinary folk don't much have fashion in mind when buying clothes. Instead we tend to be motivated by practical considerations. These include factors like availability and price, comfort and the occasion envisioned, fit and how we look, how easy it is to care for the garment, and so forth. Still, she points out, what we actually buy is less a matter of free choice than we might believe; specific social requirements and the dress codes we must conform to are as powerful as such factors as whether the item is even in stock.[109]

Yoon-Hee Kwon, in investigating motivating factors in daily clothing selection, also finds multiple elements involved in choosing clothing. But these various elements are subsumed under two predominant ones: temporal and clothing orientation factors. The former are more variable and include weather, the kind of activity envisioned, one's mood at the moment of selection, practicality, and the physical self. The clothing orientation factors are more constant and reflect personality dimensions such as spontaneity, self-actualization, self-regard, and feeling reactivity. These factors are interdependent; mood, for example, is influenced by weather. Thus, a given choice of what to wear on a particular day is affected not only by many factors, but also by how they interact. [110]

Life development probably plays an important role too. Identity formation is perhaps especially crucial during the period of adolescence.[111] With girls in mind, though presumably applicable also to boys, Thea Tselepis and Helena de Klerk advocate using dress during early adolescence as one important way of supporting development. They believe dress can facilitate formation of a positive body image, self concept, and individual identity. They suggest that clothes useful for such purpose are those whose fit satisfies her expectations, assist her in meeting peer group norms, and facilitate her sense of being in charge of herself.[112]

Suzanne Sontag, in 1982, advanced research on what she terms 'proximity of clothing to self.' Sontag thinks this concept can be assessed by the extent to which clothing correlates with six characteristics of perception of the closeness of clothing to the self:

❑ as one with the self, or an aspect of self;
❑ as part of how personal appearance both establishes and validates the self;
❑ as a significant self symbol of identity, mood, or attitude;
❑ as a way to show self-regard or self-worth;
❑ as part of how one responds affectively to self-evaluation; and,
❑ as related to body cathexis. [113]

Like the other studies cited above, this research conveys a sense of the importance as well as the complexity of the relationship between dress and individual expression. In sum, at risk of being repetitive, fully comprehending the relationship of dress and identity is a daunting task.

Yet we cannot escape trying to make some sense of the connection. On the one hand, we dare not be overly confident that we can always and perfectly assess another's personal characteristics by what they wear. On the other hand, we are going to make some judgments as a matter of course, so we might as well try to be as accurate as possible. For us, that starts by trying to isolate a few of the ways in which we might use dress to project inner qualities out into the outer world.

How do clothes extend the self?

The expressive system surrounding clothes starts with a point of origin: a person garbed in some form of dress. Kaiser notes how clothing, a highly visual system, generates cues; these we use to communicate to others, and others rely on them to understand us. She says that, "We tend to organize our actions around clothing symbols because they help us in defining situations and understanding others."[114]

But why do we choose *this* garment to wear? In the next question we will consider that our choices may reflect affiliation with some group. In a broad sense, the customs and conventions (i.e., 'the rules') of fashion in our society exert a pressure to dress like Americans—whatever that means—and to conform to our culture's rigid division between two genders. So we all tend to be constrained to stay within broad parameters drawn with respect to cultural and social expectations.

Yet, we also dress in highly variable ways. Despite general conformity to at least some broad affiliations, we remain distinct from each other in the particular clothes we wear. In short, our choices reflect a keen degree of individuality. Through dress we select, whether consciously or unconsciously, how to present ourselves. On any given occasion we may choose to express one aspect of ourselves over another. Or we may aim at some broad, overall presentation of the self. Regardless of specifics, dress offers a convenient and constant avenue for self-expression—and that expression reveals various experiencing of self and life.

Clothes are a ready adjunct to words and actions—a kind of extension of the self. Consider a few of the ways we use dress to express ourselves:
- ❑ We dress to suit and to reflect our mood.[115]
- ❑ We dress to make statements about our social status.[116]
- ❑ We dress to present ourselves in a particular way at events. [117]
- ❑ We dress to image our gender identity. [118]
- ❑ We dress to feel comfortable and to say, 'This is me.'[119]
- ❑ We may even dress at times to express a private and secret self.[120]

Each of these dress behaviors extend the self by projection into the world around us or extend the self by offering new ways to imagine ourselves, even if only in the privacy of our own bedroom.

How does dress enhance the self?

At the same time we use dress to *extend* the self we rely on it to *enhance* the self. We all want to put our best self on display, as constructed for a particular context, and we utilize dress to help us to do that. Central to our thinking most of the time is making ourselves as attractive as possible because we both feel better about ourselves when we think we look good and because we realize others act more favorably toward attractive people.[121] Though we may match good behavior with our dress, we all realize that others are likely to form an initial impression of us principally from our clothing because that is the first context in which they see our self.

That appearances matter seems common sense—and has empirical support through numerous studies. We need point only to one as illustrative of the issue that matters most here: dress is critical in manipulating perception of attractiveness. To the power of clothing we can also add other elements of dress such as the artful use of cosmetics and ornamentation, though the debate as to whether these add to or subtract from appearance is a longstanding one.[122] A study published in the early 1980s tested a variety of ideas related to whether dress influences perception of attractiveness. In the study, 69 color photos were taken of the same 21year-old woman posed in the same posture and facial expression with only variations in dress. She wore a wide variety of items in the different pictures, including T-shirts, pants, skirts, blouses, as well as wigs, hats, and cosmetics. Female undergraduate students were asked to sort the photos according to attractiveness. The results supported two general ideas: first, people have relatively different perceptions of attractiveness; second, regardless of their standards used to judge it, perceptions of physical attractiveness are changed by a person's dress.[123]

Fashion capitalizes on this awareness and seeks to manipulate it.[124] By constructing a more-or-less agreed upon sense of how one should look in certain social contexts, or as members of certain groups, fashion shapes vehicles of dress into which we are invited to fit ourselves in the effort to enhance who we are. The implicit promise possesses a certain irony: if we conform we can prove our individuality to best advantage! Inevitably, then, fashion influences our internal dialog.

How does dress influence our self-perception?

What is true in our use of dress for self-expression to others is also applicable to our expression to ourselves—which returns us to our starting point of dress as a means of self-talk about ourselves. Our clothed selves are embedded in a highly complex interactive process: we select what to wear both to generate a particular sense within ourselves and to direct our behavior, thoughts and feelings about our own self. In short, we cue our own person no less than we cue others.

How do clothes create an experience relevant to self-perception? Carole Turbin highlights the importance of the 'silhouette.' When we put on clothes they create a certain 'look' that generates a particular 'feel.' This happens because the items we wear restrict or allow various movements in different parts of our body. These, in turn, elicit bodily sensations. So, too, do the fabrics from which our garments are made. They also affect movement, but additionally engender sensations because of their texture and drape—the way they sit on us,

59

whether lightly or heavily, stiffly or fluidly. This constellation of effects, Turbin notes, result in private sensations with public implications.[125] What we experience *in* our dress affects what we express *by* our dress.

If we are thinking about such matters when we dress for public presentation we may believe we are in full command, able to faithfully express what we desire and capable of accurate interpretation of what others are saying through their clothes. We already have seen how doubtful this judgment is. But there is more to concern us than merely an exaggerated self-confidence. Not only are we not completely in charge of the process, we may be under its influence through the very items we think we have chosen. Perhaps the clothes have chosen us!

Even as we select clothes to express ourselves, fashion is exerting its pressure on us. In a certain respect, we are all slaves to fashion. As mentioned above, fashion influences serve to constrain individuality within the boundaries of what society desires (or what we think is socially desirable). In this manner, for example, gender ideals can be visibly represented in clothes and gender stereotypes reinforced through fashion pressures to conform. Eric Segal has described an example of this process at work in something as seemingly innocuous as the paintings of Norman Rockwell. Segal constructs a compelling argument that Rockwell's art displays its subjects' dress such as to create strong images of 'the sissy' and his adult counterpoint, 'the fop,' in distinction from the desired image of White, middle class, heterosexual masculinity. Across the next half-century of Rockwell's illustrations in *The Saturday Evening Post*—one of the most widely circulated publications in the world—these images persistently presented an ideal of American masculinity either affirmed or denied by clothing choices.[126]

Fashion pressures can result in conflict, too. Parental clashes with kids over appropriate clothing choices are a regular feature of life. Children use dress to express desires to be like those they admire. Imitation in dress is, after all, what promotes and promulgates fashion trends. Thus our private experiences can become tied to public clashes over our dress presentation.

One way that many of us escape such difficulties is by conforming in outerwear to others' expectations while letting our underwear carry the burden of our self-experience and expression. Thus many crossdressers only partially crossdress, and they do so by wearing the underwear of a different gender. In this manner their personal experience and expression is kept relatively hidden; the private is meant to trump the public.[127] In some ways underwear is ideally suited for this purpose. As Turbin points out, in contacting the most intimate parts of the body these become the most private of garments.[128] Because they are not meant to be seen in wider public venues, the revelation of them is likely to occur only by choice and to intimates most likely to accept the expression.

But relying on undergarments as a safety valve to escape conflicts over dress is, ultimately, a stopgap and an unsatisfying solution. It avoids rather than answers an important question:

Why is self-expression in dress controversial?

What should be less controversial than what we choose to wear? Yet society sets boundaries to what constitutes acceptable individual expression. As Philip Johnson, features editor at *Lucire*, put it when talking about men in skirts, "People are generally suspicious of individuals who appear to be different from the rest of the crowd, as most people are taught to follow the herd, blend in with everyone else and don't rock the boat."[129]

Any pronounced variation from an expected norm fetches attention, even if it is just wearing a coat on a hot summer day. The more pronounced the difference from the norm, or the weightier the norm itself, the more attention one can expect—the very phenomenon relied on at times in creating a distinctive look, as with Goth dress. In some situations persons who dress to express their individuality may find that expression rejected, which may prompt feelings of being rejected as a self. The ensuing interaction between people can, of course, lead to mutual enlightenment and acceptance—but often doesn't. As with the relation of dress to group affiliations, the use of clothing to reflect individuality is fraught with potential for misunderstanding.

Further complicating the situation is that while we dress to express ourselves, at times that expression includes the communication of our hopes or intentions for interaction with others. But this poses a puzzling situation for others who must accurately discern *if* we are trying to signal a desire for interaction, and if so, then *what* interaction we are wanting. Nowhere is this more dramatically critical than in determining if a manner of dress is meant to signal an interest in sexual interaction. Thus this expressive use of dress is the most potent and problematic of the communication functions clothes can play. [130]

Exactly what might be the relation of dress to sex and gender is a matter we have walked around in answering these first two questions. Now we must turn fuller attention to the matter. First we will consider it broadly (in answering Q. 3) as one of the ways we affiliate through clothes with groups. Then we will consider the context of values and moral judgments we form about gender-differentiated dress behavior (in answering Q. 5). By that point we will be quite ready to explore more closely the very ideas of 'sex' and 'gender' adhered to in our culture (in answering Q. 6). These things being done, we will then be ready to focus on crossdressing (in answering Q. 7). That, in turn, will lead us to related matters that will extend our understanding of what is happening in crossdressing.

Q. 3

How do clothes affiliate us with others?

The Short Answer: Dress is instrumental in forging affiliative bonds with social groups. Clothes commonly mark membership in groups, but do more than simply that. Because we are social beings by nature, affiliations are central to our sense of personal identity, and clothing that marks our belonging to a group simultaneously contributes a statement about our identity. Belonging has its privileges—but also its obligations. Dress codes, formal and informal, are mechanisms by which our social identity is signaled and controlled. While the most notable example of a dress code in operation is the formal uniform, which indicates both the particular group and one's rank, various fashion styles and particular garments or even accessories may also serve to identify membership in a particular group, though often less formally. One such group is the gender to which we are assigned at birth based on our body's visible sex. Like other groups, gender groups must reckon with status—an aspect of a group's pride of identity, but also a mechanism for creating hierarchical order within a group and between groups. In our culture, masculinity is privileged over femininity; the dress expectations for masculinity are therefore more sharply circumscribed. Despite the gender assignment made by others, we may or may not experientially affiliate with that gender. Instead we may affiliate with another gender, using dress to express that voluntary affiliation. In some cases, we may wish to create a sense of gender separate and distinct from either of the gender poles (masculinity and femininity) sanctioned in Western culture. Gendered distinctions in dress are ways gender groups are separated and to some extent defined. Crossdressing provides one way to signal variation from an affiliation imposed by gender assignment.

The Longer Answer: The prominence of the clothing industry in all cultures signals how important dress is to our manner of relating to one another. The design, production and consumption of apparel together comprise a substantial economic force in every society. In centuries past, clothing constituted perhaps the most significant personal property an individual owned and was accordingly treated with more care and respect than is typical today. Still, even in our contemporary world of disposable clothing, apparel remains a matter of some care and daily attention. The investment in dress that people make is highly visible in wardrobes that, as personal wealth allows, tend toward sizable and diverse. This phenomenon not merely shows that dress matters but, as Diana Crane observes, that it matters because clothing "performs a major role in the social construction of identity."[131] A diverse wardrobe means a sizable one; social construction means this collection is used instrumentally.

Why do we need so many clothes?

None of us gets by with a single outfit. None of us can because society expects too much of us in terms of role expectations. We are placed in gender groups, told what wear is suitable for the religious group we belong to, made to wear uniforms at school or work or sports play, and choose attire appropriate for leisure, formal affairs, and professional meetings. Because we all belong to many groups, and these groups to some extent distinguish themselves from one another by dress, we soon learn we need to alter our appearance in different social contexts. But these dress alterations for our social performances are multi-dimensional. Typically, we must somehow accomplish the following:

❏ show by our dress that we belong to the group;
❏ show by our dress *how* we belong;
❏ retain a sense and display of our individuality; and,
❏ do so with dress suitable to specific situations and functions.

No wonder we become stressed by how we look! The sum of it all, as Susan Kaiser tells us, is a complicated 'social psychology of dress.'[132] In short, we discover a genuine need for a robust wardrobe, one capable of meeting both personal and social requirements. Every group we affiliate with—by choice or by necessity—uses dress as one way to mark its members. And we all belong to many groups, some temporarily and others for a lifetime. So we need clothes, and lots of them. Moreover, we require purposeful, suitable *diversity* in our clothes to meet our affiliative needs.[133]

Diversity in clothing reflects reality: we all affiliate with a variety of groups, each with its own formal or informal dress code (see below). Within each group our clothes mark our status, which in some groups like the military is highly differentiated and structured. Dress elements such as stars, bars, or stripes are added to the basic uniform type to indicate rank. Other groups are much less differentiated, at least formally, and hence the apparel may be very generic, or rely on some basic signifier(s) to mark members. Medical professionals in a hospital setting, for example, may be harder to distinguish in status based merely on the garb worn. Gender groups are even more diverse, relying in many societies on a cluster of gender-differentiating dress elements, many of them minor (e.g., the side on which buttons appear), and most of them subject to change. Nevertheless, dress constitutes for groups a handy visible way of indicating status, whether as simple membership or separated into degrees of rank or hierarchy. Because we belong to many groups we must find ways to use of wardrobe resources to meet the requirements of membership.

Diversity in group-appropriate clothing facilitates our individual expression, too. Very few groups are so reliant on a formal narrow dress code so as to exclude a fair degree of individualized clothing choices. Accordingly, a major function in selecting apparel is to somehow simultaneously display our affiliation with a group while also showing our own uniqueness within the group. Our identity may include group affiliation, but it reaches well beyond that as well. Because dress is comprised of so many garments (e.g., underwear, outerwear), articles (accessories like belts and jewelry), and elements (e.g., color, fabric, shape, style), we enjoy many possible ways to accomplish these dual ends. Unfortunately, this very range of possibilities is what also evokes so much dress anxiety and fuels the consumer desire to possess more and more. In today's world, even people of modest means typically possess much larger and more diverse wardrobes than most folk in previous generations.[134]

Finally, diversity in apparel permits us to engage in the variety of social tasks the group enacts and the social roles we occupy while pursuing those tasks. The situational contexts may range from solemn formal affairs to casual pleasure activities, with each occasion calling for 'suitable' apparel. Moreover, we may occupy different roles in such contexts, perhaps functioning in a service capacity one time, and guest another; both roles demanding appropriate but different attire, though the situation (e.g., a formal dinner) may be the same. In sum, a diverse and well-cared for collection of clothes characterizes efforts to create a robust social identity.

While for some people a large and diverse wardrobe becomes an end in itself, for most of us it remains fundamentally utilitarian. We implicitly acknowledge that dress functions as a tool to place us within a social system, maintain us within it, and allow us movement within it according to rules formal and informal, general and specific. The critical role played by clothes is indicated by Alison Lurie's remark that "the more significant any social role is for an individual, the more likely he or she will be willing to dress for it."[135] As the social stakes increase, the role played by dress also increases. Though ostensibly a simple, even superficial tool, in actuality dress constitutes a preeminent instrument in the construction of our social identity and the conduct of roles associated with it.

How does dress draw boundaries?

If we have established the desirability of a diverse wardrobe, we have yet to spend enough attention on a fundamental aspect of what dress does for groups. Although there are various ways to conceive of how dress functions in social identity formation, we shall persist with the notion that dress acts to forge boundaries and that it is these we negotiate in expressing social personas.[136] Boundaries, whether personal or social, are complex. Rarely, if ever, do we profit from imagining a simple line between two readily discernible and distinct things. In answering the previous question we saw how dress fits within our personal boundary system because of its function as a 'second skin.' Now we shall briefly imagine how dress facilitates a social identity by creating a number of different boundaries. Each boundary can be thought of as a line, but with varying permeability and purpose. Some boundaries exist primarily to keep things inside from crossing outside, or vice versa; they are barriers, or gates. Other boundaries primarily serve as signals, indicating something is present, and giving it rough shape by the lines thus drawn.

The Primary Boundary

Among the boundaries dress can create one is of primary importance for groups. Similar to the manner in which clothing constitutes a second skin for the individual, acting as an important boundary that nevertheless manages to express personal identity, dress draws boundaries in appearance relevant to group identity. It first and foremost does this by defining the margin of the group itself: wear this and the wearer declares he or she belongs within the group. Within the expressive subsystem described earlier (see the answer to Q. 1), a person ordinarily dresses according to rules of dress customarily followed by the group the individual belongs to, or wishes to join. Clothing thus expresses an affiliation with the group—regardless of whether that group is defined by boundaries of ethnicity, class, age, gender, or other characteristics— which through some particular of dress facilitates the individual's recognition by her or his peers as someone who belongs. [137]

Certain professional or occupational groups have perfected the use of dress as a primary boundary by drawing it so sharply that there is ready recognition that *this* attire corresponds to *this* occupation. Ruth Rubinstein, a sociologist at the Fashion Institute of Technology, speaks of 'clothing signs,' attire established by those in charge to carry a single meaning and to guide behavior. She cites a four year long study at the University of Nevada that found "the more clearly certain clothing was associated with a social identity, the greater the sharing of meaning."[138] Rubenstein offers the examples of police officer, nun, and rodeo rider as clothed entities readily identifiable by others because the attire is such a strong sign of the group. Only those who belong to the group are expected— and sanctioned—to wear the clothing sign of the group.

With regard to identity, then, dress in its starkest group boundary role marks a line within which one gains inclusion through conformity and outside which one remains excluded from recognition. Though groups that use uniforms provide the most dramatic evidence of this, and while the inclusion/exclusion boundary thus drawn can be fuzzy for many groups, most (and perhaps all) groups retain some sense of this boundary with a common feeling among members that some particular kind of attire is highly desired while other kinds of apparel are completely inappropriate. Our dress thus makes more or less likely the establishment and maintenance of the social bonds we all need.

However, dress alone is seldom, if ever, enough to attain complete or continuing group recognition. Because other behavior also matters we may be inclined to diminish or dismiss the role played by dress. A simple illustration may prove instructive. A boy can dress in a scout's uniform and yet not be recognized as a scout by other scouts (although nonmembers of the scouts may accept the professed identity at face value). On the other hand, if a boy is a member of the scouts, he had better follow dress rules and be in uniform for scout gatherings. Dress often is a 'necessary but not sufficient' condition of membership.

This example illustrates the complex nature of the expressive system. What does a nonmember mean by dressing as a member? After all, as Rubenstein points out, it may be illegal to impersonate members of certain groups, like police officers or physicians, but it is not difficult—the clothing sign is readily accepted by others as token of membership, with all the rights and privileges attendant.[139] The boy in a scout's uniform who isn't a scout may want to be a scout, or may be mocking the scouts, or may not have anything at all in mind about the scouts when choosing the scout's uniform. On the other end of the system, observers will try to make sense of the expression by applying the rules they know about dress. Since an important rule is that distinctive garb like a uniform signifies membership in the group represented by that uniform, they will probably conclude the boy is a scout even if he isn't. If for some reason they know he is not a scout, then the violation of the dress rules may upset them.

The parallel to crossdressing should be obvious. A woman dressed as a man may mean to express identity as a man, but not necessarily. Others viewing the woman may mistake her for a man, thus accepting the expression as following the rules. Or they may see her as a woman but accept that she is bending the rules for a reason, such as to fit into a traditionally male occupation. Or they may view her as breaking the rules and either applaud her for challenging rules they agree are irrational, or censure her for violating rules they regard as essential to public order. Put a man in a dress and all the same possible scenarios exist, though the sense of what is at stake may be keener because of the hierarchical gender order.

Basic to the dilemma is that dress not only signifies affiliation with a group, but it simultaneously signifies exclusion. Only members are sanctioned to wear the group's distinctive, coded garb. Others appropriating the apparel are viewed as transgressing the group's boundaries. This is true for the Boy Scouts, and many believe it equally true for the genders. Thus crossdressing may be seen as an effort to claim membership in a gender group whose other members don't want the crossdresser, who is seen as an imposter. Fashion, in erecting boundary lines for group affiliation also sets borders to be guarded if distinctions—with exclusion attendant—are to be maintained.[140]

There is another dimension to this matter we should mark. We noted above that there are other characteristics besides dress important to identifying members of a group. We must note that this fact may be claimed as significant even with regard to dress itself. For instance, someone may claim that gendered dress is not a primary marker of affiliation with a gender because such dress depends on sexual differences between male and female bodies. Thus one may argue that the sex of the member is the real defining characteristic with dress accepted as a satisfactory marker as long as it is congruent with the wearer's sexual anatomy as set by cultural rules.

However, this underlying assumption may not in fact hold true in practice for the admittance of people into gender groups. Disjunction between anatomical sex and gendered clothing did not keep people from recognizing early feminists as women no matter how masculine their clothing. Disjunction between anatomical sex and gendered clothing also does not prevent some crossdressers from 'passing' *as if* their sex and gender match, and being treated as members of the gender group signified by their dress. Though exposure of their anatomical reality might cause some in retrospect to decry the 'lie' of the poser, that consequence does not alter the fact the person for a time was accepted as a member. Gender membership may maintain the fiction that it is based on underlying sexual differences, but everyday reality suggests it is actually dependent on clothes behavior and matching other social behaviors expected of the gender.

Secondary Boundaries: Identification & Control

In addition to the primary boundary that acts as a border helping to distinguish members from nonmembers, dress also draws secondary boundaries within the group. Dress details *how* we belong by signaling matters such as status or function. Uniform insignia exemplifies the former, a kitchen apron the latter. Typically it falls to particular elements of acceptable group dress to establish these kinds of boundaries and thus to differentiate members for one or more purposes. For example, organizational dress (i.e., clothing appropriate to the workplace), symbolically serves two principal functions: identification both with and of the group (e.g., its values), and control of the individual by the organization.[141] Uniforms, like those of the military or medical profession, accomplish such twin purposes visibly and well.

Researchers Craig Thompson and Diana Haytko remind us that our identity is not a matter of set-in-stone essential attributes, but something negotiated within a dynamic context of relationships with others.[142] Social identity vis-à-vis a group may be constructed through either relative conformity or relative nonconformity. The former path prizes being dressed like other members of the group, following a common fashion course. In terms of the latter, we may use dress to declare a degree of unwilling membership, or to distance us from others in the group. What motivates such decisions is multi-factorial, but resolves essentially to the manner in which we organize and practice our values.

Particularly for those of us in a culture where equality and liberty are basic bywords for foundational values, the idea of social control may be off-putting. Yet we all recognize that affiliations, whether in marriage or on the job or as part of a society, carry obligations that curtail our freedoms to some extent. Moreover, relationships rarely achieve perfect equality and when they do cannot retain it long; some relative imbalance, perhaps a give-and-take exchange of higher status, occurs even in the most egalitarian unions. So the construction of social identity through affiliation with groups requires some degree of submission. Following a dress code to show membership is one common sacrifice of autonomy. But, as sociologist Georg Simmel argues, fashion possesses the peculiar ability to let us demonstrate social obedience while still preserving individual differentiation.[143] In sum, even while conforming to the group—submitting to control—the possibilities offered by dress permit us to express our individuality.

Crossdressing, seen in light of these two purposes, poses a social problem anytime a society strives to keep the boundary between genders firmly distinct. The crossdresser who can pass as a member of the target gender, gaining acceptance by the group, comes voluntarily under the control of the gender role expectations for that gender group. A woman who desires to pass as a man must not only successfully pass dressed as a man, but also act as one in the masculine roles assigned the gender. The same pertains to a crossdressing male desiring to be seen and treated as a woman. But unlike other members of the gender, the crossdresser's voluntary association can be severed easily by giving up the affiliation and resuming the birth-assigned gender affiliation. Thus gender control can never be complete—a reality that may bother both noncrossdressers and crossdressers alike. It matters little that neither consciously think about this matter, for it remains a felt sense whether ever articulated or not.

But what of the crossdresser who does not pass as a member? Here the issues are more visible. First, observers face the problem of ascertaining whether the dress signals a genuine desire to belong to the gender, or is mere pretence for some other reason. If the former, it is a problem that the crossdresser cannot pass; the boundary excludes the person, who is likely to be punished for the attempt to cross both by members of the group he or she belongs to by birth assignment and by members of the desired group. If the crossdresser is not attempting to pass, then observers may be prone to assume the gesture is a mocking of the gender and see it as an affront to the values they associate with the gender. In either instance, whether genuinely desiring to pass or not, failure to do so also raises gender control issues.

The crossdresser who does *not* pass as a member of the targeted gender essentially attempts to step outside the gender control of the birth-assigned gender, but fails to engage satisfactory control within the desired gender. Accordingly, both gender groups will exercise those kinds of punitive measures meant to reinforce the basic boundary between genders. For example, a male crossdresser unsuccessful passing as a woman will be, upon discovery, subject to sanctions by men for trying to escape and also reproaches from women for trying to join. Such control mechanisms may include any number of behaviors—ridicule, scorn, alienation, discrimination, physical abuse, etc.—all of which have in common the weight of a negative social judgment. Ameliorating factors like the crossdresser's age, general social status, and persistence in the effort will also affect the response by others.

Drag—crossdressing meant to be seen as such and intended to be provocative (see the answer to Q. 17)—especially poses a dilemma for the general public. Drag represents both a calling of attention to the social gender boundaries in their identification and control functions, and a flaunting of those same functions. Drag uses dress to declare that gender identification relies on something easily manipulated and thereby relatively easily deceived. As gender performance, drag distorts what all of us do daily in using dress to appear as one gender or another. The distortion thus calls attention to the artifice we all rely upon; not nature (i.e., the sexual body), but performance (i.e., playing masculine or feminine) determines gender identity.

Drag also tweaks gender control. Crossdressing with no effort to hide the mismatch between sexual body and a gender other than the expected birth assignment proves that gender control is relatively impotent. Gender control relies on gendered distinctions in dress to reinforce social attitudes and expectations. Drag disrupts the ordinary workings of both. If the person in drag mimics the behavior expected of the gender presentation, then the values culturally attached to that gender are revealed as nonexclusive to one sex. If the person in drag mimics the behavior expected of the gender assigned the sexed body, then the performance mocks the cultural stereotype for the birth-assigned gender. Either way, then, drag reveals through dress that gender identification and control are precarious; the boundary between genders is highly permeable.

Cultures typically respond to this challenge by sanctioning certain outlets for drag. Throughout history various festivals such as Carnival or Halloween have featured sanctioned drag (see the answer to Q. 71). Such occasions facilitate a societal wide release of gender boundary tensions by encouraging, or at least permitting, gender reversals of identification, control, and status. Apart from such periods, society also tolerates ongoing drag performances in entertainment venues such as clubs and theaters, and through plays, movies, and television. Encouraged to laugh at the performer, the audience can discharge its unease at the message drag presents.

The use of drag by the gay community has largely been co-opted by society along similar lines. Where drag once possessed the power to provoke thought and aroused social concern, even outrage, it now largely is seen as innocuous.[144] Whether viewed as a harmless marker of homosexual identity or as a playful thumbing of the nose at gender conventions, in either instance it is no longer seen by very many folk as a serious challenge to cultural notions about gender.

That consequence today seems largely reserved for the male crossdresser who is unwillingly exposed while trying to pass as a woman.[145]

Secondary Boundaries: Status

Of many possible purposes served by dress in secondary, within-group boundaries, one particularly effective in a group's effort to exercise control of members is the granting of *status*. In society at large the highest status individuals are members of the upper class. Simmel sees class distinctions in society as essential to fashion's existence; without a social hierarchy, without status, there is no one to imitate. But because Simmel thinks fashion driven by two forces—imitation *and* individuation—those imitated must respond by finding new ways to be different from others. Accordingly, fashion starts with those who have high status as a way of maintaining that status. Imitation by lower status folk only provides incentive for new innovations, and so fashion cycles onward. Yet, at any given time, the class distinctions are preserved even as they are challenged.[146]

Similarly, on the first page of her tome *Fashion and Its Social Agendas: Class, Gender and Identity in Clothing*, Diane Crane writes, "One of the most visible markers of social status and gender and therefore useful in maintaining or subverting symbolic boundaries, clothing is an indication of how people in different eras have perceived their positions in social structures and negotiated status boundaries."[147] Crossdressing has long played a small but critical part. Crane herself notes, for example, how the adoption of masculine items in the dress of some 19th century women represented behavior that "transcended social class lines" and "constituted a symbolic statement about women's status and the debates over their status that raged throughout the nineteenth century."[148]

But before we can properly appreciate crossdressing's role vis-à-vis status and gender boundaries, we need a broader perspective. In the broadest sense, status can refer to one's hierarchical place within society as a whole, a placement that may be based on a variety of factors such as nobility of birth, gender, wealth, and so on. Historically, dress long functioned to differentiate social ranks in a society. Historian Daniel Roche, writing of France but as apt for other Western societies, notes that, "before the sixteenth century, the link between social distinction and sartorial difference was constantly affirmed."[149] Sumptuary laws represented one extreme way of institutionalizing dress as a social marker system. In more recent centuries the picture, Roche observes, has grown more complicated. Yet the relation of dress and status persists; social status influences personal tastes and habits, which help guide consumer behavior, including apparel purchases.[150]

At the broadest level today wealth (which is principally declared through very conspicuous consumptions) largely measures status, rather than nobility of birth. Clothes remain a principal tool for displaying wealth and thereby 'upper class' status. An interesting experiment conducted by social psychologist Leonard Bickman in 1971 demonstrates how dress signifies social status and influences the behavior of others. In the study, conducted at two public terminals in New York City, student volunteers were dressed as either 'upper' or 'lower class.' The former wore business suits if men, and nice dresses with coats if women. The 'lower' status men wore work clothes and carried accessories (e.g., lunchbox, flashlight) marking them as blue-collar workers; the women wore inexpensive skirts and blouses. Supplied with dimes, the volunteers would enter a phone booth, place the dime near the phone, and exit. When someone entered the booth, the volunteer would then reappear and ask if the individual had found the coin left in the booth. When the volunteers' dress identified them as high in social status, more than three-quarters (77%) got the dime back. On the other hand, only a little more than a third (38%) of the volunteers presenting as lower class received the dime back.[151] Apparently high social status is rewarded even in small matters—such as simple honesty over a dime. No wonder we are all encouraged to 'dress for success,' and seek higher status.

Of course, because dress can mark status differentiation, it can also be used to level the field in terms of status. School uniforms, for example, are intended to lessen status distinctions, with attendant social exclusions, and promote egalitarianism.[152] Androgynous dress can be used to lessen the difference in gender status. Blue jeans, for example, are accepted as wear suitable to either gender and permit a similar range of motion for a wide variety of activities.[153] Despite such things, status differentiation persists. Everyone may wear blue jeans, but not all blue jeans are equal—their labels proclaim a status hierarchy.

Sometimes status within a group is formally marked by rank, as in the military. More often it is conferred through placement in a hierarchical tier with some identifying mark in dress that is more ambiguous and creates only broader distinctions, such as apparel that marks the executive management from employees in the mailroom, cafeteria, or on the janitorial staff. Not only does the conferral of status mark an element of identity, it proves for many a potent motivator. The desire to retain or enhance status encourages conformity to the group's expectations and rules. Because some element of dress may mark status, changes in dress accompany transitions in status. For example, in a hospital setting someone who fulfils entry-level nursing care may be dressed as a 'candy-striper,' garb that visibly signals admittance into a recognized larger group (health care workers), while simultaneously showing separation from other members of the group (e.g., licensed practical nurses and registered nurses). The 'candystriper' is a volunteer of lesser rank in the hierarchy; after educational requirements and training the same person may move up within the hierarchy and don different apparel.

Status plays a part in all groups and is important in all cultures. Susan Kaiser, author of the influential book *The Social Psychology of Clothes*, says "the display of status through one's clothes and other means of adornment appears to be a universal phenomenon."[154] Obviously, within any given culture, some groups are larger than others and some occupy a more important role. In our culture gender groups are very important and status occupies a significant role within them. In societies like our own, where a hierarchical gender order prevails, status is most noticed simply by assignment to masculinity (higher rank) or femininity (lower rank). To preserve masculine privilege gendered dress distinctions must be preserved; gendered distinction in dress is an aspect of social status, or, to put it as aptly, social status is an aspect of gender as gender is understood in such societies.

Accordingly, pressure is exerted on us to conform to dress expectations meant to fit us smoothly into an assigned place that is to some extent predetermined by cultural values with respect to gender (and race, and so forth). Cross-dressing is *trans*gender with respect to boundary status; crossdressers cross a boundary in a hierarchical order. Because masculinity possesses generally higher social status than femininity, female crossdressers are more favorably received than male crossdressers. The former are 'dressing up' in social status; the latter are 'dressing down.' So it makes sense that whatever else may bother people about crossdressing, the voluntary lowering of social status—an act not only incomprehensible to most of us but also likely perceived as threatening to social order—is found objectionable. Especially those with vested interested in preserving the hierarchy status quo will exert the more stringent methods of social control.[155]

To overcome such resistance requires resources, psychological or otherwise. In terms of risking public exposure—or actually courting it—only those cross-dressers with sufficient social status are likely to escape censure and sanctions severe enough to curtail the behavior. History is replete with examples of rich and powerful males (and some females) who could crossdress in public without personal ruin *because* they were rich and powerful. Social rank has its privileges.

This same conclusion is supported by modern research. French psychological researchers Nicolas Guéguen and Alexandre Pascual found in reviewing various studies that, "many investigations underscored that we are more tolerant to infringements or offences committed by high status individuals." In their own experiment, they used a 25-year-old confederate whose appearance was altered by dress to display high, intermediate, or low social status. He then entered a bakery where only a single female employee was present. After requesting a croissant, and having it bagged, he then 'discovers' he has insufficient funds and asks for the employee's favor while looking her in the eye. The petition for a favor was either offered politely or rudely. The results across 120 bakeries found that a polite request was regularly honored regardless of whether the apparent status was high (95% of the time), intermediate (95%), or low (90%). But an impolite request dramatically changed things. High status still brought compliance most of the time (75%), but declining status brought less granting of the favor (40% for intermediate; 20% for low status). As in previous research, this experiment supports the notion that those perceived as high status are allowed more behavioral latitude than others.[156]

What do dress codes do?

Obviously, for identification, social control, and status to operate effectively within a group there needs to be a system of recognition. As we saw in outlining the elements of the expressive subsystem (see the answer to Q. 1), between a point of origin and points of reception are rules that guide, shape, and bind the communication. All of this, in turn, is bracketed within a context, a specific situational matrix that lends purpose and meaning to what is going on. Within groups, as dress is used to help shape and control identity, and signify status, the rules that make these matters clear are the group's *dress code*. These are sometimes formal, being explicit rules set down in such a form, with such regular practice, and reinforced by such potent measures that no one has any doubt about them.

Formal Dress Codes: Uniforms

The molding of specific rules to define contexts to express affiliation in dress is probably most evident in uniforms.[157] Lurie labels this use of clothing as "the extreme form of conventional dress." [158] Kaiser, with reference to school uniforms, notes how uniforms serve a variety of functions, including the often-remarked building of *esprit de corps*.[159] Curiously, Kaiser's observation about how school uniforms relatively decrease the impact of social status reminds us how even uniforms are malleable by context; in the military—a different context— uniforms serve a different purpose by distinguishing strict orders of rank, conferring a clear status within the group independent of the individual's social status in the civilian world.

Uniforms are part of many professional groups, from janitors to flight attendants to nurses. They are a way to signal membership in groups like the aforementioned Boy Scouts. They also function to exercise a degree of social control, sometimes aiming at specific objectives, such as being status equalizers or strictly stratifying a status hierarchy. Little effort is needed to multiply examples. Uniforms are an obvious way dress identifies a group affiliation, creates a measure of social control, and confers status.

Whereas uniforms make explicit and simplify at least some of the rules at the heart of the expressive system, the rules don't require uniforms, and formal dress codes can be spoken about more broadly. People know many professional affiliations by a certain style of dress, from the very formal and restrictive range of clothes identifying a health care professional to the wider dress range of professional educators.[160] The distinction between 'formal' and 'informal' dress codes in reality is less distinct than the words imply.

Dress codes can be abstracted from specific settings to broader application, while retaining the air of formality. Thus we speak of 'business attire'—dress affiliated with the workplace—and 'casual wear'—dress affiliated with leisure. Such labels are formal in the sense of marking clearly different kinds of clothing, while informal in the sense of permitting a relative degree or range of acceptable expression. These abstractions help highlight the importance of context (to which we will direct attention below). Complicating matters further, the rules associated with even formal dress codes are sometimes consciously bent, as when employers designate 'casual Fridays,' where employees can choose casual wear over business suits in the workplace and not risk censure.

The point is this: dress codes, regardless of their degree of formality, facilitate group affiliation. They are rules that construct visible boundary markers and thus serve the functions of identity, control, and status described earlier. While uniforms do this in a formal code, other less rigorous dress codes can accomplish the same ends. Following dress rules helps establish and maintain a group affiliation. Bending a rule is okay as long as the context makes it apparent that a higher rule is being followed. The significance of breaking a rule lies not in being a rule-breaker, but in calling into doubt the affiliation signified and served by the rule. In a world where we typically affiliate with many groups, the use of clothing poses a significant challenge to us all, especially when the rules for varying groups conflict in a specific setting, as we saw occurs when the gender dress code for women conflicts with the masculine dress code in a work setting.

Formal Dress Codes & Gender Issues: School Dress Codes

Formal dress codes do not necessarily provide relief from conflicts. An especially controversial example is school dress codes, especially where they mandate school uniforms.[161] School dress codes display range: some merely prohibit certain kinds of apparel or accessories; others mandate a uniform, either general in character or very specific. Such codes are often challenged on the grounds they violate a student's free speech rights—a potent recognition of the expressive nature of dress.

On the other hand, as noted by jurist Christopher Gilbert, schools offer many reasons why such codes are valuable. The reasons include simplifying the student's wardrobe, eliminating 'label competition' while fostering school unity and pride, promoting modesty, and—perhaps remarkably—creating opportunities for self-expression.[162] No difficulty impedes us seeing how such reasons fit with considerations already discussed above. School dress codes, with or without uniforms, lessen the pressure for a large and diverse wardrobe. A school uniform may promote egalitarianism in dress even as it encourages group affiliation. By discouraging immodesty in dress the learning environment may be facilitated through elimination of distraction, while one less prompt is offered for inciting verbal harassment or physical aggression—other reasons supporters use for dress codes.

Because transgender realities start early and persist through life, they raise the issue of transgender students coming into conflict with school dress codes. Anyone who pays attention to the news knows that periodically a challenge is raised to a school dress code involving a student perceived as crossdressed. Routinely, schools send the student home as having violated dress conduct expected of its students. Significantly, the issue is seldom if ever that the apparel in question would otherwise be objectionable if appearing on the body of a person whose sex and gender are paired conventionally. In other words, the same skirt that might be complimented on a girl when worn by a boy is cause to have him dismissed from the school grounds. Clearly in such cases the school is functioning as a conservator of what it believes are its community's prevailing values concerning gender and gender-differentiated dress.

How might a court rule if the school is challenged? Attorney Gilbert, a frequent participant in cases involving school dress codes, points to the test offered by a New Mexico court for when nonverbal conduct, such as wearing certain clothes, may be legally considered 'expressive conduct' and protected by the 1st Amendment. The court ruled two conditions must be met: first, that the student intended to send a particular message through his or her dress, and second, that it was very likely others would understand the message.[163] It seems reasonable to believe a transgendered student dressed in a manner others see as crossdressed has sent a message about gender expression that observers clearly comprehend.

Given the additional fact that courts tend to side with students in such disputes, we might conclude that a crossdressed student—these days invariably a male dressed in feminine apparel—would fare well in court. Yet the courts have a long history siding with the schools in such instances. Writing in the *Yale Law Journal*, Mary Anne Case cites a 1987 Ohio Court decision upholding a school's prohibiting a brother and sister attending the school's prom dressed in cross-gender attire; the Court ruled dress codes are "reasonably related to the valid educational purpose of teaching community values."[164] Yet, as fellow legal scholar Katharine Bartlett observes, such rationalizations from courts frequently have been criticized as an acceptance or legitimation of the very matters legislation such as Title VII was enacted to end—gender stereotypes.[165]

Attorney Dean Spade, a self-identified transgender person in New York City, has demonstrated one way in which crossdressers might prevail against dress codes. In the case of *Jean Doe v. Bell*, a transgender youth in a group home facility was forbidden to wear skirts or dresses. The attorneys representing 'Jean Doe' brought a claim against the Administration for Children's Services on three grounds: First Amendment rights, gender discrimination, and disability discrimination. The last named ground relied on having the plaintiff diagnosed with Gender Identity Disorder (see the answer to Q. 96). It was on this ground that the court ruled in the plaintiff's favor. But, as Spade notes, such a victory comes at the cost of calling being transgendered a disability—a claim both controversial and objectionable to many people whether transgendered or not. Yet Spade is clear that disability statutes are not about whether a person is somehow 'flawed,' but rather, "about pointing out that disabled people are capable of equal participation, but are currently barred from participating equally by artificial conditions that privilege one type of body or mind and exclude others."[166]

Such a dramatic legal strategy may not be necessary though. With the shifting of societal values and the passage by municipalities and states of protection for transgender people (see the answer to Q. 36), courts are more prone than ever to support crossdressing students. Taylor Flynn, in an essay for the *Columbia Law Review*, notes a 2000 Massachusetts Superior State Court ruling on behalf of a transgendered student. The student, anatomically male but identifying as a woman, was supported by the Court in efforts to dress in feminine apparel.[167] Although no uniformity of results in legal cases yet has emerged, the old grounds for disallowing crossdressing on school grounds seem to be giving way to a more nuanced sensibility.

Informal Dress Codes & Gender

But while formal dress codes such as one might encounter in a school offer clear boundaries where challenges and violations are more obvious, such codes do not constitute the majority. Much more often, dress codes are informal and not explicit. They are vaguely stated, but still often firmly held, expectations governing appearance. Instead of formally established by authorities who verbally or in writing set down a policy to be followed, such informal codes are developed over time, become 'traditions' ("This is how we have always done things!"), and are passed on through social learning: modeling followed by imitation. Reinforcement comes through discouraging verbal and nonverbal cues supplied offenders and praise provided compliers.

Perhaps nowhere is this clearer than among gender groups. Gender-differentiated dress establishes a largely informal dress code. Nowhere is it written that American males shall not wear unbifurcated apparel such as skirts or dresses. Yet few males venture out in public so dressed. Those that do either aim to pass as women, or understand that their dress will be seen as transgressive and so they can expect censure.

What characterizes the informal gender dress code in the United States seems to follow a grand logic, or if we prefer, a 'Golden Rule for Gender-differentiated Dress': a male must appear masculine—or at least *not* feminine.[168] In that sole respect, fashion remains androcentric. It also remains consistent with other aspects of gender expectation in the culture. As Evelyn Goodenough Pitcher put it back in 1963, "Deviations in dress, appearance, or job that reflect the feminine are immediately suspect. If a man is actually feminine in his instincts . . . he must never appear so."[169]

The corollaries to this foundational rule might be written as the following dictums, one for each gender:

☐ 'Males shall be held to a stricter standard of dress conformity.'
☐ 'Females may borrow masculine elements of dress as long as they feminize them.'

'Rules' such as these largely depend on widely shared assumptions that contribute to the preservation of gender stereotypes (e.g., men are strong but women are weak).

'Males shall be held to a stricter standard of dress conformity.' Despite the resonance of that rule for today, the gender hierarchy that privileges masculinity over femininity may once have provided men much more latitude in dress. For much of the history of fashion, masculinity was the focus. In fact, we would not be wrong to claim that virtually all the staples of feminine fashion are rooted in masculine fashion (see the answer to Q. 9). But over the last two centuries, for whatever reasons, fashion has become centered on femininity (save the exception of obedience to the ground logic that males must appear masculine). During that time the options available to men have contracted relative to those acceptable for women.

This change in fashion focus parallels a progressive narrowing of view about masculinity. It certainly appears to be more stereotypically framed than femininity, both in how it is construed in terms of personality traits and in regard to appearance traits.[170] Masculine privilege in the face of pressure from a more expansive, 'liberated' femininity has responded in the mainstream with even greater rigidity that often traps males into narrow and static expectations in many areas, including dress.[171] The fewer avenues offered for males for experience and expression may carry consequences in the often remarked upon emotional constriction seen in men.[172]

Not all men acquiesce. The so-called 'metrosexual' phenomenon represents an interesting, one-step-removed-from-the-mainstream, response. But though it tests the narrow limits of conventional masculine appearance, metrosexual fashion remains identifiably masculine, though leaning away from stereotypical masculinity. Inspired by the influence of gay men, metrosexual dress attempts to find middle ground between the transgender reality of homosexuality and the homophobia integral to conventional masculinity. Or, as it was put in *Advertising & Society Review*, "what used to be referred to as the gay sensibility has kind of diffused into a more mainstream masculinity."[173]

In this light, another, more radical manifestation of rebellion against the tyranny of masculine demands may be crossdressing. Apart from any gender relief it may provide—what some dismissively label a 'retreat into femininity'—male crossdressing may less pejoratively be conceived as a legitimate desire to increase opportunities for self-experience and expression through dress. In so doing they are following a path first forged, with great success, by women.[174] The fashion industry periodically attempts to inject unbifurcated apparel like skirts and dress for men (see the answer to Q. 9), but to date the men who appear in public so dressed still tend to be those whose social status (i.e., the rich and powerful), or social identity (e.g., entertainers) allow them to flaunt conventionality.

'Females may borrow masculine elements of dress as long as they feminize them.' Because masculine privilege in the gender hierarchy must be protected, the dress code that helps establish the boundaries of an exclusive 'men only' club must be more zealously guarded.[175] Ironically, though, the boundary permeability is greater one direction than another. Women are allowed to approach, though not quite cross, the line by adopting and adapting masculine elements in dress. By imitating men they are rewarded with a sort of second place trophy: not quite men, but more than just weak women. On the other hand, males who dress effeminately threaten to lower the whole class and so must be stopped. For them the gender boundary is like a brick wall.

Women have greater dress freedom because less is at stake. Already relegated to the lower social status they have little if anything to lose by exploring a variety of fashions. They can pursue upward mobility toward masculine privilege by dressing more like men (but not too much like them), or choose instead to explore and express more femininity. So successful have they proven at adapting masculine elements and passing them off in feminine apparel that the very notion of a crossdressing woman seems a quaint and outdated one (see the answer to Q. 14).

Still, the task is not as straightforward as a few words may make it seem. Women in the workplace face the challenge of accurately judging the organizational culture so that they can dress for success within it. Typically that means incorporating enough masculine elements to borrow the appearance of traits stereotypically associated with men, such as rationality, strong moral acumen, assertiveness, and competence. But if her dress is too masculine in appearance, she will be censored, with labels like 'pushy broad' applied to her.[176] She must retain an apparent and dominant femininity so as not to pose a threat to the cohesion and exclusivity of masculine maleness.

Magazines, television, and other media are replete with advice to both males and females about appearance. But it seems fair to sum it up as we have above: males must appear masculine. Gender differentiation matters, and dress codes must serve it. Though latitude is offered consistent with the American ideals of freedom and individualism, both are constrained by the requirement that the basic rule of knowing a boy or a man when you see one be obeyed. Dress thus remains a chief mechanism for displaying a social identity based on gender-paired-with-sex, controlling that social identity, and assigning it a status in a gender hierarchy.

What role does context play?

Everything we have discussed so far is context dependent. The *context* gives meaning to the situations it embraces; 'school,' for example, is a context that is associated with locations, specified roles, and particular tasks, though various *situations* within that context, such as lunch in the cafeteria, are not specifically connected to the *raison d'être* of the context. The nature of dress codes varies with the breadth of context. Formal dress codes are more likely where the context is more narrowly and sharply defined, such as in a school. One is only a member of the group 'students' when in some relation to the context of a 'school.' Moreover, the formal dress code only pertains when the student member is either on school grounds or engaged with other students on a school-conducted trip off-campus. The context in which the dress rules apply is sharply and consistently drawn.

Far more often the groups we affiliate with are less bound. They operate across contexts producing variable situations. Dress codes must therefore be more informal in order to accommodate the range of contexts and situations. Gender groups operate across so many contexts and situations that dress rules must be highly flexible. The resulting informal code lacks many specific rules though it retains a necessary logic in order to maintain the boundaries of the group.

Outside of agreed upon environments or situations, the same dress rules do not exert their force in the same way even though the same people may be present. For example, a group of children who attend the same class at school are students in relation to that context and may be required to wear school uniforms. In their neighborhood, after school and on the weekend, they are unlikely to either dress in that uniform or to relate to one another as students. Though it would not be completely incorrect to refer to them as students even on the weekend, apart from the context of school different group identities assume preeminence and the dress codes associated with those other groups take power.

The breadth and the centrality of gender groups in our culture mean both a largely informal dress code and one virtually impossible to escape. Relatively few contexts or situations render gender differentiation completely irrelevant. Even when we belong to groups operating in contexts where formal dress rules operate, such as school, gender-differentiated dress exercises its superior power by dictating its inclusion in the formal code. Thus, school uniforms may require white tops and blue bottoms, but for boys they will be shirts and pants while for girls they may be blouses and skirts. The cultural imperative to define personal and social identity by gender requires obedience to the dress logic of gender differentiation in virtually every other group, context, and situation.

This reality exerts enormous pressure on the transgendered. A common way of coping is to withdraw frequently from the public sphere and craft as robust as possible private realm where the demands of the gender dress code may be escaped. Of course, 'escape' is a relative term; no one really escapes the demands of this code even in private. The felt need for secrecy, the fear of discovery, and the realization of the negative consequences that might follow discovery of violation of the gender dress code all keep it a vital psychological force even when no observers are around. In that respect *all* dressing is a social act, even when done alone.

What happens when group dress expectations conflict?

While our culture expects a separation into two genders and uses gender-differentiated dress to keep the boundary visible, the multidimensional reality of life in a modern society complicates matters. In the early 19th century, for example, not only were dress differences between the genders larger, but so were the differences between social activities permitted each gender. By that century's end women and girls were making remarkable inroads into spheres of activity previously reserved for men and boys. The 20th century continued that trend. As a result, in the 21st century men and women, boys and girls, often find themselves engaged in the same or very similar activities and groups (occupational and recreational). Though effort has been made to preserve gender distinctions in dress, they are not as sharply drawn as before; there is little visible difference between a man's T-shirt and sweats and those for a woman, for example. Unisex styles offer a way to accommodate modern activity demands.[177]

This general dilemma faced by gender groups may be generalized. The groups we belong to often differ enough from one another that on occasion we find ourselves in a context where two groups are calling for expressions of our loyalty in ways that our appearance cannot easily solve. Lurie observes that when social roles conflict the individual is likely to either select dress appropriate to the role more highly esteemed or combine costume elements suitable to each.[178] We already have seen this solution at work in the instance of women in the workplace, especially when they are in occupations or positions traditionally associated with men.

When we reckon the complexity of social contexts, factor in the desires for individuality in dress, and add the ambiguity of most dress codes, we have an equation for dress *faux pas*. Any given dress expression may or may not follow the relevant rules for a given occasion, or may or may not be perceived by observers in the same way it is experienced or meant by the clothes wearer. If we can recall a situation where our own dress choice did not fit in, resulting in uncomfortable feelings and, perhaps, social censure, then we may have some sense of what many crossdressers may experience.

Yet to get the full sense of the situation faced by transgender people we must acknowledge another facet of social reality: groups are not completely discrete entities. Despite their separate existences, groups are often placed in sets. For example, we cluster social workers, psychologists, counselors, psychiatrists and perhaps others as 'mental health professionals.' Some sets are much stronger. In our culture, sex, gender, and sexual orientation are placed in a set with general expectations for predictable relationships among them.[179] If one is determined at birth to be male, then one is assigned masculinity; a heterosexual orientation is assumed as the default position. These preconceptions about how three distinct categories (or groups, as each has members) should or must relate to one another work well for many people. But they cause problems whenever there is a mismatch between any two or among all three.

In transgender realities there is a disjunction between the birth assigned gender group and the felt experience of that gender. In intersex conditions the issue is variance from the physical sex paired with the gender assignment. In homosexuality the issue is variance from the heterosexuality assigned the gender. In transsexualism the issue is variance from the assigned gender and the experienced gender. In all cases, two groups (e.g., sex vs. gender, heterosexuality vs. homosexuality, masculinity vs. femininity) are in conflict, whether mildly or strongly. The preemptive assignment at birth to a set of group assignments—sex, gender, sexual orientation—mandates conflicts whenever reality conflicts with the pre-established social agenda.

We may leave aside sexual orientation for the moment; it is the default assignment for all sexes and genders. The other two are ordered in relationship such that gender is presumed predicated on sex. This holds true for all sexes, but the higher status accorded being male allows us to distinguish between a stronger and milder imperative: Males *must* be masculine; females *should* be feminine.[180] Accordingly, conflicts between maleness and masculinity can be expected to occasion more interest and anxiety than those between femaleness and femininity.

Clothed bodies hide sexual anatomy to some extent at least. That poses a problem. Because privilege is predicated on maleness, and gender is predicated on sex, masculinity as a privileged gender depends on the underlying maleness, which may not be visible. Therefore, dress must be gender-differentiated so as to reassure observers that the body beneath the clothes is either male or female. Crossdressing upsets this neat equation. Since uncertainty of sex is thus introduced, calling into question the status of the gender presented, potentially any sexed body can occupy any gender status—an egalitarianism that forebodes doom for a gender hierarchy. Transgender people are, by nature, arguments for a more horizontal social reality, rather than a vertically constructed one. In the existing world, though, that means male crossdressing is more problematic than female crossdressing.

Not surprisingly, appearance issues for transgender people are often difficult. Mere compliance with expectations based on the set assignment (e.g., heterosexual masculine male) may preserve outward tranquility but at the price of inner turmoil. Lurie's observation about how conflict may be handled can be applied to a transgender person: the individual may either select dress appropriate to the role more highly esteemed personally, or combine costume elements suitable to each. For those who choose to remain 'in the closet,' who seek to avoid confrontations over dress, the latter route is favored. Outerwear reflects conformity; underwear displays rebellion. Or, put more accurately from the perspective of many transgendered persons, the outwear may be the fiction, the underwear the truth.

Typically it is when the crossdresser selects dress at odds with social expectation, and wears it in public, that any drama commences. Then the conflict between groups is taken from the private realm where the individual predominates and placed in the public domain, where the individual is only one voice among many. A chorus of disapproval may drown out that lone voice—unless, as we have discussed above, he or she has sufficient status to ignore or change public opinion.[181] So we have come full circle: dress draws boundaries, primary and secondary, and so serves groups, including gender groups; but those boundaries offer targets for challenge. Crossdressing is the formal name for the behavioral challenge to the gender boundaries drawn by dress.

What kinds of groups use dress to distinguish themselves?

With the above background in view, we next need to consider the range of group types that may use clothing as an aspect of marking group affiliation. We already have discussed that we all belong to a number of groups, and that dress expectations may vary from group to group. In essence, we can contend all groups (even nudists) use dress as a boundary system marking members as insiders or outsiders. We may even argue that matters of identity, social control, and status have some reflection in the dress of virtually every group. But to this point our discussion has been both rather general and short in examples. Without belaboring the matter it may be useful to briefly indicate the great range of group types that we find ourselves a part of—as often as not as a matter of assignment by others and not by voluntary petition. The group types we are about to mention all have relevance to transgender realities as various answers to questions will make plain throughout this work.

Cultural Groups

We all know that various cultural groups may become identified with special clothing. Perhaps the most famous example of this in the West is the Scottish kilt. This distinctive garb is readily recognized by others and immediately associated with the Scottish people. Similarly, in the East the Japanese *kimono* and the Indian *sari* are acknowledged distinctive cultural expressions. Though modern travel may have blurred cultural lines so that certain clothes are no longer as exclusively identified with their original groups, we still recognize that clothing can identify people as members of particular cultures.[182] This can remain true even when an individual moves from the culture of origin to a foreign one. By wearing one or more elements of dress distinctive to their native culture people can signal their ongoing identification with that culture while in a foreign land.[183]

Unfortunately, dress rules are subject to mistranslation when applied in a different culture. Though most Americans will take a second look at a man in a kilt, they are likely to eventually discern it as a cultural marker and show more tolerance toward the wearer than they would a man in a plaid skirt. On the other hand, a man in a kimono[184] is far less likely to be understood in his original cultural context and far more likely to be censured because of this culture's expectations for gender-differentiated dress. In fact, where Westerners are concerned, long prominence on the world stage has cultivated a hubris such that over the last few centuries wherever Europeans and Americans have traveled they have pressed their cultural dress expectations on the indigenous people. Much of the depiction of crossdressing in foreign lands has been the result of applying Western dress standards.[185]

Subculture Groups

Cultures as a whole may be associated with certain dress. Likewise, within any culture subculture groups may adopt a style or special feature to set themselves apart from the dominant culture. Immigrants, for instance, often cluster in communities where they can retain a distinctive sense of ethnicity and the dress of their land of origin can play a distinctive role in preserving their identity. The manner in which dress and acculturation interact can by dynamic. A study of immigrants from India to the United States found that consumption of ethnic apparel by newcomers was low compared to their purchases of the same as they became more comfortable in their new culture.[186] Apparently, adoption of American clothing was used instrumentally in adapting to the new culture, but once a degree of comfort was attained the use of Indian apparel helped retain ethnic identity; dress thus serves the membership interest in two groups for these individuals—their ethnic group and the larger society in which their ethnic group is a minority.

Just as immigrants often cluster and use dress to signify their group identity in a culture where they are a minority, so transgender people in many societies often reside where they know other transgender people are. Commonly this means around the world an influx of transgender people to cities. Crossdressing serves as a marker of transgender identity and seems more likely to occur in public when the individual has gained a degree of confidence in his or her social identity as a member of a distinct group where the practice is normal and approved.

Age Effects in Dress

Within cultures populations are also stratified by age. Cohorts—groups in which membership occurs by virtue of date of birth—broadly separate into identifiable generations and march through time together. As each developmental phase is reached, age appropriate wear is donned. What is deemed 'appropriate' clothing varies somewhat by age. In the United States, for example, we accept that young people dress somewhat differently than older folk. Thea Tselepis and Helena de Klerk observe that, "adolescents normally have a great interest in clothes and in their own appearance. They use clothes to feel better about their bodies, to conform to their peer group and to conform to specific role models . . . ."[187] While we all may do so, adolescents have their own peculiar manner of doing so in service of displaying group identity.[188]

Among youth we distinguish various looks, whether 'Goth'[189] or 'punk' or 'preppy.' Sometimes more than one characteristic is involved so that, for instance, an ethnic group may have its own unique sense of what its 'hip' or 'cool' youth will dress like.[190] Even socially deviant youth employ appearance in an affiliative way. [191] Yet this is not a phenomenon restricted to adolescents; college fraternities and sororities[192] may endorse and enforce certain codes of dress style, and among adults a similar phenomenon may be seen in social groups like churches.[193]

Crossdressing can occur at any age. We might expect that crossdressers in a generational group would choose gendered dress associated with their generation both when crossdressed and when dressed in conformity to their assigned gender. After all, most people most of the time wear clothes thought appropriate for their age. Yet research also indicates a notable percentage (12%) purposely use clothing to add or subtract years from their perceived age.[194] Anecdotal evidence and informal surveys suggest that crossdressers may be more likely to cross generational lines when crossdressing than when not. As occurs in the general population, when crossing generational lines the direction is typically toward younger styles for adult crossdressers, and toward adult styles for younger crossdressers.[195]

How may we summarize how gender groups are distinguished by dress?

Obviously the group affiliation with dress most germane to our investigation is gender. Although we have often referenced this type of group and used it to illustrate a number of ideas, we need now to provide a broad summary of basic ideas concerning the relation of dress to gender. While some of this necessarily repeats points previously raised, this discussion is meant to summarize essential matters in preparation for answering following questions.

Dress serves as a convenient way to identify gender, keep genders separate, and even partially define different genders. In the latter regard, dress by its material and fit can facilitate certain movements and actions, or restrict them. In the latter case dress becomes an instrument for discouraging various activities and can be used to keep a gender from them, as seen, for instance, in women being excluded from certain occupations in cultures where their manner of dress is enforced and their clothing would make certain work difficult, hazardous, or otherwise impractical. In cultures like our own, with a rigid gender divide, dress becomes especially valued as a way both to express and to *guard* gender affiliations. This latter function is why so many people are disoriented or offended when they encounter crossdressing. Though we will return to this subject regularly, examining it in many ways, we can start with some further general observations.

- ❑ Gender-differentiated appearance serves a culture's separation of genders; dress is a basic way of accomplishing this separation.
- ❑ Gender distinctions are not limited to two genders; dress can display multiple genders in distinct ways.
- ❑ Gender is flexible; so are gender distinctions in dress.

Gender-differentiated Appearance

First, as best we can tell, gender distinctions in appearance have been prized in different cultures throughout history. We may instantly link this phenomenon to the need of distinguishing the sexes for reproductive purposes. But it requires little contemplation to realize such an idea is insufficient. Gender is far more than a notice to interested parties of one's physical sex. It signifies a status in society replete with identity, roles, privileges and obligations. Gender distinctions in appearance are useful across multiple contexts and situations.

However, note the word 'appearance'; clothing constitutes a chief part of appearance but not the entirety of it. We can use the term dress in either a more limited or more expansive sense, depending on whether we incorporate items like cosmetics, jewelry, wigs and so forth. Any and all of these items can belong to a society's set of 'rules' governing gender appearance. Thus, if we use an expansive sense of dress, an individual can be said to 'crossdress' even if the clothing is appropriate to society's gender assignment but other features of appearance are not.[196]

Dress & Multiple Genders

Second, gendered distinctions do not always divide people into just two groups: masculine and feminine. Some cultures acknowledge what is loosely termed a 'third gender,' which is sometimes paired with a 'third sex.' In cultures like our own where only two genders are widely acknowledged, and these are paired with anatomical sex (i.e., masculine male or feminine female), individuals who do not fit cleanly within either a sex category or a gender one are, in effect, 'dirty.' They face a choice to comply with the society's effort to fit them according to its perceptions or to endure negative sanctions. In this situation, those folk who in another culture might be identified as belonging to a gender neither masculine nor feminine are often simply labeled as 'crossdressers' because they use dress, occasionally or frequently, fully or partly, to find a compromise between two categories that don't fit them.

Third, comparatively few elements of clothing style can be identified as 'masculine' or 'feminine' across the long reach of history. Put in another way, the symbols of gender in dress, while not arbitrary, are fluid. In terms of Western fashion, the elements of style that with the most consistency differentiate masculine from feminine appear to be:

- ❏ *Angular* vs. *curvaceous forms*: the former is masculine, the latter feminine, and both reflect efforts to utilize and accentuate anatomy.[197]
- ❏ *Bifurcated* vs. *unbifurcated*: both in terms of whether apparel hangs from the shoulders or is divided at the waist and in terms of divisions below the waist, bifurcated garb *per se* has been viewed as masculine and unbifurcated as either unisex (e.g., the tunic) or feminine (e.g., the dress).[198]
- ❏ *Free* vs. *restricted motion*: typically masculine clothing has provided a greater range of motion—and thus activity—than feminine clothing.[199]
- ❏ *Short* vs. *long*: feminine garments have customarily been longer than masculine ones; women's legs have been more likely to be covered.[200]

All of these are broad generalizations—and we shall return to them later (see the answer to Q. 9). Obviously, they admit exceptions and some reflect some periods of history better than others. In fact, it may be largely a waste of time appealing to any feature as unambiguously masculine or feminine. As we have seen, the underlying logic—males must appear masculine, or at least not feminine—is what really matters.

This last observation leads to our next point: gendered distinctions in appearance are both a matter of individual elements and the *Gestalt*, or whole appearance against its background, which includes personal and social factors. Perceptions and judgments about gender in dress are influenced by numerous things, including what is worn, how it contributes to the entire presentation, the social context, cultural values, and personal factors like previous experiences, degree of tolerance, awareness of clothing in general, and so forth. In this light, putting much weight on identifying reliable stylistic elements to differentiate gender is both overly simplistic and misleading.

Finally, we should note that the rigid pairing of gender with sex means that gendered dress cannot be entirely separated from expressing the sexed body. The silhouette—the overall shape presented by our dress—primarily conveys gender but also is understood by most people as meant to convey the body's sex. Every culture and society has its own sense of the ideal male and female body, as well as the acceptable range of presentations varying from the ideal. Gendered dress distinctions contribute to forming a silhouette and the silhouette both combines the various elements and anchors them in a vision of a sexed body. Later we shall explore the significance of this for crossdressing.

Q. 4

Does what we wear communicate our morals?

The Short Answer: While a relationship of dress to morals is commonly proposed, the nature of such a relationship is disputed. One thing seems clear: moral judgments of dress reflect underlying values. What we value we dress so as to experience and express. We value, for example, attractiveness and power; dress is associated with both. Obviously there is a dark side to such matters. Enhancing attractiveness may lead to illicit liaisons or invite unwanted responses. Among the most frequent themes in this regard are contentions that clothes originated in response to a sense of shame about the sexual body, that clothes are thus related to modesty and immodesty, and that certain styles of dress provoke aggressive responses by others. Using dress to show power, typically in terms of social rank or status, can be equally problematic. Dress can be used to make false claims about status, or to create and maintain harmful social hierarchies, such as a gender framework that socially favors masculinity over femininity. Given the confusion over the relationship between morality and sexuality that many of us experience, confusion over how what we wear in relation to sexuality, gender and behavior is 'right' or 'wrong' is unsurprising. Since morality is commonly conjoined with religion, much of what has been written and said about the morality of different kinds of clothed appearance has occurred in a religious context. When these various factors are combined and applied to crossdressing a variety of stances result, some accepting of this manner of dress and others rejecting it. However, rather than crossdressing behavior being discovered to be objectionable as such, inquiry into the role of values reveals two important things: first, moral evaluations of crossdressing are context dependent and, second, the role of values can lead to either positive or negative judgments.

The Longer Answer: The centrality of dress to the construction and maintenance of personal and social identity in our culture make it inescapably a matter for moral judgments. We highly value the notion of 'self,' and while we may distinguish between personal and social identities, we recognize they are reflections of a single individual. But this individual is a *gendered* person. Because dress plays such a critical role in signifying and signaling gender, and because gender is so central to identities personal and social, inescapably dress is freighted with value.

Yet, if dress is subject to moral appraisal, what about gender itself? Although we value it highly, can we say that we also pass moral judgments regarding it? Is gender a matter of ethics? These questions probably seem quirky at best. So accustomed are we to regarding gender as predicated on a 'natural' division of two biologically determined sexes, that we can scarcely entertain how being masculine or feminine is a moral matter. At least, ordinarily the matter never enters our mind; only when perceived gender transgressions occur do we contemplate the 'rightness' or 'wrongness' of someone's gender.

Are gender and dress moral issues?

John Stoltenberg, who roots himself in radical feminism, declares that masculinity is an ethical construction, built by choices and acts.[201] The logic of ethics is to justify our values—to explain why it is right and good to find something meaningful and important. Put in this light we should readily see gender as ethically constructed. We posit distinct constructs labeled 'masculinity' and 'femininity,' and assign to each meaning and importance along specific lines. Though we may buttress our contentions with appeals to a natural order or a divine command, the process is thoroughly human.

We may not be accustomed to giving much thought or weight to the role dress plays. But when we pause to consider this 'second skin' we readily assent to its importance in daily life. Certainly we comprehend that we are subject to the judgment of others about what we wear, realize that we do so about others as well, and that while these judgments may not always be framed in terms of 'right' and 'wrong' they reflect values, both personal and cultural.

British art historian Aileen Ribeiro, in her book *Dress and Morality*, demonstrates how clothing has a long history of involvement with moral judgments. Even as what we wear may be meant to reflect social class or status, or express our sexual attractiveness, there will be observers to weigh in on whether the dress is appropriate or inappropriate.[202] Sociologist Joanne Finkelstein accurately observes that, "using fashion as a code of communication makes use of appearances as if they were reliable signposts to the nature of self and to the moral character of the individual."[203] Correctly or not—appropriately or not—we judge others by what they wear. We have discussed this to some extent in previous answers but the matter requires first a brief review and then careful consideration in light of how such assessments enter into the realm of value and moral judgments. Let us begin with some research conducted in a sphere we are all familiar with: school.

A study reported in 1995 examined teacher and student attitudes in three urban public high schools. The research was investigating the influence dress has on perceptions by others of the person's intelligence, scholastic achievement, and behavior. Both teachers and students were shown photographs of models exemplifying various clothing styles. The results showed perceptions of all three measures—intelligence, achievement, and behavior—varied by style of dress. [204] In another study, participants were asked to rate 18 different personal traits associated with 4 garment styles. Results indicated both that clothing style and the clothing interest of an observer are involved in first impressions and inferring personal characteristics. [205] Similar studies have found like results: we make judgments about people (often incorrect) based on what they are wearing. Those judgments often relate to how dress affects attractiveness, which in turn is extended to how attractiveness relates to perceived competence, intelligence, personality factors, and so forth. The more attractive a person is, the more favorable a judgment is likely to be. What is going on in such appraisals?

What values does dress express?

Appraisals reflect value-driven assessments. *Values*, things we esteem and find meaning in, generate ethical systems that produce moral judgments. Because dress is involved with values it inevitably becomes a subject of moral assessments. We should not be surprised by this, especially in light of what we examined in answering the first three questions. We found that clothes matter, and that dress is instrumental in experiencing and expressing personal identity, including personality characteristics, and social affiliations. We are, simultaneously, beings that value both individuality and connection with others, and rely on dress to aid us in both. Obviously, this introduces a field of inquiry far too large for us to consider adequately. But we can and must glimpse it.

Let us do so by considering a single fundamental value: *acceptance*. We all strive to accept ourselves and to achieve acceptance by others. Our dress not only reflects this dual quest, it facilitates or frustrates it. Examine this figure:

Figure 4.1 Acceptance Values Experienced/Expressed in Dress

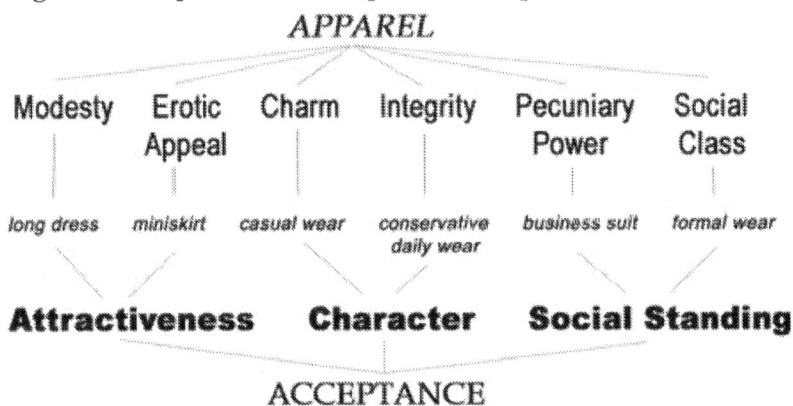

APPAREL

Modesty	Erotic Appeal	Charm	Integrity	Pecuniary Power	Social Class
long dress	miniskirt	casual wear	conservative daily wear	business suit	formal wear

Attractiveness   **Character**   **Social Standing**

ACCEPTANCE

The underlying, or basic value of acceptance generates in its quest to be ful-filled other values, such as attractiveness (physically-based), character (personal-ity-based), and social standing (property-based). Most of us admit we esteem all three of these secondary values, utilizing them to accept ourselves and seek ac-ceptance from others. But there is more than one possible path by which these meaningful things can be reached. For example, we may seek to be attractive by emphasizing personal modesty or by advertising our erotic appeal. Because these are not mutually exclusive paths we may alternate them according to con-text and other factors. Similarly, we esteem character and seek to experience and express it in various ways. We may, for instance, choose charm as the route to experience and express our character, embodying traits that say we are likable and good. Or we may emphasize integrity, demonstrating qualities we associate with personal honor. Since we typically also find meaning in our social standing we select a path to maximize our place. We may do this through pecuniary power—emphasizing our purchasing power and conspicuous consumption—or rely on our social class.

Accompanying each of these values, which are ways to experience and ex-press acceptance, are dress choices. To show modesty we select clothes that cover the body more completely, like a woman's long dress. For erotic appeal costumes are selected that reveal and highlight erogenous zones; bikinis, speedos, miniskirts, and the like all accomplish this task. Since the female body in our culture has been more associated with sensuality and sexuality, feminine dress has especially become associated with both modesty and erotic appeal. With regard to character, charm might utilize casual wear to reflect a relaxed, easy going and easy-to-get-along-with manner, even as integrity might select conservative colors and styles in clothing to show a more restrained, conscien-tious, or reserved manner.[206] In reference to social standing, the business suit has become the garb *par excellence* for portraying pecuniary power. Formal and highly refined wear meant for little or even onetime use—the more expensive the better—accompanied by ornamentation like expensive jewelry is commonly used to signify high social standing. It shows the wearer removed from the workaday world, possessing fine goods (property), and thus 'better' than the working class. While in all of the above cases we may question the validity of as-sociating certain traits with kinds of apparel, studies consistently show such as-sociations exist.

In sum, apparel must be as extensive, expensive, and diverse as possible if it is to adequately represent a variety of secondary values. If this proves true for just one basic value considered in light of only three generated secondary values, we can easily imagine how much greater the reality is for all the other primary and secondary values we find meaning in. Part of the complexity of being hu-man is experiencing and expressing a variety of values, some of which conflict, and doing so in a way that realizes our own sense of individuality while building and preserving relationships. Dress occupies a vital instrumental role in this on-going endeavor.

We would be absurd to imagine the situation any different for the cross-dresser. Nor should we imagine that a crossdresser's values are different. Cross-dressers seek acceptance, too. Attractiveness, character, and power all have a role in crossdressing choices no less than for anyone else. Though complicated by cultural conceptions about how a person's anatomical sex should fit with gender identity and roles, the crossdresser still seeks through dress an experi-ence and expression of self-acceptance. To some degree the crossdresser may also act to try to win acceptance by others through cross-gender clothing choices meant to display values like those we have discussed.

But while it is not difficult to assert these matters—which may have com-mon sense appeal—it may prove more difficult to substantiate these claims. Be-cause of their importance, and their relevance to crossdressing, we require a closer examination. For convenience, we will restrict ourselves to the three val-ues associated with winning acceptance outlined above.

Attractiveness

Clearly, as seen in numerous studies, *attractiveness* is a quality we associate with other desirable characteristics. In short, we value attractiveness. Recogniz-ing its desirability most of us expend energy daily in the effort to enhance our attractiveness. A principal way we do this is through dress—and research such as cited above seems to indicate this method can be successful. Although dress to enhance attractiveness is used both by men and women, our culture puts more emphasis on feminine fashion to increase attractiveness. Contemporary young women realize this, as indicated in a study of college undergraduates in-vestigating appearance-related social comparisons. More than two-thirds of the participating women reported clothing or style of dress as a comparison dimen-sion and it ranked as the third most frequently endorsed item in records they kept of social comparisons made over a ten day span.[207]

Given such data it seems plausible to imagine crossdressing males evincing an interest in attractive feminine clothes meant to enhance a feminine appear-ance. Though much is often made of this behavior as aimed at gaining accep-tance as a woman, that single explanation is too simplistic. Not all male cross-dressers have as their goal passing as women, and for many the proclamation that their crossdressing is to display a feminine *persona* may be little more than a conditioned response to cultural pressures to justify the behavior as something other than mere sexual fetishism.[208] We would do better to broaden our gaze and see the crossdressing as behavior not dissimilar to what we all do: seek in and through clothes both personal and social dimensions of experience and ex-pression. One aspect—but only one aspect—is the pursuit of attractiveness as a means of winning acceptance.

The fact that dress can enhance attractiveness has long been recognized[209]—and debated as to its moral merit. To some extent, as we will see presently, how we prove attractive, through dress or despite it, itself provokes debate. Often, though, the moral debate is over whether the attractiveness itself is appropriate. A seductive attractiveness, for example, may be grudgingly acknowledged at the same time it is roundly deplored. No better example may exist than the crossdressing male, whose efforts at creating a feminine attractiveness can occasion strong feeling in both men and women.

The behavior employed in becoming attractive—the time spent in selecting clothes, dressing, and working on one's appearance—may be similar among men, women, and crossdressers, but the depiction of it by others is likely to be very different. Crossdressing males are likely to be depicted as excessively narcissistic, preening before a mirror while in feminine dress.[210] While women similarly may be called vain, the judgment passed on them is mostly condescending, offered with a wink and nod that says we can only expect this from females. When masculine men, fussing to straighten a tie or coordinate a business suit ensemble spend time grooming before a mirror it is more likely styled as conscientious attention to appearance for solid professional reasons—an admirable trait showing character. Apparently only for male crossdressers does the behavior carry the weight of a pathological character trait—someone so self-centered that they have trouble relating to others. The behavior may not be different quantitatively or qualitatively from what females or other males do, but the moral judgment is significantly different. Therefore it is clearly not the behavior *per se* generating the judgment, but values.

Values tend to generate more judgments precisely because they matter to us. The more important the value, the more pressing will be the moral assessments associated with it. Because they interrelate and interact, values are context-dependent to the extent that varying contexts reorder their priority and redefine their interactions. The same set of values in one context arouses positive or neutral assessments that in another occasions moral outrage. A crossdressing male in an entertainment venue sought out by patrons will likely not be censored, though how attractive the crossdresser is will matter to the observer according to whether the appearance is supposed to be ridiculous to fetch laughs or erotically seductive. However, that same patron leaving a club may be morally offended to encounter a crossdressing male on the street, whether attractive or not.

Although most of us may be reluctant to admit it—leaving attractiveness as more a practiced than espoused value[211]—our personal appearance matters to us and we tend to provide a tinge of moral judgments to our own dress and that of others. Moreover, we rely on our own personal behavior and its context to set the standard for judging the behavior attending attractiveness. A man getting ready for work morally approves his effort, and tolerates his wife and daughter spending as much or more time since, after all, that's what females do. But the thought of another male spending an exactly equal amount of time to dress femininely will likely draw a negative judgment as a waste of time, purposeless, and/or morally reprobate. Seeking to enhance attractiveness is judged not by the behavior but by the context as circumscribed by values.

An important aspect of this is a very old debate over whether 'good' and 'right' attractiveness depends on 'natural' beauty, or whether 'artificial' enhancements are morally acceptable. Of course, the latter is marked by attractiveness that largely depends on the enhancements offered by apparel, accessories, and makeup—the elements of dress. Proponents of natural beauty are especially likely to be upset by crossdressing that succeeds in turning the appearance into a gendered being whose presumed sex is different from the actual body. However, typically debate on this issue has focused on whether women should seek by any and all means to increase their attractiveness.

It is an enduring debate. Centuries ago the Roman poet Propertius passionately spoke for the advocates of 'natural' beauty in his second elegy, addressed to Cynthia: "Why set yourself off by artificial means, to spoil the grace of nature by purchased adornment, and not suffer your limbs to shine in their own loveliness. Believe me, there is no improving beauty like yours by adventitious aid: genuine Love likes not a disguised form."[212] Similar arguments persist to the present. One might argue that such a view is a romantic one, or observe that it generally comes from men interested in truth in advertising!

Another Roman poet, Ovid, albeit with more humor than passion, argued the other side. In his *Art of Love* the poet wrote, "True beauty's a gift of the gods, few can boast they possess it—and most of you, my dears, don't. Hard work will improve the picture . . . ."[213] Similarly, centuries later, Mark Twain observed, "A large part of the daughter of civilization is her dress—as it should be. Some civilized women would lose half their charm without dress, and some would lose all of it. The daughter of modern civilization, dressed at her utmost best, is a morsel of exquisite and beautiful art and expense."[214] Less poetically, but more practically, Emily Burbank wrote in 1917, "Beauty is a wonderful and precious thing, and not so fleeting either as one is told. The point is, to take note, not of beauty's departure, but its gradually changing aspect, and adapt costume, line and colour, to the demands of each year's alterations in the individual."[215] The labor of being attractive (or at least civilized), it turns out, involves everything from clothes and makeup to hairstyle and manner. As the old saying goes, 'all is fair in love and war'; attracting a lover is justified by adding to attractiveness by any means.

Because attractiveness is desired, and because dress can enhance it, bringing favorable outcomes, most of us in practice side with Ovid. In valuing attractiveness we make an implicit moral judgment that using dress to enhance beauty is right and good. We probably assuage any guilt over the artificial nature of this act by telling ourselves that dress does not create beauty out of nothing, but merely draws forth the natural beauty already there. Thus we say things like,

'This outfit flatters me.' We dress to bring out our 'natural color,' to show off our 'real figure,' and to highlight our 'best features.'

Crossdressing often embraces this same value. While some crossdress to hide, not wanting to draw attention, others do so to express a gender reality they strongly desire, or affiliate with in personal identity, or simply that helps balance their experience of self as someone neither masculine nor feminine (but rather 'another' gender). In seeking to embody through dress a different gender the crossdresser remains a person interested in how she or he looks. Attractiveness still matters, and seeing the self as attractive while crossdressed remains associated with favorable outcomes, such as enhanced self-esteem, relaxation, greater sense of competence, and so forth.[216]

Character

Most of us, while valuing attractiveness, would judge ourselves shallow if we only sought acceptance through physical beauty. We also value character—indeed, we commonly list it as attractive! Dress often has been enlisted in the display and promotion of moral values and standards—both at individual and societal levels. For example, historian Jenna Weismann Joselit produces evidence in the America between 1890-1930 of the belief that dress is not a private affair but a public obligation to display civic virtue: "What one wore was a public construct, bound up with an enduring moral order."[217] Indeed, fashion became "the ultimate test of character—for all Americans."[218] The morality of dress lay in whether or not it showed American virtues befitting its democratic ideals.

But this was hardly an American phenomenon alone. A keen observer in England of the relationship between psychology and clothes in the 1930s wrote of masculine costume the close association sought between dress appearance and a certain character: "In the thickness of material and solidity of structure of their tailored garments, in the heavy and sober blackness of their shoes, in the virgin whiteness of their shirtfronts, men exhibit to the outside world their would-be strength, steadfastness and immunity from frivolous distraction."[219] The relation between dress appearance and character appears to be one that has persisted over a long period of time, though the strength of perceived association waxes and wanes according to time and place. Where a societal emphasis may no longer prevail, an individual importance to show character in dress may yet persist.

But is it a notion still current in the United States? Some research at least indirectly suggests it is. A report published in 2002 investigated six studies that sought in one way or another to measure the associations among self-importance of moral identity, moral cognitions, and behavior. In one study, with college undergraduates (200 men and 161 women), the subjects were presented a list of nine traits (e.g., 'caring') associated with a moral individual and then asked to imagine a person with such characteristics performing certain behaviors. One behavior strongly endorsed as likely for such a person includes dress: "I often wear clothes that identify me as having these characteristics." Interestingly, this behavior was highly associated with public action ('symbolization'), but was not central to self-concept ('internalization').[220] This may reflect a perception that dress behavior says one thing to the world but another to the self. Perhaps we use apparel to publicly proclaim character while simultaneously feeling that such behavior should not be used to judge the real self![221]

This situation puts the crossdresser in a bind. Consider once more the male crossdresser. As seen above, there is a tendency in our culture that has persisted for over a century to associate the value of attractiveness more strongly with women through feminine fashion while correlating character with men in masculine fashion. Therefore, a male who selects feminine dress in preference to masculine attire may be understood by others as choosing feminine values over masculine ones and, more pointedly, sacrificing character for the superficiality of outer appearance. Since character is strongly associated with morality, this perceived abandonment of masculine integrity or charm for the wiles of feminine dress can scarcely be seen as other than immoral.

But wait a moment. The above logic depends on accepting the questionable premises. Increasingly, we no longer so readily endorse such sexist notions as women are less morally refined than men or that men are less interested than women in appearing sexy. Changing perceptions of gender may be slow, but they are real and substantial. Indeed, the challenging of old stereotypes yields fertile soil for new ways to conceive what may be happening in male crossdressing. Seen in light of modified perceptions of the genders—and gender itself—this may in part explain both why there persists confused and contradictory impressions about crossdressing as well as a growing tolerance, if not complete acceptance.

When it comes to character, the idea that a crossdresser would choose dress designed to portray a *lack* of character, an absence of charm or integrity, seems ridiculous outside of specific contexts, such as some drag, where ridicule of conventional notions is the point. In general practice the crossdresser remains as much committed to character while crossdressing as at any other time. In fact, many crossdressers and their partners report that the personal traits associated with character actually increase, or at least become more apparent, while the individual is crossdressed.[222]

But some contend that what is objectionable in male crossdressing is character assassination: males masquerading as women are degrading caricatures. What is immoral, then, is the damage done to 'real' women. Of course, the implicit assumption in this critique is that femininity is the exclusive provenance of females. Only females can be women—another ringing endorsement of the culture's rigid pairing of sex and gender. Such criticism misses the point if femininity is a simulation; females are not 'essentially' feminine any more than males are 'essentially' masculine.[223]

Dress also often is attached to the value of *power*. The sumptuary laws of an earlier time legislated dress distinctions among social classes—a highly public way to enforce an established hierarchy. Legal scholar Alan Hunt contends that sumptuary regulations were important elements of a response to pressures on hierarchical social order. In the construction of social order and the identities of groups within society—whether organized according to gender, class, or nationality—such laws sought to clarify and preserve existing group identities despite the changes being brought by new means to wealth and other changes associated with the rise of the modern world. These laws, in effect, imagined a social order they tried to visibly construct in the appearance of its members. While such laws ultimately failed, they were instrumental in helping shape both civil law and a certain view about self-regulation.[224]

Sumptuary laws may have passed into history, and social classes both in modern democratic and Marxist societies may be widely viewed as undesirable, yet dress fashions persist as a way used to differentiate social strata. As culture scholar and fashion historian Rebecca Arnold points out about an earlier time, "members of the upper-class fought to maintain status by asserting their superior taste and financial strength, through the elitism of couture."[225] In one manner or another, those who reckon themselves in an upper-class persist in efforts to retain their status, and have it seen as such. Extravagant excess shows off the claimed superior position—in defiance of the masses unable to afford the same. Of course, as Arnold also notes, excluded groups seize the opportunity provided by "the escalating power of images" to create for themselves an 'imagined' status, replete with its own "construction of styles which mark out their own territory, immune to the taunts from their supposed betters."[226]

The modern utility of dress to craft imagined identities, coupled with modern manufacturing, also permits imitation of the fashion styles associated with the upper-class. Accordingly, dress remains a prominent vehicle for ostentatious wealth—real or imagined. In a culture built around consumption where wealth is worshipped, the surest declaration of power is the display of wealth. And nowhere is that more publicly visible across a wide range of contexts than in dress.

This same power of dress to forge imagined identities is relied upon by crossdressers. They craft a gender presentation different from the expectation for the gender assigned them at birth. This artifice depends on the power of clothes, but also is a display of personal power since nothing has more potency in our culture than the ability to mold gender. Power, then, is very much a matter of significance in crossdressing. Nor is it unrelated to the issue of social class. To the extent that social hierarchies privilege one gender over another, crossdressing unavoidably means movement upward or downward. For a crossdressing female the movement from woman to man in appearance was an effort to move up—an action easy to understand whether approved or not. For a crossdressing male the movement from man to woman appears in the social order a self-conscious decision to give up privilege and move down in the hierarchy—an action neither understandable nor easily sanctioned.

Still, the realities of social class and the powers associated with different genders are more complex than such an easy reading presents. Male crossdressers do not typically see themselves as giving up power and moving socially downward. Indeed, they may speak of claiming power, experiencing the kind of liberation associated with higher class status, and moving into the gender class they desire—or separating themselves entirely from the whole artificiality of gender and social class. Those who do not crossdress have set the agenda and rules for interpretation, but that hardly speaks well of the possibility for really understanding what is happening in crossdressing.

There are other ways in which dress involves power. The early 20th century economist Thorstein Veblen argues dress is the preeminent manner of displaying economic power: ". . . our apparel is always in evidence and affords an indication of our pecuniary standing to all observers at the first glance."[227] Veblen observes that regardless of class, the largest portion of the money spent on clothes is not for the protection from the elements they afford but for a 'respectable' appearance. Further, he contends, we operate on the assumption that the more expensive apparel is, the more desirable it becomes. Expensive clothes proclaim an economic power that can be translated into the wearer's independence from needing to make a living. Thus clothes also serve as a marker of social worth in a system where worth is predicated on economic success.

There is a gender difference Veblen notes in this regard. Feminine garb marks the woman as someone separated from 'productive employment.' He cites bonnets, shoes, and especially the corset as markers of the kind of feminine apparel that contribute to making work impossible. "It may broadly be set down," Veblen observes, "that the womanliness of woman's apparel resolves itself, in point of substantial fact, into the more effective hindrance to useful exertion offered by the garments peculiar to women."[228] Instead of work, the woman of the household consumes goods 'vicariously' for the man whose income makes consumption possible. She is the beautiful ornament upon which his wealth is lavished; her consumption of goods as shown in apparel signifies his economic power.[229]

Given this logic we might offer an observation about male crossdressing that may seem remarkable: in choosing feminine dress the male crossdresser offers the kind of display of wealth normally reserved for women! Veblen does *not* draw such a conclusion. He acknowledges that some males do dress in apparel with 'womanly' elements. He says these include priests and domestic servants, two groups similar in economic function. Beyond these fellows, he notes, there are also 'free men' whose zeal in attire brings them to transgress the gender line between men's and women's dress. But Veblen argues that such men are seen as departing from social norms and their dress is accorded as inappropriately effeminate.[230]

Why does he reach such a conclusion when his own logic could as easily have led to a different appraisal? His analysis depends on a social construction that rigidly pairs sex with gender: masculine males and feminine females, each with their own respective roles and responsibilities. In the sphere of economics, men earn the wealth and women display it. A man who both earns and displays it no less surely violates the gender boundary than the woman who goes to work. But there's the rub: the social division of the genders economically portrayed by Veblen no longer can be claimed to exist in our society—and may not have been as true for his own as he thought.

Although firmly entrenched in popular consciousness, Veblen's portrayal of the state of fashion in the late 19th and early 20th centuries may be somewhat imbalanced. Victorian scholar Brent Shannon contends that from 1860-1914 there was a trend toward cultivating British men as consumers of fashion. The effort to sell clothes and accessories was accompanied by an intense attention to distinguishing masculine shopping from that of women and to emphasize masculinity in the clothes. By the end of this period the success of this effort was marked by the accepted connection between masculine dress and professional success.[231] In short, masculine fashion appealed to power.

In this light, it appears less remarkable that some men might have been content in Veblen's day with showering their own wealth upon their own clothes. The 'dandy' was well-known, and despite frequent ridicule there were plenty enough examples. It is hardly a wild stretch to imagine men happy to select feminine fashion for themselves as an expression of personal power, regardless of what others might judge. Today, when women's involvement in the workforce is so extensive, and their economic dependence on men greatly lessened, the division depicted by Veblen seems far less credible. In fact, we have pretty much given up the idea that woman even can be crossdressed, so wide is the acceptance for whatever attire they adopt. And while males may still be seen as crossdressing, the donning of feminine apparel is not likely to be censored on the grounds that is an inappropriate extravagance on clothes! The power issues involved have changed.

Today, while we generally favor efforts made by ourselves and by others to enhance attractiveness, dressing for power remains controversial. We may see it as 'right' in some situations, 'wrong' in others; as 'harmless' or 'harmful.' When conjoined to other highly valued matters, like gender, the potential for strong moral judgments increases. For instance, to use Veblen's terms, a male wealthy enough to display pecuniary power, who dresses in a manner reflecting effeminacy, sends what a lot of folk see as mixed signals. As discussed earlier, men are above women in the gender hierarchy; wealthy men are above less wealthy men in the social order. So a wealthy man who dresses in a manner seen as effeminate has done the incomprehensible: appeared as someone weaker than his gender and wealth permit.

How strong are our moral judgments—and on what are they based?

Aside from such instances, our moral judgments about dress tend to remain mild and implicit. We feel something, but not strongly enough for the judgment to rise fully into consciousness, or to motivate a direct statement or action. Instead, we may smile approvingly or shake our head and avert our eyes. We note the dress and form a judgment, but perhaps only weakly perceive the link to the underlying value or determine the matter is not worth a stronger expression. Typically it requires the combining of two or more primary values in an upsetting fashion to generate stronger moral sentiments.

In the 19th century new impetus for such explicit judgments arose when a keen interest in the origin of clothing resulted in competing theories, two of which are particularly pertinent here: dress originated as adornment, or it was created for modesty in response to shame.[232] While these competing theories may seem to highlight the value of attractiveness, in reality the elements of character and power were strongly involved as well. Each position gave rise to justifications about the 'right' or 'wrong' of apparel choices, taking into consideration—and shaping reflection about—how we should appear attractive, what such choices say about character, and how they display entrenched positions of gender-based power. Much of the debate took place within a religious context, especially with advocates of the modesty theory appealing to the biblical book of Genesis. Such debates, however muted in public consciousness, continue.

Specifically, how much or little we wear, where it is placed, and its style are still commonly spoken about as communicating something moral—something either 'right' or 'wrong.' More specifically yet, that morality is commonly said to be about our sexuality. A great deal of what has been said about the morality of dress has devolved to this one aspect. In fact, many believe that this connection of dress to sexuality and to moral expression goes all the way back to the very beginning when human beings first covered themselves.

Is clothing a moral response to shame?

The notion that the origin of clothes is rooted in a moral expression provides a rationale for various ideas about what is appropriate in dress. In the Western world, many believe that clothing came about as a moral response to *shame*. This response took the form of covering ourselves for the sake of modesty rather than either protection from the elements or for adornment. Because clothes hide nakedness (i.e., the sexual parts of the body), which generates shame, any clothing that covers the portions of the body generating this shame is morally approved; any deficit in such covering is morally illicit. Thus modesty in dress not only explains the origin of dress, but remains its moral standard.

How did such a notion form? The idea is rooted in the story of Adam and Eve in the Hebrew Bible. The text relates that after succumbing to temptation, "the eyes of both of them were opened, and they realized they were naked; so they sewed fig leaves together and made coverings for themselves."[233] As the Puritan Philip Stubbes commented in the 1580s, before sin there was no shame in being naked; after sin, "they became unclean, filthy, loathsome, and deformed." So they "sewed them garments of fig leaves together, to cover their shame withal." But, Stubbes continues, "Then the Lord, pitying their misery and loathing their deformity, gave them pelts and hides of beasts to make them garments withal, to the end that their shameful parts might less appear . . . ."[234] Three lessons are derived by Stubbes from this: first, that sin is why clothes exist; second, that God is their originator and giver; and third, that they exist to cover our shame.[235]

For many people through the ages this biblical story and accompanying commentary like that by Stubbes has inextricably linked clothes with a sense of body shame. Many of us have been taught, if only indirectly, that we wear clothes to conceal our nakedness, and we do this because of how we feel about our bodies—specifically our sexual anatomy since that provides a noticeable distinction between man and woman. Clothes, then, signal our sense of shame, specifically with regard to our sexual bodies.[236]

We might note, however, that the Bible itself does not compel us to find this supposed connection. In fact, the text actually offers grounds for a contrary understanding. In truth, the Bible actually may lend a more nuanced explanation than that Adam and Eve felt shame—a word that does not even appear in the text. The biblical first couple was tempted by the desire to be like God, to know good and evil. What they got was knowledge of *differences*. They learned they were not only not like God, they were not even like each other!

So where do some among us derive the connection to shame? The idea calls us back to an earlier text, where after recounting the creation of male and female it is written, "And the man and his wife were both naked, and were not ashamed "(Genesis 2:25). Interestingly, the ancient Jewish translation Targum Neofiti for this text adds "as yet" in anticipation of what is to come. [237] So at least some in that Jewish community saw shame linked to what transpired in the Fall (Genesis 3). Yet all the text says is that "they knew that they were naked" (Genesis 3:7). The supposed shame comes from the link between being naked and not ashamed *before* the Fall with knowing they are naked and making clothes *after* the Fall. It seems plausible to suggest shame was the motivation.

Whatever Adam and Eve may have felt when covering themselves with fig leaves is not made explicit. But it does lead to hiding from God and a subsequent confrontation with Deity. When pressed to explain his actions, Adam offers up fear—and adds, "because I was naked" (Genesis 3:10). Why would he be afraid because he was naked? While it is possible his fear stemmed from shame, or was attached to it, perhaps a better sense remains this notion of differences. Adam naked before the Fall has no sense of differences—or perhaps more accurately, of their import—and thus neither fear nor shame. After the

Fall, he is acutely aware of his difference from God as a consequence of the knowledge he has gained. Perhaps, too, both he and Eve, perceiving their bodily differences and sensing there are important consequences in them, experience an anxiety, or nonspecific fear that leads to covering up and hiding. But whether such elements enter in or not, it is reasonably clear that the knowledge they have gained of 'good and evil,' makes it plain which they are, and how different that is from God. That alone suffices to generate fear.

Thus Adam's awareness of his physical nakedness makes a nice parallel to his awareness of his exposure before God of the deed he and Eve have done. That he became aware of sexual differences, too, was the thought of Rabbi Abba ben Kahana, who centuries later in a midrashic comment interpreted the Hebrew text as meaning the clothes they made were gender-differentiated. [238] Just a few lines later we read, in Genesis 3:21, "The LORD God made garments of skin for Adam and his wife and clothed them"—a text variously interpreted in subsequent literature. [239] Whatever the precise garb with which God clothed them, the inevitable exposure of the first couple's deed becomes the occasion of a divine provision—another manifestation of how God cares for them, as He replaces fig leaves with clothes made from animal skins.

What role does modesty in dress play?

The role of shame inspires the idea that dress is meant for modesty.[240] As we have seen, a way to view this connection is to conceive it as modesty and apparel linked in a single simultaneous act of creation. If shame arises within the breast of man, the gift of God is a covering for it; an implicit behest to modesty. It took little imagination among religious authorities to make that a mandate. But is modesty inherently bound up with dress? If it isn't, what connection might then be drawn between them?

The word itself derives from a Latin term for discretion, moderation, and restraint; it is rooted in orderliness. In English, by the 16th century it was being used to convey self-control. In the sense that it reflects a freedom from excess, in practice it came to mean austerity—not merely in dress but in manner. Thus the word itself suggests the possibility that modesty and dress might be severed in some important way. Over the years, numerous scholars have produced arguments and cultural evidences to advance the case that modesty's origin was independent of clothing. For our present discussion it is not important we retrace those arguments; we need only view the consequences.

But first we must describe what modesty in dress looks like holistically. Modest clothing is characterized as 'proper,' 'unobtrusive,' and—to borrow a word long gone out of fashion—'shamefast.' Modest dress exemplifies an orderliness of conduct—in all respects, perhaps, but especially in one sphere. Although we scarcely need it, we get a hint of this sphere in noting that in the early 18th century there was a particular garment called a 'modesty,' a veil-like piece to cover the bosom. Whatever else modesty attaches to, in clothing we must reckon with its connection to sexual body parts.

According to the argument that modesty responds to shame, we cover ourselves to keep from common viewing those body parts associated with the shame of sex. Of course, these anatomical parts are our erogenous zones, most especially the genitals. Modesty in dress puts these parts of the body in 'their proper place,' so to speak, by hiding them away. Pioneering sexologist Havelock Ellis, in his treatise on the evolution of modesty, reflects this sensibility linking modesty and sex by likening modesty to an instinctual fear that typically centers in concealment of the 'sexual processes.' Ellis regards modesty as more pronounced in women, such that it might even be counted as the chief of feminine psychosexual characteristics.[241]

However, Ellis does *not* view modesty as originating in connection with clothing. On the other hand, he does tie the origin of clothing's first psychological basis on an emotion of modesty. In his view, modesty in clothing is a defensive gesture against the strange gaze of others, and especially the act of the female shielding herself from the eyes of males. Ellis notes, though, that the defense is not against aggressive acts, but merely against sight. This fact, he thinks, reduces the defense to a playful one and facilitates "the invention of ornament or clothing as sexual lures." As Ellis points out, "the fashion of feminine garments . . . has the double object of concealing and attracting."[242] Modest dress draws the eye while concealing from it the flesh beneath.

Similarly, we may recall from earlier discussion (see the answer to Q. 1) that sociologist William Thomas argues that dress exists to attract others' attention, including signaling potential mates. In setting this notion forward, Thomas simultaneously disputes the shame theory described above and posits an erotic role for modest dress:

> The naive assumption that men were ashamed because they were naked, and clothed themselves to hide their nakedness, is not tenable in face of the large mass of evidence that many of the natural races are naked, and not ashamed of their nakedness; and a much stronger case can be made out for the contrary view, that clothing was first worn as a mode of attraction, and modesty then attached to the act of removing the clothing; but this view in turn does not explain an equally large number of cases of modesty among races which wear no clothing at all.[243]

Sociologist Thomas and sexologist Ellis concur that modesty originated independent of clothing. They also agree that modesty attaches to clothing in such a manner that erotic appeal trumps shame. This position stands in stark contrast to the religious contention that shame over the naked body, and especially the erogenous zones, motivates their concealment through the adoption of austere clothing. In fact, modesty clothing, as long as it remains gender-differentiated, remains capable of attracting attention to those parts of the body that sexually differentiate people. And that fact allows modest dress to attain some degree of erotic appeal.

Thomas might have looked no further than the United States of his own century to illustrate an awareness of this duality. Women fighting for equal rights in the middle of the 19th century made dress reform one aspect of their work. Among their arguments for dress reform was that current feminine fashions—replete with stylistic elements such as low cut bodice, bare arms, and compressed waist—excited male imagination and incited immorality.[244] From our vantage point women's dress of the 1850s may seem almost excessively modest, yet the women of the time understood perfectly well the connection between modesty and eroticism. A bare midriff is not required to make a waist alluring.

In startlingly contrast to Stubbes' Puritan perspective, Ellis and Thomas raise the possibility that modesty attaches more strongly to allure than to shame. This view retains a connection of modesty in dress to sexuality, but moves it away from shame-based consciousness of the sexed body to attractiveness-based eroticism. If modesty had no other goal than to cover the flesh, a burlap bag would be all any of us need. Yet the diversity in color, style, fabric, and fit of clothes deemed modest leaves no doubt that attractiveness still matters. What sets modest dress apart from the overtly erotic is not that it is less appealing or attractive, but that it stands in a consciously different relation to other values such as character and power. Modest dress stresses a certain range of conceptions about proper character and power, a range constrained by a view of the right order of things, including gendered relations. So where does this situation leave us?

How are clothes, morality, and sexuality related?

We have already considered the idea that attractiveness is valued by us as an important factor in winning acceptance. As outlined earlier, modesty in dress is one path to demonstrating attractiveness—whether by shame-based concealment or as artful invitation in a restrained, 'civilized' fashion. Either path may lead to enhancing attractiveness, winning acceptance, and being joined to another. That the two paths may diverge in the particular manner they accomplish this, or in important respects as to their relational outcomes, is not our concern here. What matters here is that we grasp how our values reflect one or another interpretation of how modesty and dress interact. Our moral judgments are different if we view modesty in the service of eroticism rather than shame.

Let us retreat to the broader matter of dress used to enhance or display attractiveness. While males and females may differ in what they find attractive, both sexes highlight attractiveness as a critical value in mate selection. Clothing is commonly employed to indicate interest in being favorably noticed, seen as attractive by others, and thus possibly approached in a friendly manner. Certainly a degree of sexuality figures into such clothed displays of the body. Young adults of both sexes confess they view some clothing as indicating sexual interest,[245] and this tendency is especially likely for young men[246]—the very ones most prone to be seeking sexual partners, or committing sexual aggression. Even women, though, may be prone to attribute to victims of sexual assault less compassion because they perceive the dress as having invited the aggression.[247] Thus attractiveness is not divorced from considerations of power.

Evolutionary psychology offers a rationale for changes in feminine fashion that correlate sexual attraction with economic power. In short, 'marriage economics,' as Nigel Barber puts it, should show up in fashion. As the sex ratio between males and females fluctuates, dress styles should adapt to the relatively less or greater opportunities for mating-through-marriage offered to women. Barber, drawing on data from three studies of dress fashion across the period from 1885-1976, found evidence to support his hypothesis that women dress differently depending on the sex ratio and the varying desirability for economic power of marriage as opposed to employment. When mating opportunities were lower, but employment more accessible so that economic independence was possible, necklines and hemlines went up, while waists became wider. A high value placed on marriage and marital stability favors longer dresses, lower necklines, wider décolletage, and narrower waists—signs of fertility *and* modesty.[248]

Many today accept the notion that the moral connection of dress to self-expression centers on sexuality. In short, what we wear and how we wear it is thought by some to chiefly express our sexuality. Unfortunately, even if true—and not everyone agrees that it is—this connection is complex and unclear. For one thing, research suggests that a majority of folk in our culture feel morally confused about sex. [249] Start with the confusion about exactly what clothes do or do not express, add how well or poorly dress does it, then sprinkle in the variety of ways people make moral decisions, [250] and the result is a bewilderingly murky mess.

Probably most of us, after some careful reflection, disagree that the predominant purpose of dress is to display us sexually. But we likely concur that the sexual body is rarely absent from consideration when clothes are selected. In light of various explanations for the origin of clothing we might be inclined to wonder if some harmony can be brought among the competing voices. Do we have to choose one idea—protection from the elements, shame/modesty, or mate attraction—as the sole reason for clothing?

British psychoanalyst J. C. Flugel, writing in the first third of the 20th century, combines elements we have discussed, joining the need for protection from environmental factors to the opportunistic use of apparel for erotic appeal in mate attraction, but without sacrificing the power of shame or the motive of modesty. Indeed, Flugel proposes that women's clothes, in particular, combine elements both of shame/modesty and erotic appeal. Unlike the male body, the female body is more thoroughly sexualized by virtue of her erogenous zones being more widely distributed. "It is not surprising," he writes, "that women should be at once the more modest and the more exhibitionistic sex, since both their shame and their attractiveness relate to the whole body."[251] Western culture's sense of shame over the sexual body leads to modesty in dress, which in turn can be manipulated for calculated erotic exposure and allure.

Flugel has proved immensely influential. His concept of erogenous zones is widely employed and his observations about the modern restrictiveness in masculine fashion in contrast to feminine dress remains widely endorsed. But Flugel was more than a psychologist; he also had a strong sense of history and the role of culture. He knew that in other societies men may be the ones with the leisure and opportunity for the kinds of adornment modern Western women enjoy; in earlier centuries European men also enjoyed a liberty of individuality—a kind of narcissism in fashion—since displaced: "Up till recently in human history, men were dressed as gaudily and were allowed as much individuality in clothing as were women . . . ."[252] By contrast, Flugel observes that modern fashion "allows few outlets for personal vanity among men; to be dressed 'correctly' or in 'good taste' is the utmost that a modern man can hope for. . ."; instead, what is original and beautiful in clothing is reserved for feminine fashion.[253]

Still, Flugel's is not the last word on the subject.[254] There remains the specter of gender, which though joined in our culture to sex still transcends it in scope. If there is a moral dimension with regard to clothing and the sexed body, there is also one regarding if, when, and how our manner of dress expresses gender. [255] Precisely because our culture so rigidly pairs sex and gender, the specter of one immediately raises the ghost of the other. The relation of both sex and gender to dress—as well as other related matters—is at the heart of what we need to know to comprehend crossdressing. But before we examine the relation of clothing to gender and crossdressing (Q. 6-10), we must look more broadly at sex and gender (Q. 5).

107

Q. 5

Why do sex and gender matter?

The Short Answer: 'Sex' and 'gender' are terms that in casual conversation tend to be used interchangeably. Labels like 'male' and 'female' especially are used for both sex and gender. Such usage reflects the confusion over the relationship between these two—which proves not to be as straightforward as often imagined. 'Sex' properly refers to the typing of the body based on anatomical presentation as presumably related to reproductive function. Thus, whatever the genetic code, if a body at birth looks like it will eventually provide semen it is sex-typed 'male;' otherwise it is sex-typed 'female.' Our culture recognizes only two sexes. 'Gender' refers to the presumed personal experience expected to follow from having a certain body sex, as well as the presentation of characteristics socially accepted and approved for such a body. As this suggests, gender in our culture is thought to flow inevitably from sex. Male bodies are expected to produce 'masculine' boys and men; female bodies are expected to produce 'feminine' girls and women. The key word is 'expected': based on body sex apparent at birth, individuals are assigned a gender and raised with the expectation of conformity in personal experience and social presentation to what is believed to be appropriate for the experiences and characteristics of a particular sex. Despite our culture positing a binary system pairing anatomical sex with gender in a predictable fashion, nature produces astounding variation in sex, gender, and the ways they interact. Though both sex and gender separately raise issues, the larger problem lies with the modern construction of gender. The contemporary Western view has created more problems than it has solved by insisting on only two genders. We need a more robust view. A better understanding of transgender realities such as crossdressing helps us better grasp the reality of gender.

The Longer Answer: Neither the idea of 'sex,' nor that of 'gender,' is as straightforward as we might suppose (or wish). To understand what, if anything, our manner of dress says about gender, we must spend some time wrestling with both the concepts of sex and gender. To begin with, we must wonder about these terms and how we regard them. Is our current ease with how we understand 'sex' and 'gender' merited? Do we really comprehend either in a way that warrants what we so often do—raising our beliefs to the position of universal truth? Are the modern assumptions of *only* two sexes and *only* two genders empirically established, or a socially limited and inadequate construction? Is 'gender' itself a modern social construct, or is it an accurate and adequate label for an objective reality?

These questions matter immensely if we are to rightly comprehend crossdressing. In light of the medicalization of sex (see the answer to Q. 91) transgender behaviors like crossdressing came to be regarded as 'deviant,' an 'illness'—at least as they are practiced by some. [256] In a framework where 'gender' is conceived and articulated according to a particular logic the conclusions about crossdressing may feel inevitable. But is this framework pretentious? Does it arrogate to itself an authority unwarranted by the facts? Such questions occupy contemporary scholars and they must also busy our minds if we are to be honest with our subject matter.

What is 'sex'?

Let us begin with sex. The subject is one endlessly fascinating for most of us. We use the word often and in a variety of contexts. We probably feel quite confident in our use, believing we know what it means. Nevertheless, because the term is important and because people use it in different ways, we need to take a moment to define it. But before we do, let's be clear about what sex is *not*. Sex is not the same as gender. Sex is not the same as sexuality. In this work it does not refer to sexual activities, though that is a common, popular use of the word. Although most of us are often sloppy in our use of language, we need here to clear some space and see our terms precisely.

Defining 'Sex'

In this work the term 'sex' is used in a manner conforming to general academic usage. We may or may not conclude that the usual and customary understanding needs changing. But even if we decide it does, such change will lack relevance without first understanding what it has been changed from. Since the purpose of this work does not include making such a change we shall constrain ourselves by what prevails in our culture at present. Thus, throughout this work 'sex' refers to "*anatomical presentations presumably related to reproductive capacity.*" [257] This definition roots itself in biology ('anatomy,' 'reproductive capacity'), but as importantly modified by environmental factors, such as the influence of culture on observers' judgments ('presentations,' 'presumably related').

Two allied terms are 'sexuality' and 'sexology.' Both terms are much broader than the word 'sex.' Both involve personal and social dimensions as well as biological ones. In this work, 'sexuality' refers to "attitudes, beliefs and behaviors organized around and with respect to sex." We should have no objection if the clause "and gender" is added at the end because attitudes, belief, and behaviors organized around and with respect to gender are commonly considered alongside those about sex. 'Sexology' is the study of these matters. A sexologist may belong to a discipline such as psychiatry or psychology, sociology or anthropology, or some other academic discipline, but focuses that discipline on researching and understanding sexuality.

'Sex' begins with biology, though it does not end there. At a fundamental level sex is a matter of genetic coding. The karyotype for a generic male is 46, XY; for a generic female it is 46, XX. The genetic coding guides the eventual anatomical display, but in itself does not ensure for sexual organs that all 46, XX females will look anatomically alike and all 46, XY males will present anatomically the same. Between genotype (genetic potential) and phenotype (realized presentation) are many intervening variables. For example, SRY (*sex-determining region Y*) is a specific gene on the Y chromosome that triggers critical events leading to the sex characteristics associated with being male. Later, there are specific hormonal influences that further shape ongoing development. However, despite all this rich biological background, when we talk about the sex of people we are not typically referring to their karyotype or prenatal sex development, but to their anatomical presentation at birth, and specifically those anatomical parts associated with reproduction.

We each have a body that displays certain physical characteristics associated with reproduction. These include body parts such as the breasts, penis, testes, clitoris, labia, vagina, and ovaries—some of which clearly are not directly related to reproduction. Those body parts visible for inspection in the newborn—the genitals—such as the penis or labia, are conventionally relied upon in making an assignment of sex that, contrary to logic, is relied on throughout life in social situations calling for identification. It matters little whether the observed anatomical parts accurately represent reproductive ability; they serve to separate individuals. In our culture only two such camps—'male' and 'female'—are recognized and socially sanctioned. Thus, all newborns are assigned one or the other sex status on the assumption of a particular future reproductive role, whether they will ever play that role or not. From birth forward, genital anatomy is used as the basis of sex assignment and sexual expectations.

Superficially, at least, the arrangement seems to make sense and to work. Certain body parts seem generally mutually exclusive. Someone who appears to have a penis and testes is presumed not to have ovaries; someone with a clitoris and labia is presumed not to possess testes. Where unexpected mixing of genital features occurs the presumption is that a 'mistake' is present which calls for medical intervention to 'correct.' A common standard has been visible inspection of the penis or clitoris, with length determining sex assignment. Once a determination has been made medical interventions such as surgery are used to adjust genital appearance for better conformity to the cultural expectations. As a general rule, ambiguous cases are assigned to the sex status 'female' (see below).

A Critique of 'Sex'

With a moment's reflection we might find it remarkable how easily we accept the idea of two mutually exclusive sexes. The cultural conception of sex depends on premises that prove to be dubious. Especially critical to sustaining this scheme are the following notions:

❑ Sex is about reproductive biology.
❑ The essential and central purpose of sexuality is reproduction.
❑ Only two anatomical sex representations are natural.

Each needs further examination.

Even the little we have considered thus far should indicate that sex is about more than just reproductive biology. Although the sexual body provides a foundation, upon that foundation is constructed an elaborate set of beliefs about that body. One such belief in our culture, fundamental to the others, is that only two kinds of sexual bodies are possible. We see all bodies as if they represent 46, XX or 46, XY karyotypes. Of course, throughout human history all people have had to rely on in coding people with respect to reproductive anatomy was visible inspection. The understanding of human genetics is still in its infancy. The idea that genetic differences might really matter in a way calling into questions such a neat and simple division is only slowly gaining hold.

For practical purposes we tend to ignore the importance of atypical karyotypes such those with extra X chromosomes associated with maleness (e.g. XXY, XXXY, or XXXXY), or those X chromosome differences associated with femaleness (e.g. X, XXX, XXXX, or XXXXX)—except to the degree these differences result in anatomically different presentations and impact reproductive ability. A 'male' whose karyotype features more than a single X is still grouped along with generic XY males because the genital presentation, though generally 'underdeveloped' is still more like an XY person than an XX one. Though typically sterile, these 'males' still *appear* reproductively capable (hence the notion of presentation presumably related to reproductive ability).

What emerges, then, is that *presentation* matters preeminently. Although the rubric used is that the genitalia appear capable of reproductive functioning, what truly matters is that the genitalia serve to place the individual into one or another of two camps. Thus biology matters, but the eye of the perceiver of that biology matters more. The reason sex-based differences are important lies not in intrinsic biological differentiation, real as it may be, but in the uses put to such differences. As Moira Gatens observes, "the male body and the female body have quite different social value and significance" [258]—valuations that both underscore the priority placed on anatomical presentations and that then shape gender expectations to keep people in their respective places at their respective poles.

As it presently exists in our culture, the justification for this binary system where only two sexes are recognized depends on the belief that what matters most about sex is reproduction and reproduction requires two different contributions (sperm and ovum). Since only two contributions are needed, and since each contribution comes from a person whose body is different and accommodates the meeting of sperm and egg, any further category for sex is superfluous. What presumably matters is only that one sex desires the other so that they sexually join. Therefore, only 'male' (contributor of sperm via testes and penis) and 'female' (contributor of ovum via ovaries and vagina)—and heterosexuality (the 'natural' desire between male and female)—are needed.[259]

Again, at first blush this premise seems entirely plausible. The human species depends on the sexual contributions of sperm and ovum to share genetic material and create new members. We do not reproduce asexually. Although technology allows for fertilization outside the context of sexual intercourse, it remains true that one person contributes sperm and another an egg, and that these parties look anatomically different. Without reproduction the species ends.

However, as Myra Hird points out, nonlinear biology shows us how ridiculously narrow our conception of reproduction can be even from a biological standpoint. As Hird observes, "the *vast* majority of cells in human bodies are intersex . . . . *Most* of the reproduction that we undertake in our lifetimes has nothing to do with 'sex.'" In fact, as she lists them, reproduction can occur by recombination of DNA strands, merging, meiosis, or mitosis. "Moreover," she says, "there is no linear relationship between sexual dimorphism and sexual reproduction." After all, in a number of species males can become pregnant, or the animals can be both sexes either simultaneously or sequentially.[260]

We need also to recognize that most sexual behaviors and activity prove nonreproductive in nature. Indeed, as biologist Joan Roughgarden observes, if we are to judge the success of sexual intercourse as a reproductive mechanism, its high failure rate (more than 100 couplings per conception) would compel us to see it as remarkably inefficient. [261] But then, many of us don't want conception. In fact, many of us go to some lengths to prevent it. Some of us intentionally avoid reproduction our entire lives—without foregoing sexual activity.

Inarguably, sexual activity is widely regarded as a pleasurable and meaningful activity in its own right. It is almost certainly pursued in solitary masturbation more often than in pair couplings. When intercourse does occur it often is for nonreproductive reasons, such as relationship building or the shared pleasure of genital contact. [262] Logically, in terms of actual sexual practice and the motivations involved, it is implausible to claim reproduction as either essential or central—which calls into doubt, too, the notion that only heterosexual desire is 'normal.' Reproduction may be required for human species propagation, but it is a small part of sex.

We need to put the matter the other way around: sex is essential and central to reproduction. From a logical standpoint there is no necessity to posit reproduction as a justification for assigning human beings to one or the other of two sexes. Not only is reproduction neither essential nor central to sex, the sup-

113

posed pairing of anatomical presentation to reproductive capacity is spurious. Some of us look capable of reproduction but aren't; some of us look dubious in reproductive ability but prove capable. Any way it is examined the idea that reproduction should be seen as key to sex determination proves flawed and inadequate.

This recognition leads us to reconsider the third proposition. In a system where reproduction is inaccurately made central, it is of no surprise that anything that raises doubt about reproductive ability should be seen as 'unnatural,' or 'defective.' Logically, though, it is not only unnecessary that all of us be able to reproduce, it is not even in our species best interest that all of us who can should actually do so. In short, reproduction matters more at a species level than at an individual level. Moreover, because species survival depends on variability—Nature's way of hedging the odds in a world where environments change—it is logically natural for many variations to occur that prove nonreproductive. These are neither 'unnatural' nor 'mistakes.' That is why we are better off speaking of 'generic' and 'atypical' or 'different' presentations than the current value-laden choices 'natural' and 'defective,' or 'normal' and 'abnormal.'

Our rigidly binary system is challenged both by reason and by evidence. Clearly there are individuals born whose genital presentation makes easy placement as 'male' or 'female' impossible. Once called hermaphrodites, sometimes referred to as androgynes (or androgynous in its pre-1970s use), those of us with such a presentation are now termed 'intersexed.' Unfortunately, that term retains the notion of two sexes with some folk in-between. Our allegiance to binary thinking has meant any of us in-between must be moved one direction or the other. Since sex coding starts at birth, none of us gets a choice in the matter. Others make the decision.

In our culture this is done at birth and is one of the prerogatives of the medical profession. The presiding medical official makes this life-defining judgment based principally on a single visual cue: the presence or absence of a penis. [263] This phallocentric perspective itself reflects a gendered view of the priority of the sexes. A large phallus (penis) is better than a small phallus (clitoris). Unless a phallus is clearly large enough to qualify as a penis, the bearer must be assigned status as a female. Size matters. A child with a penis is labeled male and comes under the immediate weight of social gender expectations that he be perceived and act as masculine. Absent any obvious penis the designation is female, with the expectation of perceptions and actions corresponding to a feminine gender identity and role.

But what seems easy enough to do at birth with a naked neonate becomes problematic later. We do not rely on the nude presentation of genitalia to tell us the sex of a grown person. Instead, we rely on gender. That, in turn, relies on physical cues as diverse as size, shape, and absence or presence of physical features like hair on the face or visible breasts. Still, our judgments are based on cues that only are partially about anatomy. Our cues also include behavioral expectations (such as manner of dress) for each gender stemming from culture. In fact, we can often be quite crass in how we utilize such cues, especially when we make physical ones primary. Consider, for example, the not-so-long-ago practice Anne Fausto-Sterling reminds us about: "Until 1968 female Olympic competitors were often asked to parade naked in front of a board of examiners. Breasts and a vagina were all one needed to certify one's femininity." [264]

This might seem charmingly naïve if it weren't so patently offensive. As Fausto-Sterling accurately points out:

> Our bodies are too complex to provide clear-cut answers about sexual difference. The more we look for a simple physical basis for 'sex,' the more it becomes clear that 'sex' is not a pure physical category. What bodily signals and functions we define as male or female come already entangled in our ideas about gender. [265]

A striking illustration of this is provided by what happens to intersex neonates (formerly termed true- or pseudo- 'hermaphrodites'), As Alice Dreger documents, genital ambiguity has been viewed as a social danger for a long time. Any uncertainty in sexual designation has been imagined to produce all sorts of disorder—not merely in the individual, but for the society. Hence, an immense pressure is exerted to define each individual according to a 'one body—one sex' rule, where the only allowable options are 'male' or 'female.' Science, like the culture at large, finds it difficult to tolerate challenges to this rule.[266]

Like most people, physicians who work with intersex infants generally resist ambiguity. Instead, adhering to the cultural insistence on two distinct sexes, they make observations and decisions meant to reinforce a black-and-white schema where the empirical reality is gray. Dreger observes how the births of such infants are typically treated as an emergency, with strict protocols calling for a sex-determination within 48 hours. If this means invasive surgery (e.g., clitorectomy), then so be it. The rationale is that prompt action prevents later confusion over the individual's sexual and gender identity. [267]

Susan Bradley and colleagues, writing in *Pediatrics*, summarize the guidelines for sex and gender assignment as including three important considerations:

❑ Sex appearance of normality, with the best prognosis for sexual functioning including reproduction, should be balanced with an assignment carrying the best hope for stable gender identity.

❑ Any decision on sex reassignment is better made sooner than later, and certainly by age 2 years old.

❑ Parental and professional ambiguity as well as uncertainty over the decision should be minimized.[268]

The guidelines reflect the cultural judgment that sex determines gender. In our culture, such a complex of concerns surrounding ambiguity of sex is most easily resolved by assignment of gender to match the *most apparent* sex, with a presumption as to what appears male as the basic yardstick. The determination

115

is then later buttressed with medical modifications and hormonal supplements to heighten the apparent match, together with any other support needed.

Suzanne Kessler, in her book *Lessons from the Intersexed*, concurs that cultural factors weigh heavily. She charges that medical teams working on such cases follow "standard practices for managing intersexuality, which rely ultimately on cultural understandings of gender." [269]

In fact, Kessler notes:

> [P]hysicians who handle cases of intersexed infants consider several factors besides biological ones in determining, assigning, and announcing the gender of a particular infant. Indeed, biological factors are often preempted in physicians' deliberations by such cultural factors as the 'correct' length of the penis and capacity of the vagina. . . .

Moreover, in the face of apparently incontrovertible evidence—infants born with some combination of 'female' and 'male' reproductive and sexual features—physicians hold an incorrigible belief that female and male are the only 'natural' options. [270]

If even professionals find it hard to rise beyond cultural conventions, how can we reasonably hope the rest of us will do so? Moreover, we ought to pause and ask ourselves what purpose is served by the official and legal sex identification made at birth. Attorney Martine Rothblatt, Vice-Chair of the Bioethics Subcommittee of the International Bar Association, argues that the immediate categorization at birth of an individual as either 'male' or 'female' constitutes a form of sexual segregation that should raise the specter of apartheid. Her contention is that such legal categorization, the basis of binary gender assignments, is as wrong as the legal division into races. [271] All our ordinary practice does is confirm an erroneous, limiting, and ultimately harmful view of sex and gender.

Fortunately, the above situation shows signs of changing. Intersexed people have been vigorous in giving voice to their concerns about such practices. Slowly, the medical community has begun to listen. What do intersex people want? The Intersex Initiative says:

> We are working to replace the current model of intersex treatment based on concealment with a patient-centered alternative. We are not saying that intersex babies are better off left alone; we want there to be social and psychological support for both the parents and intersex children so that they can deal with social difficulties resulting from being different than others. In the long-term, we hope to remove those social barriers through education and raising awareness.[272]

The Intersex Initiative, observing that sexual anatomy does not determine gender identity, advocates that while a child be assigned a gender based on a 'best prediction' of eventual gender identity, that irreversible surgeries be avoided and the child, when old enough, be permitted gender self-determination. [273] Not all intersex people feel comfortable being included under the gender umbrella of transgender, but like other realities described as transgender, intersex forces us to rethink what we presume to know.

Considered either separately or together, we do not have to accept such a limited, inadequate and inaccurate scheme regarding 'sex.' The ancients wisely espoused the notion that *Natura non facit salut* ('Nature makes no leaps'). Our own senses confirm that in myriad ways: we range in gradations of height, hair and eye color, and so forth. None of suggests that all people have to be one of only two heights or two hair colors. Even with eye color, where we commonly group people as blue-eyed or brown-eyed, we still easily recognize gradations so that a range of color is apparent to us. Why should Nature depart from this practice in matters of sex?

The objection might be raised that eye color and reproductive ability are hardly on a par since the latter is essential to species survival. Perhaps Nature constrains and simplifies matters in the interest of reproduction. Appealing as the idea is, reproduction is a far messier matter in reality. Many individuals are infertile, a substantial percentage of conceptions never come to term, and more than 1-in-2,000 live births are visibly intersex. Either Nature is highly inefficient in maintaining a binary system, or the idea of gradations has more merit than commonly granted. The better question is not why 'abnormalities' occur, but what purposes might be served by gradations along the sex continuum, including those grades where infertility results.

While this subject merits a lengthier treatment, we shall have to content ourselves with what we have: grounds for reasonable suspicion at least, if not also sufficient warrant for rejecting the present cultural myopia about sex. A strict binary system of sex designation does not well fit human experience. Because a rigid insistence on it has important personal and social consequences for members of our culture—and those in other cultures subject to our imposition of it on them—we should consider ourselves ethically bound to rethink this matter. We are in desperate need of a better conceptual scheme and more robust vocabulary.

What is 'gender'?

Unfortunately, because gender is pinned to sex, problems with the latter mean difficulties for the former. The first and perhaps most common difficulty arises from making 'sex' and 'gender' synonyms. This most frequently occurs with the use of the words 'male' and 'female' to refer both to sex and to gender. In this work, 'male' and 'female' are meant to convey sex, not gender. We can accept a relationship exists between sex and gender, but we must be careful not to blur the lines separating them lest we confuse our study of transgender and crossdressing beyond hope of comprehension.

In a very real sense, defining 'gender' depends on conceiving its difference from and relation to 'sex.' Because that is the focus of the next section, here we merely will offer a definition and some preliminary observations, just as we did for 'sex.' Whereas 'sex' is a term rooted in biology but mediated by personal and social beliefs, 'gender' is a term rooted in personal and social beliefs but mediated by biology. In contemporary use, 'gender' involves differentiating sex-based groups into corresponding types with distinct psychological and social markers. Once more, for better or ill, we start with the conception that prevails in our culture and consider its adequacy. Thus, in this work 'gender' is defined as "*the set of experiential and presentational characteristics associated with and culturally arising from pairing with a particular sex.*" However, often the discussion of this term will reflect some dissatisfaction with such a definition. As with 'sex,' 'gender' is accompanied by other terms, which we shall soon consider.

In our culture, because there are conceived two opposing sexes there are conceived two opposing genders. As with sex, two genders are the only accepted alternatives. These are named 'masculine' and 'feminine.' [274] The former is paired with 'male' and the latter with 'female.' Accordingly, only two groups of sex and gendered people are fully socially approved: masculine males and feminine females. Of course, in reality we know things are not so starkly divided.

In real-world parlance we accept that *both* masculinity and femininity exist to some degree in all of us. Moreover, we may even further distinguish kinds or types within a gender. There is a difference, for example, between dominant and subordinate masculinities; at any given time in a society's history a particular form of masculinity may be prized above others.[275] We also generally have a sense that gender is a 'many splendored' thing, comprised of multiple interacting factors, each varying in intensity, quality, and degree of influence for the individual. In short, with a little reflection we see that gender is not a simple matter for any human being. Yet, in general terms we still expect a preponderance of the dominant masculinity in males and a preponderance of the dominant femininity in females. Nor do we make much effort to distinguish among members of the two recognized genders, save by age. The two broad groups are linguistically referred to in age-differentiated ways: 'boys' (masculine males) and 'girls' (feminine females) in childhood; 'men' (masculine males) and 'women' (feminine females) in adulthood. [276]

A Critique of 'Gender'

Although our culture recognizes two genders, they are hardly equal. The genders exist in a hierarchy with masculinity occupying the superior position. So androcentric is Western culture that masculinity is really the only gender that matters; femininity exists as that which masculinity is not—a logic that obviates the need for other gender alternatives. Sex historian Vern Bullough puts the matter neatly when he writes, "Femininity . . . has been a catchall category for all those characteristics males have not claimed as their own."[277]

Our critique of gender must start from awareness of this disparity. When we see that femininity is so construed it becomes easier to recognize that much more than body sex is at work in constructing gender. Biologist Anne Fausto-Sterling remarks that, "labeling someone a man or a woman is a social decision."[278] She points out that scientific knowledge may be appealed to but *belief* is what proves determinative. Specifically, it is our beliefs about gender that lead us to identify a person as a boy, girl, man, or woman. We *believe* that being in the body of one sex should and does generate a certain kind of experience different from that for bodies of the opposite sex—a 'men are from Mars and women are from Venus' approach. We further *believe* that these presumed differences produce presentational differences. Boys act differently from girls; men act differently from women. Moreover, we believe they *must* act differently because of the sex of their bodies. Anatomical genitalia are thus accorded the power to determine gender experience and guide gender presentation.

Such beliefs generate consequences. Though gender is viewed as arising predictably from sex differences, it nevertheless must be proved. In this respect it is different from sex and carries a weightier load. As Vern and Bonnie Bullough cogently point out, "Gender . . . is an achieved status rather than an ascribed biological characteristic and is based on tasks performed and the significance of clothing as well as anatomical and other factors." [279] The presumed sex-based gender experience must be concretely demonstrated. It is not enough to have the body of a male—you must act like a man. The way a man (or woman) acts is itself prescribed, always along the lines believed 'natural' for a particular sexed body. In its presentational aspect gender relies on a number of cues—representational symbols (e.g., clothes) and behaviors. Cues are used both to guide and manifest our sense of our own gender and to interpret someone else's gender.

We typically possess great confidence in our ability to use gender cues to accurately determine anatomical sex. As Freud observed in the early 1930s, "When you meet a human being, the first distinction you make is 'male or female'? and you are accustomed to make the distinction with unhesitating certainty." [280] Sex is inferred from gender, which itself is based on presentation, for which we presume a corresponding internal experience. These are a lot of inferences based on questionable assumptions.

Let's be clear what the critical assumptions are:

❑ Gender arises naturally and predictably from sex.

❑ Because there are only two sexes there can only be two genders.

The first assumption posits that biological differences in sexual anatomy underlie differences in experience, which in turn underlie differences in presentation. Much effort has been invested over the years to explore to what extent body differences matter in terms of such things as personality, moral reasoning, cognitive ability, and a wide variety of behaviors. In sum, the evidence shows real but generally modest differences exist between two groups differentiated as 'male' and 'female.' However, though some differences can be seen between groups, an individual in either group may on one or more characteristics score

119

more like members of the other group. Further, the observed differences may be attributable to environmental factors rather than biological ones. For instance, the often cited finding that males as a group do better in math must be qualified both by the fact that many female individuals outperform many male persons, and the group differences may be explained by the way females are raised and treated according to a gender belief that they *should* do more poorly.

Perhaps gender differences arise not from sex-based body differences but from other causes, such as the beliefs Fausto-Sterling referred to. If gender differences are applied to sex differences rather than flowing from them, they can scarcely be termed 'natural.' Instead they are artificial—constructions made by human beings. If so they need not prove any less 'predictable.' The fact that most females turn out to be feminine and most males turn out to be masculine can be seen as the predictable result of an efficient social system begun at birth, operating at multiple levels, strongly reinforced, and almost universally endorsed by its participants.

Thomas Eckes and Hanns Trautner, in their effort to forge an integrative framework for a developmental social psychology of gender, posit three generally shared assumptions among models concerned with the nature of social influences and how men and women relate to social contexts:

❑ Social influence results from *multiple factors*, including cognitive ones (e.g., self-concept), our interpersonal orientation (i.e., self- or other-oriented), group memberships, and cultural forces (e.g., ideologies).

❑ Social influence is *heterogeneous*, arising from *multiple sources*, including interpersonal, group, and cultural environments.

❑ Gender is *multidimensional*, with various dimensions and their facets interrelated in multiple ways, some tightly knit together and others only loosely connected, and varying by individual, across time and according to context.[281]

In sum, studying gender is no easier for the scholar than for the individual who must sort out all the information, much of it conflicting, and somehow function in the world.

On the other hand, if sex is powerful enough to create gender in a predictable fashion, then why does society apply such strenuous effort to ensure the result? If Nature makes only two sexes and each has a gender, then why not relax and let Nature run its course? The fact that we don't trust to Nature suggests that gender really doesn't follow inevitably from sex. Freud's judgment is sound: "what constitutes masculinity or femininity is an unknown characteristic which anatomy cannot lay hold of."[282] Society finds so many nonstereotypical gender presentations that it must enact a plethora of safeguards to try to constrain gender expression (and presumably experience) into a range of tolerable options opposite one another at two poles.

The binary system again proves inadequate. Yet, for argument's sake, let us accept the premise there are only two sexes, male and female. Why must there then only be two genders? If gender does not arise naturally and predictably from sex, then what constrains us to two genders? Consider a different pairing: sex with eye color. Let us accept there are only two sexes and only two eye colors. We are able to have blue-eyed males, blue-eyed females, brown-eyed males, and brown-eyed females. A 2 x 2 matrix yields four logical alternatives.

The failure of the first premise deflates the power of the second. Even if we accept there are only two sexes and two genders we still have four possibilities: masculine males, feminine males, masculine females, and feminine females. Freud again proved willing to look unflinchingly at empirical evidence: "make yourselves familiar with the idea that the proportion in which masculine and feminine are mixed in an individual is subject to considerable fluctuations."[283] That such 'fluctuations' actually exist is reflected in the terminology people use: feminine males are 'sissies' and masculine females are 'tomboys' or 'butch.' The terms may be used disparagingly or approvingly, but they are used, the distinctions in gender reality noted.[284] However, they are used in service of the binary system. Rather than contemplate more than two genders, people regard feminine males and masculine females as deficient variations, with the former more seriously deficient because masculinity is prized more than femininity.

Though once more both reason and evidence offer grounds to seriously question the prevailing gender scheme, before we offer more critique we must pause to look at how gender is further elaborated conceptually in our culture. This involves becoming familiar with a number of additional terms.

Gender Identity, Gender Role, Gender Attribution, and Gender Expression

One way modern science has sought to create clarity about gender is to distinguish between *gender identity* and *gender role*. Marjorie Hardy offers the following succinct description of each:

> *Gender identity* is the personal belief that one is either a male or a female, regardless of assigned gender. Thus, a male transsexual may have been assigned a male gender at birth, but his gender identity is female. *Gender role* refers to how a person behaves as a male or female—the relative masculine or feminine characteristics as perceived by self or by others. [285]

More simply, John Money and Anke Ehrhardt posit the intrinsic unity of gender identity and gender role by describing gender identity as the private experience of gender role, and gender role as the public expression of gender identity. [286]

But the above formula has limitations. It still presumes a binary gender system. Any deviation in self-perception or public display from one's assigned gender is pathological. Further, it tacitly assumes that an individual will perform gender role consistent with gender identity though that is manifestly not the case all too often.

So these terms may not be enough. In addition to gender identity and gender role, we must speak of gender assignment (or attribution) and gender expression. *Gender assignment* refers to the labeling we each receive at birth, based on our apparent sexual anatomy, with all the rights, responsibilities, and privileges (or lack thereof) attached to the gender assigned. Gender assignment is accompanied by *gender development*, an ongoing process of being shaped to conform to our gender assignment. In the famous words of philosopher Simone de Beauvoir, "One is not born, but rather becomes, a woman." [287] As we live our lives within society others routinely use socially sanctioned cues, along with other factors, to attribute to us one or another gender—and in our adherence to those cues we present as that gender. [288] For many of us, gender assignment and development fit our gender identity (experience) and guide our gender role (presentation) in such a manner that we win and keep social approval.

In our culture, gender identity is a priority so it constitutes a primary task of childhood and a focus of parent-child interaction. The process utilizes numerous elements, but dress is central; children depend on gender-differentiated dress to help them master gender assignments and the concomitant values, attitudes, and roles.[289] Both boys and girls experience pressures to conform to their assigned gender identity. However, these pressures are more rigid and restrictive for boys because of their higher status in the gender hierarchy.[290]

A significant complicating factor for boys is the role homophobia plays in the construction of a masculinity based on heterosexuality. The irrational character of this process is summarized by health researcher David Plummer's remark: "Prior to consolidating adult sexual identity, homophobic rhetoric is used frequently and with meaning, even when there is little or no concept of what a homosexual is and a definitive target in the peer group is lacking."[291] The character of homophobia, says Plummer, is different in childhood than in adulthood. Instead of zeroing in on rigid sexual identities, it focuses on the appearances and behaviors that are unpopular and transgress a boy's peer group expectations—a process that potentially makes any boy a target.[292]

If nothing else, the constant implicit recognition that at any time one might become labeled as a member of a stigmatized group fosters an inordinate, hyper-attentiveness to any cues signaling the danger of such a judgment. There is relative safety in the harbor of vocal homophobia. If a boy visibly demonstrates he is against homosexuals—whatever that means—he safeguards against the possibility of being labeled one. The other course, steering shy of feminine company and behavioral displays (e.g., crying), is also necessary, but more hazardous. No boy can so completely avoid the feminine as to protect against homophobia unless he strongly practices homophobia.[293]

Gender expression refers to the behaviors we enact to display our gender identity. It may or may not be identical at any given moment to one's gender role. Where our gender role is socially proscribed, gender expression is highly individualized. We can choose to express our assigned gender role regardless of our

122

gender identity. We may also choose to express our experienced inner gender identity though it means violating our assigned gender role. Often enough that choice comes at a price.

One such price might be having the label of a mental disorder placed upon us even though our own congruent gender identity and expression brings personal satisfaction. Modern mental health delineates a 'Gender Identity Disorder' (still popularly known as transsexualism) to indicate the presence of a discrepancy between assigned gender at birth and subsequent gender identity. Similarly, where gender role performance does not match *gender stereotypes*—popular, sometimes rigid, notions of what belongs to masculinity and femininity—then there is a tendency to see the behavior as a 'problem.' These stereotypes attach to personality traits as well as behaviors. About the former Margaret Mead remarks that personality traits labeled 'masculine' or 'feminine' generally are "as lightly linked to sex as are the clothing, the manners and the form of headdress that a society at a given time assigns to either sex." [294] About behavior, Hardy points out that, strictly speaking, a relatively small proportion (5-10%) of total social behavior is due to gender, though many of us seem anxious about whether a person's behavior is gender appropriate or gender nonconforming. [295]

Focusing on gender role development, Hardy shows the important influence brought by parents, teachers, peers, and the media. Gender role socialization, she demonstrates, has a substantial impact on more than particular attitudes and behaviors; it also affects psychological characteristics in both children and adults. She sees socialization that reinforces gender role conformity to gender stereotypes as linked to phenomena like the higher reported incidence of depression in females, who are gender socialized in such a manner that learned helplessness is more likely than for males. She also thinks such socialization is implicated in the varying performance in school between boys and girls. But females are not the only ones handicapped by gender role socialization that enforces gender conformity. Gender socialization supporting male aggression is a factor in a number of social problems that lead to referrals for intervention. [296]

Hardy notes that social forces continue to exert pressure toward gender role conformity despite evidence that gender nonconformity characteristics may be psychologically and physically healthier. She remarks, "Perhaps it is not conformity to a particular gender role that is healthier but rather society's encouragement and acceptance of flexibility that engenders positive characteristics in its members." [297] If so, this is welcome news to those of us whose best fit is with traits and behaviors not in step with typical, expected, or stereotyped gender role characteristics.

Modern Gender as Historical Artifact

So, in light of the weighty role played by socialization, where did we go wrong in knitting gender so closely to anatomy? We have found that the assumptions holding together our present cultural view of gender are highly questionable, but we need to go again to the root of the problem, albeit with a slightly different tack. We can examine the situation both historically and philosophically.

Historically, as Helen Fischer points out, "gender differences came across the centuries, out of our distant past when ancestral men and women began to pair and raise their young as 'husband' and 'wife.'" [298] There is nothing intrinsically compelling that mandates females assume a greater burden in nurturing young or caring for others; logically, males could take the larger role, and individually some do. Likewise, no mandate from Nature compels females to attend more to domestic affairs and males to master the outside world. But more often than not, such has happened in practice. Practices became sex-linked and gave rise to socially sanctioned divisions of labor associated with separate statuses as 'man' and 'woman.' The word 'woman' owes its existence to gender-ordered thinking: a woman is a 'man's wife.'

A study published in the mid-1960s, surveying practices in 224 societies around the world, found many labors are strongly sex divided. Not surprisingly, making war proved overwhelmingly a male activity; childrearing a female one. Hunting was an exclusively male activity in 166 societies, but an exclusively female one in none. On the other hand, cooking was an exclusively female labor in 158 societies, but an exclusively male one in only 5 societies. [299] Such sex-linked divisions of labor become entrenched in gender expectations and role performance.

While we might be tempted to see these divisions of labor as 'natural,' derived from the differences in sexual bodies, any such conclusion still has to be modified by the observation that cultural variability in what is seen as appropriate sex-linked labor is just as pronounced. Consider, for example, that agricultural tasks like planting are seen as belonging to both males and females in 73 societies; this labor, though, is exclusively male in 31 societies and exclusively female in 37 others![300] As well we should remember how the division of labor can be modified, as when American involvement in World War II opened the door for women to take jobs previously held by men—and female involvement in the workforce since then has continued to erode sex-linked distinctions and gender role expectations. [301]

Modern gender designations, language, and divisions in our society reflect an outdated reality. In that sense, our genders 'masculine' and 'feminine' are relics—artifacts better displayed in a museum than in civil society. 'Women' today are much more and other than 'man's wife.' Sex-linked divisions of labor prove increasingly irrelevant as both sexes fight wars, wash dishes, cook meals, and conduct business deals. The only real utility in preserving archaic forms resides in their continued buttressing of a gender order hierarchical in nature, with masculine males (especially White ones) at the top. Contemporary retention of a bipolar scheme of sex and gender, with the former generating the latter, really serves well only the narrow interests of a few.

Where have we gone wrong? Gender theorist Judith Butler argues that we got off on the wrong foot when we made the decision that gender *is*—in other words, that gender exists as a real and fixed attribute. In fact, in the way our Western culture has come to embrace it, gender fits into the middle of a linkage between biology and desire. Biological, dimorphic sex permits only two sexual outcomes: male and female. These in turn generate only two possible genders: masculine and feminine. With only two possibilities, desire is 'naturally' the attraction of one for its opposite. This whole conception, says Butler, is wrong-headed. [302]

Butler poses some questions we may find hard to answer—if for no other reason than because we have never thought of them before. She asks:

> Is there 'a' gender which persons are said *to have*, or is it an essential attribute that a person is said *to be*, as implied in the question 'What gender are you?'? . . . If gender is constructed, could it be constructed differently, or does its constructedness imply some form of social determinism, foreclosing the possibility of agency and transformation? Does 'construction' suggest that certain laws generate gender differences along universal axes of sexual difference? How and where does the construction of gender take place? . . . When the relevant 'culture' that 'constructs' gender is understood in terms of such a law or set of laws, then it seems that gender is as determined and fixed as it was under the biology-is-destiny formulation. In such a case, not biology, but culture, becomes destiny. [303]

In fact, Butler contends, gender is *not* fixed and no matter how much contemporary culture might picture it as an essential and natural attribute, it is actually socially constructed and can change. Instead of gender-as-destiny, Butler describes gender-as-performative. Better put, gender is something we *do* rather than something we *have*. It is 'performative' in that *it makes what it names*, rather than being the result of a fixed identity. Gender is constructed relation; it unfolds in real relationships in specific contexts. Rather than being fixed, gender is fluid. 'Masculine' and 'feminine' are not fixed poles.

But if this is the case, why do so many of us feel strongly that our gender *is* fixed? Butler has an answer. She argues that "the performance of gender creates the illusion of prior substantiality—a core gendered self."[304] For most of us, performativity of gender seems seamlessly constant and fixed. We thus conclude that we *are* rather than we *do* and ignore evidence to the contrary (i.e., all the small instances where we perform in ways stereotypically associated with a gender different than the one we identify with).

Because gender is socially constructed, we all play roles. Gender performativity and performance are inevitable, but the part we play is not. Biology is *not* destiny. Most of us occupy a conventional 'masculine' or 'feminine' role; some of us do not. Once we understand that gender is performative art rather than

125

predestined, perhaps individual identities can have the freedom to find the expression most suitable for them.

Or can we? Butler cautions against our viewing the matter purely as one of individual choice and invention. "Performativity," she says, "is a matter of reiterating or repeating the norms by which one is constituted; it is not a radical fabrication of a gendered self."[305] Society presents us with gender scripts, which read well bring social approval, though within whatever box is reserved for the gender group we belong to, and provided that group fits our natal assignment. We can choose to reject the script and attempt to write our own, but social scripts are normative—they set a standard against which all other choices and constructions are judged. Though gender may be a masquerade, we switch from our assigned mask at our own risk.

With such ideas in mind we must return to the connection between sex and gender.

What is the relation between 'sex' and 'gender'?

Reprising the Current Prevailing Scheme

What is the true relation between these two? In modern Western culture both the connection and the distinction between sex and gender have come to be heavily relied upon. On the one hand, as we have seen, we assume sex and gender are paired in a straightforward and limited manner. Most of us rather naively assume there are only two biological sexes (male and female), as well as only two genders (masculine and feminine), and that nature reliably pairs them in one way (male with masculine; female with feminine), with gender subordinate to sex, and both subservient to desire.[306] Any mixing of the sex and gender, such as a male presenting as feminine, is a deviant construction—unnatural and disordered.

In this scheme, sexual anatomy provides the foundation for social expectations about gender. If one is born anatomically male, then masculinity is expected; if born female, a feminine gender is assigned. In our culture this is so familiar we may believe it always has been the way the matter has been understood. But Thomas Laqueur argues that the notion that the body determines gender differences, with a dichotomy of opposites in anatomy and psychology, is essentially a post-Enlightenment way of thinking about the matter.[307] It is neither inevitable nor eternal—despite having become our culture's perspective, with all the advantages, limitations, and problems that may entail.

Within this cultural framework, deviation from the pairing of anatomical sex with gender presentation is viewed as exactly that: *deviation*, with negative connotations affecting social status and regard of psychological health. Yet while we yoke sex and gender together, we still insist on a distinction between them. Despite the critique offered earlier, for most of us 'sex' continues to be reserved for physical matters of anatomy and physiology (as though they are all that enters in). 'Gender,' correspondingly, encompasses the much broader psychosocial elements related to how sexual anatomy and physiology enter into human affairs. Or, as sexuality educator Lisa Maurer puts it, "*Sex* has to do with body parts, *gender* with the manner in which a person puts the assignment of *male* or *female* into practice *within societal limits*."[308] This all may continue to feel very straightforward, though we have shown how it is not.

Language Problems: Usage and Limitations

Consider our common speech with regard to sex and gender. In actual usage there is an awkwardness to our handling of the terms. Inconsistencies abound. We mix and match things so easily it is little wonder we have trouble sorting them out when we need to. *The American Heritage Book of English Usage* indicates the present situation:

> Traditionally, writers have used the term Gender to refer to the grammatical categories of masculine, feminine, and neuter, as in languages such as French or Spanish whose nouns and adjectives carry such distinctions. In recent years, however, more people have been using the word to refer to sex-based categories, as in phrases such as *gender gap* (as in voting trends) and *politics of gender*. Anthropologists especially like to maintain a distinction between the terms Gender and *sex,* reserving *sex* for reference to the biological categories of male and female and using Gender to refer to social or cultural categories, such as different gender roles in a religious organization. According to this distinction, you would say *The effectiveness of the treatment appears to depend on the sex* (not Gender) *of the patient* but *In society, gender* (not *sex*) *roles are clearly defined.* A majority of the Usage Panel approves of this distinction, but opinions are mixed. In a sentence similar to the first one above, 51 percent choose *sex,* 31 percent choose *gender,* and 17 percent would allow both. Similarly, for the example *Sex/gender differences are more likely to be clearly defined in peasant societies,* 47 percent prefer Gender, 38 percent would use *sex,* and 15 percent would allow both words.[309]

It seems reasonable to suppose that as long as this state of affairs pertains in how the terms are used, difficulties both in conception and communication are likely to persist.

Basic Premises

Now we can see better why so much space has been spent discussing two deceptively complex terms. Unfortunately, our effort principally has elaborated and critiqued the view that currently handicaps us rather than setting forth a positive alternative. We shall do so in a sequence of steps. First, we shall enunciate a few basic premises. Then we shall return to the contemporary situation to further investigate some issues. As we do so we shall attempt to move past present limitations to envision broader possibilities. Specifically, this will result in suggesting how we might speak more realistically about gender. This will be followed by focusing briefly on why such attention matters in the 'real world.'

We have defined 'sex' and 'gender.' Though they can be conceived in better terms than they presently are, the definitions we have posited suffice for now. 'Sex' refers to "anatomical presentations presumably related to reproductive capacity," while 'gender' refers to "the set of experiential and presentational characteristics associated with and arising from a particular sex." Accompanying these definitions are the following premises, each based on logical deductions:

❑ Because anatomical presentations presumably related to reproductive capacity vary, it is reasonable to suggest that sexes vary beyond two in number.

❑ Because the sets of experiential and presentational characteristics associated with and arising from a particular sex vary, it is reasonable to suggest that genders vary beyond two in number.

❑ Because neither sex nor gender is solely dependent on either biology or culture, both can exhibit variability that includes relative independence from each other.

Granting the plausibility of these three premises the relation between sex and gender can be reconsidered. Based on the characteristics set out in the premises, the following statements present the basic framework for our scheme of sex and gender:

❑ Biology *cannot* be ignored or devalued; a biological component to both sex and gender is inescapable and links them.

❑ Culture *cannot* be ignored or devalued; culture shapes the perception, valuation, and application of sex and gender within both social and personal spheres.

❑ Variability *cannot* be ignored or devalued; natural variations in sex and gender place the individual at the nexus of their relationship.

Simply put, sex and gender are biologically primed, socially constructed, and individually mediated.

Towards a Better Understanding

By now it should be clear there is a need for conceptual clarity and agreement on how terms so key to human relationships are understood and applied. But for these things to happen we must spread wider more accurate information to dispute and eventually overcome the naïve—and erroneous—assumptions so many of us hold. Most of us think the way we do about sex and gender because we accept with little question the common and received knowledge of our culture, especially about our bodies, no matter whether this be accurate or not. We rely on consensus ('Everyone thinks so.') even though we know how often consensus can be wrong (e.g., the world is not flat). It requires no little effort for us to open ourselves to new information when the old assumptions are so comfortable to wear. Normally, only when the old assumptions cause discomfort at a personal level, whether because we ourselves do not fit well within them or because holding the assumptions hurts our relationships with others, do we start questioning.

Let us resolve not to let the stakes become high and tinged with passion before we challenge ourselves to better thinking. What can we discover by looking for better ways of understanding sex and gender?

First, as we have seen, we find plenty of evidence available to challenge commonly held assumptions. That evidence immediately and persistently challenges the notion of a one-to-one connection between sex and gender. Second, we discover that less rigid ways of understanding gender facilitate more realistic ways of looking at human experience; many people do not fit in dichotomous categories as 'masculine' or 'feminine.' Third, we discover that greater accuracy and more realistic perceptions encourage more humane consideration of our fellow human beings. By not insisting that every round peg fit into a square hole we are able to appreciate the round peg for its own value and contributions. Those who more comfortably fit somewhere between male and female, masculine and feminine, are more likely to be accorded respect and viewed as valuable when the stigma of not fitting limited categories is removed. In sum, better ways of understanding gender advantage us all.

Of course, all this is easier said than done. Yet we must make the effort if we are to do justice to the human experience. Clearly, we need to look more closely at the problem of gender as understood in our Western culture if we are to accurately comprehend the place transgender—and crossdressing—occupies. And rest assured, gender does pose problems in our culture.

Why is gender a problem?

The very ubiquity of gender in human experience renders it a problem in some important respects. We saw earlier Hardy's observation a relatively small proportion of total social behavior is due to gender. But we should qualify that as behavior directly derived from gender; the overall influence is much broader. Despite that long reach, we often seem surprisingly oblivious of gender. "Although gender governs the full spectrum of human behaviors," remarks Jessica Xavier, "almost all people are wholly unconscious of it. Thus gender is also an unspoken and unwritten social contract that all people enter into without much discussion or debate."[310] If this is true at an individual level, it is no less the case at a societal level. Sabrina Petra Ramet describes what she calls 'gender culture':

> . . . society's understanding of what is possible, proper, and perverse in gender-linked behavior, and more specifically, that set of values, mores, and assumptions which establishes which behaviors are to be seen as gender-linked, with which gender or genders they are to be

seen as linked, what is the society's understanding of gender in the first place, and, consequently, how many genders there are.[311] This social-cultural 'understanding' is only partially conscious, but that makes it no less binding on us.

In the social contract we find thrust upon us in our culture, as Claudine Griggs notes, "Gender attribution is generally immediate, unconscious, and dimorphic. And it carries contiguous rules about masculine/feminine protocol, which are also immediate, unconscious and dimorphic."[312] In other words, we may not be conscious about why we draw our conclusions about someone else's gender, but we make our judgments without hesitation and uniformly as 'boy' or 'girl,' 'man' or 'woman.' We see and admit to only two alternatives. We assume that gender will match sex. It is our gender culture.

How is transgender 'gender'?

What we think we know about gender is subject to change—and *does* change. Richard Ekins and Dave King, among others, describe how our conceptualizing of gender behavior and identity have changed over time. They employ the term 'gender blending' to cover, for example, the behavior of those who crossdress. Ekins and King claim:

> Prior to the categorization and medicalization of sexual 'perversions' in the latter half of the nineteenth century, gender blending could be written about in terms of simple descriptions of enjoyable experiences and preferred behavior. Medicalization, however, brought with it new 'conditions' and the emergence of new identities. Increasingly, gender blending experiences and behaviours were made sense of in terms of the categories of 'science,' most notably those of the 'transvestite' and the 'transsexual.'[313]

But 'transvestite' and 'transsexual' were not conceived as *legitimate* gender alternatives; they labeled deviations from norms. There is a world of difference between a 'condition' and a 'third gender.'[314] The 'conditions,' then, were not a matter of points along a gender continuum, but distortions of one or the other end—typically, in the modern era, of the masculine pole.

In our era, the medicalization of sex and gender into dichotomous poles, with nothing between them, and exact pairings of male/masculine, female/feminine, means that any gender presentation not conforming closely to the socially expected norm will be labeled negatively. A feminine female is rewarded with the label 'lady.' A relatively gender nonconforming female is less approvingly called a 'tomboy.' Similarly, a masculine male might be referred to as a 'real man.' But a relatively gender nonconforming male may be disapprovingly labeled a 'sissy.' Those whose nonconformity in gender identity and role is more pronounced are branded 'gender dysphoric'—a pathology reflecting such deviance from the norm of the pole that is considered 'disordered.' Of course, only a disturbed few inhabit this narrow region—and no one ever truly escapes either their anatomical sex or their assigned gender. To even try proves the absurdity of the proposition and thus warrants the negative judgment.

In our culture we are all in one box. Gender is bipolar, but one-dimensional. The linearity this creates between the poles means that those that come too closely together—or, to put it differently, are too far from the poles—risk censure for dangerously pushing or violating the culturally preferred boundary lines for the genders. In essence, the true middle ground in our culture's gender scheme is a vacuum, or desert, where no one is allowed to remain, and any who cross are transgressors. Those who dare to cross or to dwell in the wilderness are likely to be viewed by others as gender-lost, or to use the psychiatric label, 'gender dysphoric.' The situation might be pictured like this:

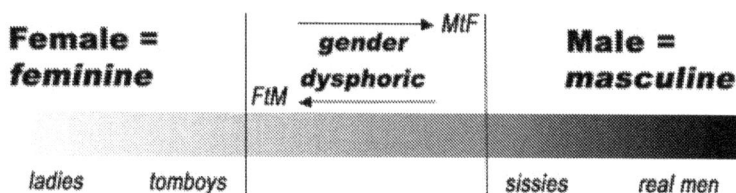

Female = feminine			Male = masculine
	FtM ← gender dysphoric → MtF		
ladies tomboys		sissies real men	

In this picture there is no room for the intersexed or a 'third gender.' Transgendered people are not genuinely trans*gendered*, because only two genders exist; they are *trans*gressors, inappropriately crossing gender lines that society insists remain clear and strong boundaries.

But the sheer persistence of a continuing group of well-adjusted, high functioning people in every generation and pretty much every place shows that this picture, whatever its simple appeal, does not work well. It neither fits the facts of experience nor succeeds in constraining human expression. Just as the indisputable reality of the intersexed has forced a more nuanced appraisal of sex, so those called transgendered (a clearly inadequate term) beckon us to a more realistic appraisal of gender. We need a new picture and a new vocabulary.

Unfortunately we continue to lack in our culture any clear and accepted parallel in gender discussions to the concept of the intersexed with respect to sex. Unlike other cultures that acknowledge a 'third gender,' ours maintains the ridiculously rigid dichotomy portrayed above. Until we can even admit to the possibility of something other than merely masculine or feminine, we can scarcely imagine what the evidence best supports—a continuum where alternative gendered realities coexist alongside those recognized as masculine and feminine. Our conceptualizations of gender continue to lag behind those of sex in this regard.

There are alternative schemes available, if we look for them. For example, Norwegian scholar Per Schioldborg proposed in 1983 that gender be ranged along *two* continua rather than one; masculinity comprises one dimension, femininity another, and intersecting at right angles they create four quadrants:

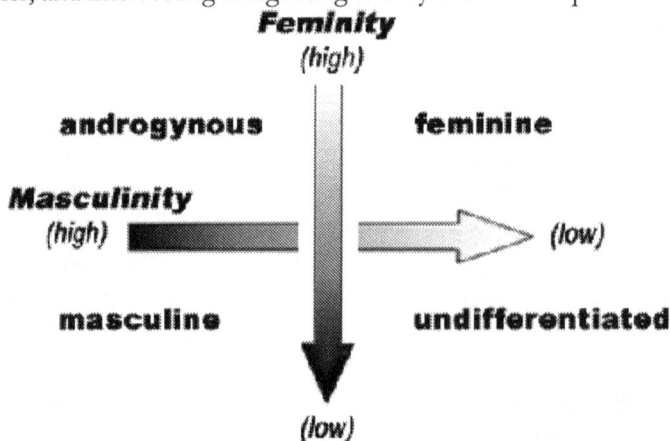

Those high in both masculinity and femininity are androgynous; those low in both are undifferentiated. One who is masculine ranks high in the masculinity dimension and low in femininity, and one who is feminine ranks high in femininity and low in masculinity.[315] This way of creating categories parallels Sandra Bem's research instrument, the *Bem Sex Role Inventory*, which has the same four gender types.

To adopt a scheme wherein gender is presented along a continuum will be advantageous over a rigid, bipolar dichotomy only when a rigid and simplistic binding of sex to gender is severed. Otherwise we end with a variant of what we have now: males are either 'masculine' or 'effeminate' ('sissies'), and females are 'feminine' or 'tomboys.' Once anatomical sex is better separated from gender genuine 'other gender' recognitions are possible.

What might such a continuum look like? Evan Eyler and Kathryn Wright propose a nine point gender scale they devised for clinical work with genetic females, which is summarized here:

- ❑ Female always identifying as a girl or woman.
- ❑ Female with maleness; at times has identified more as a boy or man.
- ❑ Genderblended (predominantly female), with identification as both woman and man, but more as woman.
- ❑ Othergendered; neither woman nor man, but of another gender.
- ❑ Ungendered; neither woman nor man nor any other gender.
- ❑ Bigendered; a combination of man and woman, where either might predominate at times.
- ❑ Genderblended (predominantly male), with identification as both woman and man, but more as man.
- ❑ Male with femaleness; at times has identified more as a girl or woman.
- ❑ Male always identifying as a boy or man.[316]

This scale retains recognition of the pairing of sex and gender but in a more flexible way.

In my own view, the conceptual underpinning of a continuum suggests fluidity. Boundaries between points on the continuum are artificial constructs, which in their extremes yield the stereotypes of masculine and feminine found at the poles. (We can retain masculine and feminine at the poles—indeed it is difficult to imagine a continuum so divorced from our present way of seeing things that other poles could be envisioned.) Between these poles other gendered realities exist. In the lived world of experience all gendered realities are fluid rather than static; our experience and expression of our gendered selves varies over time and across contexts. Yet within our own individuality the range of these changes is rarely extreme. Moreover, we all can find others whose ranges are similar to our own while being different from the rest. Thus, classifying points along the continuum as distinct gender categories merely represents an abstracted picture of experiential and expressive ranges of gendered reality.

Consider the following as one possible depiction of a gender continuum:

The continuum is ranged along two axes. One axis is gender expressiveness, the degree to which an individual presents gender. Some folk express masculinity in a very strong way (high expressiveness), while others do so more weakly (low expressiveness). The second axis is conformity/nonconformity. Some people strongly conform to social expectations about gender identity and role, while others do so more weakly. Some are nonconformists to assigned gender identity and role, either weakly and partially, or strongly and completely.

An individual might, for example, strongly express femininity and also highly conform to the social expectations for femininity—a 'real lady.' The masculine counterpart would be styled a 'man's man.' Another person might

133

strongly express femininity but be less conforming, such as a 'tomboy' who engages in rough and tumble play while simultaneously wearing makeup and unambiguously embracing her gender identity. Someone who weakly expresses the assigned masculine gender role and does not conform to gender role expectations might be called a 'sissy' even though he retains a discernible masculine gender identity. A range of gender expressiveness and conformity is possible for those who still self-identify at the poles of masculinity and femininity.

The continuum, though, reflects the reality of a 'third gender'—a cluster of other possible gendered realities distinguishable from the poles. For simplicity this cluster has been represented by just three terms: transgender, bigender, and androgynous. The androgynous person is viewed here differently from Schioldborg's scheme. In this continuum the androgynous are seen as weakly expressing gender as well as being nonconforming in a relatively mild fashion. The transgendered individual, by contrast, strongly expresses gender and gender nonconformity. Such a person may regard the 'trans' as referring to transcending the gender dichotomy, transgressing it, or merely crossing from one pole to the other at will. The bigendered person exists between the androgynous and transgendered, as well as between masculine and feminine. This individual expresses both masculinity and femininity, either weakly or more strongly, but does not conform to social expectations for either masculine or feminine. This nonconformity, too, may be greater or lesser but always accompanies a sense of being neither masculine nor feminine, or more often of being both. Because current ways of talking about gender in our culture do not use the term 'bigender,' this group is tacitly included in use of the term 'transgender' in this work.

A Multiaxial, Multidimensional Model of Gender

An even more robust picture is possible, and this next alternative represents a model put forward as better than those considered above. Gender is dependent on sex, but not as its destiny. Rather, gender *interprets* sex, and it does so in ways that may more or less reflect strong personal identification with one's sexual body (experience), more or less show strong communication of one's sexual body (expressiveness), and more or less fits expectations about one's sexual body (conformity). Consider the following image:

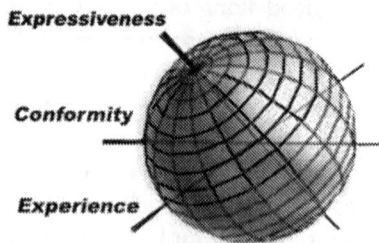

3 Gender Axes

The three axes (conformity, experience and expressiveness) are embedded in multidimensional space. Each axis has three dimensions: physical, social, and personal. In this gender universe there are also degrees (high to moderate to low) in the axes. As the axes, dimensions, and levels interact a rich matrix of gendered realities emerge.[317] For our purposes it will be enough to sketch out some of these after first elucidating further on the axes and dimensions. These remarks are all preliminary and suggestive in nature. The most important impression to gain is that gender truly is multiaxial and multidimensional, capable of division into many gender states or statuses beyond masculine and feminine, which themselves need not be viewed at polar ends.

The Three Axes

The notion of *gender conformity* is simple and practical. The axis of conformity recognizes that gender is assessed partly in terms of conformity to at least three dimensions. One is physicality. Assignment of the label 'masculine' is easier when the apparent physical body looks sexually male. Depictions of a masculine male are far more likely to show a bodybuilder than a short, slender, long-haired and beardless male. Likewise, conformity has a social dimension. Others hold expectations based on their beliefs about how a boy or girl, man or woman, should experience and express the assigned gender. In particular, more conforming gender expressions are recognized and rewarded over less conforming ones. Finally, a personal dimension mediates the others. An individual's own beliefs and expectations—whether highly, moderately, or lowly conforming to social standards—exerts a modifying influence. All three dimensions display degrees of intensity and interact. Thus any given individual may strongly, moderately, or weakly conform to the physical standard, social standard, or self standard existing for the assigned gender and/or the selected gender the person experiences and expresses.

Gender experience refers to the internal feelings and thoughts, as well as the enacted behaviors, in relation to both one's assigned gender identity and role, and one's assumed gender identity and role. Gender experience it what it means to be a gendered self as both subject and object. There is a physical dimension to this experience that entails both the perception and use of the sexual body. But this is especially the feelings, thoughts and behaviors accompanying the embodiment of the sexual body in gendered apparel, with ornamentation, hairstyle and so forth included. An individual's gender experience of the physical dimension may be strong, moderate, or weak. One may be little moved by the sexual body or attach great significance to gendered clothing; the range of possible experience is inexhaustible. There is likewise a social dimension to gender experience, a process and collection of feelings, thoughts and behaviors organized around interaction with others, or at least an awareness and accounting of others. This, too, may be strong, moderate or weak in degree. Finally, there is a personal dimension to experience; the variations in experience are as unique and many as there are individuals. But these also have degrees as individuals do not all have the same intensity or depth of felt experience, vary in their consciousness of gender, and act with more or less reserve.

Gender expressiveness refers to the display of gender, regardless of actual experience. In other words, an individual can express a gender, or degree of gender, relatively apart from any lived-in sense of it. Anyone can fake any gender experience. But anyone can also present the gender they do experience in a variety of ways and degrees. The physical dimension of gender expressiveness involves the ways an individual presents the sexual body, clothed or unclothed, so as to communicate a gender experience, whether actual, imagined, or pretended. Obviously, this may be done to a higher or lower degree. For example, not everyone who does drag does so in the same manner, to the same degree, or to reflect the same internal gender experience. Similar dynamics inform the social dimension. Gender expressed is not the same as gender experienced. Many individuals conform to social standards in their gender expressiveness despite their relative lack of gender experience for the gender being displayed. Some use gender expressiveness to glory in a rich experience of that gender. Once more variability in motivation and behavior is immense. Finally, gender expressiveness has a personal dimension. Regardless of expectations accompanying the sexual body and social standards, each person makes choices that shape how, when, to what extent, and what gender is expressed.

The above remarks, sketchy as they are, should suffice to show that the axes are each multidimensional. They are also multidimensional in the ways they interact with one another. When degrees are added in the result is a richly complex system of signification that better reflects gender reality as lived. This shall become more apparent as we turn next to the three dimensions.

The Three Dimensions

The *physical dimension* includes both the sexual body and the manner in which its appearance is constructed through things like clothing. The sexual body is never completely nude; even without clothes or makeup perceptions add layers of meaning to the biological entity. The physical dimension of gender includes both the symbolic body and the agentic body. As Erica Reischer and Kathyrn Koo summarize these, the symbolic body is "a conduit of social meaning," whereas the agentic body is "an active participant or agent in the social world."[318] The physical dimension of gender involves the ways our sexual bodies are produced, presented, and perceived as they transmit information to self and others, *and* as they exert influence on self and others. As Reischer and Koo put it, "the ideal gendered body does not merely remain in the realm of the symbolic; its power lies in its ability to directly influence behavior within the social sphere."[319]

The *social dimension* of gender refers to the matrix of relations, expectations, behaviors and so forth that give gender its widest context. Gender is always connected to some degree to the sexual body, impossible to divorce from the presentation of that body by means of dress, and inescapably personal. Yet the social dimension defines the essence of gender in ways the other dimensions cannot. It both places and connects every personal gendered body with every other one, if through no other means than the weight of shared beliefs and expectations, however derived and no matter whether reasonable or irrational. Both conscious and unconscious, the social dimension imposes the values, morality, and judgment of others. But because of how it is constructed, the social dimension evolves. It has fluidity and flexibility; it can change.

The *personal dimension* of gender refers to the individual contribution made to gender experience, expression, and conformity. Intertwined and incapable of being divorced from the other dimensions it enjoys a reciprocal interaction with them. An individual's gender is not merely the result of a sexual body, however dressed, or a social assignment, however enforced. It is always also personal, constructed in a unique configuration by personal motivations, attitudes, desires, and acts. No matter the utility of designating gender categories, the individual dimension inevitably renders them constructs unequal to life.

All of the above axes, dimensions and degrees contribute to reconceptualizing gender. We need not be terminologically confined to 'masculine' and 'feminine.' Moreover, 'masculine' and 'feminine' need not be conceived as poles at opposite ends; there may be gender statuses more extremely associated with the characteristics we have discussed. Even if we grudgingly accept division into two sexual body camps ('male' for bodies apparently like 46, XY; 'female' for bodies apparently like 46, XX), we can identify distinct gender statuses or states. Consider a few of the possibilities set out in the accompanying table; they are by no means all of the possibilities.

Table 5.1 Genders

Name (Sex assignment)	Brief Description
Gynaikine (F)	From Greek 'like a woman'; a 'lady's lady.' An individual whose sexual body represents cultural ideals of femaleness, and who embraces this body with high physicality. She possesses an exceptional experience of femaleness, strong conformity to stereotypical gender ideas associated with a female body, and exaggerated expressiveness; these axes are strongly endorsed personally though viewed socially as extreme.
Theline (F)	From the Greek 'one who suckles,' an individual whose sexual body presentation and gender traits emphasize in stereotypical fashion the attributes of 'woman-as-mother.' Her experience, expressiveness and conformity

	all stress those things associated with a female's role of bearing and nurturing children. Though socially approved, this approval is modified by a perception that the individual's identity and roles are more limited than is true for other people having female-type bodies.
Feminine (F)	A generic gender; the default label for those whose anatomical presentation appears female and whose experience, expression, and conformity fall within the social norms to win high approval as a woman who knows and keeps her gendered place.
Masimiline (F)	From Latin *mas* + *similes*, 'mannish'; an individual whose sexual body is labeled female but whose physical presentation emphasizes traits more associated with a male body. This person weakly expresses personal and social traits culturally associated with a female body, and weakly conforms to accompanying gender standards for such a sexual body. Personal experience of gender may be high, moderate, or low.
Andreiazine (F; FtM transsexual)	From the Greek for 'a manly spirit'; an individual whose sexual body is labeled female but whose expressiveness of cultural traits is much more like that expected for those whose bodies are labeled male. Nonconformity to cultural standards for gender traits associated with a female body is moderate to high. Personal experience of female sexual body may range from acceptance to discomfort or rejection (including sex change). Social disapproval is moderate to high, perhaps prompting this individual to be highly selective in expressiveness of gender, depending on context.
Neutroine (*or Anthropine*) (F or M)	From Latin *neutron*, 'towards neither side,' this gender lies midway. It is weakly associated with a sexual body, whether because of intersex condition or simply an unendorsed physical dimension. Conformity to cultural standards to either maleness or femaleness is weak, as is expressiveness of either in gender traits. The individual presents in a way where anatomical sex is not immediately apparent, or seems not to matter at all.
Gynnisine (*or gynanarine*) (M; MtF transsexual)	From Greek 'woman-man'; an individual whose sexual body is labeled male but whose expressiveness of cultural traits is much more like that expected for those whose bodies are labeled female. Nonconformity to cul-

	tural standards for gender traits associated with the male body is moderate to high. Personal experience of male sexual body may range from acceptance to discomfort or rejection (including sex change). Social disapproval is moderate to high, perhaps prompting this individual to be highly selective in expressiveness of gender, depending on context.
Muliebrine (M)	From Latin *muliebris*, 'womanish,' or 'effeminate'; an individual whose sexual body is labeled male but whose physical presentation emphasizes traits more associated with a female body. This person weakly expresses personal and social traits culturally associated with a male body, and weakly conforms to accompanying gender standards for such a sexual body. Personal experience of gender may be high, moderate, or low. Social approval tends to be lower than for gender states or statuses more conforming to cultural standards associated with a male body.
Masculine (M)	A generic gender; the default label for those whose anatomical presentation appears male and whose experience, expression, and conformity fall within the social norms to win high approval as a man who knows and keeps his gendered place.
Andrikine (M)	From Greek for 'manly'; a 'man's man.' An individual whose sexual body represents cultural ideals of maleness, and who embraces this body with high physicality. He possesses an exceptional experience of maleness, strong conformity to stereotypical gender ideas associated with a male body, and exaggerated expressiveness; these axes are strongly endorsed personally though viewed socially as extreme.
Viriline (M)	From Latin *vir*, 'a heroic man'; a 'stud.' An individual whose sexual body represents cultural ideals of male sexuality and aggressiveness, and who embraces this body with high physicality. He possesses an exceptional experience of maleness, strong conformity to stereotypical gender ideas associated with the male body as a sexual and physical instrument, and exaggerated expressiveness; these axes are strongly endorsed personally though viewed socially as extreme.

Each of these gender statuses, or states, can be operationally defined, empirically observed and tested, and described with discrete boundaries. In short, they meet the criteria for categories and thus have as much validity as 'masculine' and 'feminine.' As is, the two genders our culture endorses are conceptually overly broad, embracing gender presentations of great diversity, some with characteristics overlapping the other gender, and of increasingly less utilitarian value. If, for example, social science can continue to multiply categories of mental disorders using the logic of distinguishable traits and relatively clear boundaries, there is no reason not to apply the same logic to gender realities. In both cases the categories are artificial constructions intended to help us better sort out experiential realities. Lord knows we need some clarification for the existing muddle created by confining discussion to two genders!

The point in multiplying genders must not be to make them ends-in-themselves. The advantage of adding new gender labels, where each gender status is demarcated from the others, is to show their conceptual equality. 'Masculine' and 'feminine' not only are not the only valid gender terms, they are not qualitatively superior to other designations or statuses. One may even question their presumed numerical superiority once a continuum with enough distinct points is identified. If we are going to insist on gender labels—and there is no sign this fact is going to change any time soon—then we might as well have enough of them both to reflect gendered life as it is lived and diminish the power presently held by one privileged gender (masculinity) over another gender (feminine).[320]

Concluding Comment on Gender Models

Now, if we move away from theoretical language we can put the matter like this: people tend to cluster in recognizable gender patterns. There are those who clearly present as feminine most of the time, and whose experience and expression of femininity does not vary greatly across time or contexts. Likewise, there are those who clearly present as masculine most of the time, and whose experience and expression of masculinity does not vary greatly across time or contexts. These folk may well be the majority among us, just as unambiguously anatomically male or female persons are more common than intersexed individuals. Yet there are also those who do not fit at or even near these generic gender labels. Among such people other recognizable gender patterns may be discerned. Indeed they have been in distinguishing so-called 'third gender' groups in various cultures around the world. However, as we have seen, there is no logical reason to confine ourselves to either two or three genders—we can create as many labels as there are identifiably distinct patterns to name.

All of this modeling depends on overcoming the simplistic pairing between sex and gender, where the former invariably and predictably yields particular forms of the latter. At this point in time, evidence suggests a different conclusion: any sex can indwell any gendered reality. Hopefully we may soon come at least far enough in our thinking that we can weaken the monopoly held by a scheme limited to two sex labels and two gender labels. Perhaps even if we cling to the notion of just two basic camps we can better describe the range in each, naming gender statuses subordinate to gender states (e.g., naming 'viriline' as a status of the gender state 'masculine'). Though this seems less desirable than a thorough overhaul of our present gender scheme, at least it would be more nuanced.

Even granting legitimacy to new genders a significant linguistic challenge remains. So wed are we to dichotomous thinking that we would still need either new words to accompany terms like 'man' and 'woman,' or we would have to make those words label a range of distinct genders that share in common bodies that are more male-like or more female-like. If we become more culturally accepting of sexual bodies with mixed genital features, then perhaps we can add a third general term, like 'androgyn,' to stand alongside 'man' and 'woman.' Then, at least, there would be three camps, all body-based, but permitting a range of associated gender statuses or states.

We would still face, too, the issue of pronouns. One solution is merely to retain the present pronouns but use the one that best fits the *presentation* rather than presumed sexual body. Thus an anatomical male who lives within the gendered experience and expression of femininity should be referred to by the pronoun 'she.' The term 'transsexual' might still be appropriate if the person is transitioning in body appearance, but the term 'transgender' would not be appropriate for such a label depends on our current dichotomous system—as does '*cross*dressing'. Our own use of these terms in this book is an unwelcome concession to the limitations of current dialog.[321] Let's be clear: either anatomical males or females can be feminine; either sex can be masculine—and the same claim holds for intersexed people. Once we add new gender labels our ability to see people as they are grows, and so must our language.

Unfortunately, we are clearly not yet to this perspective as a culture. Until we can create an acceptable vocabulary to match our escape from our current dichotomous thinking we must struggle to find ways to adequately express the reality of gender for crossdressers using the limited terms already in place. But that should not hinder us from questioning and dialoging. Change happens.

So we return to the question we began this section with. If our thinking about gender changes, is it for better or worse? We are only being fair if we query whether our society's present view is the result of a better understanding of the biology of human sexuality, coupled with more clarity about social gender roles, or the reflection of cultural pressure to uphold a paradigm that has an inadequate scientific basis. If the latter is the case, it is fair to ask *why?*

What are the politics of gender?

Now we enter more fully into why all this matters. Discussions of gender are not made merely to keep academicians employed. Convictions about gender carry strong consequences socially. Kate Bornstein refers to having a clear and socially accepted gender as a "privilege." Bornstein comments: "When you have a gender, or when you are perceived as having a gender, you don't get laughed at in the street. You don't get beat up. You know which public bathroom to use, and when you use it, people don't stare at you or worse. You know which form to fill out. You know what clothes to wear."[322] Those who do not conform to our society's dichotomous scheme of gender lose that privilege and risk alienation, marginalization, and victimization.

Women in our culture generally have some sense of this. In a culture structured such that one gender (masculine) enjoys special privilege, the matter of what gender is—or is *not*—genuinely matters. This is why women have labored so long and diligently to change their perceived status. In recent decades the awareness of gender inequality has become more acute—and the controversies and debates more pointed. None of us can afford to ignore the political consequences of our society's decisions about gender because those decisions affect structures and processes that affect *all* of us.

Always in the midst of these controversies and debates are what we wear.

Both formal and informal rules about the clothes we wear help reinforce social values; to challenge the rules is to challenge certain social values. That is why so-called 'dress violations' are treated as threatening social order. An important part of our culture has been keeping sharp lines drawn between masculine and feminine—and for more than just the sexual boundary between male and female. The line is not a vertical one standing between two separate but equal groups, but a horizontal one with males (and masculinity) placed above females (and femininity). For more than two centuries dress has been an important social mechanism for keeping this line clear and the members of the groups separate—and unequal.

In recent decades this line has been challenged, and subsequently blurred. How has this happened? The primary force has been women disputing the status quo, which itself was an artificial standard granted the authority of science when medical men linked so many things to sex and gender differences. Yet that was itself only the latest in a long line of insults and injuries.

For a considerable time in Western culture females were not merely seen as subordinate to males, but as 'belonging' to them. Daughters 'belonged' to their fathers, were 'given' in marriage, and became thereby the sole property of their husbands. Keeping females sheltered from sexual experience prior to marriage safeguarded their value to a future husband. Despite the fact that such ideas persist in various guises, movements like feminism have sharply challenged this construction and brought about serious erosion to it.

Still, the more things change the more they remain the same. Despite the fact some of the crasser manifestations of gender inequality have been curbed, similar dynamics remain:

Today, male-female relationships are more likely to involve a different economic arrangement, one in which the male protects and supports the female in return for exclusive sexual rights and domestic obligations. Unrestricted female sexual independence would destroy this traditional bargain and all the institutions that it fosters. Thus a fundamental change in gender relationships would ensue, involving a diminution of the power traditionally exercised by males. Support for traditional sexual morality, then, operates to support traditional gender roles.[323]

We are living in a time when change in this arrangement continues. Men and women with their different agendas are engaged in a contest where more than reproductive strategy is in play. Those who have held power—mostly white heterosexual males—are often reluctant to share it, let alone relinquish it. Women dissatisfied with the preexisting arrangement, because it is unfavorable to them in ways that often produce violence alongside deprivation, continue to seek greater equalization of power. The resulting stress fuzzes the gender line used to keep one group above another, and that blurring of the line not only makes it less clear, but also renders it more permeable.

A highly visible way of confronting the status quo is by changing the manner of one's dress. When feminists adopted, then adapted masculine styles of dress they expressed a claim on masculine prerogatives held by males. The early feminists paid a price, enduring alienation, censure, and victimization. They were branded transgressors in dress—'crossdressers'—and 'mentally disordered' for upsetting what many believed was the natural and ordained order of male/masculine over female/feminine. Clothes were an important part of the battle because of their position in the expressive and experiencing system we rely on so heavily. Opponents certainly understood this and the battle over dress rules at school, in the workplace, and in other public arenas still persists.

Into this complex contest enters crossdressing. Although *all* statistically unlikely variations in sexual behavior or gender identification challenge the status quo, crossdressing seems to pose a particularly thorny problem for it.[324] When women crossdressed successfully, they often raised their social status. This was, in fact, a tool employed with success by women for centuries—long before the modern advent of feminism that took a largely hidden subversive act and made it public. However, in the prevailing scheme of things, when *men* crossdress they are perceived as doing the unthinkable—voluntarily lowering their social status.[325] Patriarchy remains in full force, for only within a patriarchal system, where males are valued above females and accorded higher social status, can such a judgment carry any practical force.

Q. 6

What do clothes say about our gender?

The Short Answer: Gender has both personal and social dimensions. In the experience and expression of gender the conventions of clothing fashion in a culture are utilized. We dress to experience gender and to express it. This latter aspect is in its social dimension political, being about status and power. It also is complicated both by personal intentions—the dress statements about gender we mean—and by the interpretation others make. Others often do not understand, in part or in whole, the message we send. In part that results from the multiple possibilities we have through dress to experience and express gender. These include seeking to *be* a gender, to *borrow* one through dress, to *blend* genders, to *blur* the gender lines, or to *bend* those lines. In light of the stakes involved in a culture where dress is critical to personal and social identity, society seeks to clarify messages through dress expectations along gender lines. These expectations start at birth. We immediately color code infants and then we structure their environments to encourage identity and role development thought socially appropriate for the gender assignment made at birth. But childhood is not the only time when gender differentiation in dress is expected. Adults face these expectations too, especially in the workplace. Women, in particular, seem sensitive to them. Perhaps this situation exists because their success or failure in the workplace may hinge on their dress appearance. Men, though only having to not appear feminine, nevertheless also experience pressures and stress related to dress. Everything true in general about dress is especially true with reference to underwear, our most intimate clothing. These garments are not only closest to our skin, they symbolically hold the tightest connection to both sex and gender. This opens up rich possibilities for crossdressing—possibilities often misunderstood by others.

The Longer Answer: As we have seen, cultures like our own have adopted a binary system of sex and gender. We think and speak in terms of two anatomical sexes—'male' and 'female'—and two genders—'masculine' and 'feminine'—that are thought to naturally correspond. Because sexual couplings are, for the most part, between members of opposite sexes, ways must exist for both males and females to reliably identify each other and, if possible, signal availability and interest in sexual interaction. Clothes have long been relied upon to accomplish separating the sexes for easy identification even at a distance and to signal sexual availability.[326]

However much we may enjoy sexual coupling, though, we spend comparatively little time engaged in it. Gender's functioning in culture is much broader than sexual signaling. Yet we still require aid in gender identification, and clothing still provides that help. Sociologist Gregory Stone once remarked that while gender is known silently, to dress in clothes associated with a gender is to make an announcement of one's gender—an announcement rarely questioned.[327] Dress is *behavior*, and alongside other behavior places each of us in a social matrix. Culturally, gender is a code dictating societal expectations and beliefs about identity, roles, privileges and duties.

In this light, the work of George Bush and Perry London is salient. Following in the footsteps of sociologist George Herbert Mead, they hypothesize that variability in clothing styles within a society reflect differences in social roles and self-concepts held by members within the society. They further hypothesize that changes in social roles and self-concepts will be mirrored in changes in fundamental or enduring modes of dress. Finally, they also hypothesize that the degree of variability in clothing styles parallels the greater or lesser degree of definition and conflict found in that society's social roles.[328] They found empirical evidence supporting these ideas in the disappearance of knickers; we might find more in many other dress changes.

Gender-differentiated dress, as Bush and London hypothesize, reflects our society's concern over boys and girls, men and women, filling different social roles and holding different self-concepts. But these roles and self-concepts have experienced prolonged challenge and gradual evolution, especially on the side of femininity. At the same time, conflict over these changes and a lack of consensus on definitions for masculinity and femininity, play out on the stage of fashion and clothing preferences. Though under sharp dispute today, to the degree that gender is predicated on the sex of the body, gender-differentiated clothes will continue to mean keeping male bodies displaying signals others will translate as masculinity, while female bodies are dressed to send messages received as femininity.

The fact that clothes do these things quite imperfectly has seldom slowed us down. The reason why we persist—and continue to struggle with succeeding—rests in our utter dependence on gender to define our personal and social identities, and our accompanying reliance on dress as the most prominent signifier of gender. Yet we also insist that dress fulfill other functions: it must shield us from the elements, indicate our affiliation with a wide variety of groups, and display us as autonomous individuals with unique personalities. While doing all this we demand as well that dress reflect our values, proving us demonstrably moral beings or flagrantly defying social conventions of right and wrong. With all these requirements placed on dress, inevitably demands come into conflict, confusion arises, and dress appearance fails to perfectly do what we want it to do.

What is the central dynamic in the relation of dress to gender?

In this morass of expectations dress is supposed to reliably differentiate males from females and indicate the inclusion of the former into masculinity, the latter into femininity, with nothing properly standing between. Males are to be masculine, females feminine. Yet, given the complexity of how dress functions for us, the only way we can make everything work so that all the various demands placed on it have a chance of being met is to keep the rules governing gender differentiation relatively few and flexible. But one grand exception—a single inflexible standard—serves as lynchpin to the whole. We already have indicated this as the 'Golden Rule' for gender-differentiated dress: "Males must appear masculine, or at least not feminine.'[329]

Masculinity means competence, a degree of rationality capable of imposing order on chaos, of seeing clearly where things appear murky, of narrowing a bewildering array of possibilities to the one best choice that furthers power and progress. Masculinity, in sum, is about control—of feelings, thoughts and behavior; of the personal and the social. To be a masculine male is to be in control, a situation dependent on being in position above and in front of others. So masculinity becomes about competition and strength—of mind and body, and most of all of a will that suppresses the seductive undertow of emotion that can undermine all a man's labor.

"Women's corresponding socially-ascribed image," write Joanna Brewis, Mark Hampton, and Stephen Linstead, "is of being comfortable in disturbing the masculine sense of certainty, raising questions, and opening things up."[330] Femininity is culturally constructed as antithesis to masculinity. Where masculinity must be narrow, femininity can be broad; masculinity follows an ordered course, femininity can be spontaneous and flexible; masculinity champions competition, femininity embraces nurturing cooperation. Girls and women do not have to chain creativity to the service of production. They are free to express emotions rather than constrict them.

Yes, these statements are all stereotypes. That is precisely the point. Masculinity and femininity are idealized constructs that few, if any, real individuals ever realize fully. Yet most of us, most of the time, aspire to the ideal, judge ourselves and others by the stereotypes as though they constitute a natural law, and suffer the consequences for our failures to be perfectly masculine or feminine. And if masculinity carries privilege, the loneliness at the top can be profound. The pressure of not merely keeping on top, but making the mountain higher, is immense.

Complicating matters further is the fracturing of the gender hierarchy in real world settings. To be sure, there remain bastions of masculinity. Just as sure are the continuing inequities based on gender. But to deny that genuine changes have occurred, that some progress in some quarters has been attained, would be absurd. We live today caught betwixt and between, with the allure of an orderly, if despotic regime where masculine males are everywhere in charge on the one side, and the anxiety of a chaotic, if liberating kingdom where masculinity and femininity are more fluid in personal and social lives and choices. In such a world our dress can only be what is—incredibly diverse, contradictory, and rich in possibilities that tug us toward past and future alike.

With regard to our question, 'What do clothes say about our gender?' the only essential answer pertains to males and it is: 'I am not feminine.' Females can be masculine—'tomboys'—with mild to moderate sanctions even in adulthood, depending on other contexts, such as the nature of a chosen occupation. A female police officer has more sanction to be tomboyish than does a female flight attendant. For females the dress spectrum is wide because the gender spectrum is wide. They can be feminine, androgynous, or relatively masculine. Since in a gender hierarchy there is little difference between second place and last place, how one dresses in the lower ranks is interesting, but ultimately inconsequential.

Males are restricted to a narrow dress spectrum to safeguard their perch on the single rung of masculinity. Even then their perch is precarious. A slender, particular kind of appearance of masculine maleness reaps rewards. Other masculine presentations, even those stereotypically 'macho,' face negative repercussions. For instance, the ruggedly masculine association attached to being dressed as a cowboy carries with it far less reward than a man in a business suit. Males dressed androgynously tend to be subject to bemused stares. Men dressed femininely are judged as not men (at least, *real* men) at all.

If this sounds political, it is because dress *is* political.[331]

How can dress be used to express gender?

Of course, so is gender, as we saw in the answer to the last question. In a certain respect, gender is the ultimate arena of politics. Just as there is no form of governance indisputably dictated by nature, there is no natural obligation to construe gender along the lines done in our culture. Even as politics takes varying shapes in cultures around the world and throughout history, so also do genders. Politics manifests itself in the institutions of government, the dictates of policy, the processes of law. Gender manifests itself in appearance, including a broad range of behaviors, but preeminently dress. To put it bluntly, "we concretize the nonexistence of gender in our clothing. . . ."[332]

Famed costume historian and clothes scholar James Laver cuts right to the heart of how dress and gender politics converge. In an interview in 1967, Laver remarked, "In a patriarchal society—one in which the man is dominant—the clothes of men and women are vastly different. But in a matriarchal society the clothes worn by the two sexes become more and more alike."[333] If Laver is right, we may detect the direction our society is moving through the dress of its citizens. Certainly we shall be able to see that dress provides a readily visible ground for expressing underlying social currents about gender.

The politics of gender sometimes erupt in conflict. Dress, by virtue of its omnipresence, becomes a natural and critical weapon in the gender wars. As Brewis and colleagues observe, gender-differentiated dress behavior only happens because all of us are under the sway of the power effects flowing from a discourse of gender difference.[334] All parties use it to advance their own causes. In a society like our own, where sex and gender are more neatly paired than reality warrants, clothing constitutes an arena for making a social and political statement that gender issues *can* be clear and *should be*.

For example, research shows that most of us try to align our biological sex, assigned gender and sex stereotypical clothes. Biological sex proves to be a solid predictor of choosing sex stereotypical clothing. Males are more likely to select masculine clothing and females are more likely to select feminine clothing.[335] Of course, this makes sense in a society where a strict pairing between sex and gender prevails and where violations of such a pairing in dress are predictable. Most of us, wittingly or not, are involved in sustaining the divide.

Men in power may be strongly motivated by the advantages of masculine privilege to keep the gender line clear and firm. They are likely to desire distinctly masculine and feminine dress, with men in the former and women in the latter. Women, wanting to equalize the power, may adopt masculine clothing and make it their own. But they, too, want men to remain in masculine clothing,[336] while redefining what constitutes 'feminine' dress.[337] Crossdressers, exploiting the fuzzing of the gender line by such machinations, present gendered dress in such a manner as to accent the relation of clothing and gender. Crossdressing, in an important sense, depends on the politics and conflicts of gender.

Politics involves posturing for position and power—and so does gender. With due apologies to those who use certain terms in ways other than what is said here, in broad strokes clothing can be used to express gender in one or another of at least five ways:

- ❑ *Be gender*—the use of dress to enact a gender; in its most common use this is dressing congruent to one's assigned gender and so mythically stating we *are* a gender rather than that we *do* gender.
- ❑ *Borrow gender*—the use of dress to occupy another gender temporarily.
- ❑ *Blend gender*—the use of androgynous dress or mixed gender elements to minimize or eliminate the gender divide.
- ❑ *Blur gender*—the use of dress to make gender uncertain.
- ❑ *Bend gender*—the use of dress to change or challenge the perception of gender.

149

No matter how we dress, we likely end up fitting into one of these patterns; gender and dress are inescapably intertwined.[338]

Be Gender

Most of the time we practice and observe the first pattern in its most common use. We dress congruently with our assigned gender and no fuss is raised. Our goal is clear and so is the process: we aim to present a calculated congruence between our assigned gender and apparent, designated body sex. We do so by following as best we can culturally sanctioned rules governing the use of gender-differentiated clothing. We seldom, if ever, consider that the only difference between ourselves and transsexuals is a different starting point—our congruence of sex and gender as contrasted to their incongruence between the two.

In various societies at various times this gender congruence with the paired sex is accompanied by specific and exaggerated attempts to draw attention to sexual anatomy. In this manner the tie between gender and sex is especially emphasized and gender qualities are particularly depicted in sexual language, as in the virile or potent man and the fertile or receptive woman. This plays out in dress, for example, with feminine garments designed to provide maximum exposure of the female breast or to emphasize physical features associated with fertility. In masculine fashion it occurs through garments accenting the phallus, such as the codpiece in England or the ancient Egyptian skirt starched in front to display constant aroused virility.[339]

Borrow Gender

Borrowing gender occurs far more frequently than we might imagine. We all do it imaginatively whenever we try to place ourselves in the situation of someone of a different gender—an advisable strategy in the effort to understand and get along with others no matter how difficult it may be. In terms of dress behavior it also happens more commonly than we might imagine. Non-transgender people sometimes engage in transgender behavior.

Crossdressing as a way of borrowing gender happens in a variety of casual settings. In schools often a day is set aside for students (and sometimes faculty and staff) to crossdress in ways such that their assigned gender remains obvious by their talk or other behavior. Especially for festivities, many people indulge in dress meant to represent a gender other than their own, but in such a way that there is no possibility of passing for that gender. In short, they mean for others to know that what they are wearing does *not* represent or express their gender identity or ordinary gender role. They are only borrowing the gender. Though it may be playful, it is hardly immature play; borrowing a gender at least hypothetically means putting on all the things associated with it—no light or laughing matter.

Many of us are bothered by the gender divide and gender stratification whether or not we identify as transgendered. We see how a gender hierarchy inherently disadvantages girls and women—and harms everyone. Boys and men also are trapped within their gender status and because of masculine privilege find themselves confined within narrow but weighty expectations. Ways of easing the pressure may be sought through minimizing or eliminating the gender divide.

Once more dress affords rich possibilities. Androgyny—a calculated label derived from Greek words blending masculinity and femininity—offers a balancing through blending of characteristics associated with both genders. Androgynous dress does the same thing, blending masculine and feminine elements in order to be somewhere between the two genders. This gender choice is often seen among professional women.

Consider, for example, the ethnographic and interview research conducted by Carrie Yang Costello. She studied students in two professional school settings: law and social work. Her interest was in how the appropriation of a new professional identity might be complicated by preexisting personal identity, resulting in dissonance that would show up, for example, in dress behavior. Her work reveals that the entrance into these professional groups carries with it dress expectations that, especially for women and people of color, elicit wardrobe changes that have a gendered quality. "Because," Costello observes, "Western male professional dress style is so well-established, men are able easily to approximate it. But the scenario is quite different for professional women, and I observed a lot more variation in style."[340]

As women's wardrobes changed, consistent with their striving to gain a new professional identity, their gendered self-presentation altered. In a typical scenario, Costello found that when new students determined they were dressed inappropriately they showed identity dissonance. They responded to this sense by shopping for new clothes—putting on a new skin better suited to their new identity. The trend for female students both at the law school and the school of social work was toward androgyny. But they could achieve this androgynous dress appearance by two paths. Some used what Costello terms 'subtractive androgyny': they removed signifiers of gender. Others practiced 'additive androgyny': they combined gender elements dramatically. In Costello's view, the former course was associated more with negative dissonance.[341]

Androgyny sometimes is seen as a 'third gender.' Historically, when children are seen as asexual beings, their dress tends to be either androgynous or, because of their inferior social status, like that of women.[342] In societies with a rigid gender hierarchy androgyny is likely to be judged as closer to femininity. So androgynous dress is acceptable for girls and women but only (barely) tolerated for boys and men.[343] Ironically, today many of the young people who are choosing to blend gender through androgynous dress (and use of makeup) are

151

males. This probably reflects both protest against masculine stereotypes and the lessened distance between the genders. Nevertheless, particularly among other males, androgynous dress among men and boys commonly fetches disparaging comments.

Blur Gender

Others aim to blur gender so that those who observe them are left guessing as to whether they are anatomically male or female. The motivations vary. Some may do so because they object to the artificiality of society constructed along lines drawn based on sex and gender. Others may do so because of a sense of personal uncertainty, confusion, or disturbance about their own gender identity and status. Some may find the confusion it creates to be amusing or offer opportunities they can exploit in one manner or another. All these different motivations are likely to have in common is a use of dress such that the net effect is uncertainty over the person's sex and gender. Whether that uncertainty extends to the person so dressing varies from individual to individual; it is by no means necessary to have a vacillating or ambivalent sense of gender to blur it in practice.

Bend Gender

Finally, dress can be used to bend (or even bash) gender. While all of the ways of expressing gender are political, this avenue is most likely to be seen as such. After all, it is the use of dress to change or challenge the perception of gender. Perhaps it is the intentionality of the manipulation that makes bending gender in dress so likely to be noticed and to startle observers. Most of us, most of the time, think little about matters such as whether gender is natural or artificial, reasonable or irrational, absolute or arbitrary. Dress that bends gender intends observers to know that the sex of the body is different from the gender of the dress, but it is the gender of the dress that is being championed. Most of the time people borrow gender in dress they make sure to also bend it so that all observers are clear they are enacting a gender farce.

Regardless of whether dress is manipulated to be, borrow, blend, blur, or bend gender, it results in a *Gestalt*—a perceptual whole attendant with value meanings. In dress behavior the name for this *Gestalt* is a 'silhouette.'[344] This is an optical illusion of the clothed body generated by the dress. As such it can be manipulated to achieve a desired effect.[345] The silhouette is also a figure cast against the background of personal experience and identity, culture and social identity. No matter how dress is used, for whatever purpose, a silhouette results. While there are a number of what we might think of as 'stock' silhouettes in dress, we can also more generally think of the silhouette as the individual's complete dressed form seen as though it were a shadow on the wall, an artful illustration meant to depict the body in a certain manner.

What is the effect of the silhouette?

Normally in discussions of gender and dress, including crossdressing, the conversation stays to the kinds of clothes selected and how they are worn. So, when we think of gender-differentiated apparel, we may speak of pants for men and dresses for women. Limiting our conversation to clothing items misses a significant element involved. Dress, including both clothes and costume ornamentation, holistically shapes a silhouette. In short, it drafts an overall form that is perceived by observers. That form likely is associated with a particular gender. Even more potently, it may rely on a cultural expectation of how a gender represents a sexed body, because the silhouette is principally influenced on the one side by the garment (gender-differentiated), and on the other by the physical proportions of the person (the sexed body).[346]

For example, in contemporary Western culture the most feminine females are associated with dress that in its separate elements reflects femininity while collectively shaping a silhouette unambiguously female. Gender and sex converge in the silhouette. The most desired silhouette in our culture constitutes the stereotype of the feminine female: the Barbie doll girl or woman. This silhouette reflects a slender waist, wide hips, and pronounced bust. Despite the fact that the physical reality to match the Barbie doll image is virtually unattainable and undesirable health-wise, it inspires behavior to attain it. Since the easiest way to approximate it is through dress, fashion styles accommodate the goal. Women for whom such an ideal is impossible, or undesired, seek through dress to embody one or another silhouette they regard as portraying an authentic feminine female, such as a matron, Madonna, or working woman.

Silhouettes are not merely created by stylistic elements of dress—they influence those separate elements' contribution to the whole. The silhouette suggests how a masculine male or feminine female is to sit, stand, and walk. Posture and movement are both influenced by dress designed to attain and maintain a silhouette. The silhouette draws attention to some features of the body and away from others. As various body parts are associated with one gender/sex pairing or the other, those receive corresponding fashion emphasis and contribute to the desired silhouette. For example, an item like a corset modifies the silhouette to highlight certain anatomical features that are different from those drawn attention to by another item, such as a bustle.

In sum, different uses of dress to express gender still must contend with the reality of the silhouette. Different paths affect the nature of the silhouette. The effort to be a gender, where gender is conceived as matching sex, will aim at a silhouette unmistakably male or female. The goal of blending gender, also influenced by the cultural pairing of sex and gender, will aim at a silhouette neither clearly male nor female. If, as remarked earlier, gender politics involves posturing for position and power, the posture of the silhouette makes a statement whose grammar may be made from the elements of dress, but whose semantics rests in a context of intent and interpretation.

No matter how gender is expressed, dress plays a critical role. It does so from the very beginning of life. Long before we have any inkling of gender politics and conflicts we are assigned a side to be on. At birth, or shortly thereafter, someone declares for us the gender we will belong to. We have no say in the matter and any effort later to change that assignment and designation will require tremendous effort and persistence. Throughout life this gender assignment will carry with it expectations about dress.

Make no mistake about it: among the most immediate and important cues we use in assigning gender is dress. Clothing can express gender identification and/or affiliation, either consciously or unconsciously. We use clothing to distinguish children, and expect adults to conform to 'gender appropriate' dress. Girls, boys, men and women are all subjected to cultural pressures about clothes and most of them have to do in one way or another with gender.

How is clothing related to gender in children?

Why do we find it necessary to color code infants? Obviously, a baby in wraps is androgynous in appearance; hence a convention of color-coding is convenient for declaring the child's sex. But in our culture we are at birth not merely beings-with-sex, but also beings-with-gender. Since gender assignment is made based on determination of sex, clothes that declare gender are construed in our culture to also declare sex. So dress is used to express gender assignment—a public declaration before the child can say anything on its own behalf that masculinity or femininity has been assigned as an identity and as an expectation.

Color Coding Infants & Dress Expectations for Small Children

Our society is so obsessed with this declaration that no opportunity seems too trivial to miss. Nor is there such a thing as starting too early. As Gregory Stone observed in the early 1960s, "The diaper folded in front *invests* the child with masculinity; in back, with femininity."[347] Even more obviously we rely on color cues: masculinity turns out to be blue, while femininity is pink. This situation has reached the point where even disposable diapers are color-coded!

Do we really need such gender labeling? Apparently we do. A study published in 1985 found that strangers could only determine an infant's gender if provided the visual cue of color-coded clothes. In the study, 48 infants were dressed either in gender-stereotyped clothes (pink for girls, blue or red for boys), or gender-neutral clothes. The 90% of infants dressed in gender-coded clothing were readily identified as boys or girls by observers; the same was not true otherwise.[348]

Not surprisingly, most of us want our children to be seen and known as members of the gender group they were assigned to at birth. Parents start doing what they can to ensure that right away. It isn't long into life before their children are actively involved in the process. Spencer Cahill's study of preschool children reveals how even at this tender age they "fashion themselves into gendered persons."[349] Writing of this family interaction process around gender, sociologist Emily Kane remarks that, "Parents begin gendering their children from their very first awareness of those children, whether in pregnancy or while waiting adoption. Children themselves become active participants in this gendering process by the time they are conscious of the social relevance of gender, typically before the age of two."[350]

Research indicates that children's early environments typically are gender-differentiated. For example, one study investigated the home environments of 120 girls and boys in three equal groups of 40 children at three different ages: 5, 13, and 25 months (infancy into toddlerhood). The environments for both boys and girls were filled with toys, clothes, and colors endorsed by the culture as appropriate for the gender. Thus, girls were surrounded with dolls and jewelry, and wore multicolored clothes and pink; boys' toys were sports and work related, and their clothes more often red, white or blue.[351] Early acculturation into gender stereotypes seems a social constant that both teaches gender expectations and reinforces them.

Of course, such coded declarations are convenient. But more is going on than just saving the parents from answering the question whether the child is a boy or a girl. Because our society places great emphasis on gender affiliation,[352] we begin at once inculcating in our children what we believe to be appropriate gender role behavior for the gender they were assigned at birth. An aid in reinforcing both gender identity and distinctions is provided by clothes.

This behavior, whatever benefits it may be thought to confer, comes at a cost. Gender expectations and standards are so pronounced that they lead to subtle distortions in the ways adults perceive infants. A 1974 study underscores this point. Babies of both sexes were presented for observation. The average weight of the babies was the same and the length of the girls slightly more on average. Despite these facts, the adult observers underestimated both the weight and the size of the baby girls relative to the infant boys.[353] What they saw conformed to a cultural expectation that boys be big and strong, while girls should be small and delicate. Apparently, all we need to prompt such distortions is to dress the child in a certain color, or style.

Development psychologist Carole Beale summarizes the matter well when she writes:

Gender supports many inferences about the baby's probable characteristics and behavior. Even though these initial inferences have a very high probability of being wrong, they reassure the viewer who is faced with an unfamiliar small baby. The drawback is that, as we have seen, once the baby is perceived as a boy or girl, the process of social interaction will be altered accordingly.[354]

Instant judgments, typically based on visual cues like dress, produce profoundly different patterned responses. If this process appears troubling for all children, it proves highly problematic for transgender children.

Transgender Children

Immediately in life everyone around an infant—parents, siblings, and others—facilitates the process of acculturation into the assigned gender identity and role. Typically the amount of environmental reinforcement of gender expectations is immense. Yet virtually all children exhibit some gender crossing behavior. Of course, much of this is exploratory and naïve. Parents typically respond with firm displeasure and the child learns such exhibitions are not approved. With the cognitive development of gender schemas the child ordinarily joins the throng of society, accepting, endorsing, and expressing the expected gender identity and its accompanying roles.

But what happens when a child persists in gender crossing behavior? What results from a persistent preference for articles of clothing associated with a gender different than that assigned the child at birth? Although it may be tolerated in a toddler, such behavior almost always meets increasing resistance as the child grows older, if not at home, then certainly from peers and authority figures in social institutions such as school. Moreover, in keeping with the gender hierarchy in our culture, different standards apply to boys and girls.

Sociologist Kane, interviewing a diverse group of parents of preschool children (ages 3-5), found a clear double standard. These parents welcomed gender nonconformity among girls. They often dressed them in sports clothes, provided them with masculine toys, applauded their involvement in activities associated with boys, and encouraged their ambitions to someday participate in traditionally male occupations. The term 'tomboy' was used approvingly. [355] The situation with boys proved markedly different. There the openness to nonconforming behavior was conscientiously balanced by attention to eliciting from their sons gender behavior approximating masculine ideals. Heterosexual fathers, in particular, were central to these efforts. There was approval, or at least acceptance, of boys learning to perform domestic skills or show nurturance. On the other hand, when sons engaged in certain dress behavior—wearing pink or frilly clothing, wearing skirts, dresses or tights—the parents responded with negative reactions.[356] Indeed, David Plummer's study of the role homophobia plays in the construction of a Western sense of masculinity provides evidence of how crossdressing is linked to homosexuality; to cross the gender line in dress is correlated with also crossing out of heterosexuality.[357]

If the child is a boy, he is more than six times more likely than a comparable girl to be referred to mental health professionals. At least that was the finding in a study that examined referrals of children to a clinic treating 'Gender Identity Disorder' (see the answers to Q. 93, 96) over a span from 1978-1995. Despite the fact that, if anything, the girls referred actually showed more extreme cross-gender behavior, boys were far likelier to be referred; the ratio was 6.6:1, boys to girls. The authors are surely right in viewing this as evidence of cultural factors weighing in.[358] In fact, the diagnostic system dominant among Western mental health professionals itself retains language showing a lesser threshold of tolerance for crossdressing in boys. Susan Langer and James Martin—both mental health professionals—point out that "current criteria maintain a lower diagnostic threshold for boys on preferences for wearing clothes associated with the opposite sex; girls have to insist on wearing such clothes, but boys need only to prefer them."[359]

We are returned again to the Golden Rule of Gender-differentiated Dress: "Males must appear masculine, or at least not feminine."

Developmental Process Related to Gender

Even with all the pressure to conformity provided by others and the culture at large, small children require some time to master the language of dress and other gender standards. In the first two years of life children themselves typically do not label gender—although they already have a lifetime experiencing it. Sometime between ages 2-3 most kids acquire a basic sense of gender identity, an awareness of self and others as 'boy' or 'girl.' Now gender labeling becomes a cognitive task in the child's process of socialization. From this time forward throughout childhood dress functions as a primary criterion used by children to differentiate boys from girls.[360]

While children generally are adept at knowing and adhering to gender labels and some gender standards by ages 3-4, the pace at which they develop this facility is individually varied. A longitudinal study reported in 1989 found that small children who early acquired gender labels were more likely to adopt some sex-typed behaviors. The rapidity with which they mastered this social task correlated to the nature of the emotional reaction by their caregivers. Early gender-labeling children had parents who gave more attention—positive and negative—when their children played with gender-typed toys. This wasn't a matter of instruction from parents to children about the toys, it was the emotional response of the parents, which the child picked up on. Their parent's affective weight on gender may signal to these children the importance of gender, making them more likely to apply efforts to master what seems so important to mom and dad.[361]

Gender stability—the grasp that gender identity and role should be stable over time—is reached generally by age 4, although the many children and adults with transgender characteristics indicates this concept requires some modification from the way it is generally presented as an expected and universal norm. Embracing this idea—that boys will grow up to be men and girls to be women—children realize the stakes are raised in gender role behavior, including dress. Most have not yet firmly grasped a connection between anatomical sex differences and social gender differences. Gender stability depends instead on highly visible characteristics like hair length and clothes.

In this sense, children's notion of gender remains fluid for a time. They may believe that what one wears can change a boy into a girl, or a girl into a boy. Thus it is crucial to dress and act like a boy if one wants to grow up to be a man. Gender constancy—the cultural notion that gender will not change because it rests upon biological sex—is a gradually developed social construction. By the time a child is 6-7 years old this idea is generally well-established. Kids subject each other to rigid gender standards and punish nonconformity. They also develop gender schemas—ways of thinking about information associated with gender, such as gender stereotypes and gender 'appropriate' behavior.[362]

Awareness of gender distinctions in dress doubtless precedes understanding of these differences. Development of awareness, endorsement, and expressed preferences along stereotyped expectations for dress may vary from individual to individual, but research suggests such matters are generally attained before a child starts school. A study reported in 1990 by developmental researchers Carol Lynn Martin and Jane Little found that a quarter of the 61 children (ages 3-5) tested attained a stereotyped knowledge about gendered clothing at age three, that more than half (54.5%) had done so at age four, and about three quarters (73.7%) at age five. As they put it, children need "only a rudimentary understanding of gender for preferences and knowledge to be influenced."[363] Given the pervasiveness of concern over sex and gender in our culture it might be said they are part of the very air children breathe.

Dress Preferences in Childhood

With the strong incentives to master gender, significantly coded and presented in dress, children very early form distinct notions about what they should wear and wish to wear. In 2004, *Textile Consumer* began a report on the children's apparel market by noting that as early as age three children express brand preferences. The report, based on data collected in 2003, shows that as children age from toddlers through childhood and adolescence, apparel offerings steadily increase. The report also documents similarities and differences between adults and children. For example, where adults rely far more heavily on tops (by a 3:1 ratio) to diversify their wardrobes, apparel offerings for children favor bottoms (47%) over tops (45%).[364] This may reflect, at least in part, that immature bodies are visibly sexually different below the waist and, lacking visible cues above the waist, dress accents bottoms. A skirt or dress is more important as a cue in childhood than it is in adulthood.

One thing that stays constant is the imbalance in clothing options by gender: girls at every age have more options than boys, just as women have more than men. Other gender distinctions emerge. While cotton plays a major role both in adult and children's clothing, it plays a relatively greater role for children. Further, a gender difference emerges between boys and girls: nearly three-quarters (73%) of boys' wear is 100% cotton, but this is true of only 56% of girls' apparel. The largest use of synthetic fibers in children's attire is found in girls' clothing like skirts, blouses, and dresses.[365] As we saw earlier (in answering Q. 2), fabric differences produce different physiological sensations, eliciting different psychological perceptions and reactions. It seems plausible to conclude these differences become part and parcel of our perceptions and expectations about gender.

The differences in what boys and girls are permitted to wear may prompt a variety of responses. Children of either gender may experience *dress envy*, the desire to have freedoms perceived granted to others but not to self. Girls raised always to wear unbifurcated garb—skirts and dresses—may envy the freedom of those who wear pants. On the other hand, some boys may envy the latitude most girls have to wear bifurcated or unbifurcated clothing. Moreover, as we have seen, feminine clothing embraces greater diversity of style, color, and feel. Any or all of these qualities may elicit some resentment from a boy.[366] But both boys and girls soon learn that there is too high a price to be paid for acting on such envy, so it is renounced, or at least set aside as much as possible.

A rather common response to gender differentiation is *experimentation*. Younger children, especially, enjoy more liberty to play at dressing in others' clothes. They may play at being grown-up and use items of either parent at different times. Or they may explore gender differences, only slowly being mastered, by crossdressing. Yet the risks in such activity are unequal between the genders; boys are at much more risk for censure and punishment. For example, David Plummer observes among the males he interviewed a careful retrospective distinguishing between their childhood 'dress up' play and 'crossdressing.' The same act of wearing feminine items might be involved, but the motivation—having fun, acting grownup—kept it from being transgressive (i.e., crossdressing) in their minds.[367]

The gender distinctions in dress learned in childhood are frequently relied on in a variety of social contexts throughout life. They often give rise to dress codes, informal or formal (see the answer to Q. 3). In childhood and adolescence these codes may be expressed in school uniforms that minimize many distinctions clothing might ordinarily provide while preserving the one distinction our culture insists upon—gender. Accordingly, girl's dress is always clearly distinguished from boy's dress in school uniforms. Apart from formal dress codes, informal ones among children also reinforce the gender divide. Children can be quite punitive in efforts to enforce gender conformity among peers.[368]

Gendered Dress & Adolescence

One of the features that may help distinguish adolescence from childhood is a change in orientation to dress. This change has several facets. Social scientists Jason Cox and Helga Dittmar point to one: "Although clothing tends to be gender-marked from birth, gender differences in the *activity* of shopping for

159

clothes and the *use* of clothes in terms of their peer-group relationships clearly emerge in adolescence."[369] They point out that girls begin shopping with their peers for clothes earlier than do boys, and rely more heavily on peers to evaluate clothing choices. They also observe that girls are more likely to swap clothes and, following Alison Lurie, suggest this activity can be interpreted as a mutual sharing of their identities.

While dress in recent decades has seemed to be much more important to adolescent girls than adolescent boys, the distance between the genders in the value placed on clothes and attention given to their selection appears to be narrowing. This perception has some empirical support and may reflect changes that have been taking shape over the last three decades. For example, some research shows a modest decline among girls in the percent using clothes to acquire prestige in high school between cohorts in 1978-1982 (40.6%) and in 1988-1989 (36.9%); these same cohorts for boys show an increase (15.9% to 22.2%).[370] Anecdotal reports suggest this trend has continued to the present.

With adolescent efforts to further separate and individuate—to carve out an independent identity—there often are uses of dress to experiment with gender or challenge gender norms. The contemporary interest many youth show in androgynous clothing, or dress that mixes what are seen as masculine and feminine elements, retains gender expression as central to the identity quest. Other youth cling to rigid separations of the genders, using dress to preserve the perceived status quo even if the manner in which they express gender in their clothing choices is different from their parents or from other adolescent social groups. Gender remains inescapable in clothing choices.

How is clothing related to gender in adults?

Research into the relationship between dress and gender in adults establishes it as important to both men and women. Generally, contemporary women are more involved with clothes and show a greater interest in fashion. Nevertheless, within each gender group a range of interest and involvement exists. Overall, evidence suggests men and women relate differently to their possessions, and it might be expected such differences extend to dress items.[371] Some research indicates men use dress more for self-expression while women use it more for social interrelatedness—though these differences may not be large enough to be significant.[372]

There may be important differences among men and women even when both are fashion conscious. Research reported in 1989 found that fashion conscious women tend to focus more on their public appearance and seem to be more publicly self-conscious than other women. Fashion conscious men, however, appear to be more focused on who they are as gendered beings. As the investigators phrase it, "That fashion conscious men are more gender conscious suggests that these men connect fashion with their self-identity and internalized maleness, their concept of what it means to be a man."[373]

Even where the genders converge in interest and attitude, gender lines still create differences. For example, both genders rank qualities like comfort as very important in making clothing choices. Yet the decision about what constitute comfortable clothes considers only apparel designated appropriate for the gender, despite differences in composition for many garments for men and women. Thus, even in apparently gender free or gender neutral matters, gender lines operate to constrict choices.

Nowhere in the adult world is that more apparent than in work wear. There dress codes—formal or informal—expect conformity to prevailing gender distinctions. Job environments commonly have policies, guidelines, or rules governing dress, even so-called 'casual dress.'[374] As seen elsewhere in discussing uniforms, manner of dress can be very important in identifying professional affiliations.[375] But even apart from uniforms as such, most work settings carry with them associated styles of dress. Moreover, clothing can be used to identify workplace values and characteristics so that workers in that environment dress in such a way as to not only identify their affiliation but also to influence their own self-perception.[376] This includes workers' self-perception of their feelings, sociability, and work competence.[377] The introduction of 'casual Fridays,' with their relaxed dress codes, also affords opportunities to relax the gender hierarchy.[378]

How is clothing related to gender in women?

But the gender hierarchy never disappears. As cultural studies scholar Jennifer Craik succinctly says, "Gender—especially femininity—is worn through clothes."[379] Though important to both sexes, the connection of dress to gender has been studied more with women, for whom clothes are often assumed to play a more important role.[380] Perhaps more accurately, dress may play a *different* role, rather than a more important one. They appear to rely on dress more for public and relational aspects than do men.[381] Evidence also suggests women attribute more symbolic dimensions to clothing than do men. Perhaps because of these things, and other factors such as greater choices in apparel offerings and higher expectations for wardrobe diversity, women are also more likely than men to experience dissatisfaction about their clothes (or lack thereof).[382]

At the end of the 1940s clothing researcher Mary Lou Lerch Rosencranz reported her study with a sizable and diverse group of women aimed at determining factors significant in women's interest in clothing. She found that in addition to various demographic factors (age, occupation, education, etc.), time, effort, money, and personal attention given were relevant in measuring such interest. Also, diversity of wardrobe emerged as a significant indicator of interest—a factor alongside the number and diversity of groups a woman belongs to.[383] All of these factors have been reaffirmed in subsequent studies.

Women may also attend more to dress for cues about others. One study that investigated this matter, reported in 2002, evaluated interview responses garnered from 39 adult women, ages 20-62. The research found that women form impressions about others based on appearance and dress, and believe others do the same about them. While some women acknowledged the influence of situations and specific clothing cues on the accuracy of their impressions, the majority of the women were confident that their impressions—which included assessments about personality, behavior, health, hygiene, biological traits and social roles—were reliable.[384]

Some research suggests that dress is more influential than either physical attractiveness or the kind of job being sought when a woman applies for work.[385] Yet women generally less endorse the notion that manipulating dress enhances occupational attributes.[386] Nevertheless, they often adopt a clothing strategy for other purposes, such as leveling the playing field. In a male-dominated work environment, women often turn to styles like those used by the men in similar positions or desired ones. For example, so-called 'power dressing' by women—black or navy blue suits with large shoulder pads, accompanied by high heels, and a severe hairstyle—creates a silhouette distinctly masculine.[387]

Other research also has indicated that the 'masculinity of clothing' selected by a woman may be related to a perception by others of her managerial characteristics; the more masculine the style, the more favorable the impression.[388] However, because dress also is expected to distinguish the genders, women must be careful to maintain an apparent feminine version of the masculine garb or risk censure.[389] Even feminists feel pressure to balance their values and philosophical orientation with workplace factors when choosing dress.[390]

In short, women must conform to the prevailing system in such a manner that they accomplish two ends: they remain reliably identifiable as feminine, but they simultaneously affiliate with and appropriate masculine status. The latter end is acceptable as long as it remains an evident fiction—they are, after all, still female—and as long as the assumed status does not seriously jeopardize male prerogatives. Current women's fashion for the workplace admirably accomplishes all this, thus leaving women the illusion of a shift in status that men grant them because it remains more apparent than real.

How is clothing related to gender in men?

Men also experience cultural expectations and pressures with regard to dress. But beyond the Golden Rule, is there any other reason for men to care about their clothing? Perhaps not. In 1949, Rosencranz reported earlier research involving 100 Harvard men and 59 Radcliffe women. That study found that men's interest in clothing had no relationship to their personal values.[391] Yet this conclusion may be misleading. While men may not be as accustomed as women to think of clothing reflecting personal ideals, they mostly manage to conform to the Golden Rule of dress for their gender. Moreover, longstanding social values also exert a siren-like call.

Where women are actively encouraged by fashion to shift presentation of their sexualized bodies from one erogenous zone to another,[392] thus needing grand diversity in apparel styles, men require relatively little, and quite modest garments to communicate what is important about them—status. Commensurate with their privileged position in the gender hierarchy, their dress must symbolically display the characteristics most attached to privilege: power and social standing.[393] Since these are variable, men are subject to the pressure of competition to outdo one another in power and social standing—in masculinity as it were—and to show the results in dress. To choose feminine fashion, as happens in crossdressing, is to choose clothing that accents eroticism and thus to become liable to a charge of sexual perversion as well as effeminacy.

Others judge personal qualities such as attractiveness, intelligence and popularity based on their apparel styles.[394] Like women, men need to show some concern about how they dress. In fact, it has been argued that male attitudes and concern over dress may be even more complicated than those held by women.[395] Unfortunately, the connection of men to dress as a way of expressing how they feel about their bodies is little studied. What research has been done, though, shows men also use clothing to fit cultural ideals.[396] Perhaps ironically, most of the attention men garner in connection to dress seems to come when they crossdress!

Interestingly, it may be the influence of transgender realities that lies behind today's reawakening of masculine fashion. Although men in the United States typically express a reluctance to shop for clothes or to make fashion statements in what they wear—both activities being viewed as feminine—there are signs that actual behavior tells another story. Perhaps more than at any other time in a century men are showing interest in fashion and taking a more active role in clothes purchases.[397] The so-called 'metrosexual' phenomenon, rooted in transgender reality, has helped loosen some of the restrictiveness of masculine fashion, though not without controversy and challenge. Resistance to metrosexualism focuses on its perceived threat to the Golden Rule by suggesting that it tends unacceptably toward feminine elements.

In the public arena what matters about masculine dress becomes clearest. In the workplace, even as women are granted greater freedom in dress, men sometimes find a strong expectation remains that they 'dress up' rather than 'dress down.' The terminology itself has almost a Freudian tone—men dressing in more casual fashion styles may be perceived as dressing 'down' to the feminine gender. Judith Rasband, writing for the Conselle Institute of Image management, comments:

> This whole trend toward casual dress or dressing down works to expose the male body. By taking off the tie—that longstanding symbol of male corporate power—unbuttoning the shirt, and opening the collar, men expose their neck and throat. Increased exposure more

nearly matches feminine rather than masculine stereotypes in our culture.[398]

Clearly, men no less than women confront significant cultural pressures, often
expressed in rules either formal or informal.

How is underwear related to gender?

To this point our discussion of the relation of dress to gender has implicitly
assumed a focus on outerwear. After all, if clothing is to be a principal signifier
of gender, it needs to be visible to others to be effective. So our attention has
been on outerwear in the expressive subsystem described in answering Q. 1. But
we must not leave out another important aspect of dress: underwear.

It may not be immediately apparent how underwear is related to gender.
Unlike outerwear, underwear typically remains unseen by the general public. In
fact, those who appear in public dressed only in their underwear risk arrest; they
are generally seen as disrupting public order. This situation would *prima facie* appear to render underwear a very poor signifier of gender.

Gender Differentiation in Underwear

Yet underwear is routinely gender-differentiated: men wear boxers or briefs,
women wear panties; women wear bras, men don't. Later (in answering Q. 9)
we will examine briefly the history of underwear and document some of the
relevant changes such clothing has undergone. But here our interest is in understanding why we bother to gender differentiate clothing that will more often
than not remain invisible to others. Since the notion we have been relying on is
that dress serves as a highly visible public expression of gender, we must solve
the riddle of why largely invisible dress nevertheless would become at least as
highly gender-differentiated as outerwear. To accomplish this we must revisit
some ideas.

Our Intimate Connection with Underwear

Earlier, the notion that clothing acts like a 'second skin' was introduced.
Underwear especially fits this metaphor because it resides closest to the skin.
We saw that this 'skin' functions as part of our boundary system even as it retains an independent reality. These two aspects intersect and render possible
deeply personal experiences of clothing. It is no exaggeration to regard underwear as the most personal of clothing; these are the garments we have the most
intimate association with.

There is more than one reason for this intimate connection. First, a basic
utilitarian function of underwear is to protect our natural skin from our other
clothes—and simultaneously protect those clothes from soiling produced by
our own bodies. As a 'second skin' the first boundary formed is between ourselves and the other clothes we wear—a reality that creates not only physical

distancing, but some psychological distancing as well. No such distance intervenes with underwear; as a popular advertisement proclaimed about its apparel, nothing comes between us and our under garments.

Just as we take care of our natural skin through washing it, applying lotions, and so forth in order to be healthy and comfortable, so we do with our underwear. Over time the emphasis in making and marketing underwear has changed from utilitarian and health reasons to comfort and pleasure. In fact, as comfort increases through the pure sensuousness of fabric and fit, so does the intrinsic potential to eroticize the garment by symbolic substitution for the body regions the apparel resides by. This can lead in extreme cases to fetishism (see the answer to Q. 88), but typically only elicits a felt connection between the pleasure of the garment and the pleasure felt from stimulation of the body parts beneath the garment by whatever means.

Our first reason for our intimate connection to underwear thus leads to a second. In a culture where so much of the construction of identity revolves around sex and gender, these garments cover the body's erogenous zones. We forge early in life a learned association between these clothes and our selves as sexual and gendered beings. This learned association is reinforced by the pleasures derived from comfortable, appealing underwear, the fantasy of such garments being part of a sexual encounter, and the sexual stirrings thus aroused. Precisely because gender has been predicated solely on sex, the clothing most associated with sex must also be the garb most connected to gender.

Culture describes gender in clothing, right down to the names for various apparel items. This is particularly evident in women's lingerie and underwear, where we find items like 'teddies' and 'babydoll' lingerie, and 'boyshort' panties. Such names indirectly highlight two related matters. First, womenswear, including underwear, is derived from masculine fashion (see the answer to Q. 9). Second, masculine ideals and ideas still shape conceptions of femininity, ranging feminine dress—and women—along an androcentric continuum from 'most like men' to 'most unlike men.'

The gendered nature of undergarments proves ideal for crossdressers. It means that underwear associated with a gender different from that assigned to them can be worn secretly while a connection to the desired gender is attained. This so-called 'partial crossdressing' may be for some complete crossdressing if it succeeds in creating the gender experience sought. Of course, all too often it does not fully succeed because the outerwear creates gender dissonance. Thus the normal progression in crossdressing is from underwear only to complete crossdressing.

Unfortunately, another hazard awaits the crossdresser. Because gender is viewed as founded on sex, and sexual anatomy is seen as meant for sexual activity, any crossdressing is construed as sexual in nature. The gender experience of the crossdresser is displaced by the sexual construal of the observer, leading to the generally erroneous judgment that crossdressing is a perversion intending to substitute the pleasure of clothes for the pleasure of another person. While gender trumps sex for the crossdresser, noncrossdressers generally assume that gender has nothing to do with it—all the crossdresser is out for is a guilty sexual pleasure.

That notion indirectly leads us to a third reason for the intimate nature of our connection to underwear. Because of our values with respect to sexuality, these garments also become signifiers of modesty, eroticism, and guilt. They remind us of our stance with respect to such values, or move us toward behaviors suited to our values.[399] By virtue of association with values—things that matter to us and hold meaning for us—clothing, and especially underwear, becomes subject to personal and societal taboos. The emotional stakes are thereby raised. This means we become more conscientious about how these clothes, above all others, will be regarded by others.

This step leads us to a final reason for intimacy with underwear: unlike our outerwear, open to inspection by all we encounter, our underwear is meant to be selectively revealed. Those we show our underwear to are typically those we have the most intimate relationships with.[400] Of course that often means sexual relationships, but we need not be so narrow. Since underwear covers those parts of the body most associated with sex, and sex is central to the construction of identity, nudity becomes the greatest risk of self-disclosure. When we remove our underwear we remove a boundary protecting our self and thus make that self vulnerable. Most of us are more likely to share our deepest feelings before we are to share the sight of our naked body.

We treasure underwear as both the bastion protecting our modesty and the gate to erotic pleasures. We rely on what we wear to protect us; we depend on it to reveal us. Underwear is revelation—it hides and it discloses, and in both it is the self revealed. If we are casual in our choice of the underwear we put on, it is only because we reckon the odds someone else will see it as slender. As soon as we calculate the likelihood of another seeing our underwear, our regard for what we wear rises. If we expect that the most intimate of encounters will occur, we give most special attention to our underwear—or do our best to get it hidden aside as quickly as possible! Either way our action signifies some awareness that these garments truly matter.

Given such factors it would be surprising if we did not feel differently toward our underwear than we do our outerwear.

Gender Trumps Sex

In what we have been discussing the chain linking clothes to gender to sex has been evident. Despite the primacy our culture awards sex over gender, clothing has the power to reverse the hierarchy. Through clothes gender can triumph, at least temporarily, over sex. Our intimate connection with clothing, especially with undergarments, makes possible an experience of gender more immediate and substantial than anything happening in the genitals.

166

For example, a transgendered male can choose to wear a panty with a gaff to hide his genitals and create a simulation of female sex anatomy. The biology of sex stays the same; only the appearance of bodily sex changes—yet this appearance constitutes a reality all its own. In fact, this reality suffices psychologically for many transgendered males. The superficial appearance of being female trumps the biological reality, perhaps in a manner similar to the way any of us sees what we want to see when we look at the imperfect forms of those we love.

The Eroticism of Underwear

While gender through clothing can trump sex, often enough sexuality co-opts gender. Twin factors greatly facilitate the eroticism of undergarments. First, the cultural decision that gender is completely dependent on sex, which defines it, binds gender implicitly to sexuality. Second, gender differentiation in clothing means that symbolization of gender in terms of sexuality becomes possible in dress. Being a woman, for example, means being seen a certain way as a sexual being and her clothing, particularly her undergarments, can be eroticized so that her gendered self is reduced to a sexual self.

Since sexual behavior in Western culture has come to be regarded as hierarchical and heterosexual in character, where masculine men actively pursue passive feminine females, a differentiation in roles elicits a differentiation in dress goals. For males, safeguarding masculine privilege generates the 'Golden Rule' that men must at all costs not appear feminine; if women are viewed as wantonly sexual beings (or objects), then men's own sexuality must be either downplayed or depicted in strikingly different ways. The latter course results in masculine dress fashions like the codpiece, which emphasize virility through attention to the genitals. Less crudely but no less effectively the modern business suit symbolizes virility by signifying competence, success, and status. The wearer is publicly declared as someone with resources—the very thing available females are likely to desire. At the same time, while demonstrating virility such dress presents a restrained and orderly sexuality. Unlike the wildness of women, men are portrayed as procreative producers for whom all good things must come as an order of course. Men can possess women because they first have possessed their own virile sexuality.

In this scenario, men's underwear bears no more need to be ostentatiously erotic than does masculine outerwear. Yet, in fact, men's underwear has been eroticized. A 2004 article in *The New York Times* observes that the trend in men's underwear that first gained notoriety in the 1980s with provocative Calvin Klein ads had reached a point in the early 21st century where "there are underwear boxes out there that make a man's crotch look as monumental as an Ansel Adams picture of El Capitan."[401] Since the 1930s these garments have undergone transformation in representation from utilitarian items to fashion ones. In style and color range alike men's underwear increasingly finds itself part of an erotic fashion context—masculine lingerie. Ethnologist Bo Lönnqvist is surely right in situating this development in a matrix of changes in consumer culture, gender roles, and body ideals.[402]

Perhaps principal contributors to this development have been the effect of diminished distance in the personality characteristics associated with masculinity and femininity, and the relatively greater gender equality in society. Especially with the greater admission of women into the workforce a change in sexual economy[403] has rendered desirable new strategies for men in seeking mating opportunities. Since women in general no longer need depend principally on men for access to resources, men must increase their value in the sexual economy by other means. One possibility is to mimic the strategy associated with women: accent the desirability of the body.

Western culture, at least in recent centuries, has placed the fashion burden of erotic clothing principally on women. The pairing, dubbed 'fashion and passion' by Feona Attwood, reflects in her view an increasingly sexualized culture where women are more and more targeted as sexual consumers.[404] To females are especially offered the diversity of styles and colors meant to fetch attention and signal sexual interest. Changing feminine fashions over the centuries have mirrored what societies regard at the time as principal erogenous zones. Much more than in masculine clothing, feminine apparel displays variety and is designed for erotic appeal. This is even more the case for undergarments than for outerwear.

In women's garments the bra and panty are two basic lingerie items. The former, according to Jane Ferrell-Beck and Colleen Gau, began to be associated with the erotic appeal of movie stars in the 1930s, but became more completely eroticized during the 1950s. They write, "The renewed emphasis on feminine sexuality produced brassiere designs to harmonize with body-revealing décolleté styles: plunging necklines, bare midriffs, halters, backless models, and strapless dresses."[405] The Wonder-bra, invented by Canadian designer Louise Poirier in the mid-1960s, became a cultural icon in the U.S. only in the 1990s. A marvel of technology, the Wonder-bra touted not only its comfort, but its ability to cast the appearance of a perfect breast—at least as socially construed.[406] Millions of women gained new hope for creating the kind of silhouette that passes as the erotic ideal in contemporary times.

The panty, like the bra, underwent a significant change in the 1930s by becoming a part of the cultural mainstream through wider availability and attention by retailers. Panty styles are but a microcosm of the diversity typical for women's clothes—and personalities.[407] There are bikini panties, boyshorts, briefs, culottes, g-strings, hipsters, low rise, tangas, thongs, and more. What this diversity means remains debated.

Once the motivation urged on women to wear panties was health and modesty. This gradually gave way to an emphasis on comfort and style. Now the preoccupation is with erotic appeal, even at the cost of comfort. The end result is a situation in which women are sharply at odds with one another as to whether what is available represents freedom for individuality or enchainment to a cultural one-size-fits-all view of gender as a superficial mask for a sexual body.

Just as bras and panties come in a nearly bewildering range of alternatives, so do other kinds of lingerie. There are camisoles, chemises, corsets, negligees, nighties, peignoirs, slips, and teddies—just to name a few. All these come in a variety of colors, fabrics and sizes. Since the 1970s-1980s the explosion of lingerie has expanded the erotic imagination while exerting pressure on women to present themselves not merely as sexually alluring, but erotically varied as well. Many women ask if lingerie is really made for what women want, or for what men desire—but even those asking often acquiesce if what they want is men.

Much of today's lingerie for women is so calculatedly erotic that it has sometimes been called 'porno chic'—and raises ethical issues about the role of the erotic in modern retailing.[408] When popular figures like Madonna began to wear underwear as outerwear a whole new light was shed on how such apparel can be construed. Contemporary lingerie does more than present an equation of 'feminine = erotic.' It constructs a particular notion of a sexual woman. For example, Nancy Workman argues that the revival of the Victorian corset by Victoria's Secret reinforces traditional roles as construed through the vision of a man rather than any group of women. That vision is of a woman who must be constrained and shaped to be desirable. [409]

Where fashion will head next is anyone's guess. But the eroticism of masculine and feminine underwear today reflects a cultural truth: a preoccupation with sexuality so pronounced that we appear unable to interpret gender as much more than that. We have made our most intimate garments a sexual skin. To an extent—greater for some, less for others—we have succumbed to seeing our gendered selves as principally sexual selves. Regardless of how firmly or loosely we may individually construe the tie between the sex of the body and our experience of gender, this cultural shift to merge them at the focal point of the erotic constitutes for us all a dangerous narrowing of identity, both personal and social. In a society like our own, where sexual aggression and violence run rampant, the trend to reduce the self to a sensual object is as foolhardy as it is unwarranted by the facts.

Fortunately, though clothing may be appropriated to serve problematic interests, its robust nature preserves hope. The sheer diversity of clothing available, the restless pressure of fashion, and the multiple demands we place on dress all predict that change will occur. The great attention paid these days to transgender realities also offers hope for a welcome antidote to the poison of too rigid and confining a conception of gender. The promise of crossdressing is that what it offers as alternative ways to see gender, and the relation of dress to gender, may yet free us from the prisons we seem so often bent on building about ourselves.

Q. 7

How is crossdressing related to gender and dress?

The Short Answer: In this answer our goal is an integrated comprehension of crossdressing in light of what we have learned about dress, gender, and sex. We have seen how complicated and controversial each of these subjects can be, and their intersection is no different. Crossdressing stands at a nexus of three constant fundamental and powerful forces of human experience and expression. It provides unique and significant ways of experiencing and expressing the self. Because it depends on gender differentiation in dress, inevitably some of that experience and expression becomes connected to and construed as an experience and expression of gender. For all of us the transgender reality in crossdressing at least potentially calls into question what we think we know about gender, especially its presumed reliance on sex. One result can be broadening our view of gender so as to more realistically perceive the place crossdressers occupy. But in order to fully see the relation of crossdressing to gender we must also see its relation to dress. In that respect, the way in which clothing presents and shapes gender is crucial. So, too, is the power of clothing to manipulate body shape. Dress both subverts and reinforces the connection between gender and sex. In crossdressing an individual can present a gender different than the one assigned the person and also suggest that the actual body is of the sex the clothes present. Even though the original or primary motivation for crossdressing may be unrelated to gender, the association of dress with gender makes transference of gender associations inevitable. Unavoidably, then, crossdressing assumes as its primary referent gender rather than dress, even though the nature, function, and qualities of dress continue to inform the phenomenon and constitute its first foundational context.

The Longer Answer: Perhaps it seems so much attention to clothing, sex, and gender, while each is interesting in its own right, is misplaced with regard to an effort to understanding crossdressing. Just how important is the *dress* in crossdressing? By now the answer as developed in previous questions should be obvious: dress is the first, foundational context for crossdressing. To state the obvious: without dress there is no crossdressing.

We have seen how clothes in general are central to a rich experiencing and expressive system. Consistent with what we have learned we can confidently say that dress is instrumental in crossdressing to experiencing the self and expressing both individuality and affiliations, such as a chosen association with a gender different than the one assigned at birth. Clothes are highly tactile and visual, lending themselves readily to manipulations of perception. Because they also possess gendered distinctions, clothes serve as powerful symbols embedded in physical realities. And that is where their power resides—the physical representation of ideals.

Still, while *dressing* is central to crossdressing, so is the notion that something occurs that is different from mere dressing. In common parlance 'crossdressing' has come to represent *sui generis* dress transgression. At the same time, the term has been appropriated by scholars to refer to other acts of gender crossing, such as authors who write with the voice of a member of another gender. This situation requires we take a moment to reexamine this word.

Does crossdressing just refer to clothes?

Logically, we can use the term 'crossdressing' to refer to any use of dress to cross any recognized line drawn by dress expectation or convention. As we indicated above, the word has been used metaphorically of someone (e.g., an author) 'dressing' in a gender different from the gender assigned to the person's sex. In addition to such metaphoric forms of crossdressing there are ways to literally crossdress besides those involving gender. We can speak, for example, of crossdressing as the violation of lines of social status—exactly the sort of 'crossdressing' of concern in the sumptuary laws, where those of lower class dress like members of the upper class. Or we could speak of cultural crossdressing when a member of one culture adopts the dress of another, as when a European in Japan dons the *kimono*. We could use the term of crossing racial lines, to whatever extent dress is made to identify one race apart from others. We might even extend the term to cover matters like sexual orientation as when a heterosexual male adopts items of dress viewed by others as 'gay.'

Yet, we don't often use the term 'crossdressing' for any of these matters or others we might imagine. Joanna Brewis and colleagues rightly observe how it seems less problematic for a black person to dress like a white, or a homosexual like a heterosexual, than for a man to dress like a woman.[410] The boundary drawn through dress for gender stands alone in its power to refer crossdressing to itself. By now it should be clear why this is so: the preeminent way gender shows itself is through dress. Neither race nor sexual orientation comparably rely on dress manifestation for recognition.

Thus far we have examined many aspects of dress in relation to the complex experiencing and expressing system constructed around it. As we have examined dress in this regard we have presented both a broad perspective on the matters at hand and offered some application especially to crossdressing. In a similar manner we have considered—or perhaps more accurately, reconsidered—sex and gender. We have been especially concerned throughout with the relation between dress and gender. Now, at the risk of some repetition, we will profit from putting the disparate elements together in an integrated answer to an important query:

How can crossdressing use dress for gender purposes?

Just as it is a given that without dress there can be no cross*dressing*, so we should understand that without gender differentiation there is no *cross*dressing. And because gender pairs with sex, crossdressing also must be discussed in reference to it. Further, since sex and gender differences give rise to human sexuality, crossdressing inevitably must be considered in that regard, too. In bits and pieces we have looked at multiple aspects of each of these things separately in previous answers. Now we must attempt to pull things together.

How might we sort out these various alternatives? Let us briefly return to a suggestion made in answering the previous question. There we found the following broad patterns for how clothing can express gender:

- ❑ *Be gender*—the use of dress to enact a gender; in its most common use this is dressing congruent to one's assigned gender.
- ❑ *Borrow gender*—the use of dress to occupy another gender temporarily.
- ❑ *Blend gender*—the use of dress to express more than one gender simultaneously in a manner such that the genders expressed are distinct but side-by-side (using mixed gender elements of dress), or the genders are melded androgynously (androgynous dress styles).
- ❑ *Blur gender*—the use of dress to make gender uncertain.
- ❑ *Bend gender*—the use of dress to change or challenge the perception of gender.

Crossdressing can fit into any of the patterns. Nor are the lines so clearly drawn that we can always expect an individual to always crossdress in the same way and for the same reason. This should be apparent in the following elaborations on each of these patterns.

Be Gender

Transgendered people, no less than other folk, may dress to enact gender. It just isn't the gender they were assigned. Transsexuals dress to *be* the gender signified, despite the fact it is a gender different than the one assigned at birth. The transsexual, both pre- and postoperative, aims at congruence with experienced gender identity and dresses to accomplish that goal. A transsexual female enacts a masculine gendered identity; 'he' becomes a man. A transsexual male enacts a feminine gendered identity; 'she' becomes a woman. The goal and the process

173

are no different from that pursued by nontransgender people. Only the starting point is different.

However, to the extent a culture believes we *are* a gender because of our biological sex, to that extent a transsexual will be viewed as transgressive. Such a cultural posture posits that a biological female cannot be a psychological male, or that in being a psychological male it is the mind that is disordered and not the body. Sex trumps gender. Thus despite the goal and process being the same as for others, the transsexual may be judged incapable of being the gender they say they persistently experience. The cultural din of protest may drown out the individual's voice.

Borrow Gender

Where transsexuals intend to be the gender of their dress, their experience of this gender is consistent no matter how they are dressed. The situation of many transgendered people is somewhat different. They may aim to *be* the gender they dress as, but only temporarily—when they are crossdressed. Or, they may desire in crossdressing to use the juxtaposition of one sex with another gender to create a third possibility—a gender neither masculine nor feminine.[411] Transgender people take such borrowing seriously. For them borrowing gender may be experienced both as natural and highly meaningful.

Transvestites borrow another gender, with greater or lesser identification with it.[412] Some transvestites borrow another gender for transient relief from their assigned gender; through clothes they put on and take off gender with relative psychological ease. Others find the matter more complicated. For them the gender carries its own persona—they have a masculine name and persona; they have a feminine name and persona. Some borrow the gender frequently and more intentionally aim to fully realize it, while for others it remains more superficial and intermittent. The varieties of gender experience in borrowing gender are extensive.

Blend Gender

Transgender people sometimes dress so as to blend gender. They may accomplish this by carefully mixing feminine and masculine elements to effect androgyny, which does not feel as false as presenting in their assigned gender, or by partial crossdressing. Androgyny in dress may especially suit those transgender persons who feel they fit between the gender poles and have weak connections with both femininity and masculinity. Transgender people who more strongly express one or another gender are less likely to find androgynous dress satisfactory.

Though blending gender in dress represents a compromise behavior, it often proves a sensible compromise. Anthropologist Jason Cromwell remarks, "Although passing as nontransgendered is almost always a reflection of identity, it is also safer than presenting as gender-ambiguous or androgynous."[413] Accordingly, most transgendered people play it safe. At least in their outerwear they conform to gender expectations in dress.

Partial crossdressing so as to blend gender is always a matter of wearing outerwear congruent to the assigned gender and underwear consistent with the desired gender. Since people judge us by what they see, the outerwear gains a measure of approval. Since we have the most intimate experience with our underwear the comfort of knowing that we are dressed in the underwear *we* want offers a measure of relief from having to wear outerwear expected of us. For some transgender people this compromise works; for others there remains an uncomfortable degree of dissonance because of the mixing of two genders in dress.

Blur Gender

Some transgender people dress so that gender is virtually impossible to infer. Once more this may be seen as a kind of compromise. Its advantage is that dissonance may be lessened or eliminated by creating a dress effect where neither gender is favored, but being gendered is obvious. Such efforts may be marked by favoring clothing that is very close to the gender line on both sides, or perhaps by choosing clothes associated with the opposite sex but either mixing them with articles from a different gender or using them in such a way that their original connection to a specific gender is lost. In any event, the effect is not androgyny—a clear alternative to masculinity and femininity—but calculated confusion. The goal in blurring gender is to appear gendered, but not clearly masculine or feminine.

Bend Gender

Drag queens, crossdressing entertainers, and people dressed in costumes may all bend gender—often in an outrageous fashion—to create a conflict in the eye of the beholder between the gender expressed by the clothes and the apparent gender of the wearer. But it is drag that takes pride of place as a way to dress so as to bend gender.

Drag preeminently represents the use of dress to bend gender. There is more than borrowing gender at work. When gender is borrowed, either the sex of the body is temporarily disavowed (or at least disconnected), or it is the sex that is given preeminence. When a reveler at a party appears crossdressed and makes that fact known the point is to say, 'I'm really my sex, not the gender I'm playing.'[414] When a transvestite borrows a gender the sex of the body is set at a remove, as though it does not exist, or belongs to another, or is irrelevant.

In gender bending the sex of the body matters precisely because dress is being used to say, 'I am my sex, but it's in second place to my gender.' Drag challenges the preeminence of sex. But when gender is put in first place, it is presented as performance. Its constructed nature is highlighted—often very elaborately. A drag beauty contest, for example, wonderfully tweaks all our conventional ideas about beauty, sex, and gender. Its success depends precisely on its ability to show beautiful male women or handsome female men. By bending gender the presupposed nature of the links joining sex and gender are proved highly suspect.

No less than in any other dress behavior, crossdressing—regardless of the path chosen for gender expression—casts a silhouette. The *Gestalt* thus formed is a perceptual field embracing the crossdresser's personal experience and an expression susceptible to interpretation by others. The silhouette is foreground to a rich background, one so varied and complex that the possibilities are both rich and dangerous.

What is the effect of the silhouette in crossdressing?

We saw in answering Q. 6 that the silhouette drafts an overall form that typically is associated with a particular gender that in turn relies on a cultural expectation of how that gender represents a sexed body. Dress can thus unite gender and sex in the silhouette. This fact opens new possibilities, and hazards, for a crossdresser.

In ages where manipulation of the sexual body through hormones or surgery was not available dress was even more critical to changing sex. If a person wanted not merely to express a gender different from their birth assignment, but also a different sex, dress was easily the chief means by which to do that. Changing hair length, and shaving, were accompaniments to the chief feature: gendered clothing chosen to create the desired silhouette of the society's view of a male or female body. Despite the availability of other means for changing the sexed body, the dress silhouette remains a potent force toward that end.

Although the silhouette presumably represents body sex, the actual body of the dressed person is often not what generates the silhouette. Instead it may be the apparel itself, or undergarments.[415] Male crossdressers know that a female bust line can be simulated with the artful use of a bra and inserts. The affect on the silhouette shifts the body representation away from male and toward female.

The silhouette cast by crossdressing potentially makes possible passing as a member of a different sex. While this is highly desirable for some transgender people, it can be hazardous for all who attempt it. In cultures where the gender divide helps protect a separation of the sexes, crossing the former successfully bridges the latter, too. But regardless of whether we believe gender can be altered through dress, sex clearly cannot. If the apparent sex is revealed as an illusion, disillusionment followed by unpleasant, punitive consequences is highly likely to follow. People do not like being fooled about such matters.

On the other hand, *not* passing can be equally dangerous. The silhouette that fails to create an apparent match between gender and sex raises suspicion at the very least. If observers conclude that a masquerade is being intended for deception in order to pass as a different sex, the general reflex is not to ask why but to respond negatively. Even if observers recognize that no effort is being made to pass, the dissonance created by the mismatch between sex and gender (as expected in the culture) will be felt as uncomfortable and possibly motivate unkind responses.

The crossdressing silhouette, then, matters. Given the potential for undesirable repercussions, why would anyone risk creating a crossdressed silhouette? The answer resides in what was just said: the silhouette *matters*.

The silhouette has power in expression *and* for experience. Various commentators on crossdressing have remarked that crossdressers may seem narcissistic in their use of mirrors when crossdressed. Yet if we accept that one goal of crossdressing for some is the experience of a differently sexed body then the gazing at a silhouette does not seem odd. Coupled with the feel of the clothing, which affects posture and movement in ways meant to identify a certain sexed body, the sight of the silhouette offers an important experience. Thus, for example, a crossdressed male who wears a bra relies on it both for the feel of it (which includes its affect on posture and movement), and for the contribution it makes to the look of the silhouette. Both expression and experience are at play.

The silhouette matters as well to those not trying to match a sex type. Transgender people who experience themselves as between masculinity and femininity may crossdress in such a manner as to create an androgynous silhouette. For example, a male may put on a blouse and skirt but forego a bra and so retain a male-appearing chest. The silhouette thus formed might be jarring to an observer, but satisfying to the crossdresser.[416]

Regardless of whether a transgender person seeks to use dress to be, borrow, blend, blur, or bend gender, the silhouette constitutes an important aspect. Moreover, together with the other matters we have discussed, this aspect reminds us how complex the experiencing and expressive system revolving around dress truly is. By seeing crossdressing in this context we may be able to escape erroneous evaluations. The versatility of crossdressing with reference to gender experience and expression disputes the simplistic notion of crossdressers as deviants who arbitrarily and maliciously break gender boundaries by bouncing back-and-forth between masculine and feminine poles. Melanie Yarborough and Lucy Silvay write that, "crossdressing does not mean just going back and forth between two genders. It means opening oneself up to new possibilities, being able to explore the gender continuum and find a unique space in it."[417] Of course, their remark presupposes our willingness to admit that gender is a continuum filled with potential alternatives to the stereotypes found at the extreme ends (see the answer to Q. 5).

Unfortunately, with the present prevailing system of rigid views about sex and gender, crossdressing commonly is viewed somewhere along a different continuum. It is seen on a continuum of dysfunction, with violations judged anywhere from being a benign aberration at best to a serious disturbance at worst. By blurring lines the present cultural system depends on, crossdressing challenges the system itself. If we cannot rely on expected cues like dress to make reliable judgments about gender in a framework where gender options are restricted to two exclusive alternatives, then we are in a situation where social order might well be thought threatened.

Not surprisingly, that is exactly what often happens.

What is the apparent threat posed by crossdressing?

Protecting the Gender Hierarchy

To understand the apparent threat posed by crossdressing we must retreat a moment to the foundational logic of gendered dress: males must appear masculine, or at least not feminine. In a society where access to power is largely predicated on gender status, and gender status is hierarchically arranged so as to privilege masculinity, any threat to the clarity of masculine maleness will provoke anxiety. The dread is that loss of distinct masculine maleness will endanger the very fabric of culture, calling into question personal and social identities. Women's studies scholar Jody Norton believes the threat of loss of the symbolic value of masculinity elicits "unprocessed anxiety, and unexamined, or rationalized antipathy"—the soil in which both gynephobia (fear of femininity) and transphobia (fear of transgendered realities) flourish. With regard to the latter, she writes:

> According to the hysterical logic of transphobia, insofar as transgendered persons do not accommodate themselves to a heterocentric ideology of gender that interprets reproductive functions as the naturalized basis of differential power relations, they must be made to do so. They must, that is, be institutionally and discursively disciplined, since masculinity is not a matter of anatomy but of meaning.[418]

This is a contextualized comprehension of what transgendered people face. A transgendered person whose body appears male and who has been assigned gender status as masculine poses a symbolic (*not* actual) threat. The anxiety thus aroused may—and often does—elicit antipathy, carried out in milder or more severe coercive efforts to change the individual or, failing that, punish the person. Dress operates in this context both by signaling conformity or transgression, and by presenting a tool for coercion—forcing conformity or transgression to enforce gender norms.

Another factor that perhaps exercises a modest influence on reactions to male crossdressing may be the different ways men and women relate to clothing (see the answer to Q. 6). A variety of studies have substantiated that women are more tolerant than are men when it comes to transgender realities (see the answer to Q. 37). In addition to the fact that men are more threatened by the symbolic meaning attached to transgender, they may depend more on clothes for gendered self-expression than do women.[419] In this light, crossdressing is especially worrisome because it stands as a statement of gendered self-expression directly in violation of the 'Golden Rule'—males must appear masculine, or at least *not feminine*. Just as the construction of masculinity in our culture depends in part on homophobia, it may depend also on transphobia; both homosexuality and crossdressing challenge stereotyped notions of masculinity and, by inference, maleness.[420]

Crossdressing, then, depends on two things: first, clear and hierarchical gender boundaries socially enforced and second, the utilization of dress as a principal mechanism for maintaining, or challenging, those boundaries. *Crossdressing* cannot exist unless there is a boundary to cross. But that means any and all acts of dress that create the appearance of a mismatch between assigned gender, based on sex, and the apparent gender, based on clothing, are apt to be judged as transgressive. Because only two genders are permitted, and these are predicated on apparent biological sex, dressing to express anything other than masculinity by a male or femininity by a female is to some degree transgressive.

Crossdressing as Challenge and as Reinforcement to the Status Quo

As the above indicates, there is more than one way that crossdressing and gender in this context can interact. Crossdressing can both challenge the status quo and be used to reinforce it. The theater (see the answer to Q. 44) exemplifies how crossdressing characters can be used as a double-edged sword, one that cuts against the artifice of socially constructed gender and at the same time wounds those who challenge the construction. In extreme instances, crossdressing is even used at times as a calculated tool to reinforce gender conformity.

The practice of 'petticoat punishment,' although less visible than in former times, persists as a mechanism to enforce conformity to gender dress rules by purposely violating them. In the practice a boy, or less commonly a girl (rarely an adult), is made to crossdress as a punishment for misbehavior, typically gender-related misconduct. The key is that the crossdressing is *forced* and *undesired* so that the result is shame and humiliation. The intended purpose is to restrain exaggerated (e.g., boys being too rambunctious) or inappropriate (e.g., boys being too aggressive) behavior. Anecdotal reports have indicated petticoat punishment in the background of some adult crossdressers,[421] suggesting that such practices either failed or may actually have been intended for a different purpose than the ostensible one. Although the actual practice today is rare, it remains a popular form of literature and art for many people.[422]

The premise of petticoat punishment is that all crossdressing is shameful. Of course, the reality is that not all crossdressing is automatically viewed as threatening even by noncrossdressers. Some socially tolerated, if not actually approved crossdressing has as its principal or even sole aim being transgressive. Our culture's gender dualism may desire to keep masculine males on top, and so structures dress rules to maintain this social order, but it recognizes at least implicitly that the resulting pressures must be allowed to vent. Accordingly, the existing cultural paradigm fashions outlets to offer a relative safety valve for gender pressure created by rigid hierarchical dualism by sanctioning various minor transgressions. Drag presentations, crossdressing performers, and folk at Carnival may all crossdress *because* it is a transgressive act.

Clearly a person does not have to be transgendered either in identity or body sex in order to enact a transgendered reality. Many masculine males and many feminine females occasionally crossdress. It might be in connection with a social occasion, such as a festival or costume party, but the point of the act is that it is transgressive. This transgression is apparent rather than substantial; while real, it does not matter. The context and the social rules governing the behavior make it okay to crossdress for Halloween or a masquerade ball. In so doing everyone is reassured that the gender boundaries are more permeable than everyday reality presents.

How can a crossdresser dress?

The situation we've examined puts transgendered people in a bind. Their aim is rarely to be socially transgressive but rather self-expressive. They face the dilemma of how, in this limited cultural gender scheme, to appear to themselves and others. Many among us can relate to the words penned by Kate Bornstein:

> I know I'm not a man—about that much I am very clear, and I've come to the conclusion that I'm probably not a woman either, at least according to a lot of people's rules on this sort of thing. The trouble is, we're living in a world that insists we be one or the other—a world that doesn't bother to tell us exactly what one or the other *is*.[423]

How do you dress for a situation like that?

Imperfect Choices

Some crossdressers opt to try to pass as the sex of the gender their clothing is presenting. In other words, they dress and behave in a manner meant to convey that their gender and sex match according to cultural expectations. If, for instance, they appear to be female, then they are female—at least in the way they desire to be perceived and responded to. In this manner the dilemma posed by obvious crossdressing, where observers perceive a mismatch between gender and sex, is avoided. Especially for preoperative transsexuals this solution is eminently sensible as it matches a stable gender experience and identity.

Of course not all transgendered people find this solution appealing. Some desire to express a gender different from the one assigned them at birth, which was based on their apparent sexual anatomy, but neither permanently nor with corresponding sex change. They live between the masculine male and feminine female poles prescribed by our culture. Dress for them presents problems because of cultural ideals and rules.

Clothing allows a ready way to manipulate gender, but is not entirely free of suggestions about sexuality both because of the cultural pairing of gender with sex and because apparel changes body shape. Thus the goal of retaining one's body sex, but not keeping it paired by dress with the culturally expected gender leads to a dilemma for the crossdresser: either dress to be true to a sense of self where gender and sex are paired in a way the culture does not endorse, which means obvious crossdressing, or present a unified picture to others at the cost of either one's sense of gender or of sex. None of these alternatives is particularly desirable and so compromises are sought through partial crossdressing in public, or crossdressing in private.

The crossdresser who tries to pass as the opposite sex without personally experiencing a sense of being the opposite sex is purchasing a sense of gender at the expense of their sense of sex. Put more simply, in seeking to express the experienced *gender* by dressing to pass as the opposite *sex* the crossdresser honors the gender by denying the sex. This does not 'feel right' to the person but may be accepted because it escapes social opposition and censure—if the individual successfully passes. Of course, the pressure to succeed in the masquerade can also generate anxiety, and if the effort fails the cost can be very high. In any event this solution clearly shows that gender takes priority over sex psychologically.

An alternative solution is to present in external dress a gendered self who is congruent to the sexed body. Others then see what they expect to see. In this situation either no crossdressing occurs and the person feels the loss of a gender expression suited to their internal experience, or the crossdressing is covert. In the latter instance that means either partial crossdressing that is unobserved by others, such as through wearing undergarments associated with the gender they experience, or crossdressing to whatever extent they desire in private. This solution limits the expression of experienced gender but preserves the individual's sense of the sexed body as it also protects the perception of the sexed body by others. In essence, it purchases an expression of the sexed body at some cost to the sense of gender.

If all this weren't confusing enough, some transgendered people find they do not fit comfortably with either gender, or perhaps either sex. What if the sense of gender is neither clearly masculine nor feminine, nor the sense of sex unambiguously male or female? Such individuals among us may self-identify as a third sex or third gender. In such cases crossdressing effects a compromise meant to keep the person in the no-man's land between unfriendly camps. By mixing the signs of anatomical sex with a gender not paired with that sex the crossdressed person may free the self from both conventional notions of sex and gender.[424] It may be in a culture like our own that such crossdressing is the only way to regularly maintain a third gender expression.

Why Dress Matters in Crossdressing: Doing Science

Obviously, the threat posed by crossdressing resides in its use of dress to express gender in ways not culturally sanctioned outside specific times and cir-

181

cumstances. The perception of threat evokes anxiety and defense. These reactions, potential or actual, put crossdressers in an awkward position practically, as discussed above. But another dimension further complicates life for transgender people. Transgender realities tend to be seen as inferior, deficient, abnormal, deviant, or disordered. The impetus for this widely held set of perceptions is perpetuated by mental health professionals—the very people presumably in the best position to render a sober, scientific analysis. Yet no less than the rest of us medical experts are residents within culture and subject to its forces.

The filter provided on the perception of sex and gender by the medicalization of sex has effected a muting, if not quite outright elimination, of the role of *dress* in cross*dressing*. The mental health field only nods at the obvious physical reality of the dress, but accords it little significance outside being a rather general marker of gender, which is interpreted as disturbed. This neglect of context casts serious doubt on the legitimacy of medical judgments; they label a reality imperfectly understood and removed from its foundational context. Accordingly, it becomes difficult to avoid the suspicion that something other than science has been at work and that the unintended consequence is all too often harm rather than healing.[425]

Mental health professionals (and the rest of us) need to grapple with the reality that in crossdressing questions about sex and sexuality, along with gender, gender identity and gender role all converge in the act of dressing—the wearing of clothing, with varying degrees of attendant behaviors (e.g., long hair, makeup). Just what, exactly, to make of how one dresses, though, depends to no little degree on how one conceives terms like 'sex' and 'gender,' which is why we have spent some time considering both. On these various separate matters there is no consensus, so we must not be surprised at the confusion over crossdressing often found.

If, like many medical professionals, we naively view sex and gender paired in an inflexible manner and that dictated by nature, then anything variant from clear anatomical display and culturally expected congruent behavior will be seen as a 'mistake' (in the case of intersexed individuals), 'abnormal' or 'defective' (both intersexed people and those not strictly heterosexual or gender-conforming), or 'perverted' (anyone engaged in behavior that cultural authority rejects). Though these terms may be put in the nicest possible ways, it is unlikely anyone—either in the scientific community or outside it—will see in any of such words something other than a negative value judgment. In this context, crossdressing is at best an anomaly and at worst a sin or serious illness disturbing both the individual's nature and the larger social order. This is the legacy of the medicalization of sex perpetuated in the diagnostic and classification system used by psychiatrists and others. And it is irresponsible.

The necessity to make contemporary Western distinctions and draw the conclusions common today about sex and gender is by no means obvious from empirical facts. Vern and Bonnie Bullough, among the most prolific writers on the subject of crossdressing, observe that across cultures the perception of 'masculinity' and 'femininity' are not necessarily dependent on male and female genitalia.[426] Once we dethrone the alleged determining power of sex over gender we are free to see other potent forces at work.

Among the host of factors that then enter into a reckoning of gender is clothing. The tendency of small children at a point in their development to believe that changing clothes changes gender may not be so far off. Some peoples in other cultures also regard as real and substantial changes in gender stemming from crossing gender lines by means of dress and other behavior. Some people even in our own society seem ready to accept that changes of dress, together with alterations in manner, can effect actual gender change. They see the dress and accompanying behavior as congruent expressions of a valid internal experience. Once we put dress back into crossdressing we open ourselves to numerous empirical facts waiting accounting.

The spirit of scientific inquiry requires openness to the possibility that just because crossdressing presents a challenge to conventional Western thinking about gender and dress does not make it an illegitimate challenge. Crossdressing is one of those persistent human phenomena that re-invite our attention to what we think we know. But as in all other matters of science, seeing correctly in seeing in context.

Q. 8

What happens when what clothes express doesn't make sense to us?

The Short Answer. Crossdressing would be unremarkable if it did not do two things: involve something we value and confound us. Dress is highly connected to many important personal and social values. The confound factor enters in because we think that dress can reliably communicate important things, we expect it to do so, and we believe we are well able to get the message. We become confounded when clothes express something we have trouble interpreting—like crossdressing. One immediate reaction may be a kind of shortcut response where we slap on the handiest label and act in a preprogrammed fashion. In short, we may stereotype. We may slip into a comfortable box that helps us explain what we have seen and tells us what to do. Yet when we act in this manner it may conflict with one of our value beliefs. Thus the surprising situation also might create an unpleasant psychological experience termed 'cognitive dissonance.' We experience a mismatch between what we ordinarily expect from ourselves and what we actually did. When we feel such internal discord we are motivated to eliminate it. We may respond by adjusting our beliefs to fit how we acted. Not only individuals, but groups may justify their behavior in this way. Crossdressing evokes our efforts to explain to ourselves what we are witnessing, and these efforts involve other mental processes too. Especially important may be two processes identified by Swiss developmental psychologist Jean Piaget. We tend first to make things fit what we already think we know (assimilation). If that does not work, our efforts may turn to expanding our store of knowledge to embrace the hard reality posed by the new information (accommodation). These two processes are not contradictory and work side by side. Assisting such processes are situational cues and our own values.

The Longer Answer. There are dress nonconformists all around us. Their motives may vary, but each poses to us a similar dilemma: how do we interpret and respond to whatever is being expressed? An economist, James Morgan, suggests that those who do not conform to expected customs of dress may meet with any number of interpretations. "Refusal to conform may be interpreted as stupid stubbornness or lack of good taste, or as an indication of radicalism in other and more important areas of life, or even as inability to afford new clothes."[427]

Such interpretations often are accompanied by our efforts to ignore the nonconformist. However, they are also often connected to rude remarks, discriminatory practices, or physical aggression. Amazingly enough, the simple sight of a male in a dress can generate from observers hostile behavior including violence, even murder. Even more amazingly, such acts may occur contrary to the actor's nobler aspirations and beliefs. Somehow the sight of dress nonconformists, like our dress-wearing male, sometimes evokes the worst in human behavior.

Why do we respond so negatively to dress nonconformity? Part of the answer may lie in the way such nonconformity elicits internal discomfort. We generally prefer things make sense, fit what we already know through experience, and mirror our own expectations—in short, that they be as we believe they 'should be.' When this isn't the case, the resulting disequilibrium feels unpleasant. Internal conflict that is very minor we may tolerate with little concern or action, but when it is connected with values the upset is more pronounced and prompts us to do something.

With dress at the very heart of the experiencing and expressive system we have described in previous answers, we are hardly unreasonable to expect that system to run smoothly. That means we expect dress to make sense. Because gender matters so much to us in constructing and maintaining our personal and social identities, gender-differentiated dress emerges as especially important. Above all, that manner of dress should make sense.

But it doesn't always do so. When we encounter a male in a dress we may suddenly feel like we are thrust into a movie where the actor is speaking a foreign language. We hear words, but they don't make sense. We see the dressed person, but whatever is being expressed is lost in translation. We may feel surprised, or embarrassed, or angry. We relied on the dress system to make sense, but here is an individual who seems to have beaten the system into incoherence.

Dramatically unexpected sights confound us. There is more than just the discomfort of the system not working; minor glitches happen all the time. But this situation of a crossdressed male tackles the system in such a manner it fully engages our values (see the answer to Q. 4). How do we handle such an event and our reaction?

What are 'paths of response to novel dress expressions'?

Of course, no one answer will apply to every situation. The degree of novelty will influence us, as will our mood, how surprised we are, and whom we are with. Still, there are some things that happen often enough to warrant our immediate attention. We might call them paths of response to novel dress expressions. Let's consider a few of the more prominent, which include:

- *stereotyping*—responding by assigning a ready made label and acting according to the set of programmed responses meant to accompany that label;
- *cognitive dissonance*—responding by resolving internal discord in favor of one or the other of the two sides (e.g., action and belief) of the conflict;
- *assimilation*—responding by trying to fit the experience into what we already know; or,
- *accommodation*—responding by adapting our mind to make a place for itself for new and novel information.

To keep our focus sharp we will examine each path especially in terms of our response path to a male—a boy or man—in a dress. Because in our culture this seems the most likely dress expression to be judged novel and generate upset feelings, it is a test case *par excellence*.

Why, and how, do we stereotype?

One quick and easy way to respond to a male in a dress is to activate certain cultural stereotypes about gender and gender-differentiated dress.

We are all familiar with the idea of stereotyping. The origin of the word is instructive. It derives from a late 18th century printing process that created a solid plate that could be used over and over again. That is what stereotypes provide—a preformed template that can be continually used without change. Social psychologists suggest this is what mental stereotypes, such as those about sex and gender, also accomplish. After all, it requires far less mental effort to put a label like 'male' or 'female,' 'man' or 'woman,' on a dress silhouette than to engage our attention at length in order to form a careful, nuanced, individual appraisal. Stereotyping is a mental tool readily available to quickly and efficiently sort information, especially routine or mundane information.[428]

Gender Stereotyping

Why do we gender stereotype? Psychologists Alice Eagly and V. J. Steffen suggest the motivation is the social aggregation of males into roles different than those assigned to females. Gender stereotypes, then, ultimately arise from the decision to separate people based on the apparent sex of their bodies (see the answer to Q. 5). Having done so, long habituation into these different roles presumably has cultivated different habits of thought, feeling, and action. Thus men (masculine males) and women (feminine females) form gender-differentiated personality traits.[429]

Psychologists Curt Hoffman and Nancy Hurst amend this picture by arguing that gender stereotypes do not stem from real sex differences in personality; they flow from our rationalizations rather than from valid perceptions. We generate stereotypes to explain why men and women sort into different roles—and our rationalizing includes the notion that gender personality differences make one gender better suited to certain roles than the other. It is not fact derived from observation that creates our belief in gender-based personality differences, but our need to explain the obvious separation into masculine and feminine roles.[430]

Whichever the case may prove to be, gender stereotypes posit concrete, stable differences in temperament and traits. These are then mirrored in dress. Masculine dress presumably displays masculine personality and is suited to masculine activities; feminine dress does likewise for personality and roles. Because clothing and accessories are paired with gender they both fit into the larger gender stereotypes and generate dress stereotypes. However long this took in culture, in our lives it happens very quickly.

Gender stereotypes are learned early in our development. Parents stereotype their own children, perceiving even their toddlers as conformists to gender expectations about identity and role that will bind them to masculinity or femininity in adulthood.[431] In daycare, caregivers continue gender socialization of children, reinforcing gender stereotypes.[432] And children learn the stereotypes well. In fact, in children gender stereotypes appear to become stronger (more rigid) with age.[433] Clearly, children get how important gender differentiation is and how useful stereotypes are.

Gender stereotypes continue to surround us and influence us as adults. Women and girls are expected to be caregivers, more focused on relationships such as marriage and parenthood, more emotional, more oriented to appearance, less rational, and less competent or reliable in the workplace. The workplace, in particular, is an obvious arena where gender stereotypes exercise important influence.[434] But such stereotypes are omnipresent. The media is replete with them.[435] They are present even in the daily comics we laugh at over breakfast.[436]

Stereotyping & Disconfirming Individuals

Steeped as we are in the process, we can justly call ourselves experts at stereotyping. Thus far we have discussed that expertise in ordinary matters, such as categorizing a person as male or female based on the presumption of their gender as expressed in their dress. Now along comes a male in a dress. Though the image presented does not fit our stereotype for gendered dress, we still stereotype. Like a knee jerk reflex, this mental tool flings itself out of our mind's toolbox to fix the jarring discrepancy we find before us.

Psychologists Neil Macrae, Alan Milne, and Galen Bodenhausen remark that research demonstrates "an increased reliance on stereotypes when social perception occurs under taxing or resource-depleting conditions."[437] Perhaps this is true in general of the task of sorting people into gender groups; to do each person we meet justice would be exhausting. Whether it is because we lack the ability, or merely the motivation, we fall back on stereotyping. So, in our example the crossdressed stranger, failing to fit a normal gender stereotype, still is stereotyped. In this instance the likely template, if the crossdresser is a man, will be the stereotype of a gay man. Lacking any other evidence than wearing a dress, the man is stereotyped as a homosexual in drag. As Macrae and colleagues point out about stereotyping in general, it costs us little to apply one, though those to whom it is applied may find the cost much steeper.[438]

These researchers also observe that studies have found people prove reluctant or unable to give up stereotyping in favor of seeing another as an individual unless certain factors are present. Such factors might include personal involvement (i.e., the crossdresser is someone we know), or a stake in the outcome (i.e., the stereotype affects what happens next). In sum, we are likely to stereotype in the absence of a motivation not to do so. But the efficiency of stereotyping in the moment, when the person is here now but soon gone, evaporates when the individual becomes part of the social landscape. In the face of continued exposure, which brings new information, we may be motivated to overcome the stereotype. In essence, we have traded from a generalized type to a specific instance—a process termed 'individuation.'[439]

As the last point indicates, a basic problem with stereotyping is its 'one size fits all' logic. Gender stereotypes obliterate real individual differences in favor of fixed types. All men *are* and *must be* a certain way—and so, too, for women. Of course, we know that's not true, and our stereotypes reflect this awareness. They are dimensional, typically hierarchical, with distinct subtypes contributing to the overall stereotype. Thus, our stereotype for a gay male allows for subgroups, some of which fit better with the overall stereotype[440]—a point we shall consider further in a moment.

Because we have such long and thorough exposure to gender stereotypes they become so much a part of our thinking we rarely pause to question them, in whole or in part. Instead, in common practice we reify the stereotype, mentally transforming it into something actually occurring in Nature—despite all kinds of evidence to the contrary. But that's part of the power of stereotypes. They bias our thinking such that we attend more to the things we can fit with the stereotype, and remember those things better, while ignoring other information, no matter its relevance.[441] No wonder stereotypes are so hard to overcome!

They are particularly difficult to overthrow when it comes to socially disapproved groups—like male crossdressers. Psychologists Ziva Kunda and Kathryn Oleson remark that it is possible to motivate revision of a stereotype even in such cases if, for example, the individual experiences positive contact with a member or members of the negatively stereotyped group. Unfortunately, they also cite research showing how resistant to change such stereotypes can be "even in the face of intense manipulations involving cooperation with members of the stereotyped group over extended periods of time."[442]

Why is this? Kunda and Oleson point to research suggesting what we do is avoid generalizing our positive experience of particular individuals by separating those individuals into a subtype of the group. In this way the individual remains a part of the stereotyped group but doesn't have to fill the stereotype everyone else in the group is still assumed to be like. They are 'exceptions.' Moreover, they are the proverbial 'exceptions that prove the rule.' Subtyping persons who disconfirm the stereotype actually makes the stereotype even more resistant to change.[443]

Kunda and Oleson hypothesize that this subtyping process represents an effort to preserve the stereotype (a generalization) by discounting bothersome counterexamples (individual instances). Let us reconsider our example: a male in a dress. Suppose we discover this man is happily married with children and disapproves of homosexual practices. This information disconfirms our stereotype that all crossdressed males are gay. Kunda and Oleson say that our surprise when we encounter an individual who violates our stereotype about that person's group may prompt us to try to explain away this violation. We may search for possible factors to prove this particular person is atypical—and thus irrelevant to our stereotype. Our preference for the generalized character of the stereotype over the concrete reality of the individual may be motivated by the importance the stereotype has for supporting our values, attitudes, or behaviors. Because the stereotype matters we also feel a need to justify excluding the exception, so we search for a reason or reasons that make sense to us.[444]

Attributions

In this respect we might also mention our penchant for making self-serving attributions. When we try to explain behavior—our own or someone else's—we consider two chief causal sources: internal factors (e.g., personality, values, attitudes, interests, or personal freedom), and external ones (e.g., situational factors, or socialization). So we may attribute the male crossdresser's behavior, if he is a boy, to a parent's use of petticoat punishment—a situational attribution. Or we might attribute a man's wearing a dress to his quirky personality—a dispositional attribution. Both attribution sources (dispositional or situational) are possible, but they are not equally likely to occur.

In our culture, so devoted to individualism and personal freedom, we are prone to making what social psychologists call the 'fundamental attribution error.'[445] This notion is that we have a tendency to underestimate the degree to which behavior is prompted by external causes rather than internal dispositions. In short, we favor dispositional attributions—at least for others. For ourselves we may explain behavior by elements in the environment (situational attribution); for others we tend to assume an internal factor. Still, in theory we may assume either positive or negative internal factors.

But as we have seen, when it comes to the violators of gender-differentiated dress codes—like our crossdressing male—we seem to have a pronounced tendency to render negative judgments. In fact, this tendency also applies *within* stereotype subtypes. Researchers Eric Clausell and Susan Fiske found in applying the Stereotype Content Model (SCM) to observers' perceptions of the warmth and competency of 10 gay subgroups that crossdressing gays were evaluated as lower in both dimensions than other gay subgroups.[446] Thus, while transgender people in general may suffer from being stereotyped, it seems likely not all are equally negatively stereotyped. Gender crossings may be generally frowned upon, but those involving dress are particularly disavowed.

Stigmatizing

When it comes to male crossdressing we may attribute the crossdresser's behavior to an internal disposition, which because it generates behavior foreign to our own and most people we know, we assume is deviant, delinquent, disordered, or disturbed. If we are honest, our first instinct is probably not to assume the crossdresser is on the way to a costume party (a situational attribution), but to infer the behavior represents a stable pattern reflecting some internal deficiency (dispositional attribution). We brand the male crossdresser with labels carrying pejorative connotations, shun him, or otherwise act as though he bears some mark warning us to stay away. In sum, in seeing him as undesirably different, we *stigmatize* him.

We would be remiss in our discussion of what happens when others express something in dress which we don't understand if we were to ignore the very real effects experienced by those others. Renowned sociologist Erving Goffman describes the cost paid by those we stigmatize. [447] This cost begins with a very basic price we make them pay by our judgment that their stigma makes them somehow not quite human. "On this assumption," Goffman writes, "we exercise varieties of discrimination, through which we effectively, if often unthinkingly, reduce his life chances." [448]

Goffman observes we engage in forming theories to explain why the stigma-bearer is inferior and poses a danger to us. We apply metaphoric labels to disparage them. We add imagined defects to the stigma we know. Curiously, we also may add notice of some quality generally desirable, such as the notion that the one with a stigma is supernaturally gifted with special understanding or insight—though we ourselves have no wish to obtain such a gift at the cost it carries. And then, when we witness how such a person reacts defensively toward us, we see in it a justification for our attitudes and behaviors—the person has, after all, deserved it.[449]

Goffman recognizes those with stigmas do not all fit into one group or respond the same way. Some know they bear a stigma but are neither impressed nor repentant because of it. Others make every effort to change so as to escape the stigma. Some use the stigma as an excuse for lacks of success due to other causes. Though we might enumerate a variety of possibilities, the cases are as unique as the individuals who select them.[450]

However, the gap between personal identity and social perception elicits a need for those of us who are stigmatized to respond to those of us who stigmatize. We do this, to some extent at least, by managing the flow of information known about us. Goffman points in this regard to two groups among those with a stigma. Those who are "discreditable"—who hide a stigma that may be discovered—must always be on guard to protect their secret. Those who are "discredited"—bearing a stigma either visible or otherwise known to others—are confronted by the stresses arising from how so-called 'normal' people interact with 'abnormal' people. Those who bear a social stigma constantly must reconcile their self-image with the very different one reflected by others.[451]

Male crossdressers belong to the second of Goffman's three stigma categories: stigma perceived as arising from the individual's deficit in character. Typically, the crossdresser is inferred to be weak-willed (cf. the answer to Q. 25), or possessed of unnatural passions (cf. the answer to Q. 88). To manage their stigma crossdressers may try to pass as someone belonging among the 'normals.' In the case of crossdressing this could mean either refraining from public crossdressing or attempting to successfully pass as a woman. Another possibility is retreat—avoidance of social contact in order to escape the social consequences of stigmatization. Or, conversely, the individual may seek out and align himself with others who share his stigma.[452]

As we can see, stereotyping and associated mental gymnastics provide one path of response to the male in a dress, which may be accompanied by stigmatizing the individual, with all the negative consequences that entails. So when we see the male in the dress even as our minds race to interpret it, our bodies may be engaging us in interaction. We avert our eyes, or sneer, or make a crude joke. Any number of intervening factors in the context might prompt the particular action we take, but whatever it is we instantly recognize it as violating one or another of our values or beliefs. We have been inconsistent with our own better nature—and that generates an internal reaction that elicits another path of response.

What is cognitive dissonance?

So let us imagine we have met a male in a dress and we acted rudely. Perhaps all we did was think a disparaging thought. Maybe we said something snide. Or perhaps we acted in a hostile fashion, refusing service or pushing the person away from us. Whatever it was, the act has startled us because it stands sharply contrary to our belief in general about tolerance. The behavior needs context to be comprehended.

Probably our experience of boys and men on the one side, and dresses on the other, has not put them together. In fact, we expect women, not men, to wear dresses. Males of any age we expect to be in bifurcated (divided) clothing. So the sudden presentation of one in a dress does not match our expectation—and it does not 'feel right' because it is not 'the way things should be.' Now to this we can add another jarring combination: our rudeness against a backdrop of general tolerance. Ordinarily, we expect that our behavior will reflect our beliefs;

if we believe in tolerance we *should* act tolerantly. We didn't—and it bothers us. Our internal discord has become pronounced.

In the late 1950s, social psychologist Leon Festinger explored this kind of unsettling psychological experience and introduced the notion of 'cognitive dissonance.'[453] "This theory," Festinger explains, "centers around the idea that if a person knows various things that are not psychologically consistent with one another, he will, in a variety of ways, try to make them more consistent."[454] The motivation for change is a dissonant experience—one in which incongruous or discordant combinations present themselves. In our example there is more than one discordant combination; both involve behavior and beliefs. First, there is the man clothed in a dress (behavior) set against our expectation that only females should appear in dresses (belief). In addition, there is our expectation we should be tolerant (belief) set against our actual rudeness (behavior).

According to Festinger, "the existence of dissonance, being psychologically uncomfortable, will motivate the person to try to reduce the dissonance and achieve consonance." [455] As a matter of normal course, if two things in our mind refuse to fit together, we try to eliminate the dissonance by changing either the one or the other.[456] We might expect we would reaffirm our belief in tolerance, renounce our rudeness, and move on, sadder but wiser. Surprisingly, Festinger finds that such internal conflicts can motivate us in certain situations to do the opposite—to adjust our belief to fit our behavior. We cannot change what we have done. So rather than renounce our behavior, we may renounce our belief—or at least change it enough that we can resolve our internal discord. Thus we may qualify our belief in tolerance so that exceptions can be made. In one psychological move we manage both to restore a sense of internal harmony and justify our rudeness.

Let us reflect a little further by adding depth to our context.

Suppose that we grew up believing that those who violate social norms, like expected conformity to gender-differentiated dress, deserve punishment. After all, gender dress codes exist for a reason. In fact, imagine an instance in which our actual behavior fit this belief. Our response toward such a norm violator was punitive—we made unkind remarks to a girl we thought dressed too much like a boy. We felt sufficiently uncomfortable by her dress code violation to act. Our belief prompted our behavior and, in our mind, justified it. There has been no cognitive dissonance because our behavior has been consistent with our belief.

Recently, though, we learned that some social norms are of questionable reasonableness. Specifically, we discovered that gender norms for dress have long been used to hinder and even penalize many people, especially women. This new knowledge may itself have proved upsetting and resulted in cognitive dissonance. But let us imagine that because we so strongly objected to how women were held back by gender dress codes that we resolved our internal disharmony by adopting the belief unfair social norms, like dress codes for women, should be abolished. We now regret our own unkind comments to the girl who was dressed in a fashion we did not like.

We may presently consciously adhere to our new belief, but the old belief is still there too. On the one hand, we believe that gender dress codes are unfair, punitive, and should be dispensed with. On the other hand, we also still believe these codes are necessary and so violators merit censure, even punishment. The sight of a male in a dress prompts us to act rudely. This act, caught betwixt and between two conflicting beliefs, elicits cognitive dissonance. What happens next?

Our response will be tipped one direction or another by how various factors interact and which ones prove weightiest. Not all our beliefs are equally salient to us, and neither are all our behaviors. It may be easier for us to renounce a nasty thought than our refusal of service. In the latter case, the strength of the behavior may prove greater than the belief, so it is the belief that gives way.[457] Or we may find our behavior so shockingly inconsistent with our well-formed belief that we rationalize its occurrence as due to other factors—the man acted inappropriately and we were only responding defensively; tolerance was never the issue. Or perhaps we realize that our belief in tolerance—which we now reaffirm—was incomplete. Now we have added another condition to its embrace and while regretting what occurred, we resolve to do better next time.

Other alternative courses of action might be enumerated, but they all divide along one of two basic paths: affirm the belief or affirm the behavior. The likelihood of which basic path is trod may be especially influenced by elements basic to cognitive dissonance itself. For example, if we judge our behavior was not constrained but freely chosen we may be more likely to alter our belief. If we conclude our behavior resulted from a lack of choice, we may be more likely to see it as spontaneous, revocable, and not indicative of our normal actions. We are likely also to be influenced by our behavior's consequences. If there are few or minor consequences the behavior may occur again; it is our belief that is altered. On the other hand, if the consequences are significant, we may be more motivated to change our behavior.

One particularly nasty possibility lurks in the background. Festinger notes we typically change our actions or feelings in response to the reality of an environment beyond our control. But he notes the possibility of social environments where enough control might be exercised that an individual can resolve dissonance by changing the environment.[458] What if we have the power to make a crossdressing person—perhaps our son—stop crossdressing? Such a course of action eliminates the source of our dissonance. We no longer have to be bothered by a male in a dress because the male is no longer allowed to be in a dress.

Now let us imagine another possibility: we are part of a social group with enough clout we can try to prevent cognitive dissonance from such events by repressing the behavior. If it should occur, we swiftly punish it, and so banish our own temporary discomfort. This possibility is not farfetched; we see it in modified respects rather often in any society that does not want to be discomfited by differences. Publicly endorsed sanctions can happen in a variety of situations, but most notably occur when major social institutions like religion or law enforcement lend their authority—or when modern medicine, in the form of mental health professionals, uses diagnosis and therapy to act as guardian of social convention and expectation rather than science and health.

We can properly speak of cognitive dissonance at a societal level as a potent force affecting many minorities. Military analyst and student of cultural change Marc Widdowson raises the point that cognitive dissonance in society affects social cohesion. One way this plays out, he believes, is for members of a group to reduce their cognitive dissonance by downgrading other groups and their members. "In effect," he writes, "people tell themselves that the failure of other social groups to legitimize their own beliefs and behaviours is not significant because these other social groups are unimportant and their members' opinions worthless." While this course of devaluing other groups may lead to merely ignoring them in practice, sometimes that proves ineffective. As a result bitter conflict may erupt.[459]

Not so long ago, crossdressing was illegal (see the answer to Q. 36). A host of laws were employed to arrest violators. Even today male crossdressers are likely to be held by police if caught in public. Despite the fact that courts routinely dismiss such cases, and our society has made some steps toward tolerance, there remains rather widespread dissonance among members of our society when encountering a male in a dress.

The hard truth is none of is likely to ever eliminate experiences of cognitive dissonance. Yet there may be ways we can limit their occurrences and minimize their impact. A key appears to be educational preparation. Being more conscious of our values and beliefs, reasoning out their basis and legitimacy, and practicing flexibility of mind all may help us avoid dissonance. In this light, some research findings in education are pertinent.

Teachers commonly experience in the classroom the students' dilemma over how to manage their cognitive dissonance. Educators Elisabeth McFalls and Deirdre Cobb-Roberts observe that students in a multicultural course commonly receive information inconsistent with their prior beliefs, which elicits dissonance. For many, resistance to the new information resolves the dissonance—but defeats the goal of such a course to assist students to appreciate diversity. McFalls and Cobb-Roberts find that articulating the idea of cognitive dissonance to students before presenting them with information that can elicit such a response helps diminish resistance. Because the students are alert to what can happen they are better prepared to manage the dissonance when it occurs.[460]

How do we constructively handle novel experiences?

Cognitive dissonance arrests our attention when it happens. But we must not ignore other mental processes continuously operating in the background. We are, as a matter of course, constantly faced with new information from the world around us. Normally we handle that flow very efficiently. We sort things into existing mental cubbyholes and, as needed, create new spaces. When things make sense, the operations we undertake go so smoothly we don't even notice them.

When new information does not immediately make sense, it slows us down—perhaps even stops us in our tracks. A male in a dress is likely to prove such an event. If we don't know what the expression or message we assume the crossdresser is sending means, it brings us to a temporary halt. Of course, there are aids for us to fall back upon in our effort to fill in the blanks as best we can. As we have learned, we rely on rules (the customs and conventions of society) and context (the situation and setting plus our own experiences and values). But we have also seen above there are mental operations we employ—for better or worse.

What we now need is to add a simple description of two other kinds of mental processes we may utilize as we manipulate rules and context to make sense of things. The influential developmental psychologist Jean Piaget tells us that in the first of these processes we tend to fit new information into our existing framework of knowledge—a process called *assimilation*. We rely on what we already know to make sense of new things we encounter. This includes drawing on our previous experience of situations and settings as well as applying our value system so that we can make new data fit our old framework. When we can't do that we have to shift things, open up and expand our framework. When old categories in our framework are insufficient, then new ones have to be created. Changing our mental framework to make room for new information is a process called *accommodation*. Both processes are active in our mental life as seek both stability in our thinking and mental growth.[461]

These terms are applicable to our understanding how we cope with the encounter with crossdressing. Metaphorically, two roads are open to travel: we can rely on just what we already have (assimilation), or we can expand our knowledge in the effort to make sure our conclusions are more credible (accommodation). Many of us, much of the time, don't make the extra effort required in the latter choice to make it the predominant path, even though both assimilation and accommodation operate as simultaneous processes in ordinary mental life.

What is the path of assimilation?

Let's examine a fairly ordinary course of action. When we see someone who clearly is not a member of the group we associate with the clothing they are wearing, or which expresses an individuality we are not prepared to see, or that raises questions for us about its intention, our attention is arrested. We wonder what we see means. Perhaps because we are startled and the surprise makes us uneasy, we tend to choose the shortest route to restoring our inner equilibrium. That rarely means asking the person whose clothing has caught our attention for help understanding what is going on. Instead, we scan the environment for cues to help us; if lacking any we rely on our own resources.

For many of us our first effort is to assimilate what we encounter into our existing framework for similar sights. For example, if we encounter a child dressed in military garb it may surprise us and prompt reflection. We don't ordinarily expect such a sight and we try to understand it. We may offer to ourselves explanations based on group affiliation: "The child probably belongs to a youth group emphasizing military-style discipline." Or we may see it as a form of self-expression: "That boy thinks he is G.I. Joe." Or we may interpret it as a kind of self-expression that also adds an element of intent toward others: "That kid is trying to be tough and is warning everyone to watch out." In short, we rely on situational cues to help us fit what we are observing into something we already know so that it makes sense to us. In doing so our values are fully engaged, restricting the range of our acceptable alternative explanations.

But this effort may meet with varied success depending on our own background of experiences, the richness of the situational cues, and the nature of our values. If we have no similar experiences of seeing kids in military uniforms, and if we lack any ready-made context in which to make sense of the sight, or the sight engages particular values, we may find ourselves taxed trying to make sense of it. Especially in situations where we are suddenly surprised by the sight, and we lack any relevant situational cues to aid our interpretation, we may satisfy ourselves solely with our own values and the expectations they generate. If we can't make what we observe fit our framework based on what we know about the situation, then perhaps we can make it fit based on our value system.

The same process happens if we see a male in a dress. The sight in most instances is unexpected and unusual; it therefore beckons our efforts at explanation. The situation is not likely to aid us or we would not be surprised or see the event as unusual. (After all, if we are in a place where we might reasonably expect to see such a sight, we can hardly claim surprise and at any rate the situational cues will quickly aid our interpretation of what is happening.) As with the youngster in a military uniform, we may advance the explanation that the boy or man in the dress is signaling a group identity, or is engaged in self-expression, or is both expressing himself *and* signaling some intention, perhaps about the desire for sexual interaction. Because situational cues are absent and we don't know the actual case, we fall back on what we have—our own store of

197

experience, our personal values and expectations, and immediate feelings these elicit.

This matters because the meaning we arrive at, and the judgment it generates, reflects *us*—even if we share it in common with many others. We each call on what we have to make sense of things, including our ideas about what, when, and how clothes communicate. Our feelings add color to our thoughts and we use the result to justify our judgments, rarely considering in the process that everything we are doing reflects ourselves far more than it can the male in the dress—who we have taken from the status of a mystery to that of a mystery solved. But the individual remains unknown despite our judgment. Moreover, because our feelings, ideas, experiences, values and expectations are not absolute or universal, we encounter others who do not see things the way we do and who act in ways that make sense to them but not to us. Our failure to grasp this fact can—and does—lead to misunderstandings and conflict.[462]

The trouble with assimilation can be that our insistence on making what we see fit what we already know may cause us unwittingly to distort what we perceive.

What is the path of accommodation?

But we don't have to follow a course like that just described. We may choose—or feel compelled—to expand our mental framework because of what we observe. If the sight of a child in military garb, or a male in a dress, cannot fit well into what we think we know, we may decide we really *don't know* what we are seeing. New possibilities open to us as we seek relevant information, especially as we discipline ourselves to suspend judgment until we know enough to make an informed one.

This is the path of accommodation. Even while we are trying to make what we observe fit what we already think we know, we have some portion of our mental energy preparing new ground to receive new seeds of information. If we cooperate with this process we stretch ourselves toward a new point of mental stability that rests on new information and ways of interpreting things instead of distorting things to fit what we already possess.

So, now when we encounter a male in a dress, we still may look for situational cues and draw upon our values, but we also open ourselves to more information. We actively seek to expand our framework. This might mean asking the boy or man in the dress why he is so clothed. More likely we will ask someone else. If the sight engages us enough, we may even do research (like reading this book) to find reasons for such behavior.

Obviously, this path is relatively more likely when the male in the dress is someone we know—or thought we knew. Personal relationships tend to make us more eager for explanations and concerned that they be accurate ones. The more important the relationship is to us, the greater may be our willingness to employ accommodation alongside assimilation. Between both processes we are maximizing our chances for accurately receiving whatever is being expressed in the behavior we observe.

The questions and answers in this volume assist both assimilation and accommodation. They may fit into what we already know, challenge what we think we know, or invite us to new understanding through more facts than we previously had. Of course, in the process our values might be challenged too. Since values likewise rest on experience and knowledge, accommodation can prompt value changes. If these are perceived as growth, then we can embrace them as opportunities met and fulfilled, rather than experience them as threats or harm to ourselves. As our values shift and our understanding grows, our feelings will change. So will our behavior—but only if we resolve to make it so.

Q. 9

Do clothes express something un-changeable?

The Short Answer: This question is worded carefully so that it can be read—and answered—in two ways. First, it can be understood to ask if there is something unchangeable in a person that clothes may express. With reference to the things most crucial to our inquiry, to answer 'yes' endorses the culture's position that sex and gender are naturally and reliably paired. Thus gender-differentiated clothing can be said to express paired qualities that are fixed from birth. To answer 'no' contests this view and permits seeing that dress may express equally validly fluid, shifting senses of gender, regardless of the sex of the body. Or, the initial question can be understood to ask if clothes always express the same things. In other words, are clothes a constant, so that a particular fashion, or color, or garment reliably signals the same thing time after time? In this manner, regardless of whether gender in an individual may be subject to change, or liberated from too tight a connection to sex, the clothing itself can be said to remain reliably expressive of either femininity or masculinity. Put this way, the question fetches much hedging, with some folk arguing that everything about clothing is subjective, relative, and changing. Others argue some things are more resistant to change than others and these things may serve as relatively reliable signals. There are several elements of dress suggested as stable for this purpose, both with regard to children and adults, whether feminine or masculine. To ascertain the trustworthiness of such claims we must both identify what elements are claimed to remain constant and then to investigate historically the evidence. Surprisingly few elements emerge as serious contenders for remaining stable gender differentiators and perhaps none prove to be permanently enduring.

The Longer Answer: The question before us has more than one dimension. On one hand, we can ask if an important function of clothes is to express something enduring and stable about the individual. In other words, is what we wear a reliable indicator of who we are, in terms of the groups we belong to as well as our own unique personality? On the other hand, we can ask if clothing

201

itself is meant to be relatively stable and enduring in the way it expresses certain things. Can we rely on clothing to tell us fundamental things about others that won't change with a new season's fashions? The intersection of these two queries is gender. Just as we may argue that clothing serves to express gender, so we may argue that clothing fashion has built in, constant mechanisms for reliably differentiating the genders. Whether or not these things are so is the subject of this answer.

Do clothes express something enduring and stable about us?

We already have seen (in the answers to Q. 4-5) that clothes can and do express our affiliations and individuality. Both may be relatively stable and enduring in our lives. We also have considered the relation of clothing to gender (cf. the answer to Q. 6). Now we must bring some of these thoughts together and consider whether an important part of the expressive subsystem anchored in clothing is and ought to be the reflection of enduring and stable personal qualities.

I suspect most of us will think the answer obvious. For all the reasons stated in answering earlier questions, we rely on clothes to accurately say things about us. One of the most important things we rely on dress to inform us is the sex and gender of the person, assuming—as we almost inevitably do—that anatomical sex and gender presentation, including manner of dress, will neatly align with our culture's dichotomy into male and female. A century ago sociologist William Thomas argued that objects such as clothes take on the personality of the gender they have been habitually associated with. Thus, he wrote, a "mannish woman" is one who has dropped some of the signs habitually paired with our idea of the feminine.[463] Such conclusions come because we accept the 'second skin' of clothing as an accurate, reliable indicator of what we *expect* regardless of what we may actually get.

The real rub is not that clothes do this reasonably well, because more often than not our expectations are met, but that they do not always do so and even when they do the nuances of any intended message still may be missed, twisted, or ignored. Often something is lost in translation—we may feel comfortable in what we wear as expressing who we are, but others can misunderstand what we are expressing and come to completely different conclusions about us than the ones we have reached about ourselves. Or, we see someone and draw conclusions about their presentation that may range from highly accurate to highly inaccurate—and we have no certain way of knowing what is the actual case.

For instance, a young woman may dress in a halter top and miniskirt because it feels comfortable on a hot day and expresses her comfort with her own body. An observer may conclude she is inviting sexual advances, and if the observer acts on this interpretation some unpleasantness may occur. Obviously, another classic case of this problem is the man in a skirt who means to express one thing—perhaps a feminine side, perhaps ethnic pride, perhaps rebellion against culture—and an observer, based on limited knowledge and using personal values, interprets the expression as belonging to a gay man dressed as a drag queen. If these two share their thoughts, both are likely to be offended.

At other times, the expression is accurately understood—and still judged negatively. Perhaps the young woman is intending to draw sexual attention to herself. Perhaps the man in the dress really is a drag queen. Some among us find both presentations objectionable. Yet sexuality is basic to all of us, and choosing clothing to express that is hardly remarkable. It has been going on for millennia. So what is the reason these scenarios disturb some of us?

For some of us, the answer may lie in how comfortable we are with our own sexuality. Or we may feel such displays disturb public decency and threaten the social order we depend on. We may believe that while it is appropriate for clothes to express our sexuality they should do so more in private settings and in less spectacular ways. In short, we typically adhere to unwritten 'rules' about when and how expressions of some stable and enduring personal traits should be expressed. That these rules are in part idiosyncratic we are unlikely to either see or admit because we have fitted them so comfortably into the larger framework of cultural values and conventions. In short, we personalize cultural rules. So we might be okay with a young woman wanting to dress provocatively (which cultural rules permit)—as long as it isn't at the mall, where we are (which is how we have personalized the cultural rule). We may even begrudgingly accept the drag queen (because culture does)—as long as he remains hidden from us (our own adaptation of the rule).

The crossdresser faces the dilemma posed by this situation. On the one hand, many crossdressers find that dressing in garb ordinarily reserved for the opposite gender expresses something important about themselves. They experience this piece of the self as both stable and enduring. They think this aspect merits expression through clothing no less than any other part of the self. Still, the cultural rules that surround us all mostly work against the same freedom of expression for this part of the self, which needs crossdressing, and those parts of the self that can be expressed through gender conforming dress. The culture only sanctions public crossdressing in certain settings for certain practices and not, typically, as a daily self-presentation.[464]

Whenever any of us feel the need or strong desire to dress or otherwise act in a way that we believe truly expresses who we are, but which we realize runs counter to cultural expectations and rules for us, we must choose which set of consequences we will bear. If we are true to ourselves in a way that makes us open to others we risk censure, rejection and harm. But to not do so we risk self-constriction, depression, lowered self-esteem, and limitations in our possibilities for growth. Of course, publicly expressing something outside the cultural norms won't necessarily mean all bad things, for there are almost certainly others like us and even some who are not like us will accept us. Nor does refraining from completely open expression necessarily mean we must pay a stiff price.

There is the golden mean of the middle way, the path most of us choose when aspects of the self are different from the social norm. We keep that aspect of the self and its expression largely, but not entirely private. For most cross-dressers this means refraining from disclosing this part of the self to others except in a few significant and trusted relationships. In these relationships the freedom to use clothing to express this enduring and stable aspect of self may not be without risk (cf. the answer to Q. 38-39), but the possible rewards make the risk acceptable.

So, while we probably can agree that clothing can express something stable and enduring about ourselves, we also can likely agree that the matter hardly ends there. We must weigh the mostly informal rules about dress that may mean some degree of punishment if we violate them. For crossdressers, clothing choices reflect a reality that is not as simple as gender conformity to their assigned gender or genetic sex. Sometimes masculine clothing feels right; sometimes feminine clothing feels right. But, depending on our assigned gender, only one kind of dress is generally deemed acceptable—regardless of whether it expresses us accurately. Like so many other matters in life, cultural conventions place constraints on individuality and any of us who challenge such conventions risk negative consequences.

However, challenges to cultural convention can and sometimes do result in social changes. Crossdressing women challenged social constrictions; these eventually changed. The changes included what was deemed socially acceptable for women to wear, but also extended to other spheres, such as work. After all, some manners of dress make some kinds of work unnecessarily difficult; allowing other kinds of dress for women opened up new work opportunities. Crossdressing challenges not merely fashion rules, but notions of gender, which include expectations and boundaries for social roles, including in the world of work. These challenges afford an invitation to reconsider what we think we know and possibly to expand for all genders new ways of identification and role expression.

Perhaps, then, there is a vital reciprocal action between clothing and the expression of stable and enduring personal traits. Put simply, perhaps expanding what we allow ourselves to wear also signals us to expand our very selves. Not only does what we wear express who we are, but by choosing things to wear we develop our expressing self. In this manner, the answer to the first part of our question takes on special significance. Clothing plays a pivotal role both in expressing who we are and in developing ourselves.

Is clothing itself relatively enduring and stable in what it says about gender?

If what I have suggested has merit, we can expect that such a reciprocal interaction would mean changes in broad social patterns over time. After all, *if* clothing choices expand personal development *and* such development occasionally challenges social conventions, *then* enough people changing in a certain direction of growth will erode old conventions and gradually establish new ones. This is what happened with crossdressing women. Some suggest it may be happening now with crossdressing men.

What is at stake here is broader than the idea that fashions change. The evidence of that is abundant and the cycles short enough for anyone with enough years of life to readily indicate a number of examples. However, as fashion expert Maggie Pexton Murray points out, fashion is not as ephemeral as most of us might think. She believes "the most important lesson to learn about fashion is that it repeats . . . ."[465] Perhaps, then, certain meanings persist independent of particular stylistic changes. If so, then clothing may after all offer relatively enduring and stable indications of gender.

So we have two competing hypotheses with respect to dress and gender that can be distilled to this essence: either what we wear does not reflect enduring and stable gender differentiating features or it does, despite minor and transitory changes. But to investigate which idea is correct we need evidence. Let us begin with the latter notion.

Apparel Reflects Enduring and Stable Gender Differentiating Features

We may argue that what we wear reliably differentiates the genders because we have little difficulty distinguishing boys' apparel from that for girls or women's clothes from those for men. Moreover, our ease in doing so remains despite changes in fashion. In fact, we probably have little difficulty imagining that should we travel back in time we would still be able to reliably identify men and women by their dress. Common sense, fueled by a lifetime of experience, appears to make the case a certain one.

But let us see if our certainty remains once we separate the clothing from the sexed body. If apparel reflects enduring and stable gender differentiating features we should reasonably expect to be able to tell masculine from feminine clothing even when not worn. In this regard, we might argue that a number of distinct elements provide reliable cues. These include, for instance, which side buttons appear on, whether the garment is bifurcated or not, whether there is an abundance of lace, and whether or not the garment is pink.

Unfortunately, these are not as useful as we might hope when we attempt a long, historical view. For example, buttons have not been around forever and the use of both lace and buttons has changed. Unbifurcated clothes like skirts may seem reliably feminine until we remember garments like the kilt. Pink, for awhile reserved for girls and women, appears to again be gaining favor among men—and once was seen as a strong masculine color for boys. In short, these items may work pretty well in our society right now, but may not be enduring and stable indicators of gender differentiation from a historical perspective.

Instead, we must get past the ephemeral to more subtle characteristics to argue for stable, enduring elements of gender differentiation. Are there any general features that even with the long lens of history reliably differentiate genders in clothing? We briefly examined this query earlier (see the answer to Q. 2), but it merits closer attention. The most likely candidates are the following:

- ❏ *Angularity* vs. *curves*—masculine garments accent angles while feminine garments accent curves.
- ❏ *Verticality* vs. *horizontality*—by and large, masculine garments claim vertical space while feminine garments are more expansive into horizontal space (as exemplified, for instance, by the use of fringes and expanders such as the bustle or dress hoops).
- ❏ *Free* vs. *restricted motion*: typically masculine clothing has provided a greater range of motion—and thus activity—than feminine clothing.
- ❏ *Short* vs. *long*: feminine garments have customarily been longer than masculine ones; women's legs have been more likely to be covered.
- ❏ *Rich colors* vs. *muted colors*—relatively speaking, feminine ornamentation has been more brightly (and lightly) colored, even when masculine clothing is vibrantly (though more darkly) colored. Far more often than not, masculine colors are muted and solid, with black particularly favored.[466]
- ❏ *Durable* vs. *soft* fabrics—masculine clothing traditionally has been aimed at the practical necessities of the workplace, while feminine clothing has accented softer, less durable but more sensuous tactile properties.
- ❏ *Heavy* vs. *light* fabrics—not only the texture but the weight also tends to differentiate gendered clothing, with feminine clothes being lighter.
- ❏ *Bifurcated* vs. *unbifurcated*—unbifurcated garments embracing both the whole garment (i.e., not divided at the waist), or just the legs (i.e., not divided below the waist), have been almost exclusively feminine. Bifurcated garments were typically regarded as masculine in Western societies until their thorough appropriation by women in the 20th century, but they still retain a mild masculine association.

An important caveat with even such a modest list is the relativity both culturally and historically for all these items. Exceptions may readily spring to mind and may even do so to the degree they cast serious doubt on how valid a claim can be made for them as truly enduring and stable gender differentiators.

But while exceptions come to mind so, too, should recognition of the gender stereotyping communicated. The elements above are calculated to reinforce cultural ideas about each gender's characteristics and proper domains. Women dressed in light, soft, unbifurcated garments are reinforced to appear and act gentle, passive, and demure. Their clothing excludes them from work for which heavier, more durable and bifurcated garments are clearly desirable. Obviously, male crossdressers project gender traits the wider culture discourages in men—a situation far more serious than the upward striving of women through dress in a patriarchal hierarchy.

Probably more important than the separate elements is the holistic effect they aim to contribute towards. Though we may judge articles of clothing as masculine or feminine based on individual features, we are probably more interested in the total effect: is the result more feminine or masculine? When placed in an ensemble of clothing the desired effect is typically the silhouette of a sexed body, male or female.[467] In our culture, the total effect of dress with regard to gender is to reinforce the pairing of gender with sex. Feminine clothing contributes to the silhouette of the female body; masculine apparel enhances the silhouette of the male body.

However, when we deconstruct the silhouette into separate items of apparel our attention is focused more on gender than on sex. That is one reason why we care about the elements listed above; they help reinforce gender distinctions apart from the silhouette. The fact that there are so few enduring elements is offset both by the abundance of ephemeral elements in any given historical period serving the same end and by the cumulative effect in the silhouette. In sum, whether or not the actual number of enduring and stable elements for gender differentiation is large or small, the net gain is a dependable ability to tell boys from girls, and women from men, by their dress.

Apparel Does Not Reflect Enduring and Stable Gender Differentiating Features

If the evidence for gender constant elements seems minimal, what is the case for the idea that dress does *not* reflect enduring and stable gender differentiating features? Evidence supporting this notion should first and foremost demonstrate substantial shifts in gender association so that, for example, something established as masculine over time becomes realigned and is then viewed as feminine. We might from such evidence speculate that such fashion changes in broad ways reflect different views of the genders than held previously. I alluded to one such possible judgment above: the challenge posed by crossdressing women helped change fashion and that change reflects a modified view of femininity. Obviously, fashions change and it seems reasonable to think such changes can and do reflect evolving notions about gender.[468]

On an everyday level, seeing such things is difficult. Constrained as we all are by the limited nature of the time we live in, we tend to assume that the way things are is the way they should be. We also tend to read our values back into the past. When we think about how things used to be, we use our own values as the standard by which to judge the past. At the same time, we all recognize that change does occur. We see it all around us. We certainly see it in the changing whims of clothes fashion. We also cling to some things we hold as fashion certainties—that men will never wear skirts nor women sport underwear briefs; that baby boys will wear blue and baby girls wear pink.

Too easily is history forgotten, though in this case it affords abundant evidence that apparel does *not* provide the degree of stable and enduring gender differentiation that most of us assume to be true. So let us briefly review at least Western culture's history of dress. To do so we shall examine children's clothing separate from that for adults.

Has children's wear been gender constant?

Our modern division of clothing styles along gender lines typically begins at birth with color-coding. It has not always been so. In a highly influential work, French historian Philippe Ariès argues that 'childhood', in our sense of the term, did not exist in the ancient or Medieval worlds of the West. Instead, in a major transformation extending from the late Middle Ages through the 19th century, childhood emerged first among portions of the upper class, extended throughout the upper classes, and slowly enveloped the lower classes as well. Childhood as we envision it, though, may be linked to the development in the 17th century when the child began to be dressed not as a miniature adult, but as a different entity. In Ariès' words, the child came to possess "an outfit reserved for his own age group, which set him apart from adults."[469] Therefore, our remarks are confined to the period since this transformation, especially the 19th-20th centuries.

Infants are not readily distinguished as male or female by features such as size, shape, or hair. Nor do all baby fashions particularly belong to one sex or another. So color of clothing becomes a convenient way for parents to display the gender assignment of their child. This coding also cues adult responses so that they not merely treat infants of different genders differently, and project stereotyped characteristics about gender onto the child, but they even perceive the infants' physical characteristics differently.[470]

For communication about sex and gender to be reliable it must be constant, hence the informal rule that puts boys in blue and girls in pink. Such rules must remain flexible because they express not only the mere statement of gender, but also ideas about the gender. These stereotypes establish an idealized gender standard we can seriously doubt is ever perfectly met, yet influences all of us throughout life. Blue is associated in contemporary minds with traits associated with males, while pink is joined to feminine traits.[471]

This logic has not always prevailed. Once the preference was for the opposite: pink for boys and blue for girls. Clothing historian Jo Paoletti points out that the current fashion in the United States was a French import that began in the mid-19th century but did not come into dominance until about a century later, with the post-World War II baby boom. In fact, at the end of World War I (1918) the 'debate' over what color was most appropriate for which gender had reached such heights that a trade journal, *The Infant's Department*, finally weighed in with an effort to settle the matter:

There has been a great diversity of opinion on the subject, but the generally accepted rule is pink for the boy and blue for the girl. The reason is that pink, being a more decided and stronger color, is more suitable for a boy, while blue, which is more delicate and dainty, is prettier for the girl.[472]

Clearly the associations of traits for these colors were different once than they are now.

If we retreat even a little further in time, we discover that gender distinction in infant dress was nonexistent—another clue that our contemporary way of understanding gender is not all that old. For centuries all infants and young children wore dresses. It was not until the end of the 19th century that young boys were put in trousers and many boys continued to wear dresses well into the 20th century. In fact, the white unisex dress continued to appear in catalogs until at least 1957.[473] Further, it was not unusual for boys to wear dresses until around age 6 or 7, and these would shock modern American sensibilities:

Historical clothes for boys will seem remarkable to the modern parent. Even the most fashion conscious mom will marvel at the elegant brocades, lustrous velvets, silks, taffetas, printed, striped and flowered cottons, and laces from which boys' clothes were once made.[474]

Consistent with other changes we have seen originating in the late 19th century, a new innovation came with the creation of dresses designed especially for boys.[475] These were often less lacy than designs for girls, but remained unmistakably dresses, with puffy sleeves and pleated skirts. The preferred color for a boy's dress was pink. As a general rule, as the child grew older his dresses became shorter until a 'breeching' ceremony formally transferred him from dresses to pants. This could occur anywhere between ages 3-8. At least until the 1930s, fashion magazines carried pictures of boys clothed in dresses.[476]

Various reasons have been advanced for why boys wore dresses. One is that prior to the psychological theories of the 20th century children were commonly viewed as genderless.[477] In that case, unisex garments made sense. Another explanation is that parents feared the tight constriction of pants might hinder a boy's growth.[478] Perhaps more than one reason came into play, but of the acceptability of such wear for young boys there is no doubt.

As sociologist Daniel Cook documents, as the 19th century gave way to the 20th there developed a growing interest in manufacturing and selling children's clothing. Where before 1890 factories specializing in producing children's wear were virtually nonexistent, by the end of the 1920s sale of children's clothes had led department store chains like Sears to create children's departments. Cook remarks, "Concerns about how transparently clothing indicates the sex of a child have intensified since the 1920s."[479] Arguably, we may see here the influence both of Freud's ideas and the triumphing medicalization of sex (see the answer to Q. 91). In the early decades of the 20th century there was an increasing preoccupation with gender that accompanied growing realization of children's sexuality.

After World War I, even as boy's wear was becoming more distinct and unisex garments were passing from the scene, girl's wear was changing too. The flapper style of the Roaring 20s retained the formal characteristic of being a dress, yet was accompanied by elements that signaled a more 'mannish' appearance (slender, small breasted, short hair). In the 1930s and 1940s, girls were occasionally sporting pants and shorts, though dresses and skirts remained the norm. Cries against too masculine an appearance in dress seemed less directed against girls than women. By the 1950s and 1960s, girls were able to move between pants and dresses with relative social ease. By the 1970s, girls in pants were commonplace in school; what had been casual wear was now becoming commonplace in more formal settings. By the end of the 20th century, in some societies dresses were less common than pants or slacks in a wide range of settings.

Today, girls enjoy much wider freedom of expression than boys in clothes choices. It is no longer generally acceptable for boys in Western culture to wear dresses, though sporadic news articles remind us that adolescent boys in various schools continue to push against dress codes by occasionally doing so. Girls can dress in styles ranging from what society identifies as very feminine to styles virtually indistinguishable from what boys are wearing. This freedom offers them experiences preparatory to adulthood and the fashion alternatives open to women. In contemporary Western societies like the United States, it is not until adulthood that males attain enough independence to mount more serious challenges to gender stereotypes in clothes wear. But on that matter, we shall wait a moment longer. We need to summarize the current situation with regard to children and clothing.

These days the role of clothing plays an important part in early sex-role socialization. Children associate dresses with stereotypically feminine activities and pants with traditionally masculine activities.[480] Color, too, remains important to children. As one team of researchers discovered, "Very young children may identify clothing color as one of several defining attributes of sex even before they are knowledgeable about the biological differences between the sexes."[481] Both boys and girls meet violations of social gender norms with censure.[482]

Has adult clothing fashion been gender constant?

As with children, the connection of gender to dress has an interesting history for adults. In some respects, gendered distinctions in appearance have always existed, though in terms of clothing these differences in the West, prior to the 14th century, were not pronounced; that came with the rise of fashion and, especially, its developments. Gender distinctions in dress are a function of more

210

than merely sexual anatomy—they reflect gendered social status, economic power, and so forth, too. For example, Carolyn Balkwell examined 161 preindustrial cultures to see what, if any, effect economic development had on gender distinctions in dress. She found that societies with less advanced economic activities ('folk' societies) were associated either with more ornate male dress or no appreciable difference in garb between genders. Agrarian societies, on the other hand, were more associated with ornate females.[483] Such modifiers on dress costume constitute a reminder of how robust and wide is the system with clothing at its center, and how integrally tied gender is to other matters.

A Review of Fashion History

Since our purpose in considering fashion here is a limited one, we shall content ourselves with Western fashion since the Middle Ages. Specifically we are interested in establishing the extent to which gendered distinctions have proven malleable in fashion. Transgender realities like crossdressing, which rely on dress as a crucial mechanism for the experience and expression of gender, exist within a context of changing cultural values and views, contiguous with developments in fashion. In order to crossdress an individual must appropriate elements of apparel associated in her or his social context with a gender different from the one assigned by that society to that individual.

The clothing used to identify a specific gender proves not to be as constant as we might imagine. Today we take for granted that males wear *bifurcated* (i.e., divided into pant legs) garments, like pants, but do not wear unbifurcated clothes, like skirts or dresses.[484] Yet, prior to the Renaissance (14th-16th centuries), both men and women wore basic covering garments that were unbifurcated. These were typically simple in shape and similar in appearance. For centuries the *tunic* was a basic garment for many Western peoples. It might be longer or shorter, sleeved or unsleeved, worn as an outer garment or beneath other clothing, but always it was unbifurcated. It was generally gathered at the waist, like a skirt or many dresses are.[485] The tunic generally served as a single, relatively unisex garment.

But that does not mean there were not differences among societies or, within a society, between the genders. Near the beginning of the Common Era, in the late 1st century, the Roman historian Tacitus, commenting about the German peoples, wrote:

> The universal dress is the short cloak, fastened with a brooch or, failing that, a thorn. They pass whole days by the hearth fire wearing no garment but this. The richest are not distinguished, like the Persians and Sarmatians, by a long flowing robe, but by a tight one that shows the shape of every limb. . . . The dress of the women differs from that of the men in two respects only. The women often wear undergarments of linen, embroidered with purple, and, as the upper part does not extend to sleeves, forearms and upper arms are bare.

Even the breast, where it comes nearest the shoulder, is exposed too.[486]

Every society had its parallel. Men and women were differentiated in appearance, using hair, ornamentation, and clothing. Yet, generally speaking, gendered distinctions in dress were not as pronounced as they would become. In the West, the advent of fashion in the 14th century initiated profound changes. Perhaps most significantly, technological developments made it possible for clothing styles to vary more widely and change more rapidly. The relatively static expectations and conventions of dress that prevailed in previous centuries could now be challenged and overthrown.

It was only with advances in the art of tailoring, beginning in the 14th century, that bifurcated garments began to be seen as masculine garb. However, as French fashion historian and theorist Gilles Lipovetsky points out, the first bloom of fashion in the mid-14th century, replete with gendered distinction in dress, did not produce a fixed and static divide. Apparel and attendant accessories could be—and were—swapped between the genders.[487] Fashion was predominantly men's fashion—not surprising in a cultural context where gendered distinctions reflected a patriarchal gender order and masculine needs were served first.

If fashion was men's fashion, men's fashion was bifurcated clothing, especially from the waist down. As culture scholar Steven Connor notes, this meant the acknowledgement of the male leg—and in certain cases its glorification as well.[488] In the 15th century, even as men's tunics shortened and fit more closely, outer leg-wear began to appear, particularly among the upper class. New possibilities were realized late the next century when, in 1589, Reverend William Lee of Nottinghamshire, England invented a machine that would make the production of hose, including silk hose, feasible on a new scale; Lee's production was aimed at the gentlemen of his era.

We should not think that women's fashion was of no consequence, but we should recognize it was relegated to second place for a considerable stretch of history. Men in previous centuries—especially men of the upper classes—typically showed more interest in fashion styles than would be true of men in the 20th century. Lois Banner calls medieval European history a time when both young male bodies and young female bodies were eroticised, but it remained masculine clothing that set the standard for what reflected gender and sexuality—including erotic sexuality. Not until the 16th and 17th centuries did feminine fashion gain prominence.[489]

Bifurcated clothing remained the basic gender divide in clothing, though the nature of the garb was changing. In the 16th century, men were wearing breeches; by the 19th century trousers were common. This development offered practical advantages to many tasks men pursued—and the association as masculine helped keep women excluded from both the dress and the tasks accompanying it. However, as men's clothing eventually covered the legs with pants, reducing their hosiery to ankle stockings, women's clothing increasingly showed glimpses of her legs and made more desirable hosiery to cover them. The climax of that development was reached in the 20th century with the introduction of nylon stockings.

From the advent of fashion through the next several centuries Western culture's use of dress to convey social information focused on two matters: gender and social class.[490] The 19th century was pivotal in that industrialization and other factors converged to effect a democratization of dress. Social class distinctions still existed but apparel no longer served as forcefully to show them. That left gender as the sole primary focus—and the century witnessed dramatic attention to gender differentiation through dress.

This development had dramatic repercussions for masculine and feminine fashion. Both genders were confronted with increasing pressure to conform to clothing deemed appropriate for the gender. But for men this meant fewer options, while for women their apparel options expanded. Masculine fashion became—in a word—narrow. The business suit captures the essence of the trend for men: relatively simple, uniform, and dark. In fact, bright and varied colors became almost exclusively the provenance of women. By the mid-19th century a man in brightly colored clothes was taken to show the poor taste of the lower classes, or the ignorance of a foreigner.[491]

For much of the last half millennium, it has been men who have enjoyed the greater freedom in clothing choices. During the long transition from unbifurcated common wear for men to the predominance of bifurcated garments, the former remained a part of male clothing in items like long gowns and full-skirted coats. Only in the 20th century did such unbifurcated garments finally become excluded from mainstream masculine clothing.[492] In fact, it took until the latter half of the 20th century that it could truly be argued that women had gained the greater freedom and range in clothing choices. Corresponding to that development was a disproportionate interest in fashion; in the 20th century women far exceeded men in attention to fashion. By century's end an interest in fashion was firmly established as feminine. Real men didn't care.

Nevertheless, in broad perspective across the half millennium of fashion change, masculine fashion generally proved more influential on feminine fashion than the other way around.[493] Or, as contemporary fashion designer Philippe Ducac bluntly says, "Women have always borrowed from men, whether it be for fashion or women writers at the turn of the 20th century who dressed as men in order to get recognized for their work."[494] Beginning at the dawn of Western fashion, clothing later associated predominantly with women started as menswear or unisex. So pronounced has been the influence of men's fashion on women's fashion that even the skirt—a supposedly quintessential feminine item—can be argued to have been caught up by it. Thus John Connor contends that bifurcation of the body at the waist, so that there are different garments above and below, long served as a gender divide, with men wearing bifurcated

213

apparel and women wearing dresses—a garment that drapes from the shoulders. Accordingly, the skirt, which bifurcates the body at the waist, can be said to facilitate the masculinization of female dress.[495]

Consider this brief, eclectic list, all dozen items originally made principally for men, first defined by masculine fashion, but later so appropriated by women as to either make them gender neutral or feminine:

- ❏ *Blouse*—this derivation from the masculine shirt, named by the French in the early 19th century, first referred to a short blue, loose garment made of silk or cotton and worn by workmen; similar terms for similar masculine garments are found in other languages.[496]

- ❏ *Buttons*—an item with a long history, their prominence in clothing was predominantly among men's styles; the persistent gender distinction in which side buttons appear on does not seem to have been well established before the 19th century, and buttons at the back of a garment is a distinctively feminine feature.[497]

- ❏ *Corset*—perhaps the item most often seen as thoroughly feminine, its European origin c. 1500 as an iron corset cover was for men, and padded with silk underneath.[498]

- ❏ *Hosiery*—men's legs got the early attention and even silk hosiery was made first for men.

- ❏ *Lace*—the use of lace as garment fringes has come to be associated with feminine fashion but beginning in medieval Europe it was first and foremost an aspect of masculine fashion.[499]

- ❏ *Pajamas*—brought to the West from India in the 19th century, these were made for men and replaced the earlier nightshirt—another article of clothing made in masculine fashion.

- ❏ *Pants*—pride of place in the gender divide is commonly awarded to pants, here used generically for the long history of bifurcated garments reserved for men.

- ❏ *Petticoats*—originally made for men, approximating to the waistcoat.[500]

- ❏ *Pockets*—pockets sewn into garments had replaced pouches for fashionable men by the end of the 17th century; by the 19th century they constituted a significant gender distinction in dress in English society.[501]

- ❏ *T-shirt*—now a ubiquitous unisex garment, the T-shirt originated in the 20th century as an item for men, adopted from European soldiers who used cotton undershirts in their uniform attire.

- ❏ *Underwear*—the construction of modern bifurcated undergarments focused first on men; 'panties' are derivative from underpants for men.

- ❏ *Zippers*—though invented in the 19th century, the use of zippers in clothing really began with their adoption by the U.S. army in World War I. The next big boost came in the 1920s-1930s when zippers were added to men's trousers.

In outerwear, at least, perhaps only the tie remains predominantly (though not exclusively) masculine.

In addition to items borrowed from men that in time became associated also with women, sometimes as 'feminine' rather than unisex, are items that for most of history were regarded as belonging to both genders. For example, the wig dates back thousands of years and over that long span has been popular with both men and women. While men today may still wear hairpieces, the wig itself, especially with long hair, is regarded as feminine. Similarly, the chemise—a simple shift worn next to the skin—was a unisex garment, and precursor to men's shirts. In fact, by the end of the last century the net effect of fashion trends was to reduce the inventory of masculine apparel while expanding that of feminine apparel, with the latter succeeding in part by appropriation of items previously restricted to men, or making unisex styles distinctively feminine.

Dress Reform for Women

Clearly, fashion has been and remains a prominent vehicle for envisioning and enforcing a gender divide. Women, especially, felt the brunt of its effects in previous generations.[502] But over a period of time efforts on women's behalf by both men and women aimed at and ultimately accomplished significant dress reform. The demands and opportunities afforded by the modern industrial world facilitated efforts in redefining what is acceptable for women to wear. Inevitably, over the long and arduous period of transition, women crossdressed. Some did so as part of a complete adoption of masculine identity and role, but many more did so in a way that made it perfectly plain they remained women—only their dress had changed.[503] In time they won an even greater range in what is accepted as gender appropriate clothing than men enjoy.

Resistance to this development came from many quarters.[504] Religious leaders decried the erosion of morality represented by women sacrificing their femininity by donning pants. Politicians passed laws making women dressed in clothes associated with men a criminal offense, unless they had obtained express permission. Women themselves were divided on the propriety of females in masculine attire. But even as the debates wore on, and eventually wore out, fashion was adapting to the changing reality. Women continued to dress in garb associated with men, but the manner of the clothes was changing so that a distinction could be made that preserved the gender divide. Slacks were feminized, as were shirts. Artificial but telling distinctions were made in details like the side of a shirt on which the buttons appeared. Women had successfully appropriated masculine clothing and feminized it into widespread acceptability among both men and women.

Men in Skirts

As the 20th century waned and the 21st century dawned there were signs of something similar happening for men. Already in the early 1950s, writes home economics professor and clothing scholar Mary Lou Rosencranz, beachwear for men with a wraparound, sarong-type cover-up was being offered to men. By the mid-1960s, European fashion, influenced by the popularity of the Beatles and Rolling Stones, showed men adopting clothing and hairstyles previously associated with femininity. In 1966, a Munich men's shop displayed men in miniskirts.[505] For the remainder of the century there would be periodic efforts in fashion to put men in styles regarded widely as feminine.

Entering the new millennium, Western fashion designers are still putting men in skirts (once a term reserved for menswear),[506] and other clothing with elements that contemporary people typically associate with women, like garters and touches of lingerie.[507] These bold fashion designers include both women, like Vivienne Westwood and Anna Sui, as well as noted men such as Jean Paul Gaultier, Dries van Noten, and Carlo Pignatelli. At the 2004 Paris show for men's fashion, Dior designer Hedi Slimane presented ordinary young men, rather than professional models, to wear his designs, which included skirts. The choice of wear and model was a calculated one and a pointed statement. Slimane, declaring that androgyny belonged to the late 60s, remarked that, "I wanted the clothes to feel very much like the time we're living in."[508]

That the times are opening up to men once more wearing unbifurcated garments may be indicated by the public support of highly visible celebrities. Not surprisingly, it is among male rock stars that we find the most public resistance to gender stereotyping in clothes. Nor can these artists' choices be dismissed as mere ploys to gain publicity as they publicly display an attitude of rebellion toward the culture. For that to be true the musicians would have to embrace crossdressing as travesty.

Yet Boy George, who may have attained the most notoriety for his clothing, vigorously defends his apparel as masculine and not the garb of a transvestite. He is far from alone in creative fashion statements intended to stretch the perception of what is masculine dress. David Bowie has bent gender in his garb, most notably in a dress for the cover of his album *The Man Who Sold the World* (1971), which he defended as 'a man's dress.' Other presentations are more ambiguous. A generation after Bowie, Kevin Rowland's cover for his album *My Beauty* much more provocatively depicted a crossdressed man. More notably, Curt Cobain put on a baby doll outfit that was his wife's inspiration. That he was wearing feminine clothing—and didn't care—seemed to be the point. Any number of other examples of musical artists could be put forward with various debates about what their dress intends to convey, if anything.[509]

But where much of the public expects musicians to be outlandish, they don't expect sports figures to be so. Probably the best known gender-bender in dress has been the soccer player David Beckham (inspiration for the movie, *Bend It Like Beckham*), who in 1998 sported a Jean Paul Gaulthier sarong—and liked it so well he bought several in different colors.[510] But he isn't the only athlete finding comfort in such wear. The male Balinese Olympic contingent wore

216

sarongs for their uniform at the opening ceremonies of the 1996 games in Atlanta.[511] Sometimes transgendered athletes use dress as a way to challenge stereotypes about themselves. A team comprised principally of gays, transvestites, and transsexuals—'the Iron Ladies'—won the national volleyball championship in Thailand in 1996.[512]

Male movie icons also have shown that masculinity is not compromised by putting on an unbifurcated garment, and is not wear only for period pieces. Mel Gibson donned a kilt in *Braveheart*, Samuel L. Jackson did so for his role in *The 51st State*, and the more youthful Ewan McGregor has worn one in public. Brad Pitt was garbed in skirted Greek warrior dress for the epic *Troy*. Pitt was quoted as remarking about the 'man skirts' he wore that "I'm in, I'm all for it." He also played prognosticator: "I predict it's our future."[513]

If so, the future is the past revisited. Andrew Bolton, associate curator of the Costume Institute at the Metropolitan Museum of Art, has chronicled both the history and the modern phenomena of men-wearing-skirts in his *Bravehearts: Men in Skirts*. His book emphasizes that the men in skirts described are fully secure in their masculine identities.[514] Indeed, ordinary men in many walks of life have embraced a heritage of skirts as suitable male attire, and some have even championed a new term for such garb, 'MUGS'—male unbifurcated garments— to emphasize that it is not feminine wear. Outside the world of high fashion this new term was being accompanied with advice concerning how to introduce such wear to others.[515] Men, especially young men, were venturing more often into territory previously associated with young women: fashions that challenge gender stereotypes.

This new movement is not exactly parallel to the women's movement and its association with dress reform. But it is not entirely different either and feminists offended by the suggestion there are similarities are overreacting. Women once used changes in dress behavior to challenge inadequate social conventions; some men are doing so now. Women capitalized on the status men enjoyed by copying their dress and thus borrowing some of the privilege and power associated with the wearers of masculine apparel. Some men are reacting to the success and perceived power of women by utilizing a similar strategy. Some women in appropriating elements of dress considered masculine lived with the charge of crossdressing; others denied it, claiming their dress was appropriate to their gender despite the wider public perception. Today some men—regardless of their motivation for dressing as they do—are living with the charge of crossdressing, while others are vigorously denying it and contending their apparel is appropriately masculine regardless of what many might believe.

If men are borrowing elements of dress from women, it is only fair play, since as we have seen the reverse has long been true. The real difficulty lies in the persistence of a vertical gender order seeking to keep men above women. In such a framework borrowing from women constitutes a tacit acknowledgement of their power and weakens masculine privilege. It matters not that men might do so for comfort, because they like the look or feel of a garment style, find a certain style utilitarian, or simply think men should be accorded the same right women enjoy to wear whatever they want. In order to preserve the gender hierarchy the gender divide must be maintained and that means perpetuating the idea that men in clothing culturally designated as feminine are crossdressing and that such crossdressing reflects mental illness, specifically a profound disturbance of gender identity or sexual perversity—or both!

In such a cultural climate it may be especially surprising to some of us to discover the degree of acceptance such fashion trends are finding. A survey conducted by Mark Clements Research in 2000 in Los Angeles, New York, and Chicago of women ages 21-39 revealed that slightly more than 1-in-5 (20.8%) said they would be willing to date a man dressed in a skirt. Similar levels were found for the percentage of those surveyed who stated they viewed men wearing skirts as "very" or "somewhat" acceptable (24%). Perhaps surprisingly, the survey found a similar degree of support for accepting even a brother or father who engaged in such dress (20.3%). A like percentage even expressed a willingness to share their own skirts with a man (22.3%).[516]

The question remains as to why this is happening now, and why it is happening at all. Eminent Italian sociologist Francesco Alberoni offers some hypotheses. First, the economic slump of the early 1990s provided designers incentive to be creative in the hope of sparking interest in fashion—adding feminine elements to menswear certainly accomplished that. But since there are other ways to respond to such slumps, this answer is probably not sufficient explanation. A second hypothesis, then, is that the introduction of such elements reflects either a narrowing of the gap between models of masculinity and femininity, or even a cultural dominance by women. Alberoni observes that the success of women—accompanied by their appropriation of masculine style elements—has now won the admiration and attraction of men, who are taking on feminine traits. Perhaps designers are perceiving this "urge for feminization" and responding. At the same time other forces are also at work, leading to two additional hypotheses. Ours is an increasingly multicultural world and many parts of the world are less gender divided than Western European and American societies. As Westerners tune in to other cultures they may relax more into wearing styles already acceptable elsewhere. Finally, as rigid gender lines break down, so also do rigid sexual boundaries. Radical feminists, homosexuals and bisexuals all have helped weaken "the force of heterosexual eroticism." Perhaps male clothing with feminine elements is a response to a wider anti-hetero trend—a provocation. Alberoni believes all four of these hypotheses compatible with one another. Hearkening back to Freud's notion that artistic products express different impulses it is entirely plausible to see in recent men's fashion impulses reflecting the age—and contributing to its change.[517]

What about underwear and nightwear?

Underwear

Undergarments serve several purposes, such as to protect the skin from other garb and also to protect other clothing from soiling. They have over time also acquired connections to ideas of modesty and eroticism. Such apparel has a long history, though the form it takes today is of rather recent origin. They were for a long time very simple and uniformly white.

The introduction of women's undergarments in the latter half of the 19th century can be viewed as an appropriation of men's pants,[518] and many regarded as scandalous the advent of colored undergarments in that same period.[519] Many women's garments common today have a short history: long-legged pants as undergarments were sometimes used under dresses in the early 19th century, but it wasn't uncommon for them to wear nothing at all beyond the chemise (a long shirt). Shorter pantaloons worn by women as an undergarment debuted in the mid-1860s. The modern panty, a much briefer garment, was not part of every-day use until well into the 20th century (Sears began selling them in the mid-1930s). Nylon stocking premiered at the 1939 World's Fair, but modern panty-hose—undergarment and stockings in one garment—did not appear until 1959.[520] The bra is somewhat older, having been patented in 1913,[521] and evolving into its contemporary form in the 1920s.[522]

For both men and women the period between the World Wars (1919-1939) saw a reduction in the number of undergarments worn, their extent and their thickness.[523] The 1930s in particular were a decade of important changes with regard to underwear. For both men and women there were important changes in the ways undergarments were presented and came to be perceived. For women, "items hitherto belonging to the other sex appeared in feminine guise, with, perhaps, titles jocular or slangy"[524]—a practice well-known in the contemporary market (see below). The bra during this time began to acquire greater erotic connotations through association with glamorous female movie stars.[525]

Paralleling the popularity of the panty for women was a shift in the way men's undergarments were being presented to consumers. Richard Martin succinctly summarizes this change as follows: "Health as justification shifts to comfort and social acceptance as a reason to wear the undergarment."[526] For both men and women these undergarments now fully entered the mainstream of public consciousness as desirable items and as distinctly gendered ones.

Underwear fashions in Western culture today are challenging conventions that themselves are not very old. Androgynous wear has been part of the scene for the last few decades, but it is only one part of the change occurring. Some garments, like thongs, exist in separate but similar styles for men and women. But various designers are self-consciously blending genders in their clothing as evidenced in underwear like 'boy panties' and 'boy shorts' designed for women,[527] and 'manties,' panties made for men.[528] At least one website provided directions for men to make their own male panties in various styles and colors like 'Spring Sky bikini brief.'[529]

Men are becoming major consumers of at least one item associated principally with modern women: pantyhose. A 2002 article noted that Shapings.com, a Canadian online lingerie company, reported that men accounted for 85% of their hosiery sales, prompting the company to design and market 'Comfilon,' nylon tights made for men.[530] As other companies have taken notice of this trend, some have begun targeting men, such as Leevees' 'WoMan' tights,[531] or Activskin's menswear, which includes tights, pantyhose, thigh high stockings and knee high socks all designed for men.[532] Ironically, as noted earlier, tights originated as menswear and were appropriated by women so successfully that men largely ceded the garb to them.

Nightwear

Nightwear also was not strongly differentiated for most of history. In the Enlightenment both sexes wore nightgowns:

> In the 17th and 18th centuries it was known as a nightgown and worn by both sexes as in informal housedress. It was originally based on the Far Eastern kimono or banyan. Men's dressing gowns preserved their classical style; they were made of silk or flannel and reached to the calves. They were worn for morning toilette, including breakfast. Women's dressing gowns were mostly long, so that they covered the length of the nightdress; in recent times they have also become short or of three-quarter length.[533]

Despite style differences, what men wore then would raise eyebrows now.

As in other aspects of fashion, styles have changed across the years. Paralleling the shift in underwear fashions in the 20th century were changes in the perception and marketing of night clothing, especially for women. As was the case in men and women's underwear, the 1930s represent a significant transitional period for nightwear. In feminine fashions the erotic quality of night clothing styles markedly developed.[534] This characteristic remains prominent in contemporary nightwear.

As for contemporary men's alternatives in evening wear, they are severely limited, especially when compared to that available for women. The most likely explanation for this gap—and the reason this constitutes a final frontier for men's fashion—is that the bedroom is especially associated with sex and women are stereotyped as seductresses. In our culture, men commonly justify sexual encounters as the results of seduction. In having sex, they were just giving the woman what she wanted. For enticement, the allure of sexy clothing is important—for the woman. What the man wears is immaterial. To produce lingerie for men is to challenge the rules many men and women abide by in the sexual economy of our society. The same rules that delegate to women the role of attracting attention and exciting desire through appearance tell men that dressing too sexy is to usurp a feminine role.

So, for the most part, fashion ideas of sexy male night wear are limited to thongs and silky boxers, with tank tops or body shirts if anything extra is desired. Comfort wear for bed includes pajamas (mostly cotton). Unbifurcated male garments are outerwear robes. It might well be argued that men's choices today, while perhaps wider than a decade ago, lag behind what was available more than a century ago. Still, if changes in other areas of fashion are any indication, men's lingerie may well prove to be the next creative front in fashion change.

Conclusion

We may be able to contend that what we wear differentiates the genders, but we must qualify that contention. First, the elements of differentiation we typically rely upon are neither as enduring as stable as we are apt to believe. Second, the elements we depend upon do more than signify a difference; they also reflect ideas about the genders. Third, the elements we may be able to argue persist through clothing history for differentiating genders are relatively few, arguable, and perhaps more tied to sex differentiation than gender differentiation. If we adopt the view that sex and gender need not be paired the way they often are in a rigid dichotomy, then even these differences seem less potent.

The use of prominent distinctions in dress to differentiate gender appears to be an especially modern preoccupation, one that particularly gained momentum alongside the development and triumph of the modern invention of sex. I do not claim earlier peoples were uninterested in clothing differences between men and women, but they do not appear to have been so obsessed with them as crucial markers of gender. Thus the crossdressing of earlier periods could fascinate others but rarely evoked the reaction it has in the last century or so. A difference between then and now certainly seems the valuation placed on clothes as a reliable marker of gender distinction. Yet, as we have seen, fashion is in flux in the 21st century and what constitutes 'gender appropriate' clothing is being rethought in many ways. Ironically, today we witness both a preoccupation with gender distinction in dress and the advent of fashion styles where gender lines are blurred, bent and borrowed. No one knows what yet lies ahead.

Q. 10

What does crossdressing express?

The Short Answer: Many of us would love to have an answer that works all the time for what crossdressing allegedly expresses. But crossdressing complicates an already complex expressive system in which clothes stand at the center. There isn't a universal answer to the question about what crossdressing expresses. It may prove as diverse as those who do it and variable from time to time even for them. If we are to start with defining crossdressing—'wearing dress culturally assigned to a gender different from the one assigned the wearer'—we have made a beginning, but we have done so at the middle. Crossdressing behavior sits as a link between motivation and intention at one end, and the subsequent expression effected by the behavior at the other. Unfortunately, our culture tends to diminish or dismiss both relevant contexts such as dress, and the varied nature of this chain (motivation/intention—behavior—expression), by overly focusing on the gender line crossed in the behavior. By exclusively making crossdressing about gender expression, the implicit assumption is made that gender crossing is always the motive and gender masquerade always the intended expression. Because gender and sex are so firmly knotted together, a sex and sexual component are also commonly inferred. Thus, a composite picture is popularly entertained: the crossdresser transgresses the gender line either because of a disturbed sex identity (transsexual), or a disturbed sexual orientation (homosexuality), or a disturbed sexuality manifesting in fetishism (transvestism). In whatever manner it is thus construed, crossdressing signals things to many about gender affiliation, personal identity, and individual intention that may prove not only perplexing, but troubling. Every part of the expressive system around dress is in play and no easy answers are at hand.

The Longer Answer: In answering the first several questions our concern has been to firmly seat crossdressing in the context of dress, specifically gender-differentiated dress. Toward that end we have focused on establishing a wider background in clothes, fashion, gender and sex. Although we have not ignored crossdressing, our reach has been more ambitious than merely repeating the notion that it is a simple behavior reflecting a disturbed sense of gender and perhaps also a disordered sexuality. Indeed, we have seen that clothes stand at the center of a richly varied and complex system (see the answer to Q. 1), that crossdressing depends on this system (see the answer to Q. 7), and that in and through this system important experiences and expressions, both personal and social, are made possible (see the answers to Q. 2-3).

While we have never lost sight of the significance of personal experience, more attention has been given to expression. No matter how much our own involvement with dress means to our personal exploration and sense of self, it is the expression of these things that garners the attention and often concern of others. When we talk about crossdressing we tend to devote most of our attention to speculation about what the crossdresser intends in his or her dress—and how we should respond. We grant an implicit role to personal experience as an aspect—perhaps even the central feature—of crossdressing behavior. But we typically assume that the crossdressing means to communicate something—and we want to know what that is. Whatever the crossdresser may experience takes a back seat to the public aspect of the behavior.

In sum, we presume that crossdressing is an expression meant to communicate something, rather than an expression that stands in splendid isolation, neither intending nor signifying anything. This assumption attaches itself to our interpretation of crossdressing. Sometimes overriding attention to context, we may presume a 'one size fits all' explanation. Knowing that the behavior crosses gender lines we assume such crossing constitutes an intentional statement about gender. We therefore impute this assumption to the crossdresser and adhere to it in articulating what we believe is the statement being made.

The problem we encounter rests in this: there is enough accuracy in our assumptions to render a false confidence that we fully comprehend crossdressing and the crossdresser. So we stop short. In so doing we may miss a great deal. So let us ask again:

What *is* crossdressing?

The Basics

Technically, crossdressing can be said to occur whenever some boundary set by dress is crossed. Strictly speaking, the word could be applied to social borders dress ostensibly sets for age, class status, ethnicity, profession, or any number of other things. We could say quite properly that a person who is not trained to be a doctor who dresses like a physician at a hospital is crossdressing. A Spaniard in a Scottish kilt is crossdressing, as is a European in a kimono. A poor man who dresses like a rich man is crossdressing. A middle-aged woman dressed like a teenager is crossdressing.

But we don't usually call such acts crossdressing and if we did we would probably fetch strange looks. The word today is almost entirely reserved for crossing the lines set by dress to differentiate the genders from each other. In cultures like our own where only two genders are recognized—masculine and feminine—crossdressing requires those designated masculine to dress femininely, or for those assigned femininity to dress in a masculine manner. Gender-differentiated dress functions to establish gender lines and protect them as long as we all respect the dress rules thus set. Therefore, whatever else it is, first of all *crossdressing is dress crossing gender lines.*

In crossing this line, crossdressing gains significance. Gender in our culture is critical both to personal and social identity, and largely defines opportunities and roles, so staying within gender bounds is reckoned important. The fundamental importance of gender is seen in many ways, including the fact that gender assignment is made at birth. It attains a link to sex because the assignment is based on our apparent sex. Males are assigned masculinity; females are assigned femininity. Masculinity is said to reside properly in two groups, boys and men. Femininity likewise is claimed to reside properly in two groups, girls and women. From birth forward each group faces pressures to dress in ways showing membership in that gender group and not another.

Although in actuality some boys and men might be feminine, behavior expressing that is culturally improper, just as it is culturally improper for any girls or women to show masculinity. However, because masculinity is prized more than femininity, the offense of girls or women expressing masculinity is understandable, even praiseworthy, and so sanctions leveled against such displays are often mild. Not so for boys or men appearing feminine. Cultural logic concludes a voluntary lowering of gender status, with the implicit loss of all that masculine privilege represents, is so incomprehensible as to reflect a disordered mind. So a second aspect is posited as corollary to the first: *crossdressing is transgressive.*

Because dress is a principal way to display gender, and because gender matters so much, crossdressing draws attention. An important line has been crossed and that must mean something. Most of us find it highly unlikely such an important line could be accidentally crossed, or that such a crossing is not intending to say something. In light of what we have just considered, the assumption is that what crossdressing means has to do with gender, since it is a gender line that has been crossed. So crossdressing makes a statement about gender—but what exactly is said?

Because our culture believes gender is predicated on sex, we implicitly join crossdressing to both gender and sex. This prompts the notion that crossing gender represents an attempt to cross sex lines as well. Of course, it would seem logical to presume anyone wanting to do that is confused about his or her sex identity—an attribution often made about transsexuals, who claim that their sense of gender is right but their body sex is wrong. Or we might think this sex crossing comes from ambiguity, as in an intersexed individual assigned one sex but instead identifying more with the other.

Since sex is viewed in service of sexual behavior, another presumption rears its head: crossdressing transgresses sex and gender lines in order to engage in some atypical sexual behavior. At this point the clothes make a triumphal reentry as the conclusion is drawn that the atypical behavior is seeking arousal through crossdressing rather than through interacting with a partner (transvestism). Or, the person is crossdressing to draw a same-sex partner (homosexuality). Rather than replacing the idea of disturbed sex identity, a notion of sexual deviancy is often simply added on. Thus, a third notion joined to the basic sense commonly put forward runs similar to this: *crossdressing's statement about gender reflects a disturbed sense of sex identity that manifests in aberrant sexual behavior and/or orientation.*

Through this chain of logic many of us believe we have reasoned out what crossdressing says. So if we draw everything together, we may say, 'Someone crossdresses when the gender they have been culturally assigned is different from the gender presentation associated with the clothes they are presently wearing, and that in transgressing the gender line in this manner the individual intends to make a statement about gender that also expresses something about sex and sexuality.' Perhaps this basic sense seems accurate enough to suffice. But rather than presume that it does, let us test it.

Crossdressing in Context

Thus far we have set forward only basic ideas commonly used to explain what crossdressing is. Let us now restate matters in the contexts we have established in this volume. All the familiar elements are there: clothes, gender, sex, and sexuality. These are also interconnected by our sensibility that crossdressers are pursuing some experience they value and that the result is an expression everyone else has to make sense of. We have seen one common way all these are put together which yields the stereotype of the crossdresser as a sexual deviant suffering from a disturbed sense of sex identity (and probably sexual orientation). As a stereotype this explanation can be applied to all members of the class it labels, unless more evidence causes us to further distinguish crossdressers we encounter into subtypes (see the answer to Q. 8).

How well does our basic explanation for crossdressing work?

First, let us grant that crossdressing cannot be separated from gender if only because culturally established gender lines are crossed by the clothes worn. However, we should question what this means in terms of sex and sexuality. Despite the fact that our culture statically and rigidly fixes sex and gender together, there exists no compelling reason to do so and plenty of reasons not to do so (see the answer to Q. 5). If we allow the possibility that gender is not so dependent on body sex, then two broad conclusions can be generated. First, crossdressing is not fundamentally about genitalia; a disturbed sense of sex identity may exist in some individuals but is not an inherent trait in crossdressers. Second, crossdressing also is not fundamentally about sexual behavior; fetishistic behavior may exist in some individuals but it is not a fixed feature in crossdressing. With regard to sex and sexuality we must refrain from generalizations.

Some crossdressers may have a disturbed sense of sex identity and some may seek sexual gratification through clothes, but evidence suggests neither of these things prove intrinsic to crossdressers—and both may apply to some noncrossdressers.[535]

The whole rationale behind the term—*cross*dressing—is that clothes are used to cross gender lines. Dress does serve to distinguish the sexes, but more incidentally and indirectly, relying on the presumed attachment of gender to sex. Principally, dress differentiates boys and girls, men and women—*not* males and females. If all dress needed or wanted to do was distinguish the sexes very simple coverings of the genitalia might suffice. But dress does much, much more. In differentiating genders—which need not be limited to two—dress also *characterizes* them, presenting value-laden messages about gender traits, identities, and roles. Signaling reproductive function and sexual availability are tiny parts of what dress is about.

Let us posit, for the sake of argument, that all crossdressing makes a statement about gender. That doesn't tell us what the statement is. Much crossdressing manifestly intends to say, 'This dress *isn't* my gender.' As we have learned, dress can be used to be, borrow, blend, blur or bend gender (see the answers to Q. 6-7). Sometimes, the question whether crossdressing is even occurring is pertinent. For example, two men may wear kilts; one sees the garb as feminine and wears it for that reason, while the other views it as masculine apparel that also proclaims a cultural identity. The appearance may look the same to an observer, but the statements being made are very different. Is crossdressing happening here? Is crossdressing judged by intent, or by effect?

All that reliably can be said about what crossdressing expresses with regard to gender is that it puts on display, poorly or well, a gender different from the expected one assigned at birth for the crossdresser. Whether it does so intentionally or incidentally is open to question. So we can reaffirm our first idea—crossdressing is dress crossing gender lines—but we must qualify the assertion thusly: *crossdressing is dress crossing gender lines, whether intentionally or incidentally.*

If the first assertion must be qualified, what about the second? Is crossdressing inherently transgressive? To answer this we must attend again to the experiencing and expressive system centered in dress. Crossdressing is never just about the gender line being crossed. It is also about the complex, multifaceted, deeply personal and socially significant relationship we have with clothes. In fact, crossdressing can be more about clothes than gender at times, even if the two are inseparable. It is only because of our cultural prioritizing of gender that we have such a difficult time recognizing or crediting the role of dress in its fullness. We automatically impute the role of gender (and then in a very narrow manner) with such weight that any other factor in crossdressing is inaccurately minimized.[536]

While it is fair to say that crossdressing is always about gender, both because it depends on gender-differentiated dress and because gender is the line crossed—it is *not* fair to assume that gender crossing is always the *motive* for crossdressing. Sometimes it is. And sometimes the act is meant to be transgressive. But must it be assumed so?

Calling crossdressing transgressive renders a judgment. That judgment reflects the values of the one making it, and is moral in character (cf. the answer to Q. 4). 'Transgressive' is not a neutral term; it carries a negative valence. To call all crossdressing transgressive is to call it morally wrong. But moral culpability depends on the exercise of moral will—an act for which we can be held morally accountable must be one we have willed.[537] Though crossdressing results in gender lines being crossed, this consequence need not be assumed to be the intent of the behavior.

To put the matter in moral vocabulary, using religious terms, ample evidence exists from the testimony of crossdressers that their behavior typically intends confession rather than transgression. In other words, the intent is not to cross any lines but to stay within the lines that best unify the self. Since clothing acts as a second skin, we use it to image what we imagine—a creative and constructive impulse rather than a transgressive one. In the crossdresser's mind the intent and the effect of crossdressing meet in a unified presentation of the gendered self.

What then is the message? The moral will marshaled by the crossdresser typically intends to say, '*This* dress exhibits my gender, not what others assigned me to wear.'[538] The act is positive in nature, putting forward an assertion meant to unify the self. The intended effect may accomplish this for the crossdresser while simultaneously breaking gender-differentiated dress codes. But the latter result is an unintended and incidental effect. It is a byproduct of a constructive act.[539] Accordingly, we are more accurate to claim that *crossdressing seldom is transgressive in intent though it may often result in offense where none is intended or desired.*

That leaves only the third basic assertion, that crossdressing reflects a disturbed sense of sex identity that manifests in aberrant sexual behavior. To a large extent we already addressed this idea. By loosening the perceived connection between gender and sex we need not infer either a disturbance of sex identity or the pursuit of sexual deviancy. To be sure, some crossdressers may have a disturbed sense of sex identity. Some may use crossdressing simply for sexual pleasure. But lacking evidence this is always or even normally the case the basic assertion is grievously flawed. We will be more accurate if we rework this assertion as follows: *crossdressing's expression of gender may be interpreted in ways that focus on presumed disturbances of sex identity or sexual behavior but these often are not what is intended and are highly inaccurate.*

So where are we left in answering what crossdressing is? We can agree that it crosses gender lines, but we must be careful about assuming this crossing is intentional. As we saw with the instance of two men wearing kilts, cultural considerations and intentions must also be reckoned in gauging behavior. We also have to be wary of assuming crossdressing is transgressive, or reflects disturbance in either sex identity or behavior. While the results thus stated may be frustrating—after all, we all like simple, clear cut answers—they are more nuanced and accurate. Nor is all hope lost for some basic guideline to acquiring an adequate sense of crossdressing. All of the above assertions and qualifications ultimately depend on one thing: *context*.

What crossdressing is depends on context. Better said, crossdressing depends on multiple, intersecting contexts. Both gender and dress are critical contexts, with the latter central to the presentation of the former, even as the former guides the development of the latter. Personal and social contexts (including culture) also matter greatly. As we have just described, all of these come together in our efforts to describe, or define, crossdressing.

What does intention have to do with crossdressing?

An important contextual element identified by our struggle to see how these things intermingle is intention. What, if anything, does a crossdresser intend in crossdressing? Intention flows from motivation; some force or forces set a direction that the individual goes. But motivations and intentions are treacherous waters to navigate.

We might think we are better off staying with the simplest possible definition of crossdressing and refraining from speculation as to motivation. This course may sound scientifically objective but it does not and cannot happen that way. Because the gender line is crossed, and because gender is tied so closely to sex and sexuality in our culture, any definition *sans* specification of—or at least speculation about—motivation leaves intact the implicit assumption that only one, or perhaps a narrow range of motives is present, and that the motive or motives are obvious and sexual. Human psychology is not so straightforward.

Comprehending crossdressing in context requires recognition of varying motivations and intentions. We entered this discussion at the middle element in a chain: the behavior of crossdressing. The behavior links motivation to expression.[540] This chain is not unidirectional. Sometimes an expression unintended by a behavior provides the motivation to explain our intention even when no such intention originally existed! Right now we won't concern ourselves with directionality. Nor will we explore various motivations—a task accomplished a bit later (see the answer to Q. 12).

Instead, we will reflect a moment on the importance of motivation and intention. For now, let's set aside the plethora of possible motivations and simply look at whether an intention to crossdress exists. Earlier we asked if crossdressing is a matter of intention or effect. Perhaps it is both. To determine what is the case we can consider a number of situations that might be construed as crossdressing.

Is a baby boy dressed in pink crossdressing? Is a woman intending to pass as a man by wearing jeans and a shirt crossdressing? Likely we answered 'no' to the first instance and 'yes' to the second. Even though the boy crosses the gender line in dress code, observers recognize others dressed him. Lacking intent, we may draw the curious conclusion that the boy is not crossdressing though he is crossdressed! In the other situation, though women in our culture often enough wear men's shirts and jeans without being called crossdressers, the intent to pass as a man separates this woman's behavior from that of most women engaged in similar behavior. Apparently, intention triumphs over effect; where the former is lacking, the latter is mitigated, but where the former is present, the latter is enhanced.

Yet other cases may prompt doubt that intention is really so much weightier. What about the man who wears a kilt thinking it is a woman's skirt? Here the intention is to crossdress, but a kilt is masculine apparel. Does the person's error in what he chose to wear render his behavior innocuous? Observers are unlikely to regard the behavior as crossdressing unless they, too, don't know a kilt when they see one. Does crossdressing then depend on the perception of observers who judge that gender lines have been crossed? If so, intent is determined by others than those to whom the intention belongs—an odd situation almost certain to result in numerous errors in judgment.

Shall we say instead that crossdressing depends on both intention and effect? If so, then what intention has to be present? Imagine a woman intentionally wearing men's apparel, fully aware she is crossing gender lines in dress, but resolute because these are the only clothes she can find that fit comfortably. She makes no effort to act either more or less feminine than she ordinarily does. Is she crossdressing?

By this point we may be tempted again to retreat to a refusal to speculate on intention. Our alternative is to rely on observer perceptions, but those are almost always colored by inferences of intention. No matter how we try to squirm our way out of it, trying to answer what crossdressing is, and to know it when we see it, involves us in thinking about motivations, intentions—and our own judgments. In sum, we cannot escape the experiencing and expressing system that showcases gender-differentiated dress. We need to retrench ourselves in it to comprehend crossdressing.

What is crossdressing expressing?

As we have seen (in the answer to Q. 1), the expressive subsystem involving dress has these basic elements: a point of origin, rules, points of reception, and context. Crossdressing fits into this framework. One person dons dress associated within the culture with a different gender (the point of origin). In so doing, the customs and conventions of dress (the rules) for that society, and perhaps for a cultural subgroup, come into play. Crossdressing may, depending on the situation (context), follow, bend, or break these dress rules. Witnesses to the behavior (points of reception), whether the crossdresser him or herself, or others, apply the rules in the context to assist their interpretation of the expression.

They also contribute to the context their own values and experiences. Only with all these elements in play can we speak about what crossdressing is expressing.

Crossdressing very often occurs in private and thus serves an expressive system meeting an individual's experiencing needs. In such cases, the individual is both point of origin and point of reception. Nevertheless, dress rules still apply and the crossdresser's private context structures these so that the result may be interpreted by the crossdresser as being, borrowing, blending, blurring, or bending gender.

Sometimes crossdressing occurs in the presence of others. In such cases the points of reception extend to people besides the crossdresser. It is legitimate, then, to ask what—if anything—crossdressing communicates to them. As is true with clothes in general, crossdressing selections may be meant to express an affiliation or one's individuality—or both. But whatever the crossdresser intends, the rules and context in which the crossdressing occurs serve other witnesses in the act of interpreting the expression.

Crossdressing, for many of us, confuses the vital message sending/receiving process we normally rely upon, which presupposes a fixed gender divide. On the one hand, there is the problem of deciphering what the crossdressing means from the perspective of the crossdresser (the point of origin). What is the crossdresser expressing, and is it intended as a communication to others? On the other hand, what does the crossdressing mean to those who witness it (the points of reception)? When we examine the situation and setting, do they help us? What do we do with the customs and conventions of society, as we understand them? How do we reckon with the vexing problem of getting past our own filters, which may not make it easy for us to get whatever message might be present? What do our experiences and values allow us to hear?

Let's start with the first problem. What are crossdressers expressing or communicating? As we noted above, crossdressing happens for a variety of reasons. Although it is premature to go into details right now, it is appropriate to affirm that those reasons, among many possibilities, may reflect a group affiliation, or constitute a form of self-expression, or even state an intention about sexual desire. It is legitimate to ask if some or all of those reasons are why some people get upset over crossdressing. The answer isn't hard to guess.

For people who not only do not belong to a group where crossdressing is acceptable behavior (such as within some homosexual circles), but who strongly dislike that group, the association of crossdressing with the group makes it guilty by association (e.g., 'all crossdressers are these kinds of homosexuals'). Now, if all crossdressing were correlated with the group the person objects to, then this solution would be elegantly simple and efficient. But crossdressing proves a much wider phenomenon. Assuming that a crossdresser belongs to a certain group is more often than not an error. The result is that objecting to crossdressing on this ground alone is irrational and produces judgments that are wrong and perhaps even harmful (as when the crossdresser also objects to the group that he or she has been erroneously identified with, as may happen when heterosexual crossdressers are thought to be homosexual).

A more sophisticated objection, along the same lines of rejecting cross-dressing because of the affiliation with a group, concerns gender. The argument here is that crossdressing is upsetting because it transgresses gender lines, which society presumably needs to keep distinct.[541] This assumes that in all crossdressing an affiliation with the opposite gender is made and probably intentionally so. The assumption, though, runs into the same difficulty as the previous objection: not all crossdressing is about gender. Indeed, some who 'crossdress' object that such a term is itself inaccurate and prejudicial.[542]

But let's assume for a moment that something *is* intentionally being said about gender affiliation. Even so, more than one possibility exists. Crossdress-ers may be expressing a *degree* of affiliation with a gender different than their as-signed one. This degree of affiliation can range from partial and occasional (as in transvestism), to complete (as in transsexualism). Or, if some theorists are correct, crossdressing may reflect an affiliation with a gender identity that is nei-ther 'male' nor 'female' as traditionally understood. Instead, crossdressers may occupy a position (or positions) somewhere in-between.[543]

If gender should be viewed as constructed, performative, and ranged along a spectrum (see the answer to Q. 5), then the situation gets even murkier. What gender is being expressed when both masculine and feminine elements of cloth-ing are present? Is it the clothing that matters, or the intention of the wearer, or the perception of witnesses? Can someone dress in clothes associated with the stereotype of a different gender and intend his or her assigned gender? Can such a person intend affiliation with a different gender at one point, then intend af-filiation with her or his assigned gender at another point, and be dressed the same way? Or does private intention weigh much against the visible garb and its association with one gender or another? In short, just how fluid and relative are matters of gender and fashion?

The real concern here for many folk, though, is not merely about gender af-filiation. The anxiety is over crossdressing where an intention or desire for sex-ual interaction is also being signaled. For many folk the whole thing boils down to a matter of truth in advertising. If someone dresses to signal sexual availabil-ity, then perspective suitors should have a right to know the gender of the per-son sending the message. And clothes are basic to our figuring that out.[544] In this case, the only interest in gender lies in its presumed one-to-one connection with biological sex and the viewer's assumptions about what dress says concern-ing sexual orientation (e.g., 'If someone dresses like a member of the opposite sex, then that person must be expressing homosexuality.').

Of course, we have been assuming that crossdressers are sending a message in what they wear. But what if a crossdresser isn't intending to say anything to others by this behavior? What if the crossdressing is an expression devoid of any intention to communicate to others? This is an important question because experts agree that the majority of crossdressing occurs in secret. Perhaps there isn't any message meant, or the message is purely a private one. The whole matter of what it means remains a purely personal matter until the secret is discovered.

What is being received when crossdressing is encountered?

And that leads us to the second problem: what are we willing to understand when we encounter crossdressing? Will we challenge whatever filter we already have in place that prevents us from seeing alternative explanations? Before we can answer that well we must confront the existence of the filters we rely on now. These generally reflect cultural ideas, but are also influenced by our own experiences and values to make them distinctively ours. What culture contributes—at least Western culture—are definite notions about gender and its expression that we expect people's behavior to conform to.[545]

One such idea, perhaps the most fundamental, is recognized by Helen Boyd in her book, *My Husband Betty*. In trying to understand her husband's crossdressing behavior, Boyd offers as a 'best guess' the explanation that male crossdressers are trying to experience their whole selves, especially those parts a patriarchal society denies them. And, says Boyd, that is where the rub comes in. Precisely because ours is a male-dominant culture, men are not supposed to desire giving up in any way the prerogatives that come from being on top of the social pile. To dress as a woman seems an incomprehensible lowering of social status, regardless of the price paid for maintaining that status.[546]

In an era where more and more people are concerned with gender equality, there is a profound irony here. Crossdressing can be understood as a behavior *par excellence* in gender-leveling. Certainly, women crossdressing was an instrumental part of their efforts to raise their social status. But the abiding force of patriarchy still keeps both men and women from a general acceptance of men being more like women. Hence males crossdressing as females meet with a decidedly different response than when women dress like men. This is one of the last frontiers in the battle for gender equality—but our filters are such that we rarely see it as such.[547]

Of course, the whole point is our filters, which are constructed by our values and experiences. Some filters prompt some of us to lean in one direction, just as others of us possess values and experiences that lean us in a different direction. But we all will profit from a willingness to challenge our preconceptions, broaden our experiences, and review our values.

Important to this process is information. We have, in this first question set, examined the broad context of dress. In so doing we have considered a great many ideas. We have learned that crossdressing is one aspect of a massive system built around clothes that allows us to achieve significant experiences and produce meaningful expressions. Yet in looking so much at clothes we may wonder what has happened to the people who wear them.

In the next volume we must redirect our attention to focus on crossdressers themselves. Our exploration there will begin with preliminary matters such as clarifying some basic terms commonly used. Then more detailed examination will be made of proposed causes for crossdressing and the life experience of crossdressers. In sum, we will be seeking to address two important questions: Who crossdresses—and why?

Notes

Please note: Extensive use of internet resources is reflected in these notes. Every effort has been made to supply print references alongside web addresses where both were available. Although the World Wide Web constitutes an invaluable resource for research, webpages come and go; no guarantee can be made that resources used in preparing these notes are available to the reader at a later date.

Notes for Preface

[1] *GenderPAC. First National Survey of TransGender Violence* (GenderPAC, 1997), p. 2. Accessed online at http://hatecrime.trans advocacy.com/ documents/TransViolence%20Survey%20Results.pdf. GenderPAC may be contacted at 274 W. 11th St, New York, NY 10014.

[2] What I am 'for' is all efforts to engage rationality with compassion; what I am 'against' is any irrational, reactionary disgust or hatred. The triumph of truth is tolerance.

Question Set 1 Introduction Notes

[1] Mark Twain, *The Wit and Wisdom of Mark Twain: A Book of Quotations* (Mineola, NY.: Dover Publications, 1999), p. 3.

[2] Peter Wollen, "Addressing the Century," in P. Wollen (Ed.), *Addressing the Century. 100 Years of Art and Fashion*, pp. 6-77 (London: Hayward Gallery Publishing, 1998), p. 8.

[3] The contemporary preoccupation with other aspects of gender has relegated the role of clothing to so far in the rear that it scarcely gathers any attention from most of those who study crossdressing. For example, sexologist Holly Devor consciously avoids using terms like "crossdresser" or "transvestite" when discussing female gender dysphorias because she desires to "deflect attention away from the largely moot point of what constitutes clothing socially designated as appropriate only for men, and to direct attention to more central issues of gender." (See her "Female Gender Dysphoria in Context: Social Problem or Personal Problem?" *Annual Review of Sex Research, 7*, 44-89 (1996), p. 45.) But, as we shall find, social designations relating gender to clothing are not only not "largely moot," but central to understanding crossdressing—and gender.

Q. 1 Notes

[4] Janet T. Spence, "Gender Identity and Its Implications for Concepts of Masculinity and Femininity," in T. Sondregger (Ed.), *Nebraska Symposium on Motivation*, pp. 59-95 (Lincoln: Univ. of Nebraska Press, 1985), p. 64.

[5] Carole Turbin, "Refashioning the Concept of Public/Private. Lessons from Dress Studies," *Journal of Women's Studies, 15* (no. 1), 43-51 (2003), p. 44.

[6] For a wider ranging examination of the issues involved in answering this question, see Michael R. Solomon & Nancy J. Rebolt, *Consumer Behavior: In Fashion* (Englewood Cliffs, NJ: Prentice Hall, 2003), Part II: Consumer Characteristics and Fashion Implications.

[7] Tattersall's ideas are set forth in a variety of places, including the books *Becoming Human: Evolution and Human Uniqueness* (N. Y.: Harcourt Brace, 1998) and *The Monkey in the Mirror: Essays on the Science of What Makes Us Human* (N. Y.: Harcourt Brace, 2002). Interestingly, though agreeing that there is a human need for dress (both for protection from environmental elements and for self-communication), Kate Soper argues this need has been neglected if not actually repressed. See her essay, "Dress Needs: Reflections on the Clothed Body, Selfhood and Consumption," in J. Entwistle & E. Wilson (Eds.), *Body Dressing. Dress, Body, Culture* (pp. 13-32) N. Y.: Berg, 2001.

[8] Ralf Kittler, Manfred Kayser, & Mark Stoneking, "Molecular Evolution of *Pediculus humanus* and the Origin of Clothing," *Current Biology, 13* (no. 16), 1414-1417 (2003, Aug. 19).

[9] Malgorzata Zimniewska & Ryszard Kozlowski, "Natural and Man-Made Fibers and Their Role in Creation of Physiological State of Human Body," *Molecular Crystals and Liquid Crystals, 418*, 113-130 (2004). This work is discussed further in the answer to Q. 2.

[10] William I. Thomas, "The Psychology of Woman's Dress," *American Magazine, 67*, 66-72 (1908), p. 66. Accessed online at http://spartan.ac.brocku.ca/~lward/Thomas/Thomas_1908_b.html. This paper is part of a collection of Thomas' works included in a Mead Project web site at the Department of Sociology of Brock University.

[11] See Ruth P. Rubinstein, *Dress Codes: Meanings and Messages in American Culture* (Boulder, CO: Westview Press, 1995), ch. 2 (pp. 16-30). Rubinstein identifies the three ideas—covering, modesty, ornamentation—that are discussed in this answer.

[12] I briefly set forth some of the basic ideas and divisions of magic, as well as its relation to science and to religion in G. G. Bolich, *Twelve Magic Wands. The Art of Meeting Life's Challenges* (Garden City Park, NY: SquareOne Publishers, 2003). Dress properly belongs to instrumental magic but strongly links physical magic and imaginative magic; it also can be utilized by sympathetic magic.

[13] George Bush & Perry London, "On the Disappearance of Knickers: Hypotheses for the Functional Analysis of the Psychology of Clothing," in M.

E. Roach & J. B. Eicher (Eds.), *Dress, Adornment, and the Social Order,* pp. 64-72 (N. Y.: John Wiley & Sons, 1965), p. 65.

[14] Economic historian Margaret Walsh offers a succinct and wholly appropriate remark about defining the term (and related kin): "Definitions of fashion, style, or dress, are myriad, but all suggest that it is a process of continuous change of typical modes for whatever reason." See Margaret Walsh, "The Democratization of Fashion: The Emergence of the Women's Dress Pattern Industry," *Journal of American History, 66* (no. 2), 299-313 (1979), p. 299 n. 3. For a full analysis of the "fashion process" by which new styles emerge, are accepted, and finally displaced, see George B. Sproles & Leslie D. Burns, *Changing Appearances: Understanding Dress in Contemporary Society* (N. Y.: Fairchild Books & Visuals, 1994).

[15] Gilles Lipovetsky, *The Empire of Fashion. Dressing Modern Democracy,* translated by C. Porter (Princeton: Princeton Univ. Press, 1994; original work published 1987), p. 15. While agreeing with Lipovetsky that Western fashion can be dated to this point in time, I disagree with his emphasis on its historical singularity. Call it what we might, something similar can be found in other cultures and across history so that the word 'fashion' is occasionally employed in my work without limitation to the West from the 14th century forward. See, for example, François Boucher, *20,000 Years of Fashion. The History of Costume and Personal Adornment,* expanded ed. (N. Y.: Harry N. Abrams, 1987).

[16] Ann Priest, "Uniformity and Differentiation in Fashion," *International Journal of Clothing Science and Technology, 17* (nos. 3-4), 253-263 (2005), p. 253.

[17] Joe Au, "Grounded Design Theory of Italian Fashion Designers," *Journal of the HEIA, 8* (no. 2), 24-32 (2001), p. 29.

[18] Joanne Finkelstein, "Chic Theory," *Australian Humanities Review* (1997, March). Accessed online at http://www.lib.latrobe.edu.au/AHR/archive/ IssueMarch1999/finkelstein.html.

[19] Georg Simmel, "Fashion," *International Quarterly, 10* (no. 1), 130155 (1904 translation of 1895 original), p. 133. The work is more readily available in a reprint in the *American Journal of Sociology, 62* (no. 5), 541-558 (1957).

[20] Patty Brown & Janett Rice, *Ready-to-Wear Apparel Analysis,* 3rd ed. (Upper Saddle River, NJ: Prentice Hall, 2001). See especially chapter 3.

[21] Finkelstein, "Chic Theory."

[22] This idea appears in Lancelot Hogben's book, *From Cave Painting to Comic Strip: A Kaleidoscope of Human Communication* (N. Y.: Chanticleer Press, 1949).

23 J. A. Hamilton & J. W. Hamilton, "Dress as a Reflection and Sustainer of Social Reality: A Cross-Cultural Perspective," *Clothing & Textiles Research Journal*, 7 (no. 2), 16-22 (1989).

24 Theo K. Miller, Lewis G. Carpenter, & Robert B. Buckey, "Therapy of Fashion," in M. E. Roach & J. B. Eicher (Eds.), *Dress, Adornment, and the Social Order,* pp. 269-270 (N. Y.: John Wiley & Sons, 1965).

25 Margaret C. Miller, "Reexamining Transvestism in Archaic and Classical Athens: The Zewadski Stamnos," *American Journal of Archaeology, 103*, 223-253 (1999), p. 223.

26 See, for example, G. M. Rose, A. Shoham, L. R. Kahle, & R. Batra, "Social Values, Conformity, and Dress," *Journal of Applied Social Psychology, 24,* 17, 1501-1519 (1994). In addition to the function of clothing in helping to establish belonging to a group, they also point out other important ideas, like how the way we dress reflects our values and how the fashion adopted by a group exerts a pressure toward conformity among the group members.

27 The limitation of motion by apparel is a consequence used instrumentally to discourage or prevent activities not regarded as appropriate for a gender. Dresses, for example, effectively hinder many energetic activities such as sports or certain kinds of work. By rewarding passivity they encourage the trait as a hallmark of femininity.

28 Turbin, p. 45. She characterizes dress as "double-edged, both public and private, individual and social."

29 Cf. G. G. Bolich, *Serving Human Experience. The Boundary Metaphor* [Ph.D. dissertation for Union Institute and University] (Ann Arbor, MI: AMI Dissertations, 1993).

30 We could argue that clothes constitute the first contraceptive.

31 The whole matter of fetishism associated with clothing is an important subject and all too commonly misunderstood. The subject is a matter explored in answering Q. 88

32 MiKyeong Bae, Seung Sin Lee, & Sun Young Park, "The Brand Name Effect of Consumer's Evaluation on Intrinsic Attributes: A Case Study of Clothing Market," *International Journal of Human Ecology, 4* (no. 1), 45-54 (2003), p. 45.

33 On the idea of dress as a kind of symbolic communication, see Mary E. Roach-Higgins & Joanne B. Eischer, "Dress and Identity," *Clothing & Textiles Research Journal, 10* (no. 4), 18 (1992). Their article points out some of the subtle complexity of how we rely on dress for communicating and understanding both identity and social position in our interactions with others. Cf. M. L. Damhorst,

"In Search of a Common Thread: Classification of Information Communicated Through Dress," *Clothing & Textiles Research Journal, 8* (no. 2), 112 (1990).

[34] Cultural differences also make it wise to see crossdressing in cultural context: whereas in our culture it serves principally to say things about gender as tied to sex, in other cultures it may speak to the relation of gender to divisions of labor. While it is natural and inevitable we will impose our cultural filters on other societies, we need to discipline ourselves to the task of seeing crossdressing in cultural context.

[35] Perhaps crossdressers in our culture are particularly good representatives of all three of these matters. Crossdressers may be less likely to dismiss important aspects of the experiencing that takes place, thus expanding the experiencing of dress more than most, and also perhaps more likely to consciously attribute to clothes the effects experienced.

[36] Susan Kaiser, *The Social Psychology of Clothing: Symbolic Appearances in Context*, 2nd ed., rev. (N. Y.: Fairchild Publications, 1997). Kaiser identifies also such factors as social class and ethnicity, matters touched upon in answering Q. 4.

[37] In Jung's view, the collective unconscious presents itself to us in a gendered way. To males it comes as *anima*, the feminine; to females as *animus*, the masculine. The *anima* and *animus* are both 'archetypes,' mythological motifs that together form the 'collective unconscious,' which represents an unconscious pattern of mind common to all humanity. See, among other works of Jung, C. G. Jung, *Analytical Psychology. Its Theory and Practice* (N. Y. Vintage Books, 1968 edition of the Tavistock Lectures of 1935), pp. 40-41, 99f.

[38] See C. G. Jung, *The Archetypes and the Collective Unconscious. Collected Works, Vol. IX, Parts 12.* Translated by R. F. C. Hull (Princeton: Princeton Univ. Press, 1959). We should observe how even the wording of this perpetuates the gender dichotomy of our culture. Jung has been criticized for developing depictions of the *anima* and *animus* that merely reinforce gender stereotypes.

[39] This is a notion explored by Jungian therapist Lin Fraser, "Observations About Transgendered People." Presentation to ETVC San Francisco, August 11, 1990, edited by R. Schneider. Accessed online at *GenderWeb.org* website at http://www.genderweb.org/experien/obstg. html. Fraser's ideas are also discussed in answering Q. 98. For more on a Jungian perspective, see psychologist Rachael St. Claire, "A Jungian Analysis of Transgender Identity Development and Internalized Transphobia." Presented at the Harry Benjamin International Gender Dysphoria Association Symposium XVI, August 1721, 1999. Accessed online at *Transgender Soul* website at http://www.transgendersoul.com/transgender_dreams.htm. For a Jungian perspective from a male crossdresser, see

Cathy Anderson, *Jung's Anima Theory and How It Relates to Crossdressing* (2001). Accessed online at http://ourworld.compuserve. com/homepages/cathytg/anima.htm.

[40] Craig J. Thompson & Diana L. Haytko, "Speaking of Fashion: Consumers' Uses of Fashion Discourses and the Appropriation of Countervailing Cultural Meanings," *Journal of Consumer Research, 24,* 15-42 (1997).

[41] Bae, Lee & Park, p. 48 (Table 1).

[42] Ibid.

[43] Ibid.

[44] Usha Chowdhary, "Correlates of Apparel Significance Among Older Men and Women," *Journal of Consumer Studies & Home Economics, 24* (no. 3), 150-159 (2000).

[45] Jason Cox & Helga Dittmar, "The Functions of Clothes and Clothing (Dis)satisfaction: A Gender Analysis Among British Students," *Journal of Consumer Policy, 18* (nos. 2-3), 237-265 (1995), p. 248. Among the other three factors, one explicitly relates to the social dimension ('symbolize relatedness with others and social group membership'); the other two relate to luxury and to utility.

[46] Alison Lurie, *The Language of Clothes* (N. Y.: Owl Books, 2000), p. 22.

[47] Cf., for example, Roland Barthes, *The Fashion System*, translated by M. Ward & R. Howard (Berkeley: Univ. of California Press, 1990 reprint of 1983 ed.). Barthes' detailed work explores, among other things, the relation between 'real clothing' (i.e., clothing as such), 'image-clothing' (e.g., photographs of clothing) and 'written clothing' (e.g., depictions in writing of clothing). These reflect different, but related, structures: technological, iconic, and verbal. Each has its own 'shifters' that 'transform' one structure into another 'representation.' As this brief description might suggest, Barthes is not interested in either clothes or 'fashion' *per se*, but in how a social reality—fashion—is itself garbed in language representation. While acknowledging the reality of 'real clothing' as part of a sign system, that reality is not his prime interest; it is ours.

[48] Lurie, p. 3.

[49] Fred Davis, *Fashion, Culture, and Identity* (Chicago: Univ. of Chicago Press, 1992), pp. 10-11. Cf. Fred Davis, "Clothing and Fashion as Communication," in M. R. Solomon, *The Psychology of Fashion*, pp. 15-27 (Lexington, KY: Lexington Books, 1985).

[50] This is most often the case for the heterosexual male crossdresser. Interestingly, this reality, though motivated by somber recognition of the practi-

cal risks of having other witnesses, is viewed negatively by some mental health professionals who see in it mostly narcissistic self-absorption rather than sensible caution. This kind of negative judgment, though, probably reflects the cultural bias of contemporary American mental health toward downplaying social factors such as bias and prejudice. Therapists trained in a 'traditional' (White European) model of counseling emphasize individual responsibility even to the point of unwittingly reinforcing a call to 'adjust' by conforming to often irrational social forces.

[51] These rules are dress norms—"shared standards or rules which specify what human beings should or should not think, say, or do, and how human beings should or should not look under given circumstances." Jane E. Workman & Elizabeth W. Freeburg, "Part I: Expanding the Definition of the Normative Order to Include Dress Norms," *Clothing & Textiles Research Journal, 18* (no. 1), 46-55 (2000), p. 46. Workman and Freeburg document the existence of such norms in our modern society.

[52] Lurie, p. 8.

[53] For an example of research along these lines, see Mary Lyn Damhorst, "Meanings of Clothing Cues in Social Context," *Clothing & Textiles Journal, 3* (no. 2), 39-48 (1985). Cf. Mary Lyn Damhorst, Kimberly A. Miller, & Susan O. Michelman (Eds.), *The Meanings of Dress* (N. Y.: Fairchild Books and Visuals, 1999).

[54] Sociologist Irving Goffman, in writing about our presentation of self, noted the importance of assessing situations to determine our self-presentation, including our manner of dress, to involve ourselves in the situation. Inappropriate dress to a situation can result in rejection and exclusion. See Irving Goffman, *The Presentation of Self in Everyday Life* (N. Y.: Anchor Books, 1959). Also cf. Irving Goffman, *Gender Advertisements* (N. Y.: Harper & Row, 1976), which examines how posed self-presentations are used in media to communicate and perpetuate cultural stereotypes about gender.

Q. 2 Notes

[55] Joanne Entwistle, *The Fashioned Body* (Cambridge: Polity Press, 2000), p. 6.

[56] The padded bra comes immediately to mind as a shape-altering piece of clothing, but multiple examples could be summoned. People wear black for its slimming effect, don corsets to change how their waist looks, and otherwise use clothes to manipulate the body to better fit certain clothes and project a desired silhouette.

[57] Anthony Giddens, *Modernity and Self-identity: Self and Society in the Late Modern Age* (Cambridge: polity Press, 1991), p. 62.

58 The billboard use of clothes is obvious to clothing manufacturers who use the medium to advertise their wares every time someone puts on one of their garments. Other companies are also acutely aware of this phenomenon as witnessed by the many companies who use T-shirts, jackets, hats, and other items to put their corporate logo, image, or message out to the public.

59 Entwistle, p. 7.

60 For our purposes, we will imagine the self as comprised of complex, internalized self-contents (such as personality and character attributes), protected and delineated by a complex system of boundaries, both physical and psychological. See G. G. Bolich, *Serving Human Experience: The Boundary Metaphor* (Ann Arbor, MI: Doctoral dissertation for the Union Institute, 1993).

61 Elise Dee Co, *Computation and Technology as Expressive Elements of Fashion*. A thesis for the M.S. in Media Arts and Sciences, School of Architecture and Planning, Massachusetts Institute of Technology (1998), pp. 24-25; quote is from p. 24. Accessed online at http://acg.media.mit.edu/projects/thesis/eliseThesis.pdf.

62 On this particular matter, see Li Yi, *The Science of Clothing Comfort* [*Textile Progress, 31* (nos. 1-2)] (Manchester, UK: The Textile Institute, 2001).

63 A. D. Craig, "How Do You Feel? Interoception: The Sense of the Physiological Condition of the Body" [Perspective], *Nature Reviews Neuroscience, 3* (no. 8), 655-666 (2002). Craig's piece is an argument based on recent neuroscience findings to broaden the traditional notion of interoception. For our point, the relevance of interoception lies in the immediate assessment of clothes as a 'second skin' in such a way that a global feeling is generated from the physiological inputs gathered from the tactile sensations of what is worn within a mediated psychological context.

64 Malgorzata Zimniewska & Ryszard Kozlowski, "Natural and Man-Made Fibers and Their Role in Creation of Physiological State of Human Body," *Molecular Crystals and Liquid Crystals, 418*, 113-130 (2004), pp. 114-116. In 1923, a writer opined, "When clothing is hygienically correct, the wearer is able to forget the body completely and to concentrate the attention on other things." Helen Goodrich Buttrick, *Principles of Clothing Selection* (N. Y.: Macmillan, 1923), p. 8.

65 Ibid, pp. 117-120.

66 Ibid, pp. 120-124.

67 Ibid, pp. 124-128.

68 Ritva Koskennurmi-Sivonen & Päivikki Pietarila, "Quality Clothes— An Outline of a Model for Assessing the Quality of Customized Clothing,"

Emergence of Luxury (2005), p. 5. *Emergence of Luxury* is a research project funded by the Academy of Finland. Accessed online at http://www.helsinki.fi/~rkosken/quality.pdf. This piece also appeared in *In the Making* (Copenhagen: Nordes, 2005).

[69] Gilsoo Cho, Chunjueng Kim, & John G. Casali, "Sensory Evaluation of Fabric Touch by Free Modulus Magnitude Estimation," *Fibers & Ploymers, 3* (no. 4), 169-173 (2002). The research evaluated fabric touch psychophysically, using aspects for subjective touch sensation: hardness, smoothness, coarseness, coolness, pliability, crispness, heaviness, and thickness.

[70] Wonjoung Lee & Masako Sato, "Visual Perception of Texture of Textiles," *Color Research & Application, 26* (no. 6), 469-477 (2001).

[71] Numerous works, both scholarly and popular, consider this aspect, though typically not specifically with reference to clothing. See, for example, Hilaire Hiler, "Some Associative Aspects of Color," *Journal of Aesthetics and Art Criticism, 4* (no. 4), 203-217 (1946). For a more comprehensive examination, see F. Birren, *Color and Human Response* (N. Y.: Van Nostrand Reinhold, 1978).

[72] Jayoung Cho, Chunjeong Kim, & Jiyoung Ha, "Physiological and Subjective Evaluation of the Rustling Sounds of Polyester Warp Knitted Fabrics," *Textile Research Journal, 75* (no. 4), 312-318 (2005).

[73] Mary Lou Rosencranz, *Clothing Concepts. A Social-Psychological Approach* (N. Y.: Macmillan, 1972), p. 180. The low rating for wool is not surprising given its physical properties, which affect comfort in wear. When wool is compared to other fibers like cotton, silk, polyester, or blends, for use in apparel worn next to the skin it fares more poorly in perceived comfort. See G. Wang, W. Zhang, R. Postle, & D. Phillips, "Evaluating Wool Shirt Comfort with Wear Trials and the Forearm Test," *Textile Research Journal, 73* (no. 2), 113-119 (2003).

[74] Despite the strength of this association, nylon is also used in masculine clothing, most notably in jackets and other outwear. Moreover, men have discovered the benefits of nylon hosiery and a sizable market has opened up (see the answer to Q. 9).

[75] In menswear the fiber is used in neckties. See *Acetate* at the Swicofil AG Textile Services website, accessed online at Sicofil.com at http://www.swicofil.com/products/204acetate.html.

[76] "Insight into the Children's Apparel Market," *Textile Consumer, 32* (2004, Spring). Accessed online at the Cotton Incorporated website at http://www.cottoninc.com/TextileConsumer/TextileConsumerVolume32/. Cf. the answer to Q. 6.

[77] "Checking the Pulse: Toplines on Consumer Attitudes and Preferences," [Womenswear articles], *Lifestyle Monitor* (1999, Mar. 11). Accessed online at the Cotton Incorporated website at http://www.cottoninc.com/lsmarticles /?articleID=263.

[78] Vernon Coleman, (1996). Men in Dresses: A Study in Transvestism/Crossdressing. European Medical Journal. Chilton Designs Publishers. Accessed online at http://www.vernoncoleman.com/downloads/mid.htm. See §2, 'Why Do Men Crossdress?'

[79] Frank H. Menke, *Color, Environment, and Human Response: An Interdisciplinary Understanding of Color and Its Use as a Beneficial Element in the Design of Architectural Environment* (N. Y.: John Wiley & Sons, 1996), pp. 6-9; quote is from p. 6. In this work see especially chapters 12, 4.

[80] The connection of color to gender is further explored in the answer to Q. 9.

[81] Chris J. Boyatzis & Reenu Varghese, "Children's Emotional Associations with Color," *Journal of Genetic Psychology, 155* (no. 1), 79-86 (1994).

[82] Martha Picariello, Danna Greenberg, & David Pillemer, "Children's Sex-Related Stereotyping of Colors," *Child Development, 61* (no. 5), 1453-1460.

[83] Michael G. Pratt & Anat Rafaeli, "Organizational Dress as a Symbol of Multilayered Social Identities," *Academy of Management Journal, 40* (no. 4), 862-898 (1997), p. 866.

[84] T. G. Barrett & I. W. Booth, "Sartorial Eloquence: Does It Exist in the Paediatrician-Patient Relationship?" *British Medical Journal, 309*, 1710-1712 (1994, Dec.).

[85] Pat Dillon, Wendy Moore, Rebecca Bartlett, Patricia Scully, Roger Morgan, & Christopher James, "Sensing the Fabric," in S. Brewster & R. Murray-Smith (Eds.), *Haptic Human-Computer Interaction: First International Workshop, Glasgow, UK, August/September, 2000, Proceedings*, pp. 63-68 (Berlin/Heidelberg, Germany: Springer, 2000), p. 66. Accessed online at http://www.dcs.gla.ac.uk/~stephen/workshops/haptic/papers/dillon.pdf.

[86] *Kansei* is a Japanese term and refers to a product's psychological impression or image. The term is used in engineering to describe efforts to take consumers' psychological impressions about a given product and incorporate them in design elements. Thus, for clothing, *Kansei* engineering tries to find what kind of clothing elements elicit specific emotional responses and then select the desired attributes to enhance apparel so that customers will prefer purchasing it.

[87] Nazlina Shaari, Fumio Terauchi, Mitsamori Kubo, & Hiroyaki Aoki, "Recognizing Female's Sensibility in Assessing Traditional Clothes," *Journal of the Asian Design International Conference*, E04 (2003). Accessed online at http://www.idemployee.id.tue.nl/g.w.m.rauterberg/conferences/CddoNotOpen/ADC/final_paper/175.pdf.

[88] 'Haptic' refers to the prominence played by the hand is seeking and gathering sensory information. The 'haptic system' is the functional body organization centered about touching by the hand to acquire such information.

[89] See, for example, Howard G. Schutz & B. A. Phillips, "Consumer Perception of Textiles," *Home Economics Research Journal*, 1, 214 (1976). Their research involved 46 fabrics with a wide variety of possible uses and examined women's attitudes and choices. Also see, S. M. Forsythe & J. B. Thomas, "Natural, Synthetic and Blended Fabric Contents: An Investigation of Consumer Preferences and Perceptions," *Clothing & Textiles Research Journal*, 8 (no. 3), 60-64 (1989). Many studies look at particular apparel but also examine knowledge about and attitudes toward fibers and fabrics. For instance, with reference to sport shirts and undershirts, see M. S. Byrne, A. D. W. Gardner, & A. M. Fritz, "Fiber Types and Enduses: A Perceptual Study," *Journal of the Textile Institute*, 84 (no. 2), 275-288 (1993). With reference to jeans, see J. E. Workman, "Effects of Fiber Content Labeling on Perception of Apparel Characteristics," *Clothing & Textiles Research Journal*, 8 (no. 3), 19-24 (1990).

[90] Li Chu Wang, Sze Su Soong, & Jin Jong Chen, "A Study on the Wearing Perception of Sportswear," in J. Frim, M. B. Ducharme, & P. Tikuisis (Eds.), *Sixth International Conference on Environmental Ergonomics*, pp. 102-103 (Canada: Defense & Civil Institute of Environmental Medicine, 1994). The Conference was held in Montebello, Canada, September 25-30, 1994.

[91] The accuracy or inaccuracy of such pairings is investigated in the answer to Q. 5.

[92] Diana Crane, *Fashion and Its Social Agendas: Class, Gender, and identity in Clothing* (Chicago: Univ. of Chicago Pr., 2000), p. 2.

[93] The evidence is found in self-report by crossdressers (see the answer to Q. 26), reports by those close to them (see the answer to Q. 37), and in psychological tests (see the answer to Q. 27). There simply is no reason not to attribute some changes to an experience of gender different from the birth-assigned gender.

[94] As Mandoki (p. 617) observes, the body has to fit the clothes—not the other way around.

[95] Gregory P. Stone, "Appearance and the Self," in A. M. Rose (Ed.), *Human Behavior and Social Processes*, pp. 86-118 (1962), p. 101f. Stone (p. 86)

maintains that the self is "established, maintained, and altered in and through communication."

96 Katya Mandoki, "Point and Line Over the Body: Social Imaginaries Underlying the Logic of Fashion," *Journal of Popular Culture, 36* (no. 3), 600-622 (2003), p. 616.

97 Ibid, pp. 601-605; quote is from p. 602.

98 Ivan Corsa, "Paul Smith. Talking Design with 'True Brit,'" *Air Massive* (2004, May 18). Interview accessed online at http://www. airmassive.com/smith001.html. Quote is from page 1 of the 3 page interview.

99 Joe Au, "Grounded Design Theory of Italian Fashion Designers," *Journal of the HEIA, 8* (no. 2), 24-32 (2001), p. 28. The remark pertains both to the designers and to consumers.

100 Susan Kaiser, *The Social Psychology of Clothing: Symbolic Appearances in Context* (N. Y.: Macmillan, 1985), p. 148.

101 Elizabeth Reitz Mullenix, "Private Women/Public Acts: Petticoat Government and the Performance of Resistance," *The Drama Review, 46* (no. 1), 104-117 (2002), p. 109.

102 N. H. Compton, "Personal Attributes of Color and Design Preferences in Clothing Fabrics," *Journal of Psychology, 54* (no. 1), 191-195 (1962). Cited in Mary Lou Rosencranz, "Social and Psychological Approaches to Clothing Research," *Journal of Home Economics, 57* (no. 1), 26-29 (1965).

103 Mary Lou Rosencranz, "Clothing Symbolism," *Journal of Home Economics, 54* (no. 1), 18-22 (1962).

104 R. A. Feinberg, L. Mataro, & W. J. Burroughs, "Clothing and Social Identity," *Clothing & Textiles Research Journal, 11* (no. 1), 18-23 (1992).

105 Lisa Stead, Peter Goulev, Caroline Evans, & Ebrahim Mamdani, "The Emotional Wardrobe," *Personal and Ubiquitous Computing, 8* (nos. 3-4), 282-290 (2004). Also see *The Emotional Wardrobe* accessed online at http://www.emotionalwardrobe.com/. (See especially the Themes section.) For a very brief look, see *We Make Money Not Art: The Emotional Wardrobe* (2005, Nov. 14), accessed at the WeMakeMoneyNotArt.com website, at http://www. wemakemoneynotart.com/archives/007434.php.

106 Mullenix, p. 109; the quote from Stanton is from a letter she wrote in 1857 to the Dress Reform Convention.

107 Mary Ellen Roach-Higgens & Joanne B. Eicher, "Dress and identity," *Clothing & Textiles Research Journal, 10* (no. 4), 18 (1992).

[108] Allison Guy & Maura Banim, "Personal Collections: Women's Clothing Use and Identity," *Journal of Gender Studies, 9* (no. 3), 313-327 (2000).

[109] Mandoki, p. 608.

[110] Yoon-Hee Kwon, "Daily Clothing Selection: Interrelationships Among Motivating Factors," *Clothing & Textiles Research Journal, 5* (no. 2), 21-27 (1987).

[111] This notion has prevailed largely due to the influence of Erik Erikson's psychosocial developmental model. See, for example, his *Childhood and Society*, rev. ed. (N. Y.: Norton, 1953).

[112] Thea Tselepis & Helena M. de Klerk, "Early Adolescent Girls' Expectations About the Fit of Clothes: A Conceptual Framework," *Journal of Family Ecology and Consumer Services, 32*, 83-93 (2004), p. 85.

[113] M. Suzanne Sontag & J. D. Schlater, "Proximity of Clothing to Self: Evolution of a Concept," *Clothing & Textiles Research Journal, 1* (no. 1), 18 (1982).

[114] Kaiser, p. 185.

[115] Sarah Cosbey, "Clothing Interest, Clothing Satisfaction, and Self-perceptions of Sociability, Emotional Stability, and Dominance," *Social Behavior and Personality, 29* (no. 2), 145-152 (2001). Cf. YH Kwon & S. Shim, "A Structural Model for Weight Satisfaction, Self-consciousness and Women's Use of Clothing in Mood Enhancement," *Clothing & Textiles Research Journal, 17* (no. 4), 203-212 (1999), which found a positive correlation between the use of clothing to enhance mood and public and private self-consciousness. Cf. Yoon-Hee Kwon, "The Influence of the Perception of Mood and Self-consciousness on the Selection of Clothing," *Clothing & Textiles Research Journal, 9* (no. 4), 41-46 (1991). Also see, Natasha Singer, "The Suit that Makes You Feel As Good As Prozac," *The New York Times Magazine*, 72 (2000, June 11); this article features the prediction that by 2010 there will be clothes with embedded fragrances designed to enhance mood.

[116] Crane, p. 1; see chapter 2. For a short piece see Elizabeth Wilson, "Fashion and the Meaning of Life," *The Guardian*, 34 (1992, May 18). Cf. Kaiser, p. 390.

[117] B. Henderson & M. DeLong, "Dress in a Postmodern Era: An Analysis of Aesthetic Expression and Motivation," *Clothing & Textiles Research Journal, 18* (no. 4), 237-250 (2000).

[118] Ibid.

[119] Lawrence B. Rosenfeld & Timothy G. Plax, "Clothing as Communication," *Journal of Communication, 27* (no. 2), 24-31 (1977). Also see Richard A.

Feinberg, Lisa Mataro, & W. Jeffrey Burroughs, "Clothing and Social Identity," *Clothing & Textiles Research Journal, 11* (no. 1), 18-23 (1992). For an experiment that found that the way we dress can influence our self-description, see Bettina Hannover & Ulrich Kuehnen, "'The Clothing Makes the Self' via Knowledge Activation," *Journal of Applied Social Psychology, 32* (no. 12), 2513-2525 (2002). On the relation of clothes buying behavior to personality see R. S. Sharma, "Clothing Behavior, Personality, and Values: A Correlational Study," *Psychological Studies, 25* (no. 2), 137-142 (1980).

[120] The suggestion has been made this use of dress may operate among those who like to frequently dress in costumes; see Kimberly A. Miller, "Dress: Private and Secret Self-expression," *Clothing & Textiles Research Journal, 15* (no. 4), 223-234.

[121] There is a rich, extensive literature on this topic. Research studies persistently show people make favorable judgments about attractive people. For example, research suggests this factor plays a role both in teacher evaluations of students and of teachers by students (cf. the notes in the answer to Q. 4). This tendency is found even in childhood; students asked to rank teachers who are doing the same things consistently favor the ones they find more attractive. However, some evidence suggests that the effect of attractiveness is modified by other factors so that its influence waxes or wanes depending on other contextual factors; see Lucy M. Watkins & Lucy Johnston, "Screening Job Applicants: The Impact of Physical Attractiveness and Application Quality," *International Journal of Selection and Assessment, 8* (no. 2), 76 (2000). Some research also suggests that attractiveness does, in fact, enhance achievement and psychological well-being; see Debra Umberson & Michael Hughes, "The Impact of Physical Attractiveness on Achievement and Psychological Well-Being," *Social Psychology Quarterly, 50* (no. 3), 227-236 (1987). A good overview of the elements needed to assess this matter may be obtained from Alice H. Eagly, Richard D. Ashmore, Mona G. Makhijani, & Laura C. Longo, "What Is Beautiful Is Good, But . . . : A Meta-Analytic Review of Research on the Physical Attractiveness Stereotype," *Psychological Bulletin, 110* (no. 1), 109-128 (1991).

[122] Cf., for example the New Testament injunction in 1 Peter 3:34, "Let not yours be the outward adorning with braiding of hair, decoration of gold, and wearing of robes but let it be the hidden person of the heart with the imperishable jewel of a gentle and quiet heart, which in God's sight is very precious" (RSV). The Roman poet Propertius (1st century B.C.E.) criticized the same sort of things (e.g., styled hair, fancy costumes, use of fragrances), remarking, "This doctoring of your looks is pointless, believe me; Love, being naked, does not love beauticians." See Propertius' Elegy 2 in Guy Lee (Translator), *Propertius. The Poems* (N.Y.: Oxford Univ. Press, 1996), p. 4. On the other hand, see Ovid's *The Art of Beauty*, which observes that "Art clothes all things with

beauty," and advises, "let every woman strive to look her best." See *The Art of Love and Other Love Books of Ovid* (N. Y.: Grosset & Dunlap, 1959), pp. 229-231.

[123] Hilda Mayer Buckley, "Perceptions of Physical Attractiveness as Manipulated by Dress: Subjects *Versus* Independent Judges," *Journal of Psychology, 114*, 243-248 (1983).

[124] Cf. Fred Davis' discussion of identity ambivalences as a fashion mechanism. See Fred Davis, *Fashion, Culture, and Identity* (Chicago: Univ. of Chicago Press, 1992), pp. 25-29, 57-58, 71-73.

[125] Carole Turbin, "Refashioning the Concept of Public/Private. Lessons from Dress Studies," *Journal of Women's Studies, 15* (no. 1), 43-51 (2003), p. 45f.

[126] Eric J. Segal, "Norman Rockwell and the Fashioning of American Masculinity," *The Art Bulletin, 78*, 633-646 (1996). Segal's discussion interweaves the roles played by other social forces of the time, from G. Stanley Hall's psychological description of adolescence, to the Boy Scouts and YMCA, to Teddy Roosevelt. All these forces, and others, were at work in the social construction of a certain image of masculinity that social practices were to encourage. Rockwell's illustrations center in a sartorial dimension to this broad phenomenon.

[127] Precisely because no one is supposed to know what our underwear is (unless we choose to reveal it) it possesses a special appeal, both to the wearer and to others. Since we don't know what another person's underwear is, it invites speculation or generates fantasy, depending of course on our perception of and interest in the other person. On the other hand, we can secretly delight in tweaking other people's noses by contradicting their assumptions about us through wearing underwear we know would scandalize them if they discovered we were wearing it. Underwear thus opens up many possibilities for experience and expression.

In light of such considerations, underwear fashion trends invite scrutiny. In our contemporary setting the most notable vendor of such items for men is perhaps Calvin Klein, whose advertisements for both masculine and feminine underwear have generated controversy. For women, Victoria's Secret is indisputably the most noted company. For an analysis of their utilization of Victorian motifs, especially the corset, see Nancy V. Workman, "From Victorian to Victoria's Secret: The Foundations of Modern Erotic Wear," *Journal of Popular Culture, 30* (no. 2), 61-73 (1996). Workman (p. 72) concludes, "Just as the Victorian corset united notions of respectable morality and sexuality, the modern corset defines women's bodies as sexually desirable, yet encloses women in rigid positions of cultural enslavement."

[128] Turbin, p. 48.

[129] Philip Johnson, "Men in Skirts: A Bridge too Far?" *Lucire.* (Nov. 11, 2003). [Accessed online at http://www.lucire.com/2003a/1103ll0.shtml] *Lucire* is an online magazine.

[130] As alluded earlier, the obvious concern here comes in the notion that clothes invite sexual aggression. There is a substantial literature in this regard. See, for example, Jane E. Workman & Elizabeth W. Freeburg, "An Examination of Date Rape, Victim Dress, and Perceiver Variables Within the Context of Attribution Theory," *Sex Roles, 41* (nos. 3-4), 261-277 (1999). Also see Kim K. P. Johnson, Jane E. Hegland, & Nancy A. Schofield, "Survivors of Rape: Functions and Implications of Dress in a Context of Coercive Power," in Kim K. P. Johnson & Sharon J. Lennon (Eds.), *Appearance and Power: Dress, Body, Culture*, pp. 11-32 (N.Y.: Berg, 1999).

Q. 3 Notes

[131] Diana Crane, *Fashion and Its Social Agendas. Class, Gender and Identity in Clothing* (Chicago: Univ. of Chicago Press, 2000), p. 1.

[132] "The social-psychology of clothing is concerned with the various means people use to modify the appearance of the body, as well as social and psychological forces that lead to, and result from, processes of managing personal appearance." See Susan Kaiser, *The Social Psychology of Clothing: Symbolic Appearances in Context* (N. Y.: Macmillan, 1985), p. 4

[133] Parenthetically, we may mark here the conclusion drawn by Rosencranz in the 1940s: "the range of types of garments in a person's wardrobe seems to be the most sensitive single measurement of young women's interest in clothing." See Mary Lou Lerch Rosencranz, "A Study of Women's Interest in Clothing," *Journal of Home Economics, 41* (no. 8), 460-462 (1949), p. 462.

[134] That this is possible is testament both to modern manufacturing and marketing, and to the high value placed on dress, which causes people to spend as much of their time and money as they do on clothing and accessories. In distinguishing four broad consumer categories/groups in the United Kingdom, fashion scholar Ann Priest, following Michelle Lee, names one of them 'McFashion'—inexpensive, mass-marketed clothing that whether bland or a "fast food version of a 'star trend'" facilitates the consumer's entrance into fashion trends and social groups. See Ann Priest, "Uniformity and Differentiation in Fashion," *International Journal of Clothing Science and Technology, 17* (nos. 3-4), 253-263 (2005), p. 257.

[135] Alison Lurie, *The Language of Clothes* (N. Y.: Owl Books, 2000; original work published 1981), p. 16.

[136] This assertion should *not* be construed to suggest this is all dress does, nor that social identity is solely dependent on dress. Our purpose here is

to focus on a primary function so as to better understand crossdressing, which as the very word suggests involves boundaries.

[137] Cf. Paula S. Fass, *The Damned and the Beautiful: American Youth in the 1920s* (N. Y.: Oxford Univ. Press, 1977), pp. 231-233.

[138] Ruth P. Rubenstein, *Dress Codes. Meanings and Messages in American Culture*, 2nd ed. (Boulder, CO: Westview Press, 2001), p. 57.

[139] Ibid. Rubenstein points to the power of clothing signs in their ability to allow the wearer to fabricate a social identity—a fact capitalized upon, for example, by those who go 'undercover,' posing as a member of some group they do not properly belong to.

[140] Fashion does a similar boundary-setting for things like social class. Curiously, many of the people who object to boundaries in social status, and who then dress so as to cross those boundaries, uphold their value for gender groups. Apparently the logic many of us use is that fashion boundaries are good when they preserve the groups we are already in and bad when they frustrate our efforts to join a group we want to be in. On the use of fashion to maintain social distinctions, see Fred Davis, *Fashion, Culture, and Identity* (Chicago: Univ. of Chicago Press, 1992), p. 77.

[141] Michael G. Pratt & Anat Rafaeli, "Organizational Dress as a Symbol of Multilayered Social Identities," *Academy of Management Journal, 40* (no. 4), 862-898 (1997), p. 865.

[142] Craig J. Thompson & Diana L. Haytko, "Speaking of Fashion: Consumers' Uses of Fashion Discourses and the Appropriation of Countervailing Cultural Meanings," *Journal of Consumer Research, 24*, 15-42 (1997), p. 21.

[143] Georg Simmel, "Fashion," *International Quarterly, 10* (no. 1), 130-155 (1904 translation of 1895 original), p. 141. The work is more readily available in a reprint in the *American Journal of Sociology, 62* (no. 5), 541-558 (1957).

[144] Cf. the similar contention in Joanna Brewis, Mark P. Hampton, & Stephen Linstead, "Unpacking Priscilla: Subjectivity and Identity in the Organization of Gendered Appearance," *Human Relations, 50* (no. 10), 1275-1304 (1997), p. 1290.

[145] Because society has not yet learned how to assimilate this situation as it has drag, it still labels the crossdresser thus caught as 'deviant' and/or 'disordered.' By making him mentally disturbed no effective challenge to the gender conceptions of the culture can be mounted.

[146] Simmel, pp. 133-135.

[147] Crane, p. 1.

148 Ibid, p. 106.

149 Daniel Roche, *The Culture of Clothing: Dress and Fashion in the Ancien Regime* (N. Y.: Cambridge Univ. Press, 1994 [original work published in France, 1989]), p. 39.

150 Cf. the discussion in John E. Jacobi & S. George Walters, "Social Status and Consumer Choice," *Social Forces, 36* (no. 3), 209-214 (1958).

151 Leonard Bickman, "The Effect of Social Status on the Honesty of Others," *Journal of Social Psychology, 85,* 87-92 (1971).

152 There is a rich literature on school uniforms. I recommend as a good place to start Ann Bodine, "School Uniforms and a Discourse on Childhood," *Childhood, 10* (no. 1), 43-63 (2003).

153 On the other hand, blue jeans retain gender differentiation in subtle ways. Those purchased in the men's department are not identical to those sold in the women's department.

154 Kaiser, p. 49.

155 Using this logic we can predict that men who endorse the most stereotypical views of the genders are those most likely to engage in the most radical forms of social coercion, such as verbal and physical abuse, against those who transgress the social order the punishers value and support.

156 Nicolas Guéguen & Alexandre Pascual, "Status and People's Tolerance Towards an Ill-Mannered Person: A Field Study," *Journal of Mundane Behavior, 4* (no. 1), 29-36 (2003); quote is from p. 30. Accessed online at http://www.mundanebehavior.org/issues/v4n1/gueguenpascual.htm. The authors (p. 34) point out that the gender difference between the man who presented the behavior and the subjects—all women—is important to consider, too, especially since France is a society where men are higher in social status than women.

157 Lurie, p. 17. See pp. 17-21.

158 Not surprisingly, most studies are about specific uniforms rather than uniforms in general. A good place to start is Nathan Joseph, *Uniforms and Nonuniforms: Communication through Clothing* (N. Y.: Greenwood Press, 1986). Two shorter pieces, are: Leonard Bickman, "Social Roles and Uniforms: Clothes Make the Person," *Psychology Today, 7* (no. 11), 49-51 (1974, Apr.); and, with businesses in mind, Michael Solomon, "Standard Issue," *Psychology Today, 21* (no. 12), 30-31 (1987, Dec.).

159 Kaiser, pp. 378-381.

[160] While educators are rarely expected to wear uniforms, their style of dress generally is subject to certain expectations and what they wear influences student perceptions. This has been found for both male and female teachers. See Julie Lukavsky, Sara Butler, & Amy J. Harden, "Perceptions of an Instructor: Dress and Students' Characteristics," *Perceptual & Motor Skills, 81* (no. 1), 231-240 (1995). Also see Sara Butler & Kathy Roesel, "Students' Perceptions of Male Teachers: Effects of Teacher's Dress and Students' Characteristics," *Perceptual & Motor Skills, 73* (no. 3, Pt. 1), 943-951 (1991).

[161] In recent years perhaps more attention has been given to school uniforms than any other kind of uniform; the results have varied. See, for example, Dorothy Behling, "School Uniforms and Person Perception," *Perceptual and Motor Skills, 79* (no. 2), 723-729 (1994). Also, Davild L. Brunsma & Kerry A. Rockquemore, "Effects of Student Uniforms on Attendance, Behavior Problems, Substance Use, and Academic Achievement," *Journal of Educational Research, 92* (no. 1), 53-62 (1998).

[162] Christopher B. Gilbert, "We Are What We Wear: Revisiting Student Dress Codes," *Brigham Young University Education and Law Journal, 1999* (no. 2), 3-21 (1999), p. 4.

[163] Ibid, p. 16.

[164] Mary Anne C. Case, "Disaggregating Gender from Sex and Sexual Orientation: The Effeminate Man in the Law and Feminist Jurisprudence," *Yale Law Journal,* 105 (no. 1), 1-105 (1995). The case was Harper v. Edgewood Board of Education, 655 F. Supp. 1353, 1355 (S.D. Ohio 1987). Case notes that when a male junior high school student won a concession from the Washington, D.C. school dress code to graduate in relatively feminine attire it was only because the apparel in question (blouse, bell bottoms, and flats) could be construed as reasonably unisex.

[165] Katharine T. Bartlett, "Only Girls Wear Barrettes: Dress and Appearance Standards, Community Norms, and Workplace Equality," *Michigan Law Review, 92* (no. 1), 2541-2582 (1994), p. 2542.

[166] Dean Spade, "Resisting Medicine, Re/modeling Gender," *Berkeley Women's Law Journal, 18,* 15-37 (2003), pp. 33-34; quote is from p. 34.

[167] Taylor Flynn, "'*Transforming the Debate: Why We Need to Include Transgender Rights in the Struggles for Sex and Sexual Orientation Equality," *Columbia Law Review, 101* (no. 2), 392-420 (2001), n. 68. The case in question was Doe v. Yunits, CIV No. 001060A (Mass. Sup. Ct. filed Oct. 11, 2000).

[168] This central rule is consistent with gender logic in our culture; as Bob Connell comments, "'masculinity' does not exist except in contrast with

'femininity.'" See Robert W. Connell, *Masculinities* (Berkeley: Univ. of California Press, 1995), p. 68.

[169] Evelyn Goodenough Pitcher, "Male and Female," in M. E. Roach & J. B. Eicher (Eds.), *Dress, Adornment, and the Social Order,* pp. 214-216 (N. Y.: John Wiley & Sons, 1965), p. 214. This material originally appeared in *The Atlantic* in 1963.

[170] Barbara E. Hort, Beverly I. Fagot, & Mary Driver Leinbach, "Are People's Notions of Maleness More Stereotypically Framed Than Their Notions of Femaleness?" *Sex Roles, 23*, 197-212 (1990).

[171] We have known for more than a half century that boys identify more strongly with the gender expectations set for them and simultaneously show a more homogenous conception of those expectations—signs consistent with the need to protect a higher class status. See D. G. Brown, "Masculinity-Femininity Development in Children," *Journal of Consulting Psychology, 21*, 197-202 (1957).

[172] Manuel X. Zamarripa, Bruce E. Wampold, & Erik Gregory, "Male Gender Role Conflict, Depression, and Anxiety: Clarification and Generalizability to Women," *Journal of Counseling Psychology, 50* (no. 3), 333-338 (2003), pp. 336-338. Cf. J. M. O'Neil, "Patterns of Gender Role Conflict and Strain: Sexism and Fear of Femininity in Men's Lives," *Personnel and Guidance Journal, 60*, 203-210 (1981).

[173] Craig Thompson, "Interview with Scot Cromer," *Advertising & Society Review, 4* (no. 2) (2003). Electronic journal accessed online through Project Muse.

[174] To trace this development in the United States, and to see it in relation to crossdressing, see the answer to Q. 47.

[175] This process does not begin at manhood. Research indicates boys are more likely to be censored for nonconforming gender behavior than are girls, and that peers are significantly involved in such monitoring and punishing behaviors. See, for example, Carol Lynn Martin, "New Directions for Investigating Children's Gender Knowledge," *Developmental Review, 13*, 184-204 (1993). Also see, D. B. Carter & L. A. McCloskey, "Peers and Maintenance of Sex-Typed Behavior: The Development of Children's Concepts of Cross-gender Behavior in Their Peers," *Social Cognition, 2*, 294-314 (1984).

[176] Suits brought against businesses for sex discrimination often highlight the role played by negative evaluations of the plaintiff based on the perception of her appearance, which because it was too masculine was paired with negative personality trait attributions.

[177] They also demonstrate obedience to the foundational rule that males must appear masculine, or at least not feminine; unisex styles are invariably closer to traditional masculinity than femininity.

[178] Lurie, p. 16.

[179] This matter is treated in various respects in many places throughout this work. A general treatment focused on the relation of sex to gender is found in the answer to Q. 5.

[180] Simply reflect a moment on two labels for nonconformists: 'sissy' and 'tomboy.' Clearly the former is more pejorative than the latter. It is relatively okay to be a tomboy; it is *never* okay to be a sissy.

[181] In fact, it is high status figures like popular entertainers who often provide social impetus to re-imagine transgender realities. Notable contemporary examples include Harisu in Korea (see the answer to Q. 52), and Dana International in the Middle East (see the answer to Q. 53).

[182] Obviously, a substantial number of things have been written on this matter. As examples, please see Linda B. Arthur, "Clothing Matters: Dress and Identity in India," *Journal of Developing Societies, 15* (no. 2), 251-253 (1999). [Review of Emma Tarlo's *Clothing Matters* (Chicago: Univ. of Chicago Press, 1996).] Also see Ruth Rubenstein, *Dress Codes: Meanings and Messages in American Culture* (2nd ed.) (Boulder, CO: Westview Press, 2001).

[183] Alison Lurie likens this to the insertion of foreign words or phrases into standard English. See Lurie, p. 7f.

[184] The *kimono* is discussed in the answer to Q. 52.

[185] Attention to this issue is raised at various points in this work because some of the examples of crossdressing discussed in different answers are best explained as attributions by Western observers rather than as transgender behavior in the cultural context.

[186] Ramya Rajagopolan & Jeanne Heitmeyer, "Ethnicity & Consumer Choice: A Study of Consumer Levels of Involvement in Indian Ethnic Apparel and Contemporary American Clothing," *Journal of Fashion Marketing and Management, 9* (no. 1), 83-105 (2005). Also see J. C. Forney& N. J. Rabolt, "Ethnic Identity: Its Relationship to Ethnic and Contemporary Dress," *Clothing & Textiles Research Journal, 4* (no. 2), 18 (1986). Cf. Lynne Brandon & Judith C. Forney, "Influences on Female Purchase Motivations and Product Satisfaction: A Comparison of Casual and Formal Lifestyles and Anglo and Hispanic Ethnicity," *Journal of Family and Consumer Sciences, 94*, 54 (2002, Jan. 1); also see Gwendolyn S. O'Neal, "African-American Aesthetic of Dress: Current manifestations," *Clothing & Textiles Research Journal, 16* (no. 4), 167-175 (1998).

[187] Thea Tselepis & Helena M. de Klerk, "Early Adolescent Girls' Expectations About the Fit of Clothes: A Conceptual Framework," *Journal of Family Ecology and Consumer Services, 32,* 83-93 (2004), p. 83.

[188] Maureen S. MacGillivray & Jeannette D. Wilson, "Clothing and Appearance Among Early, Middle and Late Adolescents," *Clothing & Textiles Research Journal, 6* (no. 1), 43-50 (1997).

[189] Interestingly, in Goth culture, a male who uses makeup and dresses in feminine garb is not regarded as crossdressing—at least by other Goths.

[190] The reality of multiple influences (e.g., ethnicity, peer influence) on young people is described in Jeannette D. Wilson & Maureen S. MacGillivray, "Self-perceived Influences of Family, Friends, and Media on Adolescent Clothing Choice," *Family and Consumer Science Research Journal, 26* (no. 4), 425-444 (1998).

[191] L. Richards, "The Appearance of Youthful Subculture: A Theoretical Perspective on Deviance," *Clothing & Textiles Research Journal, 6* (no. 3), 56-64 (1988).

[192] Linda B. Arthur, "Dress and the Social Construction of Gender in Two Sororities," *Clothing & Textiles Research Journal, 17* (no. 2), 84-93 (1999).

[193] For a collection of essays on this subject, see Linda B. Arthur (Ed.), *Religion, Dress and the Body.* Oxford: Berg (1999). Also, for an interesting discussion on how clothing may help reveal a person's 'implicit religion' see Eileen Barker, "A Comparative Exploration of Dress and the Presentation of Self as Implicit Religion," in W. J. Keenan (Ed.), *Dressed to Impress: Looking the Part,* pp. 51-67 (Oxford: Berg, 2001).

[194] John Fetto, "Dress Your Age," *American Demographics* (2002, Sept. 1). Archived at AdAge.com Online edition.

[195] The 'golden mean' that all ages seem to strive for is youth, as expressed in late adolescence or young adulthood. Since crossdressing may be construed as fictive anyway (or 'social imaginaries'), perhaps it is easier to adopt youthful dress when crossdressing—which is already a transgression of social expectations—than when conforming to social standards for age and gender.

[196] For example, a biological male in our society dressed in masculine apparel but sporting large earrings and facial makeup will likely be seen as crossing gender lines—as being 'crossdressed' in the widest sense of that term.

[197] Interestingly, despite the fact that men are typically taller, vertical or horizontal dimensions do not reliably pair with gendered distinctions. At times, masculine fashion has accented vertical lines only to find feminine fashion falling suit. Similarly, though feminine fashion at times accented styles that meant

filling more space horizontally, so on occasion did masculine fashion, and even put both in direct competition at the same time.

[198] I am impressed by the ruminations of culture scholar Steven Connor on the two kinds of bifurcation. See Steven Connor, "Men in Skirts," *Women: A Cultural Review, 13* (no. 3), 257-271 (2002), pp. 258-263.

[199] This tendency has had the greatest practical impact and is closely related to the distinction listed above it (bifurcated vs. unbifurcated clothing). As observed earlier in the text, restriction of motion and activity in feminine dress emphasizes passivity, a stereotyped feminine trait. The appropriation of masculine fashion, especially in the adoption of bifurcated wear, expanded women's range of motion and activity, thus promoting an equalizing of gender reflected in fashion trends toward democratization in dress.

[200] This tendency is observed in various cultures and historical periods. In ages and places where garments were essentially unisex, apparel length was a more important gender marker, but it has remained generally true that in fashion styles where little else serves to distinguish masculine from feminine length is still available as a marker.

Q. 4 Notes

[201] John Stoltenberg, *Refusing to be a Man* (London: Routledge, 2003 reprint of 2000 rev. ed.; work originally published 1989), p. 182.

[202] Aileen Ribeiro, *Dress and Morality* (N. Y.: Palgrave Macmillan, 2004; original work published 1986 by Batsford).

[203] Joanne Finkelstein, *The Fashioned Self* (Cambridge: Polity Press, 1991), p. 110.

[204] Dorothy U. Behling, "Influence of Dress on Perception of Intelligence and Scholastic Achievement in Urban Schools with Minority Populations," *Clothing & Textiles Research Journal, 13* (no. 1), 11-16 (1995). Cf. an earlier study involving 750 students and 159 teachers in six Ohio high schools, which also found that perceptions of intelligence and academic achievement are influenced by dress. See D. U. Behling & E. A. Williams, "Influence of Dress on Perception of Intelligence and Expectations of Scholastic Achievement," *Clothing & Textiles Research Journal, 9* (no. 4), 17 (1991). A broader study on teacher attire can be found in Joan Gorham, Stanley H. Cohen, & Tracy L. Morris, "Fashion in the Classroom III: Effects of Instructor Attire and Immediacy in Natural Classroom Interactions," *Communication Quarterly, 47* (no. 3), 281-299 (1999).

[205] S. L. Paek, "Effect of Garment Style on the Perception of Personal Traits," *Clothing & Textiles Research Journal, 5* (no. 1), 10-16 (1986). An example of what this study found: observers rated strangers dressed in conservative and

casual styles as more self-controlled, understanding, and reliable; strangers dressed in a more daring style were seen as more individualistic and attractive.

[206] A longstanding, but certainly overstated and inaccurate portrait of masculine/feminine differences declares that women rely on a physical basis of attraction because they are morally inferior to the integrity masculine men exhibit. The contrast thus emphasizes the irrational, feeling-based femininity that must resort to displayed or repressed sensuality versus the rational, character-based masculinity that can confidently display its power and restraint. These portraits can be drawn sharply through clothing choices as well as by behavioral manners.

[207] Heather Patrick, Clayton Neighbors, & C. Raymond Kee, "Appearance Related Social Comparisons: The Role of Contingent Self-esteem and Self-perceptions of Attractiveness," *Personality & Social Psychology Bulletin, 30* (no. 4), 501-514 (2004), pp. 509-510; note Table 3.

[208] These matters are more fully pursued in volumes 24 of this work.

[209] For a better appreciation of the complexities involved in understanding attractiveness, beauty, and apparel, see J. Fan, W. Yu, & L. Hunter, *Clothing Appearance and Fit: Science and Technology* (Cambridge: Woodhead Publishing Ltd. with The Textile Institute, 2004).

[210] This is a qualitative judgment commonly found in psychiatric literature, which never bothers to compare the actual behavior and time spent at it with that done by noncrossdressing men or women.

[211] *Espoused* values are those we verbally proclaim as meaningful and important. Typically they include such things as peace, love, and a relationship with God. *Practiced* values are those demonstrated by how we actually spend our time. Typically these include things like personal grooming, which intends to maximize physical attractiveness.

[212] Propertius, *Elegies*, Book I, Elegy II, translated by P. J. Gantillon, *The Elegies of Propertius, with Notes* (London & N.Y.: George Bell and Sons, 1895).

[213] Ovid, *The Art of Love*, Book 3, lines 103-105, translated by Peter Green, *Ovid. The Erotic Poems* (N. Y.: Penguin Books, 1982), p. 217.

[214] Mark Twain, "Woman—God Bless Her," *The New York Times* (1882, Dec. 23). Accessed online at TwainQuotes.com at http://www.twainquotes.com/18821223.html.

[215] Emily Burbank, *Woman as Decoration* (N. Y.: Dodd, Mead & Co., 1917), p. 5.

[216] For more on such matters, cf. the answers to Q. 26-27, 32.

[217] Jenna Weismann Joselit, *A Perfect Fit: Clothes, Character, and the Promise of America* (N. Y.: Henry Holt and Co., 2001), p. 2.

[218] Ibid, p. 41. Joselit (p. 40) indicates how lofty such claims for dress could be, citing for example the claim of E. Azalia Hackley, author of the advice manual *Colored Girl Beautiful*, that proper attire could even provide moral uplift. However, says Joselit (p. 194), by the 1950s-1960s fashion no longer was "a source of moral suasion," save for some Catholics, who continued to see a connection between dress and the moral order.

[219] J. C. Flugel, *The Psychology of Clothes* (London: Hogarth Press, 1950; original publication 1930), p. 75.

[220] Karl Aquino & Americus Reed, II, "The Self-Importance of Moral Identity," *Journal of Personality and Social Psychology, 83* (no. 6), 1423-1440 (2002). See especially Table III, p. 1428. Cf. the humorous piece by Florence King, "Good Ol' Clothes—Conservative Clothing and Attitudes; In Defense of Elegance," *National Review, 48* (no. 20), 50-51 (1996, Oct. 28).

[221] A logical outcome of such a view might be seen in the words of a professional actor who grasps how our public appraisal of character-through-dress results in stereotyped clichés that trap us all: "We label one another mercilessly. Our culture, preening itself so complacently on choice and tolerance, is perhaps more categorizing than at any time in my life." See Ian Flintoff, "Roles of a Lifetime: Character Quirks, Accents and Clothes Are Simply Accessories; the Real You Is Not So Easily Defined," *The Financial Times*, p. 7 (2004, May 22). One of the ironies of our time is how much we must rely on our public dress appearance to display our person while knowing that the person so displayed is inevitably distorted into a type so that the real, individual self stays undisclosed.

[222] For further information related to this matter, see the answers to Q. 26-27, and 38.

[223] Joanna Brewis, Mark P. Hampton, & Stephen Linstead, "Unpacking Priscilla: Subjectivity and Identity in the Organization of Gendered Appearance," *Human Relations, 50* (no. 10), 1275-1304 (1997), p. 1291. Cf. Dworkin's remark, which they cite (p. 1291f.): "It is commonly and wrongly said that male transvestites through the use of makeup and costuming caricature the women they would become, but any real knowledge of the romantic ethos makes clear that these men have penetrated to the core experience of being a woman, a romanticized construct." See S. Bordo, "Feminism, Foucault and the Politics of the Body," in C. Ramazanoglu (Ed.), *Up Against Foucault: Explorations of Some Tensions Between Foucault and Feminism*, pp. 179-202 (1993), p. 184.

[224] Alan Hunt, *Governance of the Consuming Passions: A History of Sumptuary Law* (N. Y.: Macmillan, 1996).

[225] Rebecca Arnold, *Fashion, Desire and Anxiety: Image and Morality in the Twentieth Century* (Piscataway, NJ: Rutgers Univ. Press, 1996), p. 4.

[226] Ibid. Arnold's analysis of the relationship between dress and power is compelling and persuasive. If the upper-class is exclusionary by virtue of the power of wealth, other groups can be just as exclusionary based on different criteria. Even as upper-class fashion signals membership, so also does the particular dress adopted by these other groups. In any instance, the power of the apparel persists—only its basis (wealth or something else) changes.

[227] Thorstein Veblen, *The Theory of the Leisure Class* (London: Macmillan, 1911; original work published 1899), p. 167. The text of chapter 7 of this work, "Dress as an Expression of the Pecuniary Culture," is part of the American Studies at the University of Virginia website, and this material accessed online at http://xroads.virginia.edu/~HYPER/VEBLEN/chap07.html.

[228] Ibid, p. 171.

[229] Ibid, p. 181. Veblen points out that the "general disregard of the wearer's comfort" found in so many feminine clothes (e.g., high heels, corset, skirt, and bonnet) signifies a woman's continued economic dependence on a man, so much so that "in a highly idealized sense, she still is the man's chattel."

[230] Ibid, p. 181f.

[231] Brent Shannon, "ReFashioning Men: Fashion, Masculinity, and the Cultivation of the Male Consumer in Britain, 1860-1914," *Victorian Studies, 46* (no. 4), 597-630 (2004).

[232] For a fuller treatment of the historical context and competing theories, see Ruth P. Rubinstein, *Dress Codes: Meanings and Messages in American Culture* (Boulder, CO: Westview Press, 1995), ch. 2 (pp. 1630).

[233] Genesis 3: 7 (NIV). All biblical quotations are from the *New International Version.*

[234] Philip Stubbes, *The Anatomie of the Abuses*, ed. F. J. Furnivall (New Shakespeare Society, 1877-1879; original work published 1583, 1585, 1595), vol. 1, p. 36. I have modernized the language somewhat, chiefly by changing spellings, but also by substituting the word 'hides' for 'felles' (which might also be rendered 'skins').

[235] Ibid. But see the next page for other purposes served by clothing, such as keeping us protected from the cold.

[236] The pervasive influence of this notion in Western culture is underscored by the findings of a study by Ronald J. Goldman & Juliette D. Goldman, "Children's Perceptions of Clothes and Nakedness: A Cross-National Study," *Genetic Psychology Monographs, 104* (no. 2), 163-185 (1981).

[237] *Targum Neofiti* 2:25, in Martin McNamara (Translator), *Targum Neofiti 1: Genesis*. The Aramaic Bible, vol. 1A (Collegeville, MN: The Liturgical Press, 1992), p. 59.

[238] *Genesis Rabbah* 19:6. Midrash is a commentary on the biblical text.

[239] For example, midrash *Yalkut Chadash* interpreted the provision as being religious garb for reciting the Shᵉma (Judaism's most basic prayer/creed). *Targum Jonathan* says God used the skin of the serpent to clothe them. Rabbi Meir, in *Genesis Rabbah* plays on the Hebrew word for 'skin' to have Adam clothed in garments of light. In each case the suggestion is meant to convey something about God's relationship to Adam and Eve as well as the change in their status because of sin.

[240] Further consideration of modesty, explicitly in connection with Christian tradition, is provided in the answers to Q. 66, 72.

[241] Havelock Ellis, "The Evolution of Modesty," in H. Ellis, *Studies in the Psychology of Sex*, vol. 1, pp. 184 (N. Y.: Random House, 1942; original work published 1905), p. 1.

[242] Ibid, p. 59. Ellis (p. 60) argues against the idea that clothing originated as protection from the environment.

[243] William I. Thomas, "The Psychology of Modesty and Clothing," *American Journal of Sociology, 5*, 246-262 (1899). Quote is from page 246. Thomas argues that the genesis of modesty has nothing to do with clothing at all. Pioneering sexologist Richard von Krafft-Ebing cites Westermarck's contention that it was the desire to make themselves more attractive that motivated the use of clothing. See Richard von Krafft-Ebing, *Psychopathia Sexualis. A Medico-Forensic Study*, 12th ed. (N. Y.: Pioneer Publications, 1939/1947; original work published 1886), p.3 n. 1.

Religious people did not automatically adhere to the modesty theory. Churches were a common site for lectures and conversation about competing ideas. For example, an article from 1894 records how Mrs. Lizzie Cheney-Ward, styled an authority on the subject, lectured on the subject at a church, telling her audience, "Clothes at first were worn for ornamentation, but with no idea of modesty. It is public opinion which makes each person ashamed unless he has on what both his own consciousness and that of others expects." See "She Wore Knickerbockers," *The New York Times* (1894, Mar. 5), p. 2.

244 Robert E. Riegel, "Women's Clothes and Women's Rights," *American Quarterly, 15* (no. 3), 390-401 (1963), p. 390.

245 Susan Haworth-Hoeppner, "What's Gender Got to Do With It: Perceptions of Sexual Coercion in a University Community," *Sex Roles: A Journal of Research, 38* (nos. 9-10), 757-779 (1998). Also see Linda Cassidy & Rose Marie Hurrell, "The Influence of Victims' Attire on Adolescents' Judgment of Date Rape," *Adolescence, 30*, 319-323 (1995).

246 This, however, is far different from saying that *any* kind of clothing invites sexual aggression and can be used to justify sexual assault. For research on this matter, see Robin M. Kowalski, "Inferring Sexual Interest from Behavioral Cues: Effects of Gender and Sexually Relevant Attitudes," *Sex Roles: A Journal of Research, 29* (nos. 1-2), 23-36. (1993).

247 See, for example, Cheryl S. Alexander, "The Responsible Victim: Nurses' Perceptions of Victims of Rape," *Journal of Health and Social Behavior, 21*, 22-33 (1980).

248 Nigel Barber, "Women's Dress Fashions as a Function of Reproductive Strategy," *Sex Roles: A Journal of Research, 40* (nos. 5-6), 459-471 (1999).

249 Albert D. Klassen, Colin J. Williams, & Eugene E. Levitt, *Sex and Morality in the U. S.,* H. J. O'Gorman, Ed. (Middletown, CT: Wesleyan Univ. Press, 1989), p. 279.

250 Though most of us seldom think about it, there are several ways we make decisions about right and wrong. These moral models range from the simple and dramatic taboo morality we learned as small children to sophisticated theories about utilitarianism. For a brief summary of some of the more common models, see chapter 23, "Models of Morality," in G. G. Bolich, B. R. Care, & G. C. Kenney, *Introduction to Religion* (Dubuque: Kendall/Hunt, 1988).

251 Flugel, p. 107.

252 J. C. Flugel, *Men and Their Motives: Psycho-Analytical Studies* (London: Routledge, 1999; original work published 1934), p. 65.

253 Ibid.

254 In fact, his concept of the "Great Masculine Renunciation," which he imputed to fashion trends for 19th century Englishmen of the middle class, has been challenged as historically inaccurate. See Brent Shannon, "ReFashioning Men: Fashion, Masculinity, and the Cultivation of the Male Consumer in Britain, 1860-1914," *Victorian Studies, 46* (no. 4), 597630 (2004).

255 Some of the complexity of the idea of "gender" is explored in the answers to Q. 36.

Q. 5 Notes

[256]As the history of crossdressing shows, the people for whom this behavior is regarded as 'perverse,' 'deviant' or 'sick' changes. Up until fairly recently the social focus was on crossdressing women. When their numbers became so large the phenomena was no longer remarkable attention shifted to crossdressing men.

[257] Like it or not—and I don't—this is the notion of sex at present. I think a more accurate definition of sex is "the differentiation of human beings along a range of genital presentations where a presumed relation to reproductive function circumscribes the poles." This definition overcomes a rigid binary system while recognizing both that reproduction cannot be entirely severed from defining sex and that the points along the continuum most associated with reproduction are the poles of male and female. However, this definition limits the role of reproduction and identifies it as having an artificial component (the occasionally inaccurate presumption of reproductive capability based on a certain presentation of genitalia). Further, it legitimizes points along the continuum and offers no names for any points, including the poles, thus allowing for either the retention of existing terms (male, female, intersex) or the creation of new ones.

[258] Moira Gatens, *Imaginary Bodies: Ethics, Power and Corporeality* (London: Routledge, 1996), p. 9.

[259] A consequence of this view is that sexual orientation becomes a junction for sex and gender; masculine male needs feminine female in heterosexual desire and behavior. Another consequence, then, is that homosexuality becomes not only unnecessary, but illegitimate. Corollary to this outcome, the construction of heterosexual masculinity incorporates homophobia. This matter is briefly considered later in the answer.

[260] Myra J. Hird, "Naturally Queer," *Feminist Theory, 5* (no. 1), 85-89 (2004), p. 85.

[261] Joan Roughgarden, "Evolution and the Embodiment of Gender," *GLQ: A Journal of Lesbian and Gay Studies, 10*, 287-291 (2004), p. 289.

[262] Ibid.

[263] Lisa Maurer, "Transgressing Sex and Gender: Deconstruction Zone Ahead?" *SIECUS Report, 28* (no. 1), 1421 (1999, Oct./Nov.), p. 14.

[264] Anne Fausto-Sterling, *Sexing the Body: Gender Politics and the Construction of Sexuality* (N.Y.: Basic Books, 2000), p. 3. The International Olympic Committee (IOC) adopted chromosomal testing in 1968, which continued through 1998.

[265] Ibid, p. 4.

²⁶⁶ Alice D. Dreger, (1998). *Hermaphrodites and the Medical Invention of Sex* (Cambridge: Harvard Univ. Press, 1998).

²⁶⁷ Ibid. See especially p. 190ff. Please note, though, the encouraging signs that things are changing among these professionals. Cf. Anne Fausto-Sterling, "The Five Sexes, Revisited," *The Sciences, 40* (no. 4), 18-23 (2000, July/Aug.).

²⁶⁸ Susan J. Bradley, Gillian D. Oliver, Avinoam B. Chernick, & Kenneth J. Zucker, "Experiment of Nurture: Ablatio Penis at 2 Months, Sex Reassignment at 7 Months, and a Psychosexual Follow-up in Young Adulthood," *Pediatrics, 102* (no. 1), e. 9 (1998). Accessed online at http://www.pediatrics.org/cgi/content/full/102/1/e9.

²⁶⁹ Suzanne J. Kessler, *Lessons from the Intersexed.* (Piscataway, NJ: Rutgers Univ. Press, 1998), p. 12.

²⁷⁰ Ibid, p. 12f.

²⁷¹ Martine Rothblatt, *The Apartheid of Sex: A Manifesto on the Freedom of Gender* (N. Y.: Crown Publishers, 1995).

²⁷² *Intersex FAQ (Frequently Asked Questions)* (2003-2004). Accessed online at http://www.intersexinitiative.org/articles/intersexfaq.html.

²⁷³ Ibid. Cf. the 'Patient-Centered Model' set forth by the Intersex Society of North America, in its FAQ section, 'What does ISNA recommend for children with intersex?' (ISNA, 1993-2005), accessed online at http://www.isna.org/faq/patientcentered.

²⁷⁴ The term 'masculine' is derived from the Latin *masculus*, which can be rendered in English as 'male' or 'masculine' depending on context. This both explains the linguistic link between 'masculine' (gender term) and 'male' (sex term), and the use of the latter as a gender term. 'Feminine,' like 'female,' is derived from the Latin adjective *feminina*, related to the noun *femina*. The same remarks offered for masculine apply to feminine.

²⁷⁵ See Robert W. Connell, *Masculinities* (Berkeley: Univ. of California Press, 1995).

²⁷⁶ The four terms 'boy,' 'girl,' 'man,' 'woman,' combine sex and gender but give predominance to gender. Consider, for example, the word 'woman.' Though it presumes the female sex, it is derived from a gendered role—'a man's wife.' In this work, such terms are typically used to refer to gender rather than sex.

²⁷⁷ Vern Bullough, *Cross Dressing, Sex, and Gender* (Phila.: Univ. of Pennsylvania Press, 1993), p. 174.

278 Fausto-Sterling, *Sexing the Body*, p. 3.

279 Vern L. Bullough & Bonnie Bullough, *Crossdressing, Sex, Gender*. (Phila.: Univ. of Pennsylvania Press, 1993), p. 5.

280 Sigmund Freud, *New Introductory Lectures on Psychoanalysis*, translated by James Strachey (N. Y.: W. W. Norton, 1965), p. 113. It is worth noting that Freud grasps better than most how problematic our gender notions are. In a 1915 footnote to his seminal work on human sexuality he comments, "It is essential to understand clearly that the concepts of 'masculine' and 'feminine,' whose meaning seems so unambiguous to ordinary people, are among the most confused that occur in science." See Sigmund Freud, *Three Essays on the Theory of Sexuality*, translated by James Strachey (N. Y.: Basic Books, 1962), p. 85, n. 1.

281 Thomas Eckes & Hanns M. Trautner, "Developmental Social Psychology of Gender: An Integrative Framework," in T. Eckes (Ed.), *The Developmental Social Psychology of Gender*, pp. 332 (Mahwah, NJ: Lawrence Erlbaum, 2000), p. 9f.

282 Ibid, p. 114. Freud believes that masculinity and femininity are constructs that no one science is adequate to explain. He examines biology, psychology and psychoanalysis, concluding even for the last a limited perception and one still dependent on a relatively straightforward connection of gender to sex.

283 Ibid.

284 Indeed, self-designations such as 'tomboy' may even be presented as third gender alternatives by children. Consider, for example, the case of elementary school-aged Jodie, who after remarking that all the girls in her class "act all stupid and girlie," declared this judgment did not apply to her "cos I'm not a girl, I'm a tomboy." However, exactly what Jodie intended is unclear. She succeeded in persuading two male classmates to identify her as a boy. The researcher concluded Jodie appeared to be operating at the boundary line between masculinity and femininity—a justifiable interpretation where no other gender alternatives are allowed recognition. See Diane Reay, "'Spice Girls', 'Nice Girls', 'Girlies', and 'Tomboys': Gender Discourses, Girls' Cultures and Femininities in the Primary Classroom," *Gender and Education, 13* (no. 2), 153-166 (2001), p. 161f.

285 Marjorie S. Hardy, "The Development of Gender Roles: Societal Influences," in Louis Diamont & Richard D. McAnulty (Eds.), *The Psychology of Sexual Orientation, Behavior, and Identity. A Handbook*, pp.425-443 (Westport, CT: Greenwood Press, 1995), p. 425.

286 John Money & Anke A. Ehrhardt, *Man and Woman, Boy and Girl* (Baltimore: John Hopkins Univ. Press, 1972).

287 Simone de Beauvoir, *The Second Sex* (N. Y.: Penguin Books, 1972), p. 295.

288 Although I understand and use the terms somewhat differently from Lisa Maurer (referenced above), her discussion of them provides a succinct introduction to some of the issues involved with such vocabulary. I particularly like her discussion of gender attribution.

289 The developmental processes at work, their progression, and the role of dress are covered in the answer to Q. 6.

290 In fact, these pressures are at the heart of one possible explanation for male crossdressing (see the answer to Q. 22). In the literature, see Manuel X. Zamarripa, Bruce E. Wampold, & Erik Gregory, "Male Gender Role Conflict, Depression, and Anxiety: Clarification and Generalizability to Women," *Journal of Counseling Psychology, 50* (no. 3), 333-338 (2003), p. 333. Cf. J. M. O'Neil, "Patterns of Gender Role Conflict and Strain: Sexism and Fear of Femininity in Men's Lives," *Personnel and Guidance Journal, 60*, 203-210 (1981).

291 David Plummer, *One of the Boys: Masculinity, Homophobia, and Modern Manhood* (Binghamton, NY: Haworth Press, 1999), p. 137.

292 Ibid, p. 138.

293 Homosexual boys and men, too, may take recourse to blatant homophobia in the effort to protect themselves, including their sense of being a masculine gendered self.

294 Margaret Mead, *Sex and Temperament in Three Primitive Societies* (N. Y.: Morrow Quill Paperbacks, 1963 reprint of 1935 ed.), p. 280.

295 Hardy, p. 326.

296 Ibid, pp. 427-435.

297 Ibid, p. 437.

298 Helen E. Fischer, *Anatomy of Love. The Natural History of Monogamy, Adultery, and Divorce* (N. Y.: W. W. Norton, 1992), p. 191.

299 George P. Murdock, *Culture and Society* (Pittsburgh: Univ. of Pittsburgh Press, 1965), p. 451; the information is nicely tabled in Martin Daly & Margo Wilson, *Sex, Evolution, and Behavior*, 2nd ed. (Boston: PWS Publishers, 1983), pp. 262-263 (Table 101).

300 Ibid.

301 However, changes in sex-linked divisions of labor in our society, as well as modifications in gender expectations and roles, have been highly selective and continue to serve the essential distinction preserved in our gender or-

der. That is why, for example, women continue to be paid less than men for equal responsibility and work; their sex and gender status alone justify the pay inequity in our gender order (despite the rationalizations actually put forward).

302 Judith Butler, *Gender Trouble: Feminism and the Subversion of Identity* (N. Y.: Routledge, 1990). Note that 'performativity' is not identical to 'performance.' Butler states that the latter presumes a subject while the former disputes even the notion of 'subject.' That which is performative brings into being what it speaks of as it speaks it.

303 Ibid, pp. 78.

304 Judith Butler, "Restaging the Universal: Hegemony and the Limits of Formalism," in J. Butler, E. Laclau, & S. Zizek (Eds.), *Contingency, Hegemony, Universality: Contemporary Dialogues on the Left*, pp. 11-43 (N. Y.: Verso, 2000) p. 29.

305 Judith Butler, "Critically Queer," in S. Phelan (Ed.), *Playing with Fire: Queer Politics, Queer Theories*, pp. 1130 (N. Y.: Routledge, 1997), p. 17. Cf. Judith Butler, *Bodies That Matter: On the Discursive Limits of Sex* (N. Y.: Routledge, 1993).

306 Thus, for example, Walter Bockting portrays *gender* identity as one of four distinct components of *sexual* identity (the other three components being natal sex, social sex role, and sexual orientation). See Walter O. Bockting, "From Construction to Context: Gender Through the Eyes of the Transgendered," *SIECUS Report, 28* (no. 1), 37 (1999, Oct./Nov.), p. 3. In this conception, Bockting both follows and adapts the work of Shively and DeCecco; see Michael G. Shively & John P. DeCecco, "Components of Sexual Identity," *Journal of Homosexuality, 3* (no. 1), 41-48 (1977).

307 Thomas Laqueur, *Making Sex. Body and Gender from the Greeks to Freud* (Cambridge: Harvard Univ. Press, 1990). Although not without his critics, Laqueur has been immensely influential in the matter of modern historical changes in our perception. This is considered a truly seminal work in the field.

308 Maurer, p. 14.

309 *The American Heritage Book of English Usage. A Practical and Authoritative Guide to Contemporary English* (N. Y.: Houghton Mifflin, 1996), p. 176: 5. Gender: Sexist Language and Assumptions, §10 gender/sex. Accessed online at http://www.bartleby.com/64/C005/010.html.

310 Jessica Xavier, "Introduction," in M. Boenke (Ed.), *Trans Forming Families: Real Stories About Transgendered Loved Ones*, 2nd ed., pp. xii-xiv (New Castle, DE: Oak Knoll Press, 2003), p. xiii.

311 Sabrina Petra Ramet (Ed.), *Gender reversals and Gender Cultures* (London: Routledge, 1996), p. 2.

³¹² Claudine Griggs, *S/He: Changing Sex and Changing Clothes*. (Oxford: Berg Publishing Ltd., 1998), p. 1.

³¹³ Richard Ekins & Dave King, "Blending Genders: Contributions to the Emerging Field of Transgender Studies," *The International Journal of Transgenderism, 1* (no. 1) (1997, July-Sept.). This is an electronic journal. The article was accessed online at http://www.symposion.com/ijt/ijtc0101.htm. Also see Richard Ekins & Dave King (Eds.), *Blending Genders: Social Aspects of Cross-Dressing and Sex-Changing* (N. Y.: Routledge, 1996), p. 5. See especially, Part III: "The Medicalization of Gender Blending" (pp. 75-118).

³¹⁴ 'Third gender' people are considered in the next volume (see the answers to Q. 20, 26).

³¹⁵ Per Schioldborg, Address at the Meeting of the Nordic Association for Clinical Sexology (NACS), Oslo, Norway, September 28-30, 1983, cited in Elsa Almas & Esben Esther Pirelli Benestad, "Norway," in R. T. Francoeur (Ed.), *The International Encyclopedia of Sexuality*, Vol. IV, pp. 460-462 (N. Y.: Continuum, 2001), p. 461. Accessed online at http://www.SexQuest.com/IES4. See §7. Gender Conflicted Persons.

³¹⁶ A. E. Eyler & K. Wright, "Gender Identification and Sexual Orientation Among Genetic Females with Gender-Blended Self-perception in Childhood and Adolescence," *The International Journal of Transgenderism, 1* (no. 1) (1997). Accessed online at http://www. symposion.com/ijt/ijtc0102.htm.

³¹⁷ I often refer to gender 'statuses' or 'states,' without elaborating further. I mean by this usage an openness to interpreting gender labels as distinctly different realities ('states') or as discernibly different gradations ('statuses') within general states, however many of the latter are numbered.

³¹⁸ Erica Reischer & Kathryn S. Koo, "The Body Beautiful: Symbolism and Agency in the Social World," *Annual Review of Anthropology, 33*, 297317 (2004), p. 298.

³¹⁹ Ibid, p. 301.

³²⁰ The proposal here is intended along the lines of the "utopian fantasy" suggested by Sandra Bem: "I propose that we let a thousand categories of sex/gender/desire begin to bloom in any and all fluid and permeable configurations and, through that very proliferation, that we thereby undo (or, if you prefer, that we de-privilege or de-center or destabilize) the privileged status of two-and-only-two that are currently treated as normal and natural." Sandra L. Bem, "Dismantling Gender Polarization and Compulsory Heterosexuality: Should We Turn the Volume Down or Up?" in R. Heasley & B. Crane (Eds.), *Sexual Lives. A Reader on the Theories and Realities of Human Sexualities*, pp. 253-261 (Boston: McGraw-Hill, 2003), p. 255.

[321] There are signs of an emerging vocabulary to accompany and accommodate a paradigm shift in the way we perceive and discuss gender. The transgender community has proliferated numerous self-descriptors to move away from those associated with psychological pathology. Author and activist Leslie Feinberg has proposed we adopt new, non-gendered pronouns like 's/he,' or 'sie' (pronounced like 'see'), or 'ze' (to replace she/he) and 'hir' (pronounced like 'here,' to replace him/her). See Leslie Feinberg, *Trans Liberation: Beyond Pink or Blue* (Boston: Beacon Press, 1998). Cf. the *Queers and Allies Dictionary* accessed online at http://www.gustavus.edu/oncampus/orgs/ queers/ main/dictionary_full.html.

[322] Kate Bornstein, *Gender Outlaw. On Men, Women, and the Rest of Us* (N. Y.: Vintage Books, 1995), p. 127.

[323] Albert D. Klassen, Colin J. Williams, & Eugene E. Levitt, *Sex and Morality in the U. S.,* H. J. O'Gorman, Ed. (Middletown, CT: Wesleyan Univ. Press, 1989), p. 272f. Even earlier, anthropologist Margaret Mead also noted how modern cultures are struggling to adapt to the changing economic position of women. See her *Sex and Temperament in Three Primitive Societies* (N. Y.: Morrow Quill Paperbacks, 1963), p. 308. Original work published 1935.

[324] Marjorie Garber writes, "For me, therefore, one of the most important aspects of crossdressing is the way in which it offers a challenge to easy notions of binarity, putting into question the categories of 'female' and 'male,' whether they are considered essential or constituted, biological or cultural." *Vested Interests. Cross-Dressing and Cultural Anxiety* (N. Y.: Routledge, 1992), p. 10. Cf. Libby Purves, "Trouser Girls, Boys in Frocks and Sequin Envy," *The Times* (1992, May 6), LT 5.

[325] This idea has become a popular explanation for why male crossdressing is not tolerated while female crossdressing is. For more on this, see the subsection on men near the end of this answer, and the answer to Q. 37.

Q. 6 Notes

[326] Numerous studies investigate this notion, frequently in terms of the perceived link between a girl or woman's attire and sexual assault. Since that has been discussed elsewhere in this work, here we will examine the broader context. In general, feminine apparel that exposes or draws attention to female erogenous zones is seen as sexually inviting. Two studies may be illustrative. One examines men's appraisal in bars of a woman's sexual availability noted that while men show an awareness that their judgment on this matter based on her dress appearance may be inaccurate, they make it nonetheless. See Kathleen A. Parks & Douglas M. Scheidt, "Male Bar Drinkers' Perspective on Female Bar Drinkers," *Sex Roles. A Journal of Research, 43* (nos. 11-12), 927-941 (2000). An-

other study, on mate poaching, found that participants identified as one strategy for women suggesting easy sexual access to themselves is to wear seductive clothing. Tactics involving disguise of mate poaching enticement also involved men manipulating clothing, including dressing conservatively, changing clothes often, and hiding new clothes from his current partner. See David P. Schmidt & Todd K. Shackelford, "Nifty Ways to Leave Your Lover: The Tactics People Use to Entice and Disguise the Process of Human Mate Poaching," *Personality & Social Psychology Bulletin, 29* (no. 8), 1018-1035 (2003), p. 1020, 1027.

[327] Gregory P. Stone, "Appearance and the Self," in M. E. Roach & J. B. Eicher (Eds.), *Dress, Adornment, and the Social Order,* pp. 216-245 (N. Y.: John Wiley & Sons, 1965), p. 236.

[328] George Bush & Perry London, "On the Disappearance of Knickers: Hypotheses for the Functional Analysis of the Psychology of Clothing," in M. E. Roach & J. B. Eicher (Eds.), *Dress, Adornment, and the Social Order,* pp. 64-72 (N. Y.: John Wiley & Sons, 1965), pp. 66-72.

[329] This matter is also discussed under the material on dress codes in the answer to Q. 3.

[330] Joanna Brewis, Mark P. Hampton, & Stephen Linstead, "Unpacking Priscilla: Subjectivity and Identity in the Organization of Gendered Appearance," *Human Relations, 50* (no. 10), 1275-1304 (1997), p. 1281.

[331] Foucault's remark about the body seems no less suited to the *clothed* body: "The body is directly involved in a political field; power relations have an intimate hold upon it: they invest it, train it, and torture it, force it to carry out its tasks, to perform ceremonies, to emit signs." See Michel Foucault, *Discipline and Punish: The Birth of the Prison,* translated by A. Sheridan (N. Y.: Vintage, 1979), p. 25f.

[332] Brewis, Hampton, & Linstead, p. 1285.

[333] Quoted in Mary Lou Rosencranz, *Clothing Concepts. A Social-Psychological Approach* (N. Y.: Macmillan, 1972), p. 176.

[334] Brewis, Hampton, & Linstead, p. 1285.

[335] L. L. Davis, "Sex, Gender Identity, and Behavior Concerning Sex-Related Clothing," *Clothing & Textiles Research Journal, 3* (no. 2), 20-24 (1985). The 174 male and female subjects completed both the Bem Sex Role Inventory (BSRI) and a Sex-related Clothing Inventory.

[336] A very common way that women participate in the construction and maintenance of masculinity is through the purchase of clothing for the boys and men in their lives.

337 The mutual desire of men and women to have men dress in masculine attire reinforces the Golden Rule, while the acceptability of women dressing more like men broadens the available choices for women. Both forces thus converge to limit masculine dress alternatives relate to feminine ones.

338 Each of these patterns are also described, with explicit reference to transgender, in the answer to the next question.

339 See Michael Hayworth, "Fashion, Clothing, and Sex," in V. L. Bullough & B. Bullough (Eds.), *Human Sexuality: An Encyclopedia* (N. Y.: Garland Reference Library of Social Science, 1994), at the Magnus Hirschfeld Archive for Sexology maintained by the HumboldtUniversität zu Berlin, accessed online at http://www2.hu-berlin.de/sexology/GESUND/ARCHIV/SEN/CH10.HTM.

340 Carrie Yang Costello, "Changing Clothes: Gender Inequality and Professional Socialization," *NWSA Journal,16* (no. 2), 138-155 (2004), p. 144. This finding is consistent with what we have seen in answering previous questions: men have only to obey a single Golden Rule; women have much greater dress freedom.

341 Ibid, especially pp. 138f., 152.

342 On the dress of children, both see below and also see the answer to Q. 9, which considers how it has changed. The androgynous character of dress for males and females before adulthood exists in many social groups and contexts, including among American slaves in the antebellum United States; see Shane White & Graham White, "Slave Clothing and African-American Culture in the Eighteenth and Nineteenth Centuries," *Past & Present, 148*, 149-186 (1995).

343 Androgynous dress by males can be tolerated because it does *not* violate the golden rule that a male must look masculine, or at least not feminine.

344 "In clothing design the term, silhouette, is used to express the effect the costume creates as a whole as it appears from a distance, when details of construction and even of color are not noticeable, and the only things observed are the boundary line of the silhouette and its general proportions." Helen Goodrich Buttrick, *Principles of Clothing Selection* (N. Y.: Macmillan, 1923), p. 53f.

345 Sarah J. Doyle, "Clothing Can Create an Optical Illusion—Good or Bad!" *Wisdom from the Professionals: A Collection of Articles* (2003), accessed online at the Fabrics.net website at http://www.fabrics. net/SarahIllusion.asp.

346 Cf. Buttrick, p. 54.

347 Stone, p. 234.

[348] Madeline Shakin, Debra Shakin, & Sarah Hall Sternglanz, "Infant Clothing: Sex Labeling for Strangers," *Sex Roles. A Journal for Research, 12* (nos. 9-10), 955-964 (1985).

[349] Spencer E. Cahill, "Fashioning Males and Females. Appearance management and the Social Reproduction of Gender," *Symbolic Interaction, 12* (no. 2), 281-298 (1989), p. 289.

[350] Emily W. Kane, "'No Way My Boys Are Going to Be Like That!' Parents' Responses to Children's Gender Nonconformity," *Gender & Society, 20* (no. 2), 149-176 (2006), p. 149f.

[351] Andrée Pomerleau, Daniel Bolduc, Gérard Malcuit, & Louise Cossette, "Pink or Blue: Environmental Gender Stereotypes in the First Two Years of Life," *Sex Roles. A Journal of Research, 22* (nos. 5-6), 359-367 (1990).

[352] Gender-based-on-sex is arguably the centerpiece in the construction of identity and relationships in our culture. No wonder we spend so much effort trying to get it right!

[353] J. Z. Rubin, F. J. Provenzano, & Z. Luria, "The Eye of the Beholder: Parents' Views on Sex of Newborns," *American Journal of Orthopsychiatry, 44* (no. 1), 47-55 (1974).

[354] Carole R. Beal, *Boys and Girls: The Development of Gender Roles* (N. Y.: McGraw-Hill, 1994), p. 45.

[355] Kane, p. 156f.

[356] Ibid, pp. 158-160. Interestingly, Kane (pp. 162-164) notes that only with sons was gender nonconformity connected with a concern about sexual orientation. Feminine behavior was viewed as a warning sign of possible homosexuality.

[357] David Plummer, *One of the Boys: Masculinity, Homophobia, and Modern Manhood* (Binghamton, NY: Haworth Press, 1999), p. 145.

[358] Kenneth J. Zucker, Susan J. Bradley, & Mohammed Sanikhani, "Sex Differences in Referral Rates of Children with Gender Identity Disorder: Some Hypotheses," *Journal of Abnormal Child Psychology, 25* (no. 3), 217-227 (1997).

[359] Susan J. Langer & James I. Martin, "How Dresses Can Make You Mentally Ill: Examining Gender Identity Disorder in Children," *Child and Adolescent Social Work Journal, 21* (no. 1), 523 (2004), p. 8.

[360] The constancy and importance of dress as a marker for children has been noted in many studies. At least as far back as 1947 a large study involving 200 boys and girls ages 412 found they relied on dress cues first and foremost in

making differentiations among peers. See J. H. Conn & L. Kanner, "Children's Awareness of Sex Differences," *Child Psychiatry, 1*, 357 (1947).

[361] Beverly I. Fagot & Mary D. Leinbach, "The Young Child's Gender Schema: Environmental Input, Internal Organization," *Child Development, 60* (no. 3), 663-672 (1989). Even as small children are learning and applying expectations about dress based on gender, these expectations are being applied to them by adults. For example, a study reported in 1993, involving 100 young women in an introductory early childhood education course found that they held expectations about preschoolers based on the children's sex-typed clothing, their perceived sex (the students were shown photos in which the clothing and child images were manipulated), and the students' own sex-role stereotypes. See K. K. P. Johnson & J. E. Workman, "Effect of Clothing, Sex, and Sex Role Stereotypes on Behavioral Expectations of a Preschool Kid," *Clothing & Textiles Research Journal, 11* (no. 2), 1-6 (1993).

[362] Consider, for example, a developmental study of 95 girls ages 2-10 using the Measure of Attitudes Toward Clothing for Play (MACP) to assess them. Four different clothing styles were matched with play activities; as the girls grew older they increasingly associated wearing jeans with more aggressive and physically active play, while frilly dress was associated with doll play. A follow-up study, involving 43 of the same subjects, focused on traits, found similar results: jeans were associated with aggression, strength and bravery; frilly clothes were associated with a concern with appearance and popularity. See S. B. Kaiser, "Clothing and the Social Organization of Gender Perception: A Developmental Approach," *Clothing & Textiles Research Journal, 7* (no. 2), 46-54 (1989).

[363] Carol Lynn Martin & Jane K. Little, "The Relation of Gender Understanding to Children's Sex-Typed Preferences and Gender Stereotypes," *Child Development, 61* (no. 5), 1427-1439 (1990); quote is from p. 1436.

[364] "Insight into the Children's Apparel Market," *Textile Consumer, 32* (2004, Spring). Accessed online at the Cotton Incorporated website at http://www.cottoninc.com/TextileConsumer/TextileConsumer Volume32/.

[365] Ibid. A Table shows, for example, that 26% of girls' skirts are made 100% from synthetic fibers.

[366] Plummer, p. 144.

[367] Ibid, p. 143f.

[368] See Carol Lynn Martin, "Stereotypes About Children with Traditional and Nontraditional Gender Roles," *Sex Roles. A Journal of Research, 33* (nos. 11-12), 721-757 (1995).

[369] Jason Cox & Helga Dittmar, "The Functions of Clothes and Clothing (Dis)satisfaction: A Gender Analysis Among British Students," *Journal of Consumer Policy, 18* (nos. 2-3), 237-265 (1995), p. 243.

[370] J. Jill Suitor & Rebel Reavis, "Football, Fast Cars, and Cheerleading: Adolescent Gender Norms, 1978-1989," *Adolescence, 30* (no. 2), 265-272 (1995), Table I.

[371] Cox & Dittmar, p. 240f. The authors conclude that these differences may be construed as reflecting, broadly, differences in masculine and feminine gender identities, with the former more self-oriented and activity centered, where the latter is more other-oriented and relationship-centered.

[372] Ibid, p. 251.

[373] Stephen J. Gould & Barbara B. Stern, "Gender Schema and Fashion Consciousness," *Psychology & Marketing, 6* (no. 2), 129-145 (1989), p. 142.

[374] Timothy M. Franz & Steven D. Norton, "Investigating Business Causal Dress Policies: Questionnaire Development and Exploratory Research," *Applied H.R.M. Research, 6* (nos. 1-2), 79-94 (2000).

[375] See, for example, Michael G. Pratt & Anat Rafaeli, "Organizational Dress as a Symbol of Multilayered Social Identities," *Academy of Management Journal, 40* (no. 4), 862-898 (1997). This article explores at some length the function of dress in relation to identity in the professional setting of a rehabilitation unit in a large hospital.

[376] Yoon-Hee Kwon, "The Influence of Appropriateness of Dress and Gender in the Self perception of Occupational Attributes," *Clothing & Textiles Research Journal, 12* (no. 3), 33-39 (1994). Also see Sherry E. Sullivan, "Do Clothes Really Make the Woman? The Use of Attire to Enhance Work Performance," *The Academy of Management Executives, 11* (no. 4), 90ff. (1997).

[377] Yoon-Hee Kwon, "Feeling Toward One's Clothing and Self-perception of Emotion, Sociability, and Work Competency," *Journal of Social Behavior and Personality, 9* (no. 1), 129-139 (1994).

[378] Feminist Carole Turbin suggests that casual wear in such contexts can temporarily modify the gender hierarchy, signaling less formality in authority relationships and permitting more display of sexual interest. See Carole Turbin, "Refashioning the Concept of Public/Private. Lessons from Dress Studies," *Journal of Women's Studies, 15* (no. 1), 43-51 (2003), p. 46f.

[379] Jennifer Craik, *The Face of Fashion: Cultural Studies in Fashion* (N. Y.: Routledge, 1994), p. 56.

380 A sizeable number of studies have been done on the role of dress in the lives of girls and women. One such is by Alison Guy & Maura Banim, "Personal Collections: Women's Clothing Use and Identity," *Journal of Gender Studies, 9* (no. 3), 313-327 (2000). In this article they cluster the 'dynamic relationship' women have with their clothes around three distinct but coexisting views of the self: 'the woman I want to be,' 'the woman I fear I could be,' and 'the woman I am most of the time.' For a more extended treatment see Ali Guy, Eileen Green, & Maura Banim, *Through the Wardrobe: Women's Relationships with Their Clothes* (N. Y.: Berg, 2001).

381 Gould & Stern, p. 142.

382 Cox & Dittmar, pp. 254-257. They conclude (p. 256) that social psychological functions of clothes are, for women, much greater predictors of clothing satisfaction.

383 Mary Lou Lerch Rosencranz, "A Study of Women's Interest in Clothing," *Journal of Home Economics, 41* (no. 8), 460-462 (1949), p. 462.

384 Kim P. Johnson, Nancy A. Schofield, and Jennifer Yurchisin, "Appearance and Dress as a Source of Information. A Qualitative Approach to Data Collection," *Clothing & Textiles Research Journal, 20* (no. 3), 125-137 (2002).

385 Kim K. P. Johnson & Mary Ellen Roach-Higgins, "Dress and Physical Attractiveness of Women in Job Interviews," *Clothing & Textiles Research Journal, 5* (no. 3), 18 (1987).

386 Yoon-Hee Kwon, "The Influence of Appropriateness of Dress and Gender on the Self-perception of Occupational Attributes," *Clothing & Textiles Research Journal, 12* (no. 3), 33-39 (1994).

387 Brewis, Hampton, & Linstead, p. 1287. See their discussion on power dressing, pp. 1287-1288, 1292-1293.

388 S. M. Forsythe, "Effect of Clothing Masculinity on Perceptions of Managerial Traits: Does Gender of the Perceiver Make a Difference?" *Clothing & Textiles Research Journal, 6* (no. 2), 10-16 (1988). The answer to the title's question was that there is not a significant difference between males and females, although the latter tended to see the women subjects being examined as more forceful and self-reliant.

389 Kim P. Johnson, C. Crutsinger, & Jane E. Workman, "Can Professional Women Appear Too Masculine? The Case of the Necktie," *Clothing and Textiles Research Journal, 12* (no. 2), 27-31 (1994). At least as late as 1977, women were still having to go to court for the right to wear pants at work; see the United Kingdom case of Schmidt vs. Austicks Bookshops Ltd.

390 K. E. Koch & L. E. Dickey, "The Feminist in the Workplace: Applications to a Contextual Study of Dress," *Clothing & Textiles Research Journal,* 7 (no. 1), 46-54 (1988).

391 Rosencranz, p. 460.

392 Cf. James Laver, *Modesty in Dress. An Inquiry into the Fundamentals of Fashion* (Boston: Houghton Mifflin, 1969).

393 Cf. Susan Kaiser, "Minding Appearances: Style, Truth, and Subjectivity," in J. Entwhistle & E. Wilson (Eds.), *Body Dressing,* pp. 79-102 (Oxford: Berg, 2001).

394 E. L. Bell, "Adult's Perception of Male Garment Styles," *Clothing & Textiles Research Journal,* 10 (no. 1), 8-12 (1991).

395 Kate Soper, "Dress Needs: Reflections on the Clothed Body, Selfhood and Consumption," in Joanne Entwistle & Elizabeth Wilson (Eds.), *Body Dressing. Dress, Body, Culture* (N. Y.: Berg, 2001), pp. 13-32.

396 Hannah Frith & Kate Gleeson, "Clothing and Embodiment: Men Managing Body Image and Appearance," *Psychology of Men & Masculinity,* 5 (no. 1), 40-48. Frith and Glesson identify four themes in men's use of dress: practicality, unconcern about appearance, dressing to conceal or reveal the body, and using clothes to fit cultural ideals.

397 In the U.S. the market for men's clothing has been volatile in the early 21st century with a decline in 2000‑2003, but followed by an upswing in 2004-2005. In the United Kingdom men's designer wear expenditures in 1997 constituted 39% of the market; in 2001 they were 43% (Priest, p. 258).

398 Judith Rasband, *Real Men Don't Wear Tees!* (Conselle L. C., 2000). Accessed online at Conselle.com at http://www.conselle.com/Business_Programs /real_men.html. Rasband argues that, taken together, the woman who wears business casual attire (i.e., pants), which assumes a traditionally masculine appearance, and the man who dresses casually, thus becoming less covered and appearing more feminine, both appear to reflect changing gender roles. Resistance to men wearing casual attire, she thinks, indicates a fear of the feminization of the workplace.

399 For example, we might be motivated by modesty to adhere to our mother's advice to always wear clean and plain underwear that might in an emergency be seen by strangers—who we would not wish to form an impression of us as loose or wanton! Similarly, we may choose to wear underwear we view as erotic to cultivate inside ourselves a feeling of being sexy—and perhaps with the hope of a sexual encounter, in which the sight of our apparel will boost our partner's libido (or our own!).

[400] When couples feel less intimate with one another they are likely to change their dress habits so that they no longer dress or undress in front of one another; their underwear, like their inmost self, becomes invisible.

[401] Guy Trebay, "When Did Skivvies Get Rated NC17?" [Cultural Studies] *The New York Times* (2004, Aug. 1). Accessed online at *The New York Times'* 'Fashion & Style' webpage, at http://www.nytimes.com/2004/08/01/fashion/01SKIV.html?ei=5090&en=f0088a3b25fa1e4b&ex=1249185600&partner=rssuserland&pagewanted=all&position=. Trebay traces this development to the influence of a portion of the gay community.

[402] Bo Lönnqvist, "Fashion and Eroticism: Men's Underwear in the Context of Eroticism," *Ethnologia Europaea, 31* (no. 1), 75-82 (2001).

[403] The idea of a sexual economy depicts sexual exchanges as economic ones: a female grants access to her body in exchange for the male granting access to his resources. Thus men will desire sexually attractive, fertile women while women will desire successful, virile men.

[404] Feona Attwood, "Fashion and Passion: Marketing Sex to Women," *Sexualities, 8* (no. 4), 392-406 (2005).

[405] Jane FerrellBeck & Colleen Gau, *Uplift: The Bra in America* (Phila.: Univ. of Pennsylvania Press, 2002), p. 116; cf. p. 56.

[406] For an interesting perspective, see Garry S. Brody, "The Perfect Breast: Is It Attainable? Does It Exist?" *Plastic & Reconstructive Surgery, 113* (no. 5), 1500-1503 (2004).

[407] For a look at the history of panties and panty fashion, as well as speculations about what various panty styles suggest about their wearers, see Sarah Tomczak & Rachel Pask, *Panties: A Brief History* (London: Dorling Kindersley, 2004).

[408] Tony Kent, "Ethical Perspectives on the Erotic in Retailing," *Qualitative Market Research: An International Journal, 8* (no. 4), 430-439 (2005).

[409] Nancy V. Workman, "From Victorian to Victoria's Secret: The Foundations of Modern Erotic Wear," *Journal of Popular Culture, 30* (no. 2), 61-73 (1996); see especially pp. 68-70.

Q. 7 Notes

[410] Joanna Brewis, Mark P. Hampton, & Stephen Linstead, "Unpacking Priscilla: Subjectivity and Identity in the Organization of Gendered Appearance," *Human Relations, 50* (no. 10), 1275-1304 (1997), p. 1286.

[411] In cultures like our own, where only two genders are recognized, such creative manipulation of cultural views of both sex and gender are neces-

sary to construct a 'third gender' alternative. Crossdressing then erects a space using both the boundaries of the body and of clothing to inhabit the experience of a gender neither masculine nor feminine. In this situation it may be accurate to say that a conventional gender is being borrowed in order to *be* a third gender.

[412] This quality was briefly explored in the previous answer.

[413] Jason Cromwell, *Transmen and Ftms: Identities, Bodies, Genders, and Sexualities* (Urbana: Univ. of Illinois Press, 1999), p. 128.

[414] Cf. Butler's comment, ". . . drag says 'my "outside" appearance is feminine, but my essence "inside" is masculine." Judith Butler, "Gender Trouble, Feminist Theory and Psychoanalytic Discourse," in L. J. Nicholson (Ed.), *Femiinism/Postmodernism*, pp. 324-340 (N. Y.: Routledge, 1990), p. 336.

[415] Women and girls have long manipulated their silhouette by the style and fit of what they choose as outerwear and by the artful use of underwear like chemises, petticoats, hoops, corsets, and other garments. We also may remind ourselves that males, too, manipulate their silhouette; even the quintessentially masculine dress of the business suit affects a silhouette not exactly corresponding to the real body underneath. Both men and women alter their silhouette so as to approach a desired idea silhouette of masculinity or femininity as they conceive of it and desire it.

[416] Because the silhouette is the foreground figure against a background that includes cultural expectations and judgments about dress few crossdressers appear in public without doing all they can to ensure a socially satisfactory silhouette will be cast. When they willingly create a discordant one it is likely in service to some particular agenda where the risk is minimized or acceptable given the possible gain.

[417] Melanie Yarborough & Lucy Silvay, "California Dreamin' '99 Keynote Speech: Our Transgender Family" (1999). 'California Dreamin' is an International Foundation for Gender Education (IFGE) sponsored event. Available online at http://members.fortunecity.com/melanie4/ keynote.htm.

[418] Jody Norton, "Transchildren and the Discipline of Children's Literature," *The Lion and the Unicorn, 23* (no. 3), 415-436 (1999), p. 416 (both quotes).

[419] Cf. Jason Cox & Helga Dittmar, "The Functions of Clothes and Clothing (Dis)satisfaction: A Gender Analysis Among British Students," *Journal of Consumer Policy, 18* (nos. 2-3), 237-265 (1995), p. 251.

[420] Because of the cultural decision to make gender so dependent on sex, gender challenges inevitably threaten perceptions and values tied to the physical body. If we are made to doubt even that, the unconscious worry goes,

what else is left? On the role of homophobia in the construction of Western masculinity, see David Plummer, *One of the Boys: Masculinity, Homophobia, and Modern Manhood* (Binghamton, NY: Haworth Press, 1999).

[421] In psychiatry's DSM model, petticoat punishment was included in DSMIIIR as a 'predisposing factor' for 'transvestic fetishism.' See American Psychiatric Association, *Diagnostic and Statistical Manual of Mental Disorders, 3rd ed., Revised* (Washington, D. C.: American Psychiatric Association, 1987), p. 289. For more information, see the answer to Q. 96.

[422] This kind of literature has existed at least since the 19th century. A famous late 19th century example is M. Le Compte Du Bouleau (Stanislas Matthew de Rhodes), *The Petticoat Dominant, or Woman's Revenge: The Autobiography of a Young Nobleman as a Pendant to Gynecocracy* (1898). The internet provides many contemporary examples. See, for instance, *Petticoat Discipline Quarterly*, accessed online at http://www.petticoated.com/. For art, see *The Art of Petticoat Punishment*, by Carole Jean, accessed online at http://www.petticoat punishment art.com/.

[423] Kate Bornstein, *Gender Outlaw. On Men, Women, and the Rest of Us* (N. Y.: Vintage Books, 1995), p. 8.

[424] Another, but more difficult way to accomplish this end is to manipulate the physical body. Altering the sexed body can occur through very minor manipulations such as shaving or hair removal to more dramatic changes by hormone ingestion or surgery. When combined with dress any number of presentations become possible to represent a third sex and/or third gender self.

[425] A major aim of our time together is to put the dressing back into crossdressing—and why should be abundantly apparent to anyone who has read the answers to the previous questions. Attention to the experiencing and expression made possible uniquely by clothes (and adjunctively by other ornamentation) places crossdressing back into its proper context. Crossdressing, like other transgender realities, is not separable from either gender or apparel. The consequences within the mental health field from removing crossdressing from important contexts is covered in volume 4 of this work.

[426] Vern L. Bullough & Bonnie Bullough, *Crossdressing, Sex, Gender.* (Phila.: Univ. of Pennsylvania Press, 1993).

Q. 8 Notes

[427] James N. Morgan, *Consumer Economics* (N. Y.: Prentice-Hall, 1955), p. 312. Quoted in Mary Lou Rosencranz, "Clothing Symbolism," *Journal of Home Economics, 54* (no. 1), 18-22 (1962), p. 18.

428 C. Neil Macrae, Alan B. Milne, & Galen V. Bodenhausen, "Stereotypes as Energy-Saving Devices: A Peek Inside the Cognitive Toolbox," *Journal of Personality & Social Psychology, 66* (no. 1), 37-47 (1994).

429 Alice H. Eagly & V. J. Steffen, "Gender Stereotypes Stem from the Distribution of Women and Men Into Social Roles," *Journal of Personality & Social Psychology, 46,* 735-754 (1984).

430 Curt Hoffman & Nancy Hurst, "Gender Stereotypes: Perception or Rationalization?" *Journal of Personality & Social Psychology, 58* (no. 2), 197-208 (1990).

431 Jacqueline McGuire, "Gender Stereotypes of Parents with Two Year-olds and Beliefs About Gender Differences in Behavior," *Sex Roles. A Journal of Research, 19* (nos. 3-4), 233-240 (1988).

432 Kay A. Chick, Rose Ann Heilman-Houser, & Maxwell W. Hunter, "The Impact of Child Care on Gender Role Development and Gender Stereotypes," *Early Childhood Education Journal, 29* (no. 3), 149-154 (2002). The researchers noted that while the boys in their study received more attention from the caregivers than the girls did, the girls were more likely to be reinforced for their dress behavior (p. 151).

433 Carol Lynn Martin, Carolyn H. Wood, & Jane K. Little, "The Development of Gender Stereotype Components," *Child Development, 61* (no. 6), 18911904 (1990).

434 Studies focus on how women are disadvantaged by gender stereotypes. This occurs for women regardless of where on the economic ladder they stand. For instance, women in welfare-to-work programs may face gender stereotypes that hardly encourage growth and economic liberation. See Natalie G. Adams & James H. Adams, "'Bad Work Is Better Than No Work': The Gendered Assumptions in Welfare-to-Work Training Programs," *Journal for Critical Education Policy Studies, 4* (no. 1) (2006), accessed online at http://www.jceps.com/index.php? pageID=article&articleID=61. On a much higher rung, women managers disciplining subordinates are more likely than their male counterparts to be perceived as unfair and ineffective. See Leanne F. Atwater, James A. Carey, & David A. Waldman, "Gender and Discipline in the Workplace: Wait Until Your Father Gets Home," *Journal of Management, 27* (no. 5), 537-561 (2001).

435 Paul Lester (Ed.), *Images That Injure: Pictorial Stereotypes in the Media* (Westport, CT: Greenwood, 1996). See especially 'Part III. Gender Stereotypes,' pp. 69-106.

[436] Jack Glascock & Catherine Preston-Schreck, "Gender and Racial Stereotypes in Daily Newspaper Comics: A Time Honored Tradition?" *Sex Roles. A Journal of Research, 51* (nos. 7-8), 423-431 (2004).

[437] Macrae, Milne, & Bodenhausen, p. 37.

[438] Ibid, p. 44.

[439] Ibid, p. 44f.; individuation is introduced on p. 37.

[440] Eric Clausell & Susan T. Fiske, "When Do Subgroup Parts Add Up to the Stereotypic Whole? Mixed Stereotype Content for Gay Male Subgroups Explains Overall Ratings," *Social Cognition, 23* (no. 2), 161-181 (2005).

[441] Galen V. Bodenhausen, "Stereotypic Biases in Social Decision Making: Testing Process Models of Stereotype Use," *Journal of Personality & Social Psychology, 55* (no. 5), 726-737 (1988).

[442] Ziva Kunda & Kathryn C. Oleson, "Maintaining Stereotypes in the Face of Disconfirmation: Constructing Grounds for Subtyping Deviants," *Journal of Personality & Social Psychology, 68* (no. 4), 565-579 (1995), p. 565. The research referred to in the quote references W. G. Stephan, "Intergroup Relations," in G. Lindzey & E. Aronson (Eds.), *Handbook of Social Psychology*, 3rd ed., Vol. 2, pp. 599-658 (N. Y.: Random House, 1985).

[443] Ibid, p. 565f.

[444] Ibid, p. 566. Kunda and Oleson's own research reported in the article concerns this subtyping process, demonstrating experimentally how people justify holding on to stereotypes in the face of individuals who apparently disconfirm it.

[445] For more on this concept, see *Psychological Inquiry, 12* (no. 1) (2001), an issue devoted to reconsidering the idea.

[446] Clausell & Fiske, p. 173. The crossdresser subgroup's low competency/low warmth ranking put this subgroup in a cluster of one other gay subgroup also scoring low in both dimensions: the leather/biker gay subgroup. However, even this latter group outscored the crossdressers in perceived competence.

[447] Erving Goffman, *Stigma: Notes on the Management of Spoiled Identity* (N. Y.: Touchstone Books, 1986; original work published 1963). Goffman (p. 3) delineates a stigma as "an attribute that is deeply discrediting within a particular social interaction." He distinguishes three types (abominations of the body, blemishes of character, and tribal stigma of race, nation, religion).

[448] Ibid, p. 5.

[449] Ibid, p. 5f.

450 Ibid, pp. 610.

451 Ibid, p. 41f.; see chapter 2.

452 Ibid, chapters 23. Goffman (p. 23), in words prescient of what has happened among transgender people, writes, "the members of a particular stigma category will have a tendency to come together into small social groups whose members all derive from the category."

453 Leon Festinger, *A Theory of Cognitive Dissonance* (Stanford, CA: Stanford Univ. Press, 1957). Also see Leon Festinger, *Conflict, Decision, and Dissonance* (Stanford: Stanford Univ. Press, 1964). Cf. E. Harmon-Jones & J. Mills (Eds.), *Cognitive Dissonance: Progress on a Pivotal Theory in Social Psychology* (Washington, D.C.: American Psychological Association, 1999).

454 Leon Festinger, "Cognitive Dissonance," *Scientific American, 207* (no. 4), 93-102 (1962), p. 93.

455 Festinger, *A Theory of Cognitive Dissonance*, p. 3.

456 Ibid, p.18.

457 Cf. the idea of self-perception theory, which suggests we infer our beliefs from our behavior when we aren't sure what we believe. It may be that in forming a belief about tolerance we never considered situations like men in dresses, so we aren't sure what we believe. Our negative feeling plus our nasty behavior then prompt us to conclude we don't believe tolerance toward such folk is required by our belief in tolerance.

458 Festinger, *A Theory of Cognitive Dissonance*, p. 19.

459 Marc Widdowson, *The Phoenix Principle and the Coming Dark Age. Social Catastrophes—Human Progress 3000 B.C. to A.D. 3000* (2002), chapter 15, "Social Cohesion." Accessed online at http://www.darkage.fsnet.co.uk/Book.htm. This is an ongoing project.

460 Elisabeth L. McFalls & Deirdre Cobb-Roberts, "Reducing Resistance to Diversity Through Cognitive Dissonance Instruction. Implications for Teacher Education," *Journal of Teacher Education, 52* (no. 2), 164-172 (2001).

461 For a nicely illustrated presentation of Piaget's idea of 'equilibration,' which includes the use of assimilation and accommodation to effect a balance between cognitive stability and change, see Ed Labinowicz, *The Piaget Primer* (Menlo Park, CA: Addison-Wesley, 1980), pp. 36-41.

462 Truthfully, many of us prefer the man in the dress remain personally unknown. Our judgments compel us to see him as representing things we want no part of, regardless of how well or poorly we understand those things. Of course, we have as much right to our feelings, thoughts, and judgments as the

man in the dress. But we need to grasp that our response might cause *unnecessary harm*. And we can't morally justify that.

When our feelings, thoughts, and judgments lead us to unwarranted behavior, such as aggression toward others based on what they are wearing, then we are morally wrong regardless of the moral standing of the person we are victimizing. As my mother put it, "Two wrongs do not make a right." Even if we conclude that crossdressing is sometimes or always wrong, we are not thereby justified to put a stop to it by any means necessary.

Of course, we are rarely so crass. The more common danger is the harm generated by silently assenting to a larger cultural judgment that needlessly afflicts its minorities—and men in dress are certainly a minority! We are all familiar with the sobering experience of racism, where a silent majority consents to cultural attitudes, institutions, and practices that keep one or another minority group in an inferior position of regard, or opportunity, or reward. We are acquainted, too, with the homophobic reactions of the few who still represent an extreme example of a more widely felt unease, fear, or dislike toward openly homosexual people, which in turn perpetuates cultural attitudes, institutions, and practices oppressing them. In both instances the weight of sober empirical evidence has exposed the common anxieties as neurotic rather than realistic. Neither members of racial minorities nor of a homosexual orientation pose a threat justifying oppression or violence of any kind.

The same is true of those who crossdress.

I'll tell you this plainly right now: regardless of whether we conclude that crossdressing is morally right or wrong, religiously acceptable or abominable, psychologically sane or aberrant, in no instance are we justified in assenting to working harm against crossdressers. It is one thing to disagree, quite another to be disagreeable—and in this matter we all must aim at civility. Lacking compelling evidence of a clear and present danger posed by crossdressers, non-crossdressers cannot justify oppression, either overt or in the guise of culturally sanctioned prejudice and disdain.

Q. 9 Notes

463 William I. Thomas, "The Psychology of Woman's Dress," *American Magazine, 67,* 6672 (1908), p. 68. Accessed online at http://spartan.ac. brocku.ca/~lward/Thomas/Thomas_1908_b.html. This paper is part of a collection of Thomas' works included in a Mead Project web site at the Department of Sociology of Brock University.

464 Of course some individuals win an exception to the rule, but they may then find that they are trapped by the expectation to always be cross-dressed in order to retain their acceptance as an exception. In this manner the

culture bends one rule in service of a more fundamental rule: constancy. Cross-dressing by itself presents what a gender dichotomous culture like our own interprets as an inconstancy, especially since the crossdresser typically varies between crossdressed and non-crossdressed states. Society may not like a crossdressed presentation, but may prefer that as a dependable, constant presentation to the uncertainty of presentation offered by someone who goes back and forth between gender presentations in dress. So the general strategy seems to be to exert pressure to keep crossdressing from happening, or at least keep it hidden away, but if public presentations are persistent and draw wide attention, then society exerts pressure to make the crossdressing the constant presentation and thus eliminate uncertainty.

[465] Maggie Pexton Murray, *Changing Styles in Fashion. Who, What, Why* (N. Y.: Fairchild Publications, 1990), Preface.

[466] "What remains undeniably striking as one observes the evolution of men's clothing fashions is how one unchanging feature persists over time and space: the fondness for black. Black forms a constant in menswear, despite the not inconsiderable changes in the cut of male clothes between the sixteenth and the twentieth centuries." Marco Belfanti & Fabio Giusberti, "Global Dress: Clothing as a Means of Integration (17th – 20th Centuries)," p. 11. Paper presented at the XIII Economic History Congress, Buenos Aires, July 22-26, 2002. Accessed online at http://www.eh.net/XIIICongress/cd/papers/64Belfanti Giusberti170.pdf.

[467] The silhouette is discussed at more length in the answer to Q. 7.

[468] However, we must be mindful of Fred Davis' warning that, "temporally, too, there is reason to be cautious about ascribing precise meanings to most clothing. The very same apparel ensemble that 'said' one thing last year will 'say' something quite different today and yet another thing next year." We are constrained by this awareness to take as long a historical reach as we can and to limit ourselves to careful, if general, propositions. See Fred Davis, *Fashion, Culture, and Identity* (Chicago: Univ. of Chicago Press, 1992), p. 6.

[469] Philippe Ariès, *Centuries of Childhood: A Social History of Family Life*, translated by R. Baldick (London: Jonathan Cape, 1962), p. 48.

[470] J. Z. Rubin, F. J. Provenzano, & Z. Luria, "The Eye of the Beholder: Parents' Views on Sex of Newborns," *American Journal of Orthopsychiatry*, 44 (no. 1), 47-55 (1974). This research is briefly discussed in the answer to Q. 6.

[471] Of course, the resurgence of interest in pink as a color for men qualifies this generalization. On the early 21st century use of pink in masculine clothing, see Kelly Grannan, "Pink Moves Into the Masculine Mainstream," *The Daily Texan* (2004, Oct. 4), accessed online at http://www.dailytexan

online.com/media/paper410/news/2004/10/04/Entertainment/PinkMoves.In to.The.Masculine.Mainstream740552.shtml. Cf. "Real Men Wear Pink," *The Early Show* (CBS) (2005, Apr. 27), accessed online at http:// www.cbsnews.com/stories/2005/04/27/earlyshow/living/beauty/main691184. shtml.

[472] Jo Paoletti, *Dressing for Sexes* (n.d.). Accessed online at http:// www.gentlebirth.org/archives/pinkblue.html. Also see Jo Paoletti, "The Gendering of Infants' and Toddlers' Clothing in America," in Katharine Martinez and Kenneth Ames (Eds.), *The Material Culture of Gender/ The Gender of Material Culture* (The Henry Francis du Pont Winterthur Museum, 1997); "Clothes Make the Boy 1860-1910," *Dress, 8* (1983); "Clothing and Gender in American Children's Fashions 18901920," *Signs, 13* (no. 1), 136-143 (1987, Autumn); "Comment: Children's Clothes and Gender," *Threads, 19*, 98 (1988, Oct./Nov.). Paoletti holds a Ph.D. in textiles and teaches American Studies at the University of Maryland College Park. Cf. the short comment in Marjorie Gerber, *Vested Interests. CrossDressing and Cultural Anxiety* (N. Y.: Routledge, 1992), p. 1.

[473] Ibid. Interestingly, the first appearance in the Sears Catalog of gender specific infant wear did not occur until 1962. See K. Huun & S. B. Kaiser, "The Emergence of Modern Infantwear, 1896-1962," *Clothing & Textiles Research Journal, 19* (no. 3), 103-119 (2001). The authors view the changes in young children's clothing between 1896-1962 as an aspect of male "flight from femininity" as society constructed its modern binary system of gender.

[474] *Boys' Historical Clothing: Introduction* (Christopher Wagner's Historical Boys Clothing website). Accessed online, with numerous photographic examples, at http://histclo.hispeed.com/intro. html.

[475] Ibid.

[476] Jane Ellen, "Historic Costuming Series: Why Boys Wore Dresses," *What's New at Jane Ellen's, 3* (no. 1) (2000, February). Accessed online at http://www.dressmaker.com/ezine0200.shtml. Cf. Kristina Harris, *The Child in Fashion 1750 to 1920* (Atglen, PA: 1999). Some evidence exists that boys on occasion wore dresses until nearly puberty. The implicit notion was that all children and women were more alike to one another than any of these groups were like men.

[477] "Why Did Mothers Outfit Boys in Dresses?" *Boys' Historical Clothing.* Accessed online at http://histclo.hispeed.com/style/skirted/dress/dresswhy. html.

[478] Jane Ellen.

[479] Daniel Thomas Cook, *The Commodification of Childhood: The Children's Clothing Industry and the Rise of the Child Consumer* (Durham, NC: Duke Univ. Press, 2004); quote is from p. 101.

[480] Susan B. Kaiser, Margaret Rudy, & Pamela Byfield, "The Role of Clothing in Sex-Role Socialization: Person Perceptions Versus Overt behavior," *Child Study Journal, 15* (no. 2), 83-97 (1985). Also see the answer to Q. 6.

[481] Martha L. Picariello, Danna N. Greenberg, & David B. Pillemer, "Children's Sex-related Stereotyping of Colors," *Child Development, 61*, 1453-1460 (1990). Quote is from p. 1459.

[482] Judith E. Owen Blakemore, "Children's Beliefs About Violating Gender Norms: Boys Shouldn't Look Like Girls and Girls Shouldn't Act Like Boys," *Sex Roles: A Journal of Research, 43*, 411-419 (2003). As might be expected, perceptions and reactions among children are inconsistent and vary with age. However, of relevance to us, this research found that children ages 3-11 are more tolerant of girls with clothing and hairstyles like that of boys than of boys whose clothing and hairstyle is more feminine.

[483] Carolyn Balkwell, "On Peacocks and Peahens: A Cross-Cultural Investigation of the Effects of Economic Development on Sex Differences in Dress," *Clothing & Textiles Research Journal, 4* (no. 2), 30-36 (1986).

[484] My use of 'bifurcated' here is limited to clothing that divides below the waist, though Steven Connor makes the valid point that bifurcated can also refer to the division that occurs at the waist, so that there is a vertical bifurcation as well as a horizontal, bilateral one. See Steven Connor, "Men in Skirts," *Women: A Cultural Review, 13* (no. 3), 257-271 (2002), p. 258.

[485] Thomas, p. 69, contends that emphasis of the waist line became the dominant idea in women's fashion.

[486] Tacitus, *Germania*, 17, in *Tacitus on Britain and Germany*, Translated by H. Mattingly (Middlesex, England: Penguin Books, 1951 reprint of 1948 ed.), p. 114f.

[487] Gilles Lipovetsky, *The Empire of Fashion. Dressing Modern Democracy*, translated by C. Porter (Princeton: Princeton Univ. Press, 1994; original work published 1987).

[488] Connor, p. 259.

[489] Lois Banner, "The Fashionable Sex, 1100-1600," *History Today, 42* (no. 4), 37-44. Cf. Thomas, p. 70, who views the transition of fashion focus from male to female as reflective of men moving their focus and energy to the realm of business, where wealth is attractive enough without ornament and the importance of appearance is transferred from their persons to their goods.

490 Diana Crane, *Fashion and Its Social Agendas. Class, Gender and Identity in Clothing* (Chicago: Univ. of Chicago Press, 2000), p. 3. Cf. her remarks on the 19th century, pp. 3-6.

491 Sara Melissa Pullum-Piñon. *Conspicuous Display and Social Mobility: a Comparison of 1850s Boston and Charleston Elites* [Ph.D. dissertation] (Austin: The University of Texas, 2002), p. 147f. Pullum-Piñon (p. 148) also notes that too excessive display in this respect among women was also frowned upon as it came to be associated with women of low repute such as prostitutes, entertainers, or working women.

492 Cf. the "Men in Skirts" exhibit at the Victoria & Albert Museum website accessed at http://www.vam.ac.uk/exploring/collections/fashion/short_stories/men_in_skirts/?view=Mainframe. Interestingly, the current revival of male interest in—and appropriation of—unbifurcated garments is raising considerable attention and controversy.

493 Cf. Davis, pp. 34-37.

494 Dubuc quoted in Siobhan O'Connor, "Philippe Dubuc Pushes the Limits of Masculine Fashion," *Montreal Mirror* (2001, Mar. 29), accessed online at http://www.montrealmirror.com/ARCHIVES/2001/032901/fashion3. html .John Connor (p. 268) regards this statement as mostly true only from the mid19th century on.

495 Connor, p. 263.

496 The German *Blusen* has applied to masculine clothing. The Luftwaffe uniform, for instance, included a 'field blouse.' The English 'blouse' early on referred to a garment either a male or female might wear; boys in the 19th century typically wore blouses where men wore shirts.

497 The positioning of buttons on the left side, which makes for ease for right-handed people—the majority of the population—was allocated to masculine fashion. Award winning artist and writer David Lance Goines remarks in his history of the button that as an article of clothing, the button *per se* was "an inviolate masculine preserve for three hundred years and more." See David Lance Goies, *Button, Button* (1999), accessed online at http://www.goines.net/Writing/button _button.html.

498 Substantiating claims for the corset at an earlier date is difficult, though it is common to see the corset attributed to Cretan and Greek women of antiquity. The term's connection to men in armor is evident in its original meaning as a 'breastplate.' Men have worn corsets throughout history; President John F. Kennedy used one to help with back pain. For more information see *History of Corsets—An Overview Through the Centuries,* a webpage on the European

Corset Society's website, accessed online at http://www.eucosy.org/uk/corset/history/.

If one wishes to be ingenious, even the brassiere—an irrefutably feminine article of clothing—can be regarded as derived from male clothing if its origin is seen as an offshoot from the corset and the latter is accorded its start in men's armor.

[499] Male clergy in particular used lace. On the early history and use of lace in Europe, see Wim J. Lauriks, "Birthplace of Lace," *LACE Magazine International,* Issue 49, pp. 33-35 (1999, Spring). Cf. Wim J. Lauriks, "Growth of Lace," *LACE Magazine International,* Issue 50 (1999, Summer).

[500] Connor, p. 260. He writes (p. 260): "The phrase 'petticoat breeches' could actually be used of two slightly different things: either long underdrawers with deep flounces of lace that fell out over the knee from underneath breeches; or a skirt or petticoat worn short enough to show the fringes of the bloomer-type breeches worn underneath."

[501] Barbara Burman, "Pocketing the Difference: Gender and Pockets in Nineteenth-Century Britain," *Gender and History, 14* (no. 3), 447-469 (2002). With reference to the gendered body, see the discussion on pp. 460-464. Cf. Connor, p. 267.

[502] Thomas, pp. 71-72, sees the development of women's fashion—so fully incorporated within the business of man—as having an "altogether bad" effect on the character of women by reinforcing negative stereotypes such as their helplessness. In effect, he says, it makes her a thing rather than a person, an object for male manipulation. Yet already in 1908 he could see that change would come as women asserted independence.

[503] Numerous works exist documenting this struggle. See, for example, P. C. Warner, "Feminism and Costume History: Synthesis and Reintegration," *Clothing & Textiles Research Journal, 18* (no. 3), 185-189 (2000).

[504] Cf. Thomas, p. 71, who quotes the remark of Sir Henry Maine that the greatest calamity that might befall our modern society would not be war, pestilence or famine, but a revolution in fashion where women would dress as men—in one material of one color.

[505] Mary Lou Rosencranz, *Clothing Concepts. A Social-Psychological Approach* (N. Y.: Macmillan, 1972), pp. 172, 175.

[506] Although the early 21st century witnessed a fair amount of publicity for this trend in both Europe and the United States, it was at least as far back as the Fall of 1984 that fashion shows in London and Paris had men wearing skirts. An American designer, Stephen Sprouse, had earlier placed a male model

in a black denim miniskirt over black denim jeans in an April, 1983 show. See John Duka, "Skirts for Men? Yes and No," *New York Times* (1984, October 27th). For examples of the recent trend, visit any of a number of websites. While this volume was being prepared I sampled various places online, such as a German fashion site accessed at https://ssl.kundenserver.de/menintime.de/start_en.php3?VID=pwYIqgr5sRhjtLvF&PID=no. Also see the German fashion site Persus de accessed at http://www.persus. de/index2.htm. Cf. the British site for Midas Clothing in Manchester, England, accessed at http://www.persus.de/index2.htm. For a U.S. example, see the site for Macabi Skirt, Salt Lake City, Utah, accessed at http:// www.macabiskirt.com/.

[507] Cathy Horyn, "Face Off," *Men's Fashions of the Times. The New York Times Magazine, Part 2*, pp. 48-52 (2004, Spring).

[508] Ibid, p. 52.

[509] Bowie also sings of erotic crossdressing, as in "Cactus" when he solicits a lover to send her sweat-soaked dress for him to wear. Pictures of Bowie's and Rowland's album covers can be found on the internet. I accessed them online at rateyourmusic.com site *Album Cover Art: Homoeroticism* at http://rateyourmusic.com/lists/list_view/list_ id_is_5842. A picture of Cobain in a dress, with comments from fans, can be found at NirvanaPhotos.com, accessed online at http:// www.nirvanaphotos.com/photos. php?Cat=8&Idx=6. A dress worn by Kobain was also featured as part of an exhibit at the New York Metropolitan Museum. Cf. "Men in Skirts."

[510] David Beckham, *David Beckham: My World* (London: Hodder & Stoughton General, 2000).

[511] Laurel Wellman, "Skirting an Issue," *SF Weekly* (1996, Sept. 4). Accessed online at http://www.sfweekly.com/issues/19960904/news.html.

[512] Jean Lowerison, "The Reel Story: 'The Iron Ladies.' Volleyball-Playing Drag Queens," *San Diego Metropolitan Uptown Examiner and Daily Business Report* (2004, June; original article printed 2001). Accessed online at http:// metro.sandiegometro.com/ reel/index.php?reelID=300.

[513] Alex Feld, "Style Sheet: Grecian Formula," *Entertainment Weekly* #767 (2004, May 28), 28. Cf. Erik Kirschbaum, "Pitt Says Men May Start Wearing Skirts After 'Troy,'" *Reuters* (2004, May 9). Accessed online at http://www.reuters.com/newsArticle.jhtml?type=entertainmentNews&storyID =5082571. Cf. the answer to Q. 44. Pitt, it should be noted, proved a lousy prophet for the immediate future, and refrained from any post-*Troy* displays of skirt wearing, suggesting his remarks were generated for publicity.

[514] Andrew Bolton, *Bravehearts: Men in Skirts* (London: Victoria & Albert Museum, 2003). Cf. the museum exhibit which the book accompanies, accessed

online at http://www.vam.ac.uk/resources/press/press09?section=index&page =press09.

[515] Phillip D. Johnson, "Men in skirts: A bridge too far?" *Lucire* (2003). Accessed online at http://www.lucire.com/2003a/1103ll0.shtml.

[516] Judith Thurman, "Would You Be Caught Dead with This Guy?" *Mademoiselle* (2000). Accessed online at http://users.pandora.be/tripticdesign/ skirt10.html.

[517] Francesco Alberoni, "A Freudian Skirt," *Mono Uomo, 79*, 44-45 (1994, March).

[518] Anne Hollander, *Sex and Suits* (N. Y.: Alfred A. Knopf, 1994).

[519] C. Willett Cunnington & Phillis Cunnington, *The History of Under-clothes* (London: Michael Joseph, 1951), p. 154. The Cunningtons point out that the functioning of underclothes throughout the Middle Ages and earlier was "purely utilitarian" and used "only very indirectly to enhance sex attraction" (p. 21). This situation changed only with the Renaissance, when "the modern con-ception of 'fashions' in the costumes of both sexes began to appear in the sec-ond quarter of the 14th century . . . ." (p. 22)—but then only with visible gar-ments.

There are many recent publication focusing on undergarments, most offering brief histories with more complete attention to the modern period. See, for example, Catherine Bardey & Zeva Oelbaum, *Lingerie: A History & Celebra-tion of Silks, Satins, Laces, Linens, & Other Bare Essentials* (N. Y.: Black Dog & Leventhal Publishers, 2001). They point out that the term 'lingerie' originated in the latter half of the 19th century. Cf. the well-illustrated Gilles Neret, *1000 Des-sous. A History of Lingerie,* Trans. Sue Rome (L.A.: Taschen America Llc, 1998).

[520] For a brief history, see inventor Mary Bellis' online article *The History of Pantyhose?* at http://inventors.about.com/library/ inventors/blpantyhose.htm.

[521] Mary Bellis, *The History of the Brassiere,* accessed at http:// inven-tors.about.com/library/weekly /aa042597.htm.

[522] Jane FerrellBeck & Colleen Gau, *Uplift: The Bra in America* (Phila.: Univ. of Pennsylvania Press, 2002), p. 56.

[523] Cunnington & Cunnigton, p. 236.

[524] Ibid, p. 241.

[525] FerrellBeck & Gau, p. 56. Also see p. 116.

[526] Richard Martin, "Feel Like a Million!' The Propitious Epoch in Men's Underwear Imagery, 1939-1952" *Journal of American Culture, 18* (no. 4), 5158 (1995), p. 57.

527 In outerwear there are also 'boy cut' denim jeans, which advertisements also stress are 'all girl.'

528 For more about manties (sing. manty), visit http://www. manties.net/.

529 See Runo, *Snake Charmer Men's Underwear* accessed online at http://www.max.hiho.ne.jp/hotaru/underwear/. Runo's featured panties were made from handkerchiefs.

530 Matthew Temple, "Men in Tights," *FT.com Financial Times* (2002, June 7). Accessed online at http://news.ft.com/home/us.

531 Advertising accessed at http://www.mytights.com/mytights/browse/manu/WoMan.html.

532 Advertising accessed at http://www.comfilon.com/activskin/.

533 "Dressing Gown, Undress Gown, Nightgown, Negligee," in Ludmila Kybalova & Milena Herbenova, *The Pictorial Encyclopedia of Fashion*, trans. Claudia Rosoux (N. Y.: Crown Publishers, 1968).

534 Cunnington & Cunnington, p. 253.

Q. 10 Notes

535 Fetishism involving clothes is not the same as transvestic fetishism.

536 Is it possible to select apparel associated with a different gender without intending to express that gender? And if it is possible, is the behavior then crossdressing? For example, could a man choose to wear feminine garments merely because he likes the way they look and feel, and not because they proclaim femininity? We seem to permit this for women—why not men? Even if the individual recognizes that the society designates the apparel as gendered, must that judgment be concurred in? And even if it is agreed to, why can't it be decided that such a judgment is less important than the comfort or appeal of wearing the clothes? Further, why can't it be allowed that a person might intentionally try to set aside gender issues by only wearing such clothing in private? In that case, the intent is not to express gender but to disavow it!

537 The law distinguishes between moral culpability and legal culpability. The former depends as much on intention as on the results of an action.

538 We should note there is no requirement to see only two genders involved. Dress can say, '*This* displays my gender,' without meaning that the gender association is the gender being claimed. In other words, a male may wear feminine apparel without claiming femininity as the gender being expressed. This happens in crossdressing where a man intends to be seen as a man dressed in woman's clothes rather than as a woman. Though wearing feminine clothing

his dress statement still proclaims masculinity. Or the male may experience gender as something other than either masculine or feminine. The feminine apparel may then intend to make the statement that dress conformity is misleading and that only crossdressing, by confounding the culture's tight connection between gender and sex, offers a way through clothes to be another gender.

[539] We can easily imagine many instances in life where unintended consequences cross one or another line. For example, a person driving a car who swerves to avoid hitting a child running into the street may crash into a parked car. The intention—to miss the child—is morally good, as is one result. A secondary result—hitting the parked car—is unintended, unfortunate, and damaging. Though the driver may bear legal culpability for the consequence, there is no moral culpability, regardless of how unhappy the owner of the parked car might be. Of course, someone might argue this example is not a good parallel because it is clear that saving a child's life is more valuable than preserving someone's property. Is the congruence a crossdresser, a single individual, achieves worth the distress experienced by those dismayed at the crossing of the gender line? Do the needs—or desires—of the many outweigh those of the few, or individual? This question remains a perpetual moral conundrum, though our own individualistic culture leans a certain direction.

[540] The link is also made to *experience*. However, this answer is restrained to the question of expression—the aspect of experience open at least potentially to observation and interpretation by others.

[541] Though the argument might be made that keeping the lines clear is essential for sex identification, a more compelling argument is that maintaining the divide preserves the gender hierarchy, thus preserving privilege for those assigned (or successfully claiming) masculinity.

[542] Presently, men who favor wearing MUGs—male unbifurcated garments, such as kilts—are making this argument. Previously women could have made the same contention when they adopted ostensibly male styles of dress such as jeans and were widely viewed as crossdressing and inappropriately blurring gender lines. These matters will be considered more fully later.

[543] As Anne Fausto-Sterling puts it concerning gender: "There is no either/or. Rather, there are shades of difference." See her *Sexing the Body: Gender Politics and the Construction of Sexuality* (N.Y.: Basic Books, 2000), p. 3.

[544] Similar dynamics may happen in the more private context of a marriage. The spouse of someone who crossdresses may worry about what that says. Is the crossdresser adopting the same gender as the spouse, so that one partner is pursuing heterosexual behavior while the other is expressing homo-

sexuality? If not, what is going on? (The dynamics of the marital relationship are discussed in the answer to question 58.)

[545] See the answers to Q. 36 for more on the cultural influence with regard to gender and the role clothes play.

[546] Helen Boyd, *My Husband Betty. Love, Sex, and Life with a Crossdresser* (N. Y.: Thunder's Mouth Press, 2004). See chapter 2, "Crossdressed Lives." With reference to the idea that male crossdressing is a voluntary lowering of social status, it must be pointed out this depends on one's perspective. A male crossdresser may hold the view that femininity represents a higher social class. Such male crossdressing would parallel the historic motivation of crossdressing women seeking to enhance their social position.

[547] I agree with those who adopt the logic that 'what's sauce for the goose is sauce for the gander'—that contemporary male crossdressing should be viewed as openly, sympathetically, and supportively as women might have wished when they were the ones subjected to scrutiny for crossdressing. Others, though, argue the two situations are fundamentally different. They view women crossdressing as a battle for gender equality, but see male crossdressing as about sexuality and men trying to pass as women. I think we must avoid sweeping generalizations concerning either female crossdressers of the past or male crossdressers of the present. Just as some women then crossdressed to pass as men, so some men crossdress with no interest in being anything other than men. And in both situations, some probably crossdressed to reflect the experience of being neither 'man' nor 'woman' but a 'third gender.' Thus, a qualified position is best: the present *can* be viewed as parallel to the past, but the reality both then and now is too complex to reduce to global judgments.

Appendix

Table of Contents for 5 Volume Set

Q. 17   Why do some homosexuals crossdress?

Q. 18   What is 'transvestism'?

Q. 19   What is 'transsexualism'?

Q. 20   What does 'transgender' mean?

Question Set 3: What causes crossdressing?

Q. 21   Is crossdressing 'natural'?

Q. 22   Is crossdressing learned behavior?

Q. 23   Is crossdressing developmental (i.e., "just a 24phase")?

Q. 24   Is crossdressing caused by sexual abuse?

Q. 25   Is crossdressing a choice?

Question Set 4: What is it like to be a transgendered crossdresser?

Q. 26   How do crossdressers describe themselves?

Q. 27   What is the profile of a 'typical' crossdresser?

Q. 28   When does crossdressing usually start?

Q. 29   What is childhood and adolescence like?

Q. 30   What is adulthood like for a crossdresser?

Q. 31   Does crossdressing lead to a sex change operation?

Q. 32   Is crossdressing harmful?

Q. 33   What is involved in crossdressing?

Q. 34   Where do crossdressers find support?

Q. 35   Are all crossdressers homosexual?

Question Set 5: How are transgender realities regarded by others?

Q. 36   What is the legal status of crossdressers?

Q. 37   How are crossdressers treated in public?

Q. 38   How do partners handle the crossdressing of their significant others?

Q. 39   How does crossdressing affect families?

Q. 40   Why does society tolerate crossdressing?

Volume 3: Transgender History & Geography

Volume 4: Transgender & Religion

Q. 64   What do Christian commentators say?

Q. 65   What constitutes a 'reasonable' position to take?

Question Set 9: What does Christianity say about crossdressing?

Q. 66   What does the New Testament say?

Q. 67   What did the Church Fathers say?

Q. 68   Are there crossdressing saints?

Q. 69   Are there notable crossdressing Christian women?

Q. 70   Are there notable crossdressing Christian men?

Q. 71   Are there Christian festivals where crossdressing is accepted?

Q. 72   Has the Church said anything "officially" about crossdressing?

Q. 73   What do Christians today who oppose transgender realities say?

Q. 74   What do transgender Christians and their supporters today say?

Q. 75   Are there resources for transgender Christians?

Question Set 10: What do other religions say about crossdressing?

Q. 76   How did crossdressing figure in ancient and pre-modern religions?

Q. 77   What stance does Judaism take on crossdressing?

Q. 78   What role has crossdressing played in Islam?

Q. 79   How does Hinduism regard crossdressing?

Q. 80   Is Buddhism tolerant of crossdressing?

Q. 81   Is crossdressing found in Japanese religions?

Q. 82   Can transgender elements be found in other Eastern religions?

Q. 83   What roles do crossdressing and transgender play in African religions?

Q. 84   Are transgender realities found in Native American religiosity?

Q. 85   What role does crossdressing play in religion?

Volume 5: Transgender & Mental Health

Index

A

Abba ben Kahana, Rabbi, 103

Accommodation, 196f., 198

Adam and Eve, 22, 101, 102

Adolescence, 159

Alberoni, Francesco, 218

Androgynes, 114

Androgyny/Androgynous Dress, 50, 72, 114, 132, 134, 148, 149, 151, 152, 154, 160, 173, 174, 175, 216, 271

additive and subtractive, 151

Apparel. *See* Clothes

Ariès, Philippe, 208

Arnold, Rebecca, 98

Assimilation, 196f.

Attractiveness, 19, 58, 59, 89, 90, 91, 92, 93-97, 100, 101, 105, 106, 107, 161, 163

Attwood, Feona, 168

Au, Joe, 24, 53

B

Bae, MiKyeong, 31

Balkwell, Carolyn, 211

Banim, Maura, 56

Banner, Lois, 212

Barber, Nigel, 106

Bartlett, Katharine, 76

Beale, Carole, 155

Beckham, David, 216

Bickman, Leonard, 71f.

Bifurcated Clothing, 50, 77 78, 87, 159, 192, 206-207, 211-214, 216-217, 221

Bodenhausen, Galen, 188

Bolton, Andrew, 217

Bornstein, Kate, 142, 180

Boundaries, 6, 35, 39, 60, 61, 66-73, 77, 79, 80, 83, 131 133, 140, 177, 179f., 204, 218

especially see:

primary, 66-68

secondary, 68-73

Bowie, David, 216

Boy George, 216

Boyd, Helen, 233

Bradley, Susan, 115

Brewis, Joanna, 147, 149, 172

Brown, Patty, 25

299

Bullough, Bonnie, 119, 182

Bullough, Vern, 118, 182

Burbank, Emily, 95

C

Cahill, Spencer, 155

Childhood

  origin of, 208

Clausell, Eric, 190

Clothes

  as entry into gender, 50

  as self-boundary, 38

  color and, 45

  enhancing the self through, 58

  extension of the self and, 57

  fibers and fabrics, 40, 42, 47, 158

  gender and (also see Dress

    gender and, 148

  gender differentiation and, 49

  gender-differentiated dress in child-

    hood, 158

  health and, 40

  impact on physiology, 39ff.

  men in skirts, 215

  origin and purpose of, 19, 22, 28

  personal experience and, 26

  psychological benefits of, 31, 32

  self-expression and, 34

  sexual differentiation and, 22

  social affiliations and, 23

Bush, George, 24, 146

Butler, Judith, 125, 126

  symbolic meaning and, 29

  synthetic fibers and, 42

  underwear (also see

    separate entry), 163

  uniforms (see separate

    entry)

  ways to express gender,

    149

  wealth and, 71

Clothing

  gender stable traits and,

    205f.

Clothing Orientation Scale,

  31

Co, Elise Dee, 39

Cobain, Kurt, 216

Cobb-Roberts, Deirdre, 195

Cognitive Dissonance, 193ff.

Coleman, Vernon, 44

Color, 45f., 210

  color coding infants, 46,

    154, 208, 229

Connor, Steven, 212, 213

Context, 6-7, 19, 25, 31, 33,

  35, 37, 40-41, 46, 58, 61,

interprets sex, 134

Gender Development

definition of, 121

Gender Expectations, 154f.

Gender Expression, 122f.

Gender Identity Disorder (GID), 76, 123, 156f.

Gender Labels, 157

Gender Stability, 157f.

Gender Stereotypes, 147, 158, 187-190 208, 210, 216

Gender-differentiated Dress, 49, 50, 61, 76, 77, 80-84, 86, 103, 104, 122, 146, 147, 149, 152, 155, 157, 164, 186, 187, 190, 193, 201, 223, 225, 227, 228, 230

elements of, 87, 206

Gender Constancy, 157

in adulthood, 210-218

in childhood, 208-210

in infancy, 208f.

Genesis, 101-103

Gestalt of Dress, 48f., 53, 87, 152, 176

Gibson, Mel, 217

Giddens, Anthony, 38

Gilbert, Christopher, 75-76

Goffman, Erving, 191-192

Golden Rule of Dress, 77, 147, 157, 162-163, 167, 179

Griggs, Claudine, 130

Guéguen, Nicolas, 73

Guy, Alison, 56

H

Haytko, Diana, 31, 68

Hermaphrodites, 114-115

Hird, Myra, 113

Hoffman, Curt, 187

Homophobia, 78, 122

construction of masculinity and, 78, 122, 156, 179

Homosexual. *See* Homosexu ality

Homosexuality, 78, 82, 122, 156, 172, 179, 189-190, 218, 223, 226, 231-232

Hunt, Alan, 98

Hurst, Nancy, 187

I

Interoception, 40

Intersex, 81, 113, 115, 116, 131, 138, 140, 141, 182, 225

hermaphrodites and, 114-115

incidence of, 117

Intersex Initiative, 116

Intersexed. *See* Intersex

J

Jackson, Samuel L., 217
Johnson, Philip, 61

Joselit, Jenna Weismann, 96
Jung, Carl, 30

K

Kane, Emily, 155-156
Karyotype, 111-112
King, Dave, 130

Koo, Kathyrn, 136
Kunda, Ziva, 189-190
Kwon, Yoon-Hee, 56f.

L

Langer, Susan, 157
Language of Clothes, 34
Laver, James, 148f.
Lefebvre, Henri, 52
Lessons from the Intersexed, 116

Lingerie. *See* Underwear
Lipovetsky, Gilles, 212
Lönnqvist, Bo, 167f.
Lurie, Alison, 33, 34, 65, 74,
   81-82, 160

M

Macrae, Neil, 188
Mandoki, Katya, 52, 56
Manties, 219
Martin, Carol Lynn, 158
Martin, James, 157
Martin, Richard, 219
Masculine Lingerie, 167f.
Masculinity, 147, 225
   homophobia and, 78
   masculine privilege, 55, 73, 78, 79, 149,
   151, 217
Maurer, Lisa, 127
McFalls, Elisabeth, 195

Mead, George Herbert, 146
Mead, Margaret, 123
Medicalization of Sex, 7, 110,
   130, 182, 210
Menke, Franke, 45
Mental Health Professionals,
   7-8, 44, 81, 156, 182, 195
Metrosexualism, 78, 163
Miller, Margaret, 26
Milne, Alan, 188
Modesty, 19, 22, 23, 49, 75,
   89, 92, 101, 103-107, 166,
   168, 219

Rosencranz, Mary Lou, 42, 53f., 161, 162, 216

Rothblatt, Martine, 116

Roughgarden, Joan, 113

Rowland, Kevin, 216

Rubinstein, Ruth, 66

S

Second Skin (Clothing as . . .), 28, 32, 35, 38, 39, 66, 90, 164, 202, 228

Segal, Eric, 60

Sex, 110-117

definition of, 110f.

presentation, 112, 114f.

Sexology, 111

Sexual differentiation, 22, 23

Sexual Orientation, 81, 82, 172, 223, 226, 232

Sexuality, 113, 167

definition of, 110

Shaari, Nazlina, 47

Shannon, Brent, 100

Silhouette, 48, 59, 87, 152-154, 162, 168, 176-177, 187, 207

crossdressing and, 176-177

Simmel, Georg, 25, 69, 71

Slimane, Hedi, 216

Smith, Paul, 52f.

Social Psychology of Clothes, 72

Sontag, Suzanne, 57

Spade, Dean, 76f.

Spence, Janet, 20

Stanton, Elizabeth Cady, 55

Stereotype Content Model (SCM), 190f.

Stereotypes, 46, 55, 60, 70, 76-78, 97, 123, 133, 147, 152-155, 158, 164, 177, 179, 185, 187-192, 208, 210, 217, 220, 226, 232

Stigmatizing, 191-192

Stoltenberg, John, 90

Stone, Gregory, 51, 146, 154

Sui, Anna, 216

Sumptuary Laws, 71, 98, 172

T

Tacitus, 211

Targum Neofiti, 102

Tattersall, Ian, 22

Thematic Apperception Test (TAT), 54

Third Gender, 86, 131-132, 134, 140, 151, 181

Thomas, William, 23, 104-105, 202

Thompson, Craig, 31, 68

X

Xavier, Jessica, 129

Y

Yarborough, Melanie, 177

Z

Zimniewska, Malgorzata, 40f.

www.ingramcontent.com/pod-product-compliance
Lightning Source LLC
Chambersburg PA
CBHW031500270326
41930CB00006B/177